JUSTIFIED IN CHRIST

JUSTIFIED
IN
CHRIST

God's plan for us in Justification

K. Scott Oliphint, ed.

MENTOR

The Imputation of Adam's Sin by John Murray is reprinted by permission of Wm. B. Eerdmans Publishing Company and P&R Publishing.

ISBN 1-84550-246-9
ISBN 978-1-84550-246-1

10 9 8 7 6 5 4 3 2 1

Published in 2007
in the
Mentor Imprint
by
Christian Focus Publications, Ltd.,
Geanies House, Fearn, Ross-shire,
IV20 1TW, Great Britain.

www.christianfocus.com

Cover design by Danie Van Straaten

Printed and bound by
CPD, Wales

Contents

How great presumption is it to condemn the supreme Judge when he freely absolves, so that this answer may not have full force: "I will show mercy on whom I will show mercy"? And yet Moses' intercession, which God restrains in these words, was not to the effect that he should spare no one but that he should wipe away the charge against them even though they were guilty, and absolve them all equally. And on this account, indeed, we say that those who were lost have their sins buried and are justified before God because, as he hates sin, he can love only those whom he has justified. This is a *wonderful plan of justification* that, covered by the righteousness of Christ, they should not tremble at the judgment they deserve, and that while they rightly condemn themselves, they should be accounted righteous outside themselves.

John Calvin, *Institutes*, 3.11.11

Introduction:
The Justification Crisis

Sinclair B. Ferguson

One does not need to be a seer to recognize that evangelicalism today is experiencing a crisis of fragmentation.

Fifty years ago, to be an evangelical implied a deep commitment to the great creedal verities of historic Christianity. But it also included certain distinctive views about the nature of the work of Christ and how the blessings of salvation are received.[1] At the heart of these lay the authority of Scripture and the twin convictions that the death of Christ involved penal substitution, and that the beginning of the Christian life was marked by justification by faith alone.

Of course there were differences among evangelicals. But by and large there remained much common ground.

The map has now changed, perhaps beyond recognition and possibly permanently. The question "What is an evangelical?" would today receive a wide variety of answers, many of them much less robust than the historical definition.

It has been commonplace in contemporary analyses to comment that evangelicalism has experienced a series of seismic shocks, ranging from the charismatic movement (whose influence is today felt everywhere either in expression or reaction) to the (not unrelated) "worship-wars" with their attendant issues of seeker sensitivity and, in their wake the emerging/emergent church movement. But, all the while, something deeper has been taking place under the surface, the full force of which is now becoming increasingly evident.

---

[1] See, for example, the taxonomy of evangelicalism in D. W. Bebbington, *Evangelicalism in Modern Britain* (London, 1989); D. M. Lloyd-Jones *What is an Evangelical?* (London, 1971)

One index that this "something else" would soon emerge should have been evident from the books produced by evangelical publishers, by the nature of pulpit rhetoric, and the themes of the conferences and seminars evangelicals organized and attended. One great theme tended to be overlooked. Sadly, it was one of the defining themes of historic evangelicalism: *Jesus Christ, his Person and Work.* Doubtless it was always assumed. But throughout the middle period of the twentieth century evangelical literature paid scant attention to this central theme of the gospel or to the way in which union with Christ brings the Christian every spiritual blessing (Eph. 1:3). The most substantial literature published in the period tended to be reprints of earlier works. Despite the best efforts of a small number of scholars (particular tribute should be paid here to the late Leon Morris) it was probably not until the publication in 1986 of John Stott's *The Cross of Christ* that a prominent evangelical drew attention to the theme that had been so missing from book catalogues. And it would surely be safe to say that the sales of even Dr. Stott's widely praised and appreciated work pale by comparison with the sales of *The Purpose Driven Life*. It would be fascinating to know how well a book entitled *The Cross-Driven Life* would have sold.

There have been signs of hope, of course. Some of them have taken publishers by surprise (when J. I. Packer's *Knowing God* was first published in England the print run was about as small as was viable and the publisher was heard to say that they did not know whether there would be many people really interested in a volume with such a title). But that notwithstanding, gone was the conviction that what people needed most of all was the knowledge of God the Trinity, and an understanding of Jesus Christ and his work and the grace and truth that are to be found in him. Martin Luther's cry, "Blessed be all those prophets who say to the people of Christ, 'Cross, cross' ..."[2] was relegated to a lower division. "How to" deal with fears, problems, pain, and low self-esteem, and having a good marriage and raising model children became the new evangelical agenda.

Without realizing that it was happening, evangelicalism had developed into a caricature of itself. Something inherently and

[2] Thesis 92 of The Ninety Five Theses of Martin Luther

importantly present in its genetic structure became exaggerated out of all proportion: expressing things charitably, how salvation becomes mine now obscured how salvation was accomplished by Christ. In technical theological terms the *ordo salutis* concerns (how does salvation work out?) obscured *historia salutis* (what did God do in history to accomplish salvation?). At its worst the theme of *my life* obscured knowledge of the significance of *Christ's death*.

Curiously – or was it so strange after all? – this style of evangelicalism expressed patterns of thought that had certain parallels to the earlier liberal theology of Friedrich Schleiermacher (1768–1834).

In his own way, Schleiermacher had patented and branded a "seeker sensitive" theology that (he certainly believed) made the gospel relevant to his contemporaries – "the cultured despisers of religion"[3] who, under the spell of the Enlightenment had given up on the possibility that Christian doctrine could be true. For them the knowledge of God was no longer attainable. Kant's critique of reason had limited it to the knowledge of the phenomenal realm; access to the noumenal was barred. Schleiermacher, refusing to believe that all was lost, turned things on their head, stressing that the essence of true Christian faith was the feeling or sense of absolute dependence upon God.

Schleiermacher thus fathered modern theology and launched a trend that would lead to that theology eventually becoming little more than religious anthropology, the study of religious experience. Thus in our own day departments or faculties of theology or divinity in many centers of higher learning have undergone a name-change to become departments or faculties of religion. The detritus of this in the modern world is the extent to which – not least among Christians – the "self" and its development has become the great (and very individualized) project of the hour. The knowledge of the person and work of Christ, clear thinking about the nature of justification and its grounds, and its relationship to and differences from sanctification – the issues to which Christians in earlier generations had given so much attention – were now

---

[3] The allusion is to his famous earlier work, *Religion: Speeches to its Cultured Despisers* (1799).

regarded as of marginal practical relevance. The Trinity – once the very foundation of the theological encyclopaedia – now, in Schleiermacher's theology, was relegated to what was virtually an appendix to his magnum opus *The Christian Faith* (1821–22, 2nd edition 1830). Somewhat unnervingly, the results in every recent poll of what evangelicals today apparently believe (or don't believe) suggest that a turning to the self and a de-centering of the Trinity has become pervasive in the subculture that was thought to be immune to liberalism.

When this is the ethos of the evangelical church, it is in no fit state to deal with any new wind of teaching. Hence the importance of this book.

The authors of these essays are bound together by their association with Westminster Theological Seminary in Philadelphia. They stand in a noble tradition of evangelical and reformed scholars. They share a love of learning and their very considerable academic gifts range from biblical exegesis to systematic and historical theology, from philosophical and cultural apologetics to homiletics and pastoral theology. They also share a common love for the church and aspire to serve the Christian community. They are actively involved in the life of the church, and in their own local congregations. Each of them exercises a broader influence by writing and speaking in both scholarly and popular contexts. They share the conviction that these two contexts are intimately related, and that what takes place in the academy eventually filters through to influence the preaching and teaching heard by congregations and the popular literature that Christians read.

This combination of love of learning, a passion for the gospel, and a love for the people of God brings these eight men to share a common concern that evangelicalism today lies open to influences which will damage its health and eventually destroy the coherence of its theological system and style of life.

The authors also stand in a particular epoch in the development of evangelical scholarship, and it may be worth pausing to comment on some of these trends.

Fifty years ago evangelical scholarship was small and weak. Evangelical students had few books to help them through the onslaught of liberal scholarship. Now that has dramatically changed. Evangelical scholarship virtually dominates the marketplace and conservative works of encyclopaedic length and learning are readily available. The growth in strength of numbers and scholarly output has been little short of phenomenal – from a trickle in the 50s and 60s to a flood in the 90s. Evangelical scholarship has also grown in confidence as it has come of age. Now there is less shame attached to being "evangelical" in the sense of having an interest in Scripture as the Word of God. In the academy it is less frequently said that to be an evangelical it is necessary to lose one's mind (although it might still be said as a "put-down" of young students).

But largely unnoticed, as evangelical scholarship grew strong, two things were happening. There was a – perhaps naïve – conviction that if a new race of *biblical* scholars could be produced then theology – particularly *systematic theology* – of an evangelical kind would benefit from the knock-on effects. What was sometimes overlooked was the fact that Scripture is not pre-theological nor is biblical interpretation a-theological. It contains its own theological controls, its own "form of doctrine" (Rom. 6:17) to which believers are committed by the gospel. The theology taught in Scripture in turn provides an underlying framework for exegesis and biblical theology. The unity of Scripture makes that possible and in fact demands it. Sadly, however, the adage that scholars were "simply following the text" did not always take account of the fact that the text ought never to be isolated from its theological framework.

Without these theological controls it was only too possible for scholars who believed that they were simply following the text of Scripture where it led not to recognize the fact that the lenses they often wore for their work were ground in the historical-critical laboratory. Furthermore, much academic work involved entering the stream of scholarship at a particular point in the river, learning the rules, and playing according to them. That river offered few signs warning of the danger of the rocks that lay just under the water's surface. The presuppositions expressed in a methodology can too easily be overlooked.

Over the decades, "new" positions have emerged in evangelical biblical scholarship. Those who developed them continued to affirm that these approaches were consistent with a confession of evangelical faith. What was too often overlooked was how similar were the methods now used, and the conclusions now drawn by "evangelicals," to those of nineteenth-century scholars who were the father figures of *non-evangelical* and eventually *anti-evangelical* scholarship over a century ago.[4]

Eventually what is taught in the academic world filters down into the popular literature in which evangelicalism abounds, and into the pulpits and classrooms of the church.

A parallel movement can be discerned in the discipline of theology. Where there is no middle ground to speak of, and the cutting edge is found in either liberalism or evangelicalism, almost inevitably evangelicalism attracts into its orbit individuals who are less than comfortable with the verities of a past generation. They see their task, by definition, not to seek a deeper understanding of the old but to advance the new. The more imaginative and creative the mindset, the more likely it is that the old will seem confining; the envelope must be pushed out further.

These two strands have now begun to run together. Thus some members of and speakers at what were founded as evangelical academic societies or conferences, have bade farewell to the distinguishing features of historic evangelicalism (while often remaining under its banner). Inevitably this has begun to trickle down into more ground-level, grass roots writing and speaking. It would seem likely that this will continue, and that many different points of evangelical theology will be questioned and eventually the map of evangelical theology will be redrawn – almost unrecognizably.

The result of these various influences and tendencies is that the term "evangelical" is no longer as fully or as clearly articulated as it once was. Indeed the value of the term itself has come into question. If it is possible to express reservations or even deny penal, substitutionary atonement, yet remain an evangelical then the term no longer denotes what it once did. A critical concern is associated with this, because the connected issue, "What is the evangel?" is not merely an academic one; on it hangs the message of salvation the church proclaims.

---

[4] The words attributed to Thomas Carlyle were perhaps more prophetic than many of his contemporaries cared to admit: "Have my countrymen's heads become turnips when they think that they can hold the premises of German unbelief and draw the conclusions of Scottish Evangelical Orthodoxy?" John Macleod, *Scottish Theology* (Edinburgh, 1943), p. 310.

Against this background the particular cluster of issues on which this book focuses involves the obedience of Christ in his penal substitutionary sacrifice, how that obedience is imputed to individuals, and what this implies in terms of justification by faith. These intimately related issues belong to the kernel of what it means to be an evangelical, and (so evangelicals have maintained) belong to the very heart of the gospel.

The authors, it should be stressed, do not believe that salvation is received by a mere affirmation of the doctrine of substitutionary atonement and the imputed righteousness of Christ. But they do believe that unless the gospel is articulated in these terms (or worse, if they are denied) the good news about the Christ who does save and what it means to believe in him is distorted and the gospel is compromised.

As these eight essays indicate, debate over the work of Christ and its application has become a *cause celèbre* in much contemporary literature and discussion. That is true with respect to the objective aspect of the gospel: What was actually transacted on the cross in order to effect our salvation? But it is also true with respect to its application: What does it mean to be "justified" and by what means does this take place?

The more specific background to this whole book – as will soon become evident – is the authors' shared concern about the influence of what is usually referred to as "The New Perspective on Paul." It may therefore be helpful to readers less familiar with it to provide some hints to understanding what this nomenclature denotes, and to give some preliminary indication as to why it has become such a live issue among evangelical Christians today.

It is worth saying that what is in view here is a *perspective* rather than an agreed set of dogmas. It is shared by people whose views of specific Christian doctrine may differ substantially (e.g. for example, on the nature and the reliability of Scripture). For that reason, aspects of it, and its proponents, constitute something of a moving target.

The "New Perspective" began life as a new perspective on Jewish faith and religion around the time of Jesus and Paul. In essence its contention is that the Judaism of this period of the second temple was – contrary to Protestant interpretations of the past – actually a religion of grace. It was *most certainly not* a religion of "works-righteousness." It did not teach that salvation is earned by self-effort. Rather, it held that salvation, or entry into the covenant community, was entirely a matter of grace. Thereafter obedience to the law was the way of remaining in the community whose principal external "boundary" markers were observing the Sabbath, the rite of circumcision, and the food laws. Consequently the teaching of Jesus and especially of Paul must be read (or re-read) in that light.

Hovering in the background here is a view not only of the Judaism of the first century but also of the history of the Western church since the time of the Reformation. Proponents of the New Perspective tend to emphasize that Western biblical scholarship was historically deeply influenced by the ghost of Augustine and the categories within which Martin Luther, the great German reformer, understood the gospel.

For Luther the great personal issue was how a sinful man can be justified before God. The "problem" the gospel solves was essentially that of his guilty condition before a righteous and holy God who abhors sin. Luther held that justification, being accounted righteous before God, takes place when the individual trusts in Jesus Christ who was "made sin for us, who knew no sin, that we might be made the righteousness of God in him" (2 Cor. 5:21). Like Calvin, Luther was awestruck by the wonderful exchange, in which our sins were accounted ("imputed") to Christ on the cross, and his righteousness was accounted ("imputed") to us through faith. For the Reformers, then, this "wonderful exchange" meant that a double imputation lies at the heart of the gospel. Thus justification was seen as "the standing or falling article of the church" (Luther) and "the hinge on which all religion turns" (Calvin).

Both Luther and Calvin believed that the late medieval church had distorted the gospel to the point of destroying it. They saw parallels and analogies between, on the one hand the Judaism which opposed Jesus and the Judaizers Paul encountered, and on the other the teaching of the late medieval church. They believed that in their exposition of the gospel over against Rome they were simply echoing the teaching of Jesus and Paul, and in their polemics against Rome were standing foursquare within apostolic teaching.

In the past century, the trickle of scholarship that once suggested this was not the whole story – or even the true story – has become a river. Notable protests were issued almost a century ago by Claude Montefiore (a Jewish scholar), and George Foot Moore. They argued that Judaism was a religion of grace, exhibited in delight in Torah. This position would later be developed in the post World War II era by three individuals.

In 1948 a Welsh scholar, W. D. Davies published *Paul and Rabbinic Judaism*, in which he argued that Saul of Tarsus was essentially simply a rabbi who found in Jesus the fulfillment of the prophecies about the Messiah. In this – admittedly a dramatic enough *volte-face* for someone who had persecuted Jesus' followers, but not in any works-grace antithesis – lay the distinguishing feature of his gospel.

In 1963 the Swedish scholar Krister Stendahl, Dean of Harvard Divinity School and later Bishop of Stockholm, published a paper in *The Harvard Theological Review* entitled "Paul and the Introspective Conscience of the West." Interestingly, in the light of its title and approach, Stendahl's essay had originally been a lecture given to The American Psychological Society in 1961. But its chief impact would not be so much on psychologists as on New Testament scholars.

Stendahl argued that the idea of the guilty conscience in Paul was a construction – a fabrication, really – of Western Christianity, in particular due to the influence of Augustine. It has always been – he believed significantly – absent in the Eastern church. Far from suffering from a burden of guilt prior to his experience on the Damascus Road, Paul in fact considered himself in a right relationship with God, "as to the law, blameless" (Phil. 3:6). His so-called "conversion" was in fact not a conversion from "guilt" to "grace" at all. Rather it was a realization that Jesus was the Messiah. Whatever he experienced on the Damascus Road, it was not a Western sinner's conversion, but rather a "call" to recognize Jesus as Messiah. Responding to this, Paul began to believe in Jesus and to proclaim him as Messiah. Paul's "sin" was not the guilt of spiritual and moral failure, but the error of persecuting the church and failing to recognize that it was the community of the Messiah. He was not a prototype Luther longing to have his guilty conscience relieved. One important development of this for

Stendahl was the contention that the heart of Paul's great Letter to the Romans (and therefore, the heart of his gospel) was therefore to be found not in Romans 1–4, but in Romans 9–11.

A sea-change came with the work of E. P. Sanders (son-in-law to W. D. Davies). His work *Paul and Palestinian Judaism*[5] took further the trajectory of his predecessors in a way that has revolutionized the map of New Testament, and particularly Pauline, studies in the past quarter century. Sanders' study focused on comparing *the pattern of religion* in Paul with that in Jewish literature between 200 BC and AD 200.[6] Judaism, Sanders argued, was a religion of "covenantal nomism." A right relationship to God is established by his gracious covenant. Obedience preserves the individual in that position. The sacrificial system provides for failure. The key element in his thesis was that this "pattern of religion" is not dissimilar to the pattern of religion which we find in Paul the Christian – a pattern of grace, not a pattern of self or works-righteousness.

How does such a view impact the way Paul and his teaching are interpreted? It immediately raises a question about how his conversion is to be analyzed.

Sanders argued that our access to this is by reasoning from the solution to the problem. What was unveiled to Paul on the Damascus Road (i.e. what was the solution?)? It was: Jesus is the Messiah. Saul's problem therefore was not that he was seeking salvation by his own works, nor that he was racked by a guilty conscience; it lay, rather, in his failure to recognize Jesus as Messiah for all, and in the implications (persecution) that resulted from his blindness. In summary, in perhaps Sanders' best-known sentence: "*this is what Paul finds wrong with Judaism: it is not Christianity.*"[7]

This being the case Paul's problem with the Judaizers was not that they were smuggling works-righteousness into salvation, but that, by their insistence on the traditional boundary markers, they were *excluding* those whom the Messiah *included* in his community. For if salvation required the observance of those markers, (i) Gentiles would be excluded from God's people, and therefore (ii) Christ would have died in vain.

---

[5] London, 1977.

[6] Significantly, the book carried the subtitle *A Comparison of Patterns of Religion*.

[7] *Paul and Palestinian Judaism*, p. 552. The emphasis is Sanders' own.

Sanders' work became the starting place for much contemporary rethinking of the New Testament. For scholars, of course, a Copernican revolution is always a highly productive event. Indeed it would be difficult today to write a paper or monograph on New Testament theology without at least paying lip-service at the shrine of the New Perspective. While some who once did so have changed their minds as their thinking has progressed, in the English-speaking world (where the New Perspective has most rapidly gained ground) the output of two British scholars has attracted a great deal of attention: James D. G. Dunn, formerly Lightfoot Professor at the University of Durham (usually attributed with coining the expression "new perspective on Paul") and N. T. Wright, coincidentally now Bishop of Durham in the Church of England. Without the influence of these two high-profile scholars it is likely that the New Perspective would have taken much longer to impact the evangelical church.

Like a considerable number of contemporary scholars, both of these authors have evangelical backgrounds, were active as students in the Inter-Varsity Fellowship (now Universities and Colleges Christian Fellowship) and in the British scholarly society associated with it, The Tyndale Fellowship. They draw differing exegetical and theological conclusions from their new perspective – and this underscores the importance of the term "perspective." But in general they share the view that Paul's concern (e.g. in Galatians and Romans) was not that of grace over against works, or the pursuit of a self-righteousness, but the requirement, for fellowship, of the works of the law, in particular, the familiar "boundary markers" of circumcision, Sabbath, and the kosher food laws, contrary to the gospel way of faith in Messiah Jesus. For them too, Judaism was essentially a religion of grace, not of works-righteousness. Thus, when Paul speaks about "justification" he is not in fact talking about "the way in" but describing the status of those who already are in.

In essence, therefore, Saul's conversion was not at all like Augustine's, or Luther's, or Bunyan's, nor are his polemics like that of Augustine against Pelagius, or Luther against Rome, or for that matter Bunyan's against high Anglicanism.

The obvious implication of this, however guardedly or palatably stated, is that traditional Protestantism has misunderstood Paul and with him Judaism. It has read Jewish religion and especially the Pharisees through Lutheran eyes, and mistakenly viewed Judaism through the lenses of the errors of Rome.

The "New Perspective" is seen to offer several benefits to the contemporary church. For one thing, it alleviates the charge that the Christian gospel, and in particular the apostle Paul, are guilty of anti-Semitism in the sense of misrepresenting true Judaism. For another, its implication would seem to be (and is sometimes virtually stated to be) that the conflict of the Reformation could have been avoided if both Roman Catholic and Reformation theologians had been able to understand the true nature of the gospel. Then both could have recognized their errors and arrived at... yes, a new perspective! The New Perspective then becomes a great – perhaps *the* great – ecumenical alchemy. Moreover, its focus on Jesus' Lordship as Messiah is seen to provide a solid foundation for a this-worldly Christianity that engages in social and political action.

The critical side of this emerges in the conviction that this perspective recovers the true biblical gospel, and saves evangelicalism from part of its own history. Evangelicalism can live and breathe because it knows that salvation is by grace; but it has employed a false anatomy to understand and express how the heart of the gospel functions. This is particularly clearly articulated by N. T. Wright. Critiquing the view that the doctrine of justification by faith is the gospel, and that the gospel is "an account of how people get saved" he affirms, rather, that

> 'The Gospel' is the announcement of Jesus' lordship, which works with power to bring people into the family of Abraham, now redefined around Jesus Christ and characterized solely by faith in him. 'justification' is the doctrine which insists that all those who have this faith belong as full members of this family, on this basis and no other.[8]

Several things are worth noting here.

The first is that the implied critique of evangelicalism is a caricature. Doubtless the caricature exists – we have already noted the evangelical slide into focusing on experience. At that

[8] *What St Paul Really Said*, pp. 132-133.

level we can agree. But it is, nevertheless, a caricature, not the real thing. For the idea that justification by faith (or thinking that one is justified by believing in justification by faith) *is* the whole of the gospel has never been the foundation of historic evangelicalism.[9] The work of Christ has always been foundational to everything else. Nevertheless, evangelicalism has always maintained that the "way in" is justification by faith.

The second thing to note here is not so much what is said – which, by its use of biblical language and categories may seem to be nuanced towards the language of historic evangelicalism – but what is *not* said. There is here no specific reference to the atonement, far less an explicit confession of Christ's death as penal and substitutionary. It is not denied. It might be said that this is surely covered by the way "Jesus' lordship ... works with power." But its absence is telling. There are elsewhere references to key evangelical ideas (propitiation, for example, although in this writer's view not adequately set within the context of a thorough exposition of divine wrath that evokes the horror of Romans 1:18ff, or Revelation 6:12ff). What is clear is that central to this vision of the work of Christ is not so much atonement as penal substitution but Christ's victory over the "principalities and powers." This view, when popularized by the Swedish theologian Gustav Aulén's book *Christus Victor* (1931), certainly had in view a reconfiguring of the gospel – and in Aulén a de-emphasizing (even repudiation) of penal substitution as the heart of the atonement and therefore of the gospel.

It should not be surprising, therefore, that also associated with this view is a denial of the imputation of Christ's righteousness to believers. This is argued in part on the basis that righteousness is an *attribute* of God and in the very nature of the case, attributes cannot be "imputed." The implication of this view is – logically and inevitably, even if not always recognized – that our sin cannot

---

[9] In an illuminating personal note Bishop Wright comments on the "vital and liberating point" which he first met in the work of the sixteenth-century Anglican theologian Richard Hooker, that one is not justified by faith by believing in justification by faith (*What Saint Paul Really Said*, London, 1997, p.159). What strikes one as curious about this statement is that while such a discovery would indeed be liberating, one would be hard pressed to find an intelligent evangelical in the history of the church who has taught such a distorted view of the gospel.

therefore be imputed to Christ. For my sin is also an *attribute* – *my* attribute! – and if an attribute cannot be imputed to another, it is not only Christ's righteousness that cannot be imputed to me but, alas, my sin cannot be imputed to Christ. Thus the very heart of the evangelical faith is eviscerated.

A third thing should be mentioned here. It has been implied and sometimes stated by adherents of the New Perspective that the Reformers were mistaken in virtually equating the Judaizers who plagued the church with the "salvation without grace" teaching they saw in late medieval church life. But this seriously misconstrues if not misrepresents the historical situation.

In fact the late medieval church was almost obsessed with grace – and how the individual gets "more" of it by doing what he can. The Reformers well understood that Roman Catholic theology did not outright deny the necessity of grace. Rather they recognized that the "grace" referred to was really not grace at all – since its reception was so conditioned on a man's good works. To say "grace" is by no means the same thing as to understand or teach "grace." One should never be misled by the regular occurrence of the word "grace" into assuming that a biblical understanding of grace is well understood.

The result of this – paradoxically – is that at times one has the impression that the New Perspective fails to notice a strikingly similar phenomenon in Second Temple Judaism, or glosses over it when it appears: the use of the language of "grace," when in context the "grace" in view is conditioned on man. It is in fact compromised grace, not true grace. It turns out, after all, that while the pattern of the Old Testament's teaching is that fellowship with God is by pure grace, that grace is at times greatly dis-graced in the rabbinical literature, as it frequently was in the history of the covenant people. Even the notion that the reason Yahweh is so gracious to his poor people is *because* they have suffered so much turns out to be grace compromised by its conditionalism: there is a reason to be found in man to "explain" why, or to whom, God is gracious. But true grace cannot thus be qualified without being distorted.

More might be said about the question of whether or not Paul experienced a "guilty conscience" before he yielded to Christ. It seems to the present writer that the relationship between Saul of Tarsus and Stephen, the likelihood that they were members of the same synagogue (or synagogue group) in Jerusalem, the fact that Saul had never been excelled by any of his peers ... until he met Stephen, and the role that the law against coveting seems to have played in Saul's life, all suggest that much more was involved in his Damascus Road experience than a call to recognize Jesus as Messiah.

The New Perspective has proved to be attractive to a number of evangelicals who are concerned about the state into which historic evangelicalism has fallen, with its focus on the self and subjective experience. For with the New Perspective comes an emphasis on Scripture as story, on the history of redemption, on biblical theology, on the objective rather than the subjective, and a renewed emphasis on the community of the church and sacraments and on the social implications of the Lordship of Jesus Christ.

The authors of these essays share these concerns. They belong to an old tradition, indeed an older tradition, that has long guarded redemptive history, biblical theology, the life of the church, and the implications for the redeemed of the Lordship of Christ. Readers may readily spot here the influences of Abraham Kuyper and Herman Bavinck, Geerhardus Vos and Cornelius Van Til, Herman Ridderbos and John Murray, and behind them all John Calvin. It would be hard to find a group of evangelicals more aware of the dangers of a subjectivism or a pietism that focuses on faith rather than on Christ, on an experience of justification rather than on the cross. They are well-versed in the gospel, and its maintenance is their chief concern. In all of their discussions of justification in Pauline theology, historical theology, confessional theology, and in its philosophical, cultural, and pastoral implications they are concerned to guard what is of "first importance": "That Christ died for our sins in accordance with the Scriptures ..." (1 Cor. 15:3).

Much more could be said here, even by way of introduction. But before raising the curtain for the contributors to this volume to step on to center stage, it may be helpful to provide a road map to the journey on which the following pages take us.

Richard B. Gaffin Jr. opens this symposium with an important essay on the relationship between justification and eschatology, underlining that justification has a "last day" quality about it, because it is integrally related to the resurrection-justification of Christ. Like adoption, with which it goes hand-in-hand in the gospel, justification is a present and perfect reality which anticipates a future realization. But how are these two "moments," the present day and the last day related to each other? Dr. Gaffin proves a safe guide home for the Christian in insisting that the final declaration of justification, as the fruition or publication of present justification, is never rooted in anything but the finished work of Christ.

Lane G. Tipton then builds upon Dr. Gaffin's work in expounding the importance of union with Christ. Rooted in a careful study of several important passages of Scripture, Dr. Tipton articulates the genius of this union in terms of the New Testament's teaching on the distinct but inseparable, contemporaneous but eschatological nature of all soteriological benefits. He then discusses how well, or otherwise, this apostolic teaching is reflected in a variety of theologians, including an extended discussion of the work of N. T. Wright in this area,

This sets the scene for a series of historical-theological contributions. The first of these is authored by Peter A. Lillback, the current President of Westminster Seminary and also a Reformation scholar in his own right. He examines the views on justification of various Reformation figures, including Lutheran, and points to the genius of Calvin's formulation of the dual, distinct yet inseparable covenant benefits of justification and sanctification. Thus Calvin teaches a forensic justification that can never be confused with sanctification, yet never exists without moral renewal.

Two contributions follow which draw upon and explore the rich theological discussions of justification in the seventeenth century. Carl R. Trueman develops the study of the Calvinist tradition with a careful essay on the teaching of John Owen the great English Puritan theologian (perhaps the greatest English theologian, period). Setting his exposition of justification against the background of the theological subcultures in the seventeenth century (not least that of Socinianism), Dr. Trueman underscores the clarity and depth of Owen's exposition of Christ's active and passive obedience and righteousness. Here is "Reformed orthodoxy at its best."

Before leaving the seventeenth century, Jeffrey K. Jue invites us to linger at the Westminster Assembly's debates and discussions of justification. This, as will soon be clear, is of more than merely historical interest in view of current claims that the Westminster divines glossed over the classical distinction of active and passive obedience in their statements on the work of Christ and in their exposition of imputation. Dr. Jue patiently lays out not only the historical evidence from the debates of the Assembly, but also sets them within the historical-theological context without which they have been misinterpreted. By way of conclusion he draws a striking parallel between views associated with the "New Perspective on Paul" and that of seventeenth-century Arminians.

William Edgar not only advances the discussion into the following century and beyond, but also takes us into the climate of the French Revolution and the rise of the modern world. Moving easily in the philosophical and cultural milieu of Europe, he offers some illuminating reflections on humanity's need of – and substitutes for – atonement. Arguing, in the words of one of his subheadings, that "Warm embrace is not justification" Dr. Edgar calls us back to the foundation of the finished work of Christ.

This leads us to an essay by K. Scott Oliphint on covenant faith. Justification is "by faith." But what is "faith" and in what sense is it related to justification? Dr. Oliphint takes up the question (much discussed in the work of proponents of the "New Perspective") of the meaning of Paul's phrase *pistis Christou*. He brings forward important considerations for maintaining the classical understanding that this refers to the faith of the believer in Christ, not to the faith or faithfulness of Christ.

Finally, J. Stafford Carson brings these discussions to a conclusion by examining the pastoral implications and value of the doctrine of justification by faith. In passing he notes ways in which the dilution of the doctrine not only involves an abandonment of traditional formulations but actually endangers the truth of the gospel.

Two "bonus tracks" complete this volume. The first is a valuable bibliography of reformed works on justification, compiled by Professor Alexander Finlayson. This provides an essential starting point for further study. The second is the brief but seminal monograph by the late Professor John Murray, entitled *The Imputation of Adam's Sin*. In a variety of ways Professor Murray's influence and mantle have fallen on the contributors to this book, some because they were his students, all because they have taught at Westminster Theological Seminary, Philadelphia, Pennsylvania. The inclusion here of this careful study of imputation makes a fitting appendix to this catena of contemporary studies on a theme which lay close to Professor Murray's heart and was a crucial aspect of his life and work.

Now all that remains is to echo the famous words that once led to the conversion of Augustine: *tolle lege* – pick up this book and read on.

Justification and Eschatology

Richard B. Gaffin, Jr.

Some Initial Considerations

The Reformation doctrine of justification recaptures the eschatological heart of the gospel. This appreciation, largely implicit and however often compromised or inadequately appreciated, is definite and clear in its effect. In fact, it probably does not overstate, this rediscovery is perhaps what is most important about the Reformation soteriologically. Certainly nothing is more important.[1]

For instance, in a verse like Romans 8:1, "There is therefore now no condemnation for those who are in Christ Jesus," Luther and others, instinctively and implicitly if not explicitly, heard an eschatological pronouncement. They understood that the "now" (νῦν) there is nothing less than eschatological in its force; it is the "now" of eschatological realization.

Late medieval Roman Catholicism left the future verdict at the final judgment the ever anxious and uncertain outcome of the Christian life. In contrast, the Reformers grasped that the verdict, belonging at the end of history, has been brought forward and already pronounced on believers in history, and so, constituting the certain and stable basis for the Christian life, provides unshakeable confidence in the face of the final judgment.

This Reformation understanding, I take it, is true to the New Testament and, in particular, to Paul's teaching that believers have already been justified by faith. In this chapter that teaching, eschatological to its core, is not my primary concern, and will be

[1]This chapter adapts material, slightly modified, from Richard B. Gaffin Jr., "*By Faith, Not By Sight.*" *Paul and the Order of Salvation* (Milton Keynes, England: Paternoster, 2006), primarily 79-100.

presupposed rather than argued, though some of its important aspects will emerge in the course of the discussion that follows.[2] Instead, in light of clear New Testament teaching on justification as realized and a present reality for believers, I want here to focus on the question of justification as future. Addressed for the most part as an issue in Paul's teaching, what about justification and the "not yet" of our salvation? Should we, according to him, think of our justification as in some sense still future? Should we, in other words, see his teaching on justification in terms of his already –not yet outlook on salvation as a whole and within what I take to be the controlling anthropological grid provided by the "inner self"–"outer self" distinction explicit in 2 Corinthians 4:16?[3]

It might seem, at least as an initial reaction, that our answer should be in the negative, and an emphatic "no" at that. The reason for such a reaction is not only understandable but bound to be appreciated. To speak of justification as in any sense future or "not yet" appears to take away from its "already," definitive character. To view it as in some sense still future seems to threaten its present, absolute finality and so to undermine its settled certainty in the life of the Christian. It would surely betray or misrepresent Paul, then, if anything I say here would be heard or allowed to call into question that settled certainty. That is no more or less the case, for instance, than it would be to call into question for him, because the resurrection of the body is still future, the settled certainty of the believer's already having been resurrected with Christ (e.g. Eph. 2:5-6; Col. 3:1; Gal. 2:20). In fact, as we will presently see, this observation about the resurrection has particular, inner relevance for justification.

---

[2]The New Perspective on Paul holds, characteristically, that the primary concern of justification is ecclesiology (who belongs to and what defines the church as the eschatological people of God); its soteriological significance is, at most, second order and derivative. That view for the most part will be outside our purview, except to state here that, to the contrary, justification is at the heart of Paul's soteriology – to be sure, with inalienable ecclesiastical, corporate implications.

[3]This distinction (cf. Rom. 7:22; Eph. 3:16), I take it, reflects, in basic anthropological categories, the dual, realized–still future structure of salvation in union with Christ by faith, in the interim between his resurrection and return. For some substantiation and further elaboration, see Gaffin, *By Faith, Not By Sight*, 53-58.

Explicit references in Paul to a still-future justification for believers, if present at all, are minimal. Among passages usually cited are Romans 2:13; 5:19; Galatians 5:5; 2 Timothy 4:8, but all are contested. My own view is that at least some of these passages and perhaps others are plausibly, even most likely, to be read as referring to an actual future justification for believers, or a future aspect of their justification. However, I am not able here to enter into the kind of detailed exegesis that would be necessary to make treatment of them profitable, especially in view of the intensive attention that Romans 2:13, in particular, is currently receiving in this regard. This means that our discussion here, in taking the direction it does, has a somewhat partial character and so, at places, no doubt needs to be amplified.

In fact, there is value in bracketing the passages noted in the preceding paragraph from our consideration in the interest of showing, as the following discussion seeks to do, that the case for a future aspect to the Christian's justification or, put another way, the case for a decisive future aspect to the forensic side of salvation that is tantamount to justification, does not rest on such passages alone or even primarily. There are four components to that case, as I make it here: 1) a presumptive consideration stemming from the structure of Paul's soteriology and eschatology; his teaching on 2) the forensic significance of both death, including bodily death, and resurrection; 3) adoption; and 4) the final judgment.

The Perspective of the Westminster Standards and Reformed Orthodoxy

Before considering these four components, it will be useful to introduce into our discussion, as background, a historical-theological perspective that has been given confessional status in the Westminster Standards. *Larger Catechism*, 90 asks, "What shall be done to the righteous at the day of judgment?" In a similar vein is *Shorter Catechism*, 38, "What benefits do believers receive from Christ at the resurrection?" In both instances the answer includes the affirmation that on the day of judgment believers, as they are said to be righteous, shall be "openly acknowledged and acquitted."[4]

---

[4]The supporting texts cited, in order, are Matt. 25:33 and 10:32 (*Larger Catechism*) and Matt. 25:23 and 10:32 (*Shorter Catechism*).

The point, plain enough, in both catechisms is that Christians will be included in the final judgment. At the risk of belaboring the obvious, for them it will have forensic or legal significance, it will be relevant as judgment; they will in fact be judged at the final judgment. Specifically, for them the outcome contemplated or, we may also say, the verdict to be rendered, will be their acquittal; they will be "openly acquitted." In other words, of any charges to the contrary conceivably contemplated, they will be declared not guilty and that will happen publicly. It is not to be missed that in the *Shorter Catechism* this acquittal is among the "benefits" received from Christ. Also, that it is said to be "open" or public is an important factor that will occupy us in detail below.

To be "acquitted" and to be "justified" are largely interchangeable. While, considering biblical teaching as a whole, the two are not fully synonymous – justification includes a positive forensic standing as well as acquittal as the judicial removal of the guilt incurred by sin – they do overlap in meaning. Acquittal is at the heart of justification. So these Catechisms teach, in effect, that for believers the final judgment, as it involves their being acquitted, will have justifying significance. In some sense it will be their justification, their being declared to be righteous. We may conclude, then, by clear implication, that the notion of the believer's justification as in some sense future or having a future aspect has confessional grounding in Reformation orthodoxy. That notion does not stem from the historical-critical study of Paul in the modern era. Nor is it a recent discovery bound up with the New Perspective on Paul. It is not foreign to or in conflict with the heritage of the Reformation but rather is given with that heritage.[5]

---

[5]The scope of this concluding generalization should probably be narrowed to reformed orthodoxy, since I am unaware, though without extensive study, of similar statements in Lutheran confessions and theology.

This generalization also warrants the careful sort of documentation and amplification that I am unable to give it here. It is my growing impression that the notion of justification as in some sense future has been widespread in reformed theology in the past, beginning in the seventeenth century, or at least much more prevalent than is often recognized and acknowledged today. Among reformed writers who speak of justification as future are R. Dabney, *Systematic Theology* (Edinburgh: Banner of Truth, nd/1871), 645; J. Fisher, *The Assembly's Shorter Catechism Explained, by Way of Question and Answer* (Glasgow: William Smith, 1779/1753), 251-52; J. Flavel, "An Exposition of the Assembly's

Justification as Future: A Presumptive Consideration

But now, what about Paul? How does this confessional position square with his theology? I begin addressing that question with what might be viewed as a presumptive consideration, one bound up with the structure of his theology or, more particularly, the basic pattern of his soteriology. Put negatively, there is no place in Paul for a justification that a) would fall outside of union with the exalted Christ by faith, that is, would not be a benefit given with that union; b) would fall outside of the already–not yet pattern of receiving salvation that qualifies that union; and c) would fall outside of the scope of the "inner–outer" anthropology of 2 Corinthians 4:16 that corresponds to b). In other words, a future justification of the Christian at Christ's return – in the resurrection of the body and at the final judgment, as we will see – is a "good and necessary consequence," fully consonant with Paul's teaching. To argue the contrary is faced with a difficulty, substantial, if not insuperable, in my judgment. It must show how isolating justification from the already–not yet structure of receiving salvation, in particular from the "not yet" aspect of salvation, would be compatible with or coherent within Paul's soteriology centered on union with Christ and involving the "inner–outer" anthropology reflected in 2 Corinthians 4:16.

This observation, I recognize, is one that may not be persuasive to everyone, at least at this point in our discussion. But it will carry weight with those who recognize that the Pauline corpus presents its readers with a structure of theological thinking and the corresponding need to wrestle with the full dimensions of that theology. Whatever the seeming liabilities to some, then, Paul's teaching on justification, we may fairly anticipate, has its place

---

Shorter Catechism," in *The Whole Works of the Reverend Mr. John Flavel* (Edinburgh: Andrew Anderson, 1701), 832; J. Owen, *The Doctrine of Justification By Faith* (*John Owen, The Works of John Owen*, ed. W. H. Gould [Edinburgh: The Banner of Truth Trust, 1977], V.159-60); Francis Turretin, *Institutes of Elenctic Theology*, vol. II, ed. James T. Dennison Jr., trans. George Musgrave Giger [Phillipsburg, New Jersey: Presbyterian and Reformed Publishing Company, 1994], II.685 [16:9:11-12]; H. Witsius, *The Economy of the Covenants Between God and Man* [Phillipsburg, NJ: Eng. trans., Presbyterian and Reformed Publishing Co., 1990/1677], 1.418-24 [book 3, chapt. 8, para. 63-77]. These materials repay careful reading and reflection. My thanks to Robert Tarullo and Peter Wallace for alerting me to some of these sources.

within and reflects the already-not yet pattern of his eschatological soteriology.[6] But we are not left only with this presumption.

Death and Resurrection

Secondly, few will dispute that union with Christ in his resurrection, being united to the resurrected Christ by faith, grounds in its entirety Paul's teaching on sanctification and the renewal of the Christian. But union with Christ as resurrected is not only renovative. That union also has judicial or forensic significance, as does Christ's own resurrection.

The judicial importance of Christ's resurrection is plain from Romans 4:25, "who was delivered up for our trespasses and was raised for our justification." Here a direct connection is drawn between the resurrection and justification. In the light of the immediate and broader context of Paul's teaching, that connection is best understood as follows. As the representative sin bearer and righteous substitute (Rom. 3:25; 8:3; 2 Cor. 5:21), in his full obedience culminating in his death (Phil. 2:8), Christ's resurrection is his own justification in the sense that the resurrection itself is God's *de facto* declarative recognition, on the ground of that obedience, of his righteousness (cf. 1 Cor. 1:30). As an event, his resurrection, we may say, "speaks" and it does so judicially, in a legal manner. For Christians, then, Christ's justification, given with his resurrection, becomes theirs, when united, by faith, to the resurrected Christ, that is, the justified Christ, his righteousness is reckoned as theirs or imputed to them.[7]

The resurrection as Christ's own justification is confirmed by 1 Timothy 3:16, "manifested in the flesh, justified in the Spirit," where the reference, almost certainly, is to the Holy Spirit's activity in raising Jesus from the dead. While most translations

---

[6]Among the best and most helpful overall treatments of this soteriology as well as of the basic structures of Paul's theology in general are Geerhardus Vos, *The Pauline Eschatology* (Grand Rapids, Mich.: Baker, 1979), see esp. 36-41, and Herman N. Ridderbos, *Paul: An Outline of His Theology*, trans. John Richard DeWitt (Grand Rapids, Mich.: W. B. Eerdmans Publishing Co.,1975), esp. 44-90.

[7]To speak of union, as I have at the beginning of this paragraph, as having judicial or forensic significance, is not to exclude imputation or make it redundant. Union *or* imputation, either–or, but not both, as it is sometimes put in discussions current and in the past in depreciating or dispensing with imputation, poses a disjunction for Paul altogether false.

render the verb, "vindicated," the vindication in view is surely judicial; it is to be seen in terms of Christ's righteousness manifested in his obedience "in the flesh," that is, his earthly life prior to the resurrection. So there is no need or compelling reason to abandon the usual translation of the verb, "justified" (KJV, NKJV). "Shown to be righteous" (NLT) also gets at the sense. With that said, it must be kept in mind, of course, that Christ's justification, unlike the believer's, does not involve the imputation to him of the righteousness of another. The ground of his being declared righteous, unlike theirs, is his own righteousness and obedience.[8]

A direct connection between the believer's justification and the resurrection is present in Romans 5:18 in the expression, "justification of life" (δικαίωσιν ζωῆς). That this refers specifically to the life given with Christ's resurrection is beyond doubt from "eternal life" in verse 21 and the parallel statements in 1 Corinthians 15:21-22. The thought here is either that justification consists in life, resurrection-life as *de facto* justification, or, alternatively, that life is the consequence of justification. On either understanding and in the light of the other passages we have noted, the resurrection is inalienably forensic. The resurrection is exponential of Christ's justification based on his righteousness, and the believer's justification is a function or manifestation of union with Christ in his resurrection.

Resurrection is of course meaningless apart from death. In a standard biblical expression, it is always life "from the dead." Accordingly, the forensic, justifying significance of the resurrection we are considering is bound up with its antithetical outcome, death, an outcome that is as judicial in its significance as is resurrection-life. For Paul, briefly,[9] human death is the judicial consequence of sin. Death is neither the merely natural, inevitable outworking of sin nor the cumulative effect of sinning. It is not only sin's own reflexive "reward" or pay-off. As the "wages of sin" (Rom. 6:23), death is not merely pecuniary. As sin is the violation of God's will revealed in his law, death is sin's due, that is, its penal recompense.

---

[8]For further discussion of the resurrection as Christ's justification, see Richard B. Gaffin Jr., *Resurrection and Redemption. A Study in Paul's Soteriology*, 2nd ed. (Phillipsburg, New Jersey: Presbyterian and Reformed Publishing Co., 1987), esp. 119-24.

[9]For a longer survey, see Gaffin, *"By Faith, Not By Sight,"* 30-35.

Death, as God's response to sin, is a response that is judicial in nature. Death, as his ultimate curse on sin, is his just punishment of sin. Death for Paul, it does not overstate, is inalienably penal. Romans 5:16–18 is decisive on this point. On the Adam side of the contrast, the central thread of the argument is not simply from sin to death, as the power unleashed by sin. Rather, that thread moves from sin directly to condemnation and only then to death as the consequence of that condemnation, as the explicitly judicial consequence of sin.

A forensic dimension, therefore, is endemic to both sides of the polarity between death and resurrection. They are, respectively, the judicial consequence of and seal on condemnation and its antithetical counterpart, justification. We are bound, then, to relate that forensic dimension to the already–not yet structure of the resurrection, resulting in this conclusion: as believers are already raised with Christ they have been justified; as they are not yet resurrected they are, in some respect, still to be justified. In terms of the anthropological profile of 2 Corinthians 4:16, considered as "the outer self," subject to decay and wasting, mortal and destined for death, that is, as still unresurrected, the believer's justification is in some sense still future.

Romans 8:10 substantiates this conclusion: "But if Christ is in you, though the body is dead because of sin, the Spirit is life because of righteousness."[10] Here Paul has in view the present situation of believers. On the one hand, his primary accent is on their being indwelt and enlivened by Christ through the Spirit, closely identified here with Christ as "the Spirit of Christ" (v. 9; cf. "the Spirit of life in Christ Jesus," v. 2 and Christ as "life-giving Spirit," 1 Cor. 15:45). In other words, they have already been raised with Christ.

At the same time, however, the imprint of the dual, "inner–outer" anthropology of 2 Corinthians 4:16 is unmistakable in the

---

[10]The translation of v. 10c, " ... the/your spirit is alive ... " (e.g. NIV, NAS) can certainly be given a Pauline sense but is not likely, if for no other reason because here Paul uses the noun "life" (ζωή), not an adjective ("alive"); on the exegesis of this verse, underlying my treatment here, see esp. John Murray, *The Epistle to the Romans: The English Text with Introduction, Exposition, and Notes*, in *The New International Commentary on the New Testament* (Grand Rapids, Mich.: Wm. B. Eerdmans Publishing Co., 1959), 288-291.

way verse 10 is formulated. Or, expressed alternatively in the terms of the related profile in 6:12-13, the believer is "alive from the dead" (v. 10c – the Spirit is life because of righteousness) but is that only "in the mortal body" (v. 10b – the body is dead because of sin).

On the one side of this two-sided state of affairs, then, the "outer," the body, is said to be "dead because of sin." But that can only mean, in the light of Paul's overall teaching, that the body of the believer is mortal as a consequence of sin. Further, that consequence, the believer's mortality, we are bound to say in the light of what we noted above in 5:16-18, is the specifically judicial consequence of sin. Even as, we may note, on the other side, seen in terms of the "inner," it is "because of righteousness" that the Spirit is the life of the resurrected Christ indwelling the believer (cf. Gal. 2:20; Col. 3:4). That is, righteousness, embodied in Christ as we will presently note, is the judicial ground of that life. That this consequence on the side of the "inner," too, is specifically judicial is clear from "the justification of life" in 5:18, as noted above. The righteousness in view in verse 10c, in other words, is justifying righteousness.

It needs to be stressed that this righteousness is not a result of God's renovating work in believers, righteousness as produced in them. Rather, it is Christ's righteousness as distinct from theirs, from anything being done in them. If that were not the case, then Paul would be saying, in effect, "the Spirit is life as a consequence of inwrought righteousness." But that would have things precisely backwards for him. Such Spirit-worked righteousness in the believer is ever the reflex or manifestation of life in the Spirit. That life is never "because of" that righteousness, and that righteousness is never the ground of that life.

In order to head off potentially serious confusion and misunderstanding, I need to be clear at this point where our reflections are *not* headed. I am not arguing, in terms of the inner–outer distinction, that Paul sees the believer as only partially justified as part of an ongoing process that is not yet complete or uncertain as to its outcome. In the immediate context of verse 10, verse 1, like a lodestar, provides a fixed and invariable point of reference. The removal of condemnation, the justification, affirmed there is true of the believer, not just in part but as a whole person. For sinners united to Christ by faith, in the judgment rendered by God, the previously existing state of being found guilty and of being condemned has been reversed by their being found not guilty, by their being declared just. That judicial reversal applies to the believer as a person, not just to a part or aspect. In the terms of 2 Corinthians 4:16, it is the single, total subject of that verse, the person who does not "become discouraged," who has been justified, not just "the inner self" of that person. It would be perverse toward Paul to conclude anything less.

At the same time, however, in verse 10 we are bound to take into consideration the distinction, indeed the nothing less than life-and-death *disjunction*, in view just as it is applied specifically to *Christians*, and to do so in terms of Paul's teaching on the realized–still future pattern of their resurrection. In that light, it seems fair to observe, for believers, as death is inalienably penal ("because of sin"), its removal – as the judicial consequence of the reversal of judgment already effected in justification – does not take place all at once but unfolds in two steps, one already realized and one still future. Correlatively, the open or public declaration of that judicial reversal, that manifest declaration attendant on their bodily resurrection and the final judgment, is likewise still future. In that sense, put in the terms of 2 Corinthians 5:7, "we walk by faith, not by sight," corresponding as it plainly does to the anthropological distinction of 4:16, believers are already justified – by faith. But they are yet to be justified – by sight.

An illustration may help to make this point clear. The situation is analogous to that of a prisoner whose conviction has been overturned and, with that reversal, his imprisonment terminated. But the procedure by which the court implements its decision, irreversible and sure in its execution, is such that the actual release from prison takes place in two stages, one immediate and the other at a point in the future (here the analogy breaks down because of the "inner-outer" anthropology involved). To apply the analogy further: as to their inner self, sinners, when justified by faith, are instantaneously released into resurrection-life from the prison/punishment of death; so far as their outer self is concerned, there is a delay, until the resurrection of the body, in their being released from that prison.

These observations are reinforced by 1 Corinthians 15:54-56, "When the perishable puts on the imperishable, and the mortal puts on immortality, then shall come to pass the saying that is written: 'Death is swallowed up in victory.' 'O death, where is your victory? O death, where is your sting?' The sting of death is sin, and the power of sin is the law" (ESV).

Here Paul is discussing the believer's bodily resurrection, in other words, the resurrection of the "outer self."[11] In that regard (bodily resurrection), for the believer "death [being] swallowed up in victory" is *not yet* a reality. "Then," that is, at a time still future, "*shall* come to pass the saying that is written: 'Death is swallowed up in victory'" (v. 54).[12] Again, in terms of the controlling metaphor of the chapter (vv. 20, 23), so far as the Christian's place in the "harvest" of bodily resurrection is concerned, death is not yet "swallowed up in victory."

That this victory over death for the church is still future is confirmed by verses 25-26. "He," that is, the already resurrected Christ, "must reign *until* he has put all his enemies under his feet," with death being the "last" of these enemies "to be destroyed." Given the immediate context, the present tense of the Greek verb (καταργεῖται) plainly has a future force, as virtually all English translations recognize. By his own bodily resurrection, as the "firstfruits," death's final and complete destruction has already occurred for Christ personally and so is assured for the rest of the harvest. But for them their actual, bodily participation in that destruction has yet to occur. Further, verses 50-52 make clear that the future victory over death in verses 54-55 will be at the time of the "last trumpet," that is, the final judgment (cf. 1 Thess. 4:16; Matt. 24:31).

In this setting, then, where the destruction of bodily death is still future for believers, verse 56 affirms, "the sting of death is sin, and the power of sin is the law." Here, with reference to the present, continuing mortality of the believer, an explicit link is made between death and sin, and specifically as the latter is in view as violation of the law. Sin is "the sting of death," the "kiss" of

---

[11]It needs to be kept in mind that the resurrection of unbelievers is outside Paul's purview throughout the whole of 1 Cor. 15 (as is also true in 1 Thess. 4:13-17; cf. Acts 24:15, where he affirms the resurrection of the "unjust" as well as the "just").

[12]I leave to the side here Paul's interesting use of the OT here and in v. 55 (Isa. 25:8 and Hos. 13:14).

death, we might say. That is, for believers in their present bodies, sin retains its virulent, death-dealing potency and does so, Paul says, just as the law stipulates death as the punishment for its violation. In other words, the continuing mortality of believers, as the consequence of sin, has legal, forensic significance. Here, we should conclude, their bodily mortality is seen as the still present, yet unremoved penal consequence of sin.

To be sure, in dying for them Christ has fully borne and so secured the removal of the punishment their sins justly deserves (e.g. Rom. 3:25-26). Nothing Paul says even remotely suggests anything else. But for them death, as the just punishment for sin, has not yet been removed so far as the body is concerned. For Paul, however certain its eventual removal for believers, while death remains, and to the degree death is operative, to that extent the effects of punishment for and curse on sin continue. In that respect, death, as punishment for and curse on sin, is not yet removed.

The culminating note of exhortation on which the chapter ends (vv. 57-58) is consonant with this conclusion. Paul assures Christians, "your labors are not in vain in the Lord," and that is so because of "God, who gives us the victory through our Lord Jesus Christ." But, from the immediately preceding verses (the references to victory in vv. 54-55), for them that death-destroying victory, while secured and certain, is still future.

These reflections, I should be clear, do not lose sight of nor do they intend to eclipse that for every Christian, as for the apostle himself, "to die is gain" (Phil. 1:21). Surely it is a provision of God's fatherly love that the believer's bodily death becomes the gateway to the blessing of a being with Christ that is "far better" (v. 23). Death, for believers, is the means of access to the perfecting of the "inner self," with the burdens of present bodily existence left behind. Also, Christians, even in death, body as well as soul, remain united to Christ. This appears to be a fair inference from 1 Thessalonians 4:14, "For if we believe that Jesus died and rose again, even so God will bring with him those who have fallen asleep in Jesus."[13]

---

[13]On the basis of this verse the *Westminster Shorter Catechism*, answer 37, speaks of the dead bodies of believers as "being still united in Christ"; similarly *Westminster Larger Catechism*, answer 86, "waiting for the full redemption of their bodies [Rom. 8:23], which even in death continue united to Christ [1 Thess. 4:14]."

Furthermore, nothing, not even death itself, can separate them from the love of God in Christ (Rom. 8:38-39). For them, though they are still presently subject to the penalty of death, God is no longer a wrathful and unreconciled judge but their loving heavenly Father. And so far as suffering and bodily dying are concerned, present ultimately because of their sinfulness rooted in Adam (Rom. 5:12ff.) and their remaining complicity in it, he, in the words of the hymn, "sanctifies to [them] this deepest distress." In fact, in an important strand of Paul's teaching that I am unable to take up here, the present sufferings of believers can and do become an expression of their already having been raised with Christ. Suffering with Christ itself is the medium that manifests his resurrection-life.[14]

Still, bodily death, though a transition to greater blessing, is not, as such, in itself, a blessing. In expressing the preference to be "away from the body and at home with the Lord" (2 Cor. 5:8), Paul at the same time recoils, with intensity ("we groan"), from the ultimate "nakedness" this disembodied existence involves, and his deep desire is to be spared such disembodiment (vv. 2-4).[15] For the creature made bodily in God's image, and awaiting in hope the full restoration of that image in the resurrection of the body (1 Cor. 15:49), to be deprived of bodily existence is a deep and distorting abnormality that has its only adequate explanation in death as the judicial consequence of sin.

To ameliorate bodily death for believers, the fact of their dying, to view the experience itself less starkly or more positively for them, is to be on the way to romanticizing death in a way that is foreign to Paul and, for that matter, the rest of the biblical writers. God's love for believers is not manifested in death as such, but in sustaining them, despite the ultimate and ugly trauma of death, in the unbroken fellowship of his fatherly love and care (cf. Rom. 8:38-39), until this last vestige of the wages of sin is removed in the resurrection of the body.

To summarize this second point, the "outer self" of the believer does not yet experience the saving benefits of union with Christ, either transformative or forensic. So far as I am "outer self," I

---

[14]See esp. 2 Cor. 4:10-11; Phil. 3:10; cf. 2 Cor. 12:9-10; Phil. 1:29; for a discussion of these and related passages, primarily in Paul, see my "The Usefulness of the Cross," *Westminster Theological Journal* 41 (1978–79): 228-46.

[15]On the interpretation of these verses, see esp. Vos, *Pauline Eschatology*, 186-98.

am not yet justified – openly – any more than I am resurrected – bodily. And that is so, without diminishing either the reality that I am already and irreversibly justified or the absolute future certainty of my being justified in the resurrection of the body at the final judgment. Here again, the principle of 2 Corinthians 5:7 holds: I am justified "by faith," but not (yet) "by sight."

Adoption

Thirdly, this conclusion regarding the present–future structure of the Christian's justification is reinforced by a basic aspect of Paul's teaching on adoption. In Paul, adoption, like justification, is a forensic reality. Briefly here, as sinners alienated from God, human beings are not naturally God's sons. Quite the opposite, they are "by nature children of [his] wrath" (Eph. 2:3). This divine wrath is inalienably judicial; it is always his just wrath (Rom. 2:5, 8; 2 Thess. 1:8-9). Accordingly, the removal of that wrath and restoration to fellowship with God as his sons, involves a legal aspect. Christians are not God's sons either inherently or by virtue of creation. Neither is that identity the outcome of a renovative process. Rather, the believer has the status of being God's son by his decisive, declarative act. Adoption, like justification, is judicially declarative.

In Romans 8:14-17 Paul is emphatically clear that believers have already been adopted. They are now, by adoption, "sons of God," and among the consequent privileges they enjoy, the Spirit, who indwells them, is "the Spirit of adoption," assuring them that now, presently, God is their Father and they, as his adopted sons, may address him as such.

But then just a few verses later, he writes, "we wait eagerly for adoption, the redemption of our bodies" (v. 23). Now adoption is future, at the time of the resurrection, given with or realized in bodily resurrection. Here, too, for adoption, as we saw to be the case for justification, the future resurrection of the body is invested with *de facto* forensic significance.[16] The resurrection of believers will be declarative of their adoption.

In basically the same context, within the scope of a few verses, then, adoption, as a forensic, declarative reality, is seen as both

[16]The description, only here in Paul, of the resurrection as a "redemption" reinforces this forensic significance.

present and future. Initially this could seem confusing, even incoherent. How can it be both? By the nature of the case, it would seem apparent, either I am adopted or I am not. If I am adopted, how can I be awaiting adoption?

Paul, we can be sure, has not become unsure of himself here. Nor is he involved in some kind of double-talk. He is not speaking in paradox, where adoption as future renders uncertain adoption as present and settled. The left hand of the "not yet" of adoption does not take away or cancel out, in dialectical fashion, what the right hand of the "already" of adoption gives. Rather, the respect in which he distinguishes present and future is clear from the immediate context. What is still future, and the entire creation longs for, is "the revelation of the sons of God," that is, fairly glossed, "the *open* revelation of the sons of God" (v. 19). Again, what is in prospect is "the freedom of the glory of the children of God," that is, the free and open manifestation of their glory (v. 21). Believers await the open manifestation of their adoption in the resurrection of the body.

Here, yet again, the principle of 2 Corinthians 5:7 is present and controlling. For now, until Jesus comes, Christians have their adoption "by faith," but not yet "by sight." They are God's adopted children in the mode of "believing," but not (yet) of "seeing." It is in fact the case, they are not yet *openly* adopted. A fair commentary on Paul at this point is I John 3:2, "now we are the children of God, and what we will be has not yet been revealed."

Paul's statements on adoption, we may conclude, provide a window on how he would have us view the closely related forensic blessing of justification. As adoption is both present and future, so too is justification. We have already been justified by faith but not (yet) by sight. Like our adoption, our justification has still to be made public or openly manifested. We have not yet been "openly acquitted."

The Final Judgment

Fourth and finally, while explicit references in Paul to justification as future may be minimal and debatable, in a number of places he either speaks of or clearly indicates the relevance of the final judgment for Christians. Further, as it includes them, it will be a judgment "according to works." That is, as we will see, at the final judgment "works" will serve as an essential criterion.

The clearest passages in this regard are Romans 2:5-16 and 2 Corinthians 5:10.[17] The latter is the capstone declaration to a section (vv. 1-10) where Paul speaks of the hope, penultimately, that Christians have of being present with the Lord apart from the body at death but is concerned primarily with their ultimate hope of bodily resurrection. "For we must all appear before the judgment seat of Christ, so that each one may receive what is due for the things he has done in the body, whether good or evil." Believers, too, face final judgment, and for them, too, that judgment will involve the just adjudication of the things they have done bodily, in "the outer self."

In Romans Paul is intent in the first major section primarily on establishing the universality of human sin (1:18–3:20). His basic assessment, summarized, just beyond this section in the words of 3:23, is that "there is no distinction" [between Jews, despite their privileged possession of the law, and non-Jews], "for all have sinned and fall short of the glory of God." In the course of this argumentation reference is made, in 2:5, to "the day of wrath and revelation of God's righteous judgment," and verse 6 adds that on that judgment day "he will render to each one according to his works."[18] Verses 7-11 then detail the two sides of the judgment in view, with their respective outcomes.

The perennial question at issue in verses 5-11, or if verses 12-13 are included, is whether on their positive side they have in view a scenario that is actual or one that is unrealized and true only in principle. That is, on the one side, is Paul describing Christians and the actual outcome of the final judgment for them or, alternatively, is he speaking hypothetically? The former reading, it seems to me, is almost certainly right.

For the hypothetical view, the view that Paul is speaking, on the positive side, of what is true in principle but not in fact realized, one of the main arguments advanced is that reference in these verses to the gospel or to provisions and consequences of the gospel would be out of place, foreign to the larger context

---

[17]Among others that could be mentioned, Acts 17:31; Rom. 14:10; 2 Tim. 4:1, 8.

[18]Quoting from the Greek OT, Ps. 61:13 (Heb., 62:13; Eng., 62:12) and Prov. 24:12; cf. Eccles. 12:14.

(1:18–3:20) where Paul's concern is with the law and with sin as universal. The gospel and salvation, in particular justification by faith without the works of the law, do not come into view until 3:21ff.

As a generalization, there is a large element of truth in this "pre-evangelical" view of 1:18–3:20. But it is subject to certain qualifications and these have a bearing on how to understand 2:5-11. For instance, 2:29 speaks of "circumcision of the heart, in the Spirit," marking the one who is Jew "inwardly." Despite efforts to see this, too, as a description of what is also true only in principle without affirming that there are actually such persons, particularly in view of the reference to the Spirit it can hardly be read other than as a referring to Christians. That understanding is supported, perhaps put beyond question, by the description of the church in Philippians 3:3 as "the [true] circumcision, who worship by the Spirit of God and glory in Christ Jesus and are not confident in the flesh." Our point here is that Paul's argumentation is such that an outcome of the gospel, and an important one at that, is in view prior to 3:21ff. Moreover, and even more directly related to 2:6ff., the final judgment, just as it is in view in these verses, is, Paul says, "according to my gospel" (v. 16). Apparently, then, Paul sees the positive side of the judgment described in verses 5-11 as having not just legal but gospel significance.

Another major argument for the hypothetical view is a negative one, that to take this passage on its positive side as referring to the final judgment for Christians, especially if verses 12 and 13 are included, creates a basic contradiction with Paul's clear and consistent teaching elsewhere that justification is not by works but by faith. Pointedly, it is argued, to apply to Christians the latter half of verse 13, "the doers of the law ... will be justified," flatly contradicts 3:20, "by the works of the law no one will be justified in his [God's] sight," and many other like passages. However, as I hope our discussion will show, even if verse 13b is to be properly applied to believers, which I am leaving an open question here, contradiction need not be the result.

The hypothetical reading of verses 5-13, or at least verses 5-11, is beset with a substantial difficulty. The future judgment in view here, including the principle or role of works involved, is no different from the descriptions or allusions we find in numerous places elsewhere in Scripture. The following may be cited among such New Testament passages.[19]

> "For the Son of Man will come with his angels in the glory of his Father, and then he will repay each person according to his works." (Matt. 16:27)
>
> "For an hour is coming when all who are in the tombs will hear his voice and come out, those who have done good to the resurrection of life and those who have done evil to the resurrection of judgment." (John 5:28-29)
>
> Before the great white throne, picturing the final judgment, "the dead were judged by what was written in the books, according to their works." (Rev. 20:13)
>
> "I am coming soon, and my reward is with me, to repay everyone according to his work." (Rev. 22:12)

Elsewhere, to cite one more example in Paul, he exhorts believers not to grow weary in doing what is good,

> "for whatever one sows, that will he also reap. For the one who sows to his own flesh will from the flesh reap corruption, but the one who sows to the Spirit will from the Spirit reap eternal life." (Gal. 6:7-9, ESV)

If Romans 2:5ff. are interpreted hypothetically, then the perceived problem of conflict with biblical teaching on justification by faith simply defaults to these and other like passages and they will also have to be interpreted hypothetically on their positive side. But consideration of them will show, as John Murray says pointedly, "the impossibility of such a procedure."[20] The broader biblical context shows that the positive outcome in view in Romans 2:5ff., at least in verses 5-11, if not verses 12-13 as well, is best seen as describing what will be true of Christians at the final judgment.

---

[19]For the OT, e.g. in addition to the references cited in n. 18, Job 34:11; Jer. 17:10, 32:19.

[20]Murray, *Romans*, 63. Among the vast commentary and monograph literature on theses verses, Murray's treatment remains particularly helpful and has especially shaped my own approach.

Looking now within this passage, it is apparent that on its positive side, for Christians, what is at issue is not some penultimate outcome, say, relative degrees or levels of reward, as this and related passages are sometimes understood. Rather, as is also clear on the negative side, at stake is final judgment in nothing less than its ultimate issue, the all-or-nothing of final, eternal destiny. That is evident from the ring composition that marks verses 6-11. God's impartiality as judge in verses 6 and 11 brackets an a-b-b-a chiasm, with verse 10 corresponding to verse 7, verse 9 to verse 8.

On the positive side, in the case of "those who by perseverance in doing good [good work] seek glory, honor and immortality" (v. 7), that is, for "everyone who does [works] what is good" (v. 10), the outcome of the judgment in view is "eternal life" (v. 7) and "glory, honor and peace" (v. 10). That, for them, is the ultimate outcome, and it stands in unrelieved antithesis to the only other alternative in view, the eternal destruction of the self-willed and disobedient, described as "wrath and fury" (v. 8) and "anguish and distress" (v. 9).

Within the larger context of Paul's teaching as a whole, then, the question is unavoidable. How are we to relate this future judgment according to works, as spelled out in this passage and others, to his clear and emphatic teaching elsewhere that justification, as already pronounced eschatological judgment, is a present reality, received by faith alone and on the sole basis of the imputed righteousness of God revealed in Christ?

With an eye to a long and somewhat complicated discussion that we are not able to survey here in any detail, the answer to this relational question does not lie in the direction of distinguishing two *different* justifications. This view has variant forms: one present, by faith and one future, by works; or, present justification by faith alone, future justification by faith plus works, the former based on Christ's work, the latter based on our obedience, even if seen as Spirit-empowered; or, yet again, present justification based on faith in anticipation of future justification on the basis of a life time of faithfulness.[21] All such views undermine or eclipse, whether or not intentionally, the full graciousness of justification according to Paul.

---

[21]E.g. the view, apparently, of N. T. Wright. "Present justification declares, on the basis of faith, what future justification will affirm publicly (according to [Rom.] 2:14-16 and 8:9-11) on the basis of the entire life" (*What Saint Paul Really Said* [Grand Rapids, Michigan: William B. Eerdmans Publishing Company,

The answer, rather, lies where by now we should expect to find it, in the already–not yet structure of union with Christ by faith and in the nature of that faith, particularly as "faith working through love" (Gal. 5:6). There can be little question that this phrase describes justifying faith. In the immediate context justification is at issue, specifically whether circumcision is necessary for justification (vv. 2ff.), so that it is in terms of that issue that the contrast within verse 6 has its sense ("neither circumcision or uncircumcision counts for anything, but faith working through love").

For Christians, future judgment according to works does not operate according to a different principle than their already having been justified by faith. The difference is that the final judgment will be the open manifestation of that present justification, their being "openly acquitted" as we have seen. And in that future judgment their obedience, their works, are not the ground or basis. Nor are they (co-)instrumental, a coordinate instrument for appropriating divine approbation as they supplement faith. Rather, they are the essential and manifest criterion of that faith, the integral "fruits and evidences of a true and lively faith," appropriating the language of the *Westminster Confession of Faith*, 16:2. It is not for nothing, I take it, and not to be dismissed as an overly fine exegesis to observe, that in Romans 2:6 Paul writes "according (κατά) to works," not "on account of, because of (διά)," expressing the ground, nor "by (ἐκ) works," expressing the instrument.[22]

Resurrection and Final Judgment

Toward the beginning of our discussion, I cited the two catechism answers from the Westminster Standards that speak of believers being openly acquitted at the final judgment. The wording of those questions, readers may have noted, differ. *Larger Catechism*, 90 asks, "What shall be done to the righteous at *the day of judgment*?"; *Shorter Catechism*, 38 reads, "What benefits do believers receive from Christ at *the resurrection*?" (italics added). These different phrasings

---

1997], 129). If, as some maintain, this statement has in view what is no more than the "evidentiary basis" of future justification, that is at least not clear from the context of this statement (nor, so far as I have seen, elsewhere in his writings).

[22]Among the vast literature on this and related passages and on the issues they raise, particularly helpful are Ridderbos, *Paul*, 178-181 ("Judgment According to Works") and the concluding observations of Murray, *Romans*, 78-79.

raise the question, how are bodily resurrection and final judgment related? So far as Paul is concerned, it seems clear (as *Larger Catechism*, 88 affirms), especially in the light of 2 Corinthians 5:10, that the resurrection precedes the final judgment. In other words, believers, in union with Christ, will appear at the final judgment as already resurrected bodily. That is, they will appear there in their "spiritual" bodies, that is, bodies that are enlivened and transformed by the Holy Spirit and so are as imperishable as they are glorified and powerful (1 Cor. 15:42-44). Christians will appear for final judgment as fully conformed, by bodily resurrection, to the image of their brother, the exalted Christ (v. 49; cf. Rom. 8:29).

This carries an implication, as important as it is obvious, for understanding, and for ministering, Paul's teaching on justification as future. If believers appear at the final judgment as already resurrected bodily, then they will appear there as *already openly justified*. Their future justification, as we have been speaking of it, will have already taken place in their resurrection, with the *de facto* declarative, forensic, justifying significance it has in Paul, as we have pointed out above. This means, further, we may say, that, for believers, the final judgment, as it is to be according to works, will have for them a reality that is reflective of and further attests their justification already openly manifested in their bodily resurrection.

It would be perverse to an extreme, then, to read Paul's teaching on the final judgment, as well as my discussion of it here, as leaving Christians in this life, in the face of death, uncertain of the future – unable to know for sure the outcome for them at the final judgment and wondering whether they have produced enough "good works" in this life for a favorable verdict entitling them to eternal life. To the contrary, everything at stake here, including their assurance, depends on Christ, specifically his finished righteousness imputed to them, in union with him, and received by faith alone. At the same time, Paul's teaching on the final judgment and the role it will have for believers does put in ultimate perspective the integral, unbreakable bond he sees between justification and sanctification, and on the truth that faith as "the alone instrument of justification ... is ... not alone in the person justified" (*Westminster Confession of Faith*, 11:2).

Union with Christ and Justification

Lane G. Tipton

Introduction

By accenting the centrality of the death and resurrection of Jesus Christ (*historia salutis*), and by incorporating faith union with Christ into the deepest structure of its soteriology (*ordo salutis*),[1] Reformed theology in the tradition of John Calvin offers an expansively rich conception of salvation in Christ,[2] and affirms a robust theology of justification in Christ. Believers are justified in Christ by receiving through faith alone the imputed righteousness of the crucified and resurrected Son of God.[3] Reformed theology therefore affirms the central redemptive significance of union with Christ and maintains staunchly the imputation of Christ's righteousness, received by faith alone, as the sole ground for the believer's justification.

The primary focus of the present essay is to ask and answer the following question: how does union with Christ bear on justification? Put with greater precision, how does the imputation of Christ's righteousness, understood in terms of his active and

---

[1]Soteriology is the study of the application of redemption to believers in Jesus Christ. *Historia salutis* focuses on the once for all accomplishment of salvation in the humiliation and exaltation of Christ. *Ordo salutis* concerns the definitive and ongoing application of redemption in Christ to believers. What has been accomplished *by Christ* in his death and resurrection (*historia salutis*) is given *in Christ* to all believers (*ordo salutis*).

[2]For an excellent summary of this development within reformed soteriology, consult Sinclair B. Ferguson's *The Holy Spirit* (Downers Grove, Illinois: IVP, 1996), 93-114.

[3]Cf. *The Westminster Confession of Faith*, chapter 11, sections 1-2, along with *The Westminster Larger Catechism*, Q&A 65-69, for classic statements of union with Christ and justification.

passive obedience,[4] relate to union with Christ? This essay will attempt to specify the proper relationship between union with Christ and the imputation of righteousness given to the believer in justification.

The thesis of this essay is twofold. First, union with Christ furnishes the organizing structure in terms of which the Spirit applies to believers all of the realized redemptive benefits in Christ distinctly, inseparably, simultaneously, and eschatologically. Second, the imputation of Christ's righteousness is best understood as the aspect of union with Christ that supplies the judicial ground of justification. Union with Christ and the imputation of Christ's righteousness therefore remain distinct-yet-inseparable facets of what it means to be justified by virtue of faith union with Jesus Christ. These two points encapsulate a biblical and reformed theology of justification in Christ. Implied in these observations, then, is the additional point that reformed theology offers a categorically distinctive conception regarding the relationship between union with Christ and justification that cannot be reduced to the formulations of either the post-Reformation Lutheran or so-called New Perspective approach of N. T. Wright.

Union with Christ and Justification: Biblical and Systematic-Theological Considerations

If the imputation of Christ's righteousness is best understood as that aspect of union with Christ that supplies the judicial ground of justification, then it seems critical to examine the biblical lines of argument that support such a conclusion. In this section we will examine six distinct lines of argument that together confirm the notion that imputation is the judicial ground for justification and is given distinctly, inseparably, simultaneously, and eschatologically in union with Christ.

First, *all saving benefits of the gospel, including justification, sanctification or adoption, are given to believers only in terms of faith-union*

[4]Active obedience designates Christ's conformity to the positive precept of God's moral law in both its Adamic and Mosaic administrations. Passive obedience indicates Christ's bearing of the penal sanctions of the broken law of God in both its Adamic and Mosaic administrations. Active and passive obedience culminate in the exaltation/glorification of the Son of God.

with the crucified and resurrected Christ of Scripture. Paul reminds the Ephesian Christians, and believers more generally, that they have "every spiritual blessing in the heavenly realms in Christ Jesus" (Eph. 1:3). Every blessing in the Spirit that can be given in this age is a present possession of the church in Christ Jesus. A little reflection sustains this observation quite convincingly.

Believers are elected and predestined in Christ (Eph. 1:4, 5), die and rise with and in Christ (Eph. 2:4-6; Col. 2:11-13; 3:1-4), are called in Christ (1 Cor. 1:9; 2 Tim. 1:9), regenerated in Christ (Eph. 2:5; Col. 2:13), justified in Christ (Rom. 8:1; Gal. 2:17; 1 Cor.1:30), sanctified in Christ (1 Cor. 6:11; Rom. 6:5ff.), persevere in Christ (Rom. 6:4; 1 Cor. 4-9; Phil. 1:6), die in Christ (Rev. 14:13; 1 Thess. 4:17), and will be raised and glorified in Christ (1 Cor. 15:22; Rom. 8:30). Herman Bavinck, in *Our Reasonable Faith*, offers characteristic in-sight. He observes that,

> There is no sharing in the benefits of Christ unless we share in his person, *because the benefits cannot be separated from the person*; the benefits are not deposited in a merely human person, or a priest, or in a church (i.e. the sacraments) ... the treasury of the blessings of Christ has been deposited nowhere but in Christ ... there is no fellowship with the person of Christ without sharing with his person ... *Christ himself and all his benefits* belong to the church through the Holy Spirit.[5]

By virtue of union with the person of the crucified and resurrected Christ, believers receive every soteric benefit, whether justification, sanctification or adoption, because the benefits of redemption cannot be separated from the person of the crucified and resurrected Christ.

Believers are united to the person of Christ. But more specifically believers are united to his person as crucified and resurrected. Therefore, extending the preceding observation, *union with Christ is a soteric replication in the structure of the believer's life-experience of what happened antecedently in the life-experience of Christ, namely, death and resurrection.*[6]

---

[5]Herman Bavinck, *Our Reasonable Faith: A Survey of Christian Doctrine* (Grand Rapids, Michigan: Eerdmans, 1956), 399-400 (italics mine).

[6]Two qualifications seem necessary. First, the replication in view occurs in the life-experience of the sinner, which means that an analogical relationship

Ephesians 2:5-6 proves particularly instructive along these lines. In perhaps its broadest description, Paul presents the believer's personal experience of salvation as being made alive with Christ (2:5) and raised into the heavenly realms in Christ Jesus (2:6).

In Ephesians 2, Paul refers in verses 2, 3, and 5 to the course of the believer's life-experience prior to union with Christ. The references to a previous walk in verse 2 (cf. Col. 3:7; 2 Cor. 5:7) involve a customary form of life, accenting a characteristic ethical orientation. Paul's language in 2:3 regarding "former conduct" confirms that he has in view life-experience of sinful disobedience prior to being made alive together with and raised up together in Christ (cf. 2 Cor. 1:12; 1 Tim. 3:15). These observations reinforce Paul's baseline conviction that union with Christ has a "before" and "after" in life-experience (cf. Rom. 16:7). The "before" and "after" of union with Christ involves the most basic transition conceivable in Christian experience: a transition from death in sin and trespasses (Eph. 2:1-3) to resurrection life in Christ Jesus (Eph. 2:4-6).

And Ephesians 2:6 amplifies the point that the new life given in Christ has a decisively resurrection structure: "And He raised us up and seated us in the heavenly places in Christ Jesus." The act of resurrection, by which believers become possessors of new life, cannot be isolated from union with Christ. There is no notion of redemptive life apart from the more basic category of resurrection life, and this resurrection life is given in terms of union with Christ. Hence, when Paul specifies the sense in which we have been made alive in Christ (v. 5), it is natural and necessary that he invoke the category of resurrection life in Christ (v. 6). To be made alive with Christ consists in being raised up together with and in Christ. The believer's death and resurrection with and in Christ replicates on a soteriological level the resurrection of Jesus Christ from the dead.

This critical point that governs Paul's soteriology becomes transparent when we read Ephesians 2:5-6 in light of Ephesians 1:19-20.

---

exists between the death and resurrection of Christ, on the one hand, and the death and resurrection of the believer in Christ, on the other hand. Second, both the structure and redemptive reality of what is replicated in the believer's life-experience are nothing less than the resurrection life of Christ, given to believers in the act of union with Christ.

There is a replication in the structure of life-experience of the believer of what occurred in the life-experience of Christ. As Christ was dead on account of believers' trespasses reckoned as his own (1:20), so the believer, prior to union with Christ, was "dead in trespasses" (v. 5). As Christ is "raised from the dead" (1:20), so also the believer is "raised up together in Christ Jesus" (2:6). As the resurrected Christ is "seated at God's right hand in the heavenlies" (1:20), so also the believer is "seated in the heavenlies in Christ Jesus" (2:6).[7] What obtains in the life-experience of Christ as resurrected and seated in the heavenlies pertains to the church's life-experience in union with Christ. This principle of soteric replication explains the resurrection structure of union with Christ. It is resurrection life in Christ – the very resurrection life of Christ – believers possess in union with Christ. Therefore, replication of the resurrection life of Christ in believers occurs by means of union with Christ.[8]

Third, and supplying the basic redemptive-historical rationale for both the point that precedes and the points that follow, *Christ's bodily resurrection, as an eschatological event in redemptive history, includes within it his own justification, adoption and sanctification* (cf. 1 Tim. 3:16; Rom. 1:4; 6:9-11). Not only does Paul speak of Christ's death and resurrection as the basic redemptive category that structures union with Christ, but he also thinks in concrete categories about the nature of Christ's own bodily resurrection. Paul understands Jesus' resurrection as his justification, sanctification, and adoption,

---

[7]A complementary formulation appears in Romans 6:1-14, in which Paul presents the believer's sanctification as a soteric replication of Christ's own death to sin and resurrection to walk in newness of life (v. 4). Paul can reason directly from Christ's death to sin and resurrection unto life toward God (v. 10) to the believer being dead to sin but alive to God in Christ (v. 11).

[8]This language must be understood in such a way that safeguards the Creator/creature distinction, while preserving the resurrection structure of union with Christ. Because Christ's ontic status is utterly unique as the second person of the Trinity, and because in his incarnation as second Adam he remains a divine person, accent must fall on the *creaturely* replication of resurrection life in those united to Christ. Hence, the relationship between Christ's own death and resurrection, and the believer's union with Christ, his death and resurrection must be *analogical*. Yet this must not eclipse the fact that the believer's salvation is most basically understood as a sharing in the resurrection life of Christ himself through union with the crucified and resurrected Savior.

and each benefit is a distinct-yet-inseparable aspect of the one eschatological act of resurrection.

1 Timothy 3:16 focuses on Jesus' justification.[9] At the time-point of his resurrection, Christ was justified in the Spirit. Regarding the structure of this verse, which is actually a stylized poem, I see no compelling reason to depart from the majority position that there are three stanzas composed of two lines, with antithetical parallels present in each couplet.[10] Hence, contrast one is the flesh–Spirit; contrast two is angels–nations; contrast three is world–glory. The structure of the poem subserves the fundamental theological message of the text, which focuses attention not the two natures of Christ, but the two states of Christ, namely, humiliation and exaltation.

Consequently, the contrasts in view are fundamentally eschatological in character. The contrast in couplet three between world and glory gives us some insight into the nature of the contrast in the first couplet between flesh and Spirit. Just as world is related to glory as the sub-eschatological is related to the eschatological (i.e. the preliminary to the final, the provisional to the complete), so also the contrast in the first couplet between flesh and Spirit.

While the incarnation of the Son of God "in the flesh" in 1 Timothy 3:16 does not involve sin, it does denote that mode of existence qualified as temporary, transitory, and provisional. Flesh stands in antithetical contrast to Spirit. The Spirit stands over against the flesh as the agent of the New Creation. George Knight is helpful on this point:

> Romans 1:4 serves as the best commentary on this compact statement (see the commentaries of Cranfield, Murray and Ridderbos). In Romans 1:4 the πνεῦμα would appear to be the Holy Spirit. There, too, a vindication or demonstration is in view (declared to be the Son of God in power) and the means of the declaration is 'by the resurrection from the dead ... If these are

---

[9]1 Timothy 3:16 "Great indeed, we confess, is the mystery of our religion: He was manifested in the flesh (Ὃς ἐφανερώθη ἐν σαρκι), justified in the Spirit (ἐδικαιώθη ἐν πνεύματι), seen by angels, preached among the nations, believed on in the world, taken up in glory.

[10]For a helpful overview of interpretive options, consult William Mounce's *Pastoral Epistles*, Word Biblical Commentary, (Nashville: Thomas Nelson Publishers, 2000), 215-18.

> true parallels, then here Paul is speaking of the vindication of Jesus by the Holy Spirit through his resurrection.[11]

Moreover, we must not overlook the contrast between the Son "being believed on in the world (ἐν κόσμῳ) and "being taken up in glory (ἐν δόξῃ)." The same sort of contrast present between world (as it presently exists) and glory (the realm of the eschatological future, presently realized in the resurrection order) is present in the flesh/Spirit contrast in couplet one. Therefore, when put in view of our text in 1 Timothy 3:16, Spirit and glory are clearly coordinates of one another – the Spirit standing in eschatological contrast to the flesh as glory does to world.[12]

Christ's appearance "in the flesh" accents his identification with humanity in its weakness and frailty and gives expression to his assumption of human nature in its sub-eschatological mode of existence. To speak of Christ as justified in the Spirit invokes his relation to the Spirit-wrought eschatological act of re-creation that dawns in his own resurrection. Paul therefore lays bare the fundamentally eschatological character of Christ's resurrection. Jesus, as resurrected, is identified not with the fleshly, weak and provisional order, but becomes a participant in the pneumatic order of glory and imperishability (cf. 1 Cor. 15:42-49).

And this is true of Christ not only as resurrected, but as justified (ἐδικαιώθη) in his resurrection (3:16b). The eschatology of Jesus' resurrection sheds a great deal of light on the nature of his justification. Just as Jesus is raised to an eschatological order, never to return to the frail, provisional and transitory, so also with respect to the justifying aspect of his resurrection. Jesus' resurrection as his justification places him as second Adam and Messiah permanently beyond probation and in full possession

---

[11]George Knight, *The Pastoral Epistles* (Grand Rapids, Michigan: Eerdmans, 1992), 184-85.

[12]This observation is not intended to blur the distinction between Spirit and glory – the former a reference to the person of the Holy Spirit and the latter a predicate of the age to come and a function of the Spirit's work. The point is simply that Spirit and glory indicate the presence of the eschatological order, as opposed to the sub-eschatological order of flesh and world. But this point in no way blurs the absolute and fundamental distinction between the Spirit (i.e. the uncreated and self-contained third person of the Trinity) and glory (i.e. the created and dependent eschatological order).

of eschatological righteousness.[13] Jesus' justification in the Spirit is an irreversible and declarative act that demonstrates his eschatological righteousness.[14]

The same verb (ἐδικαιώθη) appears in other contexts – one in Paul and the other in a synoptic Gospel – and carries the forensic, declarative, and demonstrative sense of open acquittal or vindication (Rom. 4:2; Matt. 11:19). When we grasp that Jesus is justified (ἐδικαιώθη) in his resurrection, the judicially demonstrative and forensically declarative character of his resurrection from the dead becomes obvious. Jesus' resurrection is an eschatological demonstration and judicial declaration that the Son of God has been vindicated as righteous.

The resurrection of Jesus as his justification follows from the fact that Jesus died as a substitutionary sacrifice for his people, bearing the wrath and condemnation of God for sins not his own (Heb. 2:17; Rom. 3:24-25; 4:25; 2 Cor. 5:21; Heb. 9:26-27). Jesus bore in his sacrificial death the reckoned guilt of his people that requires their condemnation. Hence, the person of Jesus *per se* is without sin, but Jesus as a substitutionary sacrifice actually bears in his death the guilt of reckoned sin and the judicial reality of eschatological condemnation. Because this is the case, we must speak of Jesus' resurrection as his justification. The judicial declaration of justification *alone* reverses the judicial verdict of condemnation, and the verdict

---

[13]Any attempt to allow the already/not-yet of justification to introduce a synthetic element into the formulation, so that covenant faithfulness or good works provide a ground for the future (second) justification, has missed the most critical point about the believer's justification. Just as Jesus' resurrection places him forever beyond probation as the justified second Adam and Messiah, so also believers in union with Christ are forever beyond probation and in possession of eschatological righteousness. Nothing in the not-yet can compete with the foundational gospel truth that *the believer's present justification in Christ is just as definitive and irreversible as the justification of Jesus Christ*. Any discussion of the future eschatology of justification must begin and cohere with the irrevocable and unalterable character of the believer's present justification in Christ (cf. *The Westminster Larger Catechism*, Q&A 70-71, 90).

[14]For an exegetically rigorous and theologically suggestive treatment of Jesus' resurrection as his justification, adoption, and sanctification, see Richard B. Gaffin, Jr., *Resurrection and Redemption: A Study in Paul's Soteriology* (Phillipsburg, New Jersey: P&R, 1987), 119-23.

of justification in Jesus' case is manifest in his resurrection in the Spirit.

And when we recognize the covenantal character of Jesus' obedience as a second and last Adam (Luke 4:1-13; Rom. 5:12-19; 1 Cor. 15:45, 47), and the way that his active and passive obedience satisfies the just demands of the covenant of works, then the resurrection of Christ as his justification *must* involve a judicial declaration that the Son of God has met perfectly the demands of justice, both in terms of the positive precept and penal sanction of the covenant of works.[15] Thus, the resurrection of Christ as his justification is a forensic declaration that the Son of God has offered the *ex pacto*, meritorious obedience required under the covenant of works both in life and in death.[16] The resurrection of Christ as his justification is the necessary outworking of the meritorious obedience offered by the Son of God under the covenant of works.

Since the covenant of works invests the work of the Son of God with both an eschatological and meritorious character, it follows that the resurrection of Christ includes eschatological justification. Covenant theology demands nothing less, and Paul in 1 Timothy 3:16, consistent with the corpus of his entire theology, teaches the eschatological justification of Jesus Christ by virtue of his resurrection in the Spirit.

Dissatisfaction with understanding the resurrection of Christ as including his justification could easily betray an implicit permutation of a docetic Christology.[17] The reality of Jesus'

---

[15]All denials of the active obedience of Christ must presuppose a denial of the covenant of works, because the covenant of works originally held forth to Adam the prospect of eschatological life on the condition of active obedience alone. Therefore, references to Christ as a second and last Adam (explicitly in 1 Cor. 15:45, 47, and implicitly in Rom. 5:12-19 and Luke 4:1-13) demand we understand the obedience of the Son of God as possessing both active and passive aspects.

[16]For insightful treatments of the meritorious character of Adam's obedience under the covenant of works, consult M. G. Kline, *Kingdom Prologue* (Overland Park, Kansas: Two Age Press, 2001), 107-117, and Francis Turretin, *Institutes of Elenctic Theology*, vol. I, (Phillipsburg, New Jersey: P&R, 1994), 578.

[17]I use docetic in a modified sense in the development of the argument below. Traditionally, advocates of docetism contend that the Son of God only appeared to have a true human nature. What I intend by docetic in this context amounts

condemnation demands that resurrection include a justifying aspect. This is so because the judicial verdict of justification alone answers to the judicial verdict of condemnation, and the verdict of justification in the resurrection of Christ signals an eschatological reversal of the verdict of condemnation he suffered on the cross.[18] Just as Jesus was *truly condemned* in his death, so also he was *truly justified* in his resurrection. Paul accents the appearance of Jesus in the flesh in the context of his justification in the Spirit, which rules out any form of docetic Christology, or implications consistent with a docetic Christology.

Fourth, *Jesus Christ, as crucified and resurrected, contains within himself – distinctly, inseparably, simultaneously and eschatologically – every soteriological benefit given to the church* (cf. 1 Cor. 1:30 "And of him you are in Christ Jesus, who became for us wisdom from God, that is, our righteousness, holiness and redemption").

Demonstrating the Christological character of God's wisdom, and elaborating on the fact that no flesh can boast before God (vv. 17-29), Paul argues that God has originated a state of affairs in redemptive history in which Christ, by virtue of his death and resurrection, has become eschatological wisdom for his people. That this is the case turns on the fact that Christ "*became* wisdom from God for us."[19]

And it is "of his doing" that you are "in Christ Jesus." The point is that no flesh can boast before God, because, for one

---

to an implicit denial that the Son of God actually bore eschatological wrath and condemnation in his substitutionary atonement on behalf of his elect people.

[18]Along these lines, Vos incisively observes that in the case of Christ "...resurrection had annulled the sentence of condemnation" (*The Pauline Eschatology* [Grand Rapids, Michigan: Eerdmans, 1961], 161). Gaffin is no less clear when he says that "... the eradication of death in his resurrection is nothing less than the removal of the verdict of condemnation and the effective affirmation of his (adamic) righteousness" (*Resurrection*, 122).

[19]Two brief points of elaboration seem in order. First, the other place in 1 Corinthians where Paul speaks of a "becoming" in the case of Christ appears in 1 Corinthians 15:45, where Paul has in view what Christ became in his resurrection and, more specifically, ascension (i.e. life-giving Spirit). Apart from his resurrection from the dead, Christ has not become eschatological and soteriological wisdom for us any more than he has become life-giving Spirit. Second, the pneumatic references in 1 Corinthians 2:4ff., which qualify the wisdom in 1 Corinthians 1:30, assume a functional identification of Christ and the Spirit and therefore presuppose the categories of both death and resurrection.

thing, it is of him or of his doing that believers are in Christ Jesus. It is sovereign power or activity of God, and nothing resident within the flesh, that effects union with Christ. Therefore, a decisive, divine activity lies at the basis of the believer's union with Christ, and the language "in Christ Jesus" provides a comprehensive soteriological formulation that sums up globally the difference between those who know God's wisdom and those who do not.

Paul uses the "in Christ" phrase pervasively to convey the multi-faceted reality of the salvation heralded in the gospel of Christ. But what more specifically does 1 Corinthians 1:30 tell us about the nature of the Christ with whom the believer is united? In terms of his developed argument in 1 Corinthians, Paul provides in 1:30 a preview of the 1 Corinthians 15:45ff. formulation in a greatly compressed and encapsulated form, bringing a different set of concerns into view. 1 Corinthians 1:30 previews 15:45ff. in the sense that "life-giving Spirit" is the broadest redemptive category that describes the resurrection life given to those in union with the ascended Christ (with a decided focus on *future* eschatological blessing), but 1:30 describes that same redemptive-historical reality in the narrower categories of specific soteric benefits (with the emphasis lying on realized blessings). This means that what Christ "became" in his death and resurrection can be explained in broad (i.e. life-giving Spirit) or narrowly aspectival soteric categories (i.e. righteousness, holiness, and redemption).[20]

How, then, are we to understand the predicate nominatives that follow the relative clause, i.e. righteousness, holiness, and redemption? The basic insight to grasp is that the "wisdom" Christ has become for his people in 1 Corinthians 1:30 is characterized by the soteric categories of righteousness, holiness, and redemption. Gordon Fee argues that the true wisdom is to be understood in terms of three different aspects of the same saving reality, namely, what was accomplished for us in the redemptive

[20]In 1 Corinthians 1:30 Paul brings into view the definitive aspect of sanctification, by which sanctification is viewed as a permanent breach with the power of sin. As such, Christ clearly contains within himself our holiness in that, as crucified and resurrected, he has entered into a permanent state of death to sin, and this same truth is predicated of believers in Christ (Rom. 6:9-11; Col. 3:1-4).

work of Christ.[21] What Fee suggests, then, is that the additional nouns that Paul uses after the relative clause function to accent the various aspects of the one fundamental saving reality that Christ has become for us in his death and resurrection.

In 1 Corinthians 1:30, then, Paul speaks of union with Christ in terms of Christ becoming for us wisdom from God, understood aspectivally in distinct-yet-inseparable categories of righteousness, holiness, and redemption. When we keep these things in mind, we can make the following inference: just as Christ himself has become for us the life-giving Spirit (1 Cor. 15:45), so also Christ contains within himself – inseparably, distinctly, simultaneously, and eschatologically – righteousness, holiness, and redemption (1 Cor. 1:30). To be in Christ is to be in the one who has become for believers the crucified and resurrected embodiment of all saving benefits. Therefore, there are no benefits of the gospel apart from union with Christ.

Fifth, and turning the focus now upon union with Christ and the imputation of his righteousness, we need to make the following observation: *the sin of Adam, understood as trespass and disobedience, elicits condemnation and consists in death, both in Adam and those he represents; but in antithetical contrast to this reality, the righteousness of Christ, understood as one meritorious act of righteousness and obedience, elicits justification that consists in eschatological life, both for Christ and those he represents* (Rom. 5:12-19).[22]

First, notice that the sin, transgression, and disobedience of Adam are closely and inseparably correlated to one another and provide the context by which we understand both his and our condemnation in him. The sin of Adam (v. 12) is first and foremost to be viewed as trespass of the divine will (cf. 5:15, 17a). Sin is certainly a relational concept, but it is a relational concept in view of the covenantal Creator/creature relationship. Sin, at its core, consists in a violation of God's righteous will, a violation of God's covenantal revelation (cf. *Westminster Shorter Catechism*, Q&A 14).

Second, in explicating this close connection between sin and transgression of the divine will, Paul brings into view another

[21]Gordon Fee, *The First Epistle to the Corinthians*, New International Commentary on the New Testament, eds. Ned B. Stonehouse, F. F. Bruce, Gordon D. Fee, (Grand Rapids, Michigan: Eerdmans, 1987), 86.

[22]For many of these insights, I am deeply indebted to Dr. Richard B. Gaffin, Jr.

complex of issues that are equally interrelated to one another: *trespass and condemnation* (cf. 5:18 "the trespass of the one man led to condemnation for all men"). The covenantal transgression of the divine will renders Adam and all men comprehended in him or represented by him judicially liable to condemnation.

Third, and speaking now more globally, Paul broadens his focus and summarizes in verse 19 as follows: "by the disobedience of the one man the many were made sinners." In the developing context, the sin in view is sin as trespass, sin as guilt, sin that brings an objective judicial declaration of condemnation against Adam and his posterity. It is by the disobedience of the one that the many were rendered judicially liable, guilty, and condemned before God. What this line of argument turns up is this: the sin of Adam, understood as trespass and disobedience, elicits condemnation and consists in death. Adam's sin renders both Adam and the sinner judicially liable to God. Sin elicits a forensic, judicial declaration of condemnation.

Fourth, in antithetical contrast to sin as trespass and disobedience, eliciting condemnation and death, notice the righteousness of Christ as obedience, eliciting justification and life. Along these lines notice two points. First, sin stands in direct contrast to righteousness, as each is descriptive of the work of either Adam or Christ (5:18). The work of Adam is described as sin and presented as trespass and disobedience. But the work of Christ as second Adam is described in *direct contrast* to sin as trespass and disobedience as "one (man's) righteous act." Adam's sin as transgression and disobedience stands *over against* Christ's one act of righteousness.

Righteousness therefore answers to sin as that which renders the sinner judicially liable to God. Hence, righteousness must involve that which *reverses* the liability to guilt and condemnation. Paul makes this very point explicit in 5:18: "Then as one man's trespass led to condemnation for all men, so one (man's) righteous act leads to justification and life for all men."[23] *The one man's righteous act answers directly to the one man's trespass.* And if the trespass

[23]For a brief but useful discussion of the translation of δι᾽ ἑνὸς δικαιώματος, consult volume one of C. E. B. Cranfield, *The Epistle to the Romans*, International Critical Commentary, eds. J. A. Emerton, C. E. B. Cranfield, and G. N. Stanton, (Edinburgh, T&T Clark, 1998), 288-90.

involves a violation of the divine will and invokes condemnation, then righteousness involves conformity to the divine will and invokes justification.[24]

Fifth, and building on this last point, focusing in particular on Romans 5:18, notice that growing directly out of the contrast between the trespass of the one and the one act of righteousness is a further contrast: condemnation as consequence of the trespass and justification and life as the consequence of the one act of righteousness. 5:18: "Then as one man's trespass led to condemnation for all men, so one man's righteous act *leads to justification and life for all men.*" Condemnation, which is forensic and declarative, is the result of the one man's trespass. Justification, which is likewise forensic and declarative, is the result of the one act of righteousness. Antithetical parallels are drawn between sin and righteousness, on the one hand, and condemnation and justification, on the other hand. As a result, just as Adam's act of disobedience results in condemnation for those he represents, so also Christ's one act of righteousness results in justification and life for those he represents. And the terminology classically employed by reformed theologians to communicate the "reckoning" of Adam's trespass for our condemnation or Christ's act of righteousness for our justification is *imputation.*[25]

Finally, notice how Paul broadens the considerations in verse 19: "as through the disobedience of the one man the many

---

[24]This text presupposes the active obedience of Christ for at least two reasons. First, the sin of Adam involves the trespass of God's righteous will, which is revealed to Adam in the covenant of works. It is the character of Adam's sin as trespass that brings into view his failure to conform in trust and obedience to the positive precept of God's revealed law. Hence, the one act of righteousness of Christ as second Adam must *at least* include conformity to the positive precept of the law as a covenant of works. Second, Jesus' one righteous act brings about justification that consists in righteousness and *life* (εἰς δικαίωσιν ζωῆς, cf. Rom. 5:18). Life is *first and foremost* a function of the eschatological focus of the covenant of works, by which eschatological advancement was held forth to obedient Adam (cf. Vos, *Biblical Theology*, 28f.). Active obedience under the covenant of works was the original and exclusive way to eschatological life. This fact is clearly articulated in 1 Corinthians 15:45ff., where Paul argues that the prospect of pneumatic life was implicit in the Adamic order. Life as the outcome of Christ's righteousness and obedience as the second Adam therefore requires active obedience.

[25]Cf. *The Westminster Shorter Catechism*, Q&A 33.

were constituted sinners, so also through the obedience of the one, shall the many be constituted righteous." Paul now construes the verdicts of condemnation and justification on the basis of disobedience and obedience, respectively. Adam's disobedience is that federal, representative act that grounds the judicial sentence of condemnation for those he represents. But Christ's act of meritorious obedience, including as its outcome his resurrection for our justification (cf. Rom. 4:25), grounds the judicial sentence of justification for those he represents. Consequently, justification on the basis of the obedience of Jesus Christ (as second Adam) answers directly to the problem of condemnation on the basis of the disobedience of the first Adam.

Sixth, and in light of all the preceding, we can make sense of the fact that *Christ's obedience and resurrection have absolutely decisive significance for believers' justification.* It is along these lines that we can understand quite naturally how Paul can reason that Christ was "delivered over for our trespasses but raised for our justification" (Rom. 4:25). If Jesus is not justified until the time-point of his resurrection (1 Tim. 3:16), and if his resurrection is a solidaric event that co-implicates his people as it comprehends them within it (Rom. 4:25), then clearly Jesus' resurrection has unique relevance for the justification of all believers. Consequently, it is insufficient merely for Jesus to shed his blood for the justification of believers (Rom. 5:9), because Jesus' eschatological acquittal is tethered to his resurrection from the dead (1 Tim. 3:16).

Paul simply combines in Romans 4:25 the twin notions of Jesus' resurrection as his justification and Jesus' resurrection as a solidaric event that includes believers in its compass. And the result is that Jesus rises not only for his own justification (1 Tim. 3:16) but for the justification of believers as well (4:25). This formulation anticipates the solidaric roles played by the two Adams in Romans 5:12-19.

Geerhardus Vos comments in detail on this passage in a sermon entitled "The Joy of Resurrection Life." Vos argues that the resurrection of Christ "stands in the center of the gospel as a gospel of justification – or deliverance from the guilt of sin."[26] He observes,

---

[26]Geerhardus Vos, *Grace and Glory* (Carlisle, Pennsylvania: Banner of Truth Trust, 1995), 157.

> by raising Christ from death, God as the supreme Judge set his seal to the absolute perfection and completeness of his atoning work. The resurrection is a public announcement to the world that the penalty of death has been borne by Christ to its bitter end and that in consequence the dominion of guilt has been broken, the curse annihilated forevermore.[27]

Christ was delivered over for our trespasses, but raised for our justification. By virtue of faith union with the resurrected Christ, all of his meritorious active and passive obedience, all that he is as crucified and raised unto justification, is reckoned to believers. Thus, in the deepest structures of Pauline soteriology we grasp the perfect convergence of union with Christ and the imputation of righteousness. Christ's own resurrection is his justification, and by virtue of faith union with the resurrected Christ, believers are justified in Christ (by means of faith) and receive his righteousness.

The imputation of Christ's righteousness, the reckoning of Christ's righteousness as the believer's own, occurs simultaneously with union with Christ, but can be distinguished from union with Christ, given its uniquely forensic and judicial nature. Perhaps one way of putting the matter is that incorporation into Christ includes within it the possession of Christ's own righteousness, which is imputed to the believer by virtue of his solidarity with the crucified, resurrected, and righteous Son of God. Union with Christ allows Paul to speak in relational and judicial categories simultaneously, without conflating either into the other. Forensic and participationist motifs in Paul's theology do not stand over against one another; rather, they mutually supplement and inform one another. In the final analysis, the imputation of Christ's righteousness is best understood as that aspect of union with Christ that supplies the judicial ground of justification.

The preceding exegetical observations are designed to provide a normative basis for assessing the historical formulations in the next section of this essay. Sustained reflection on the biblical material warrants the soteriological formulations found in Calvin and the reformed tradition.

---

[27]Geerhardus Vos, *Grace and Glory* (Carlisle, Pennsylvania: Banner of Truth Trust, 1995), 161.

Union with Christ and Justification: Historical-Theological Formulations

This section will outline three different ways of relating union with Christ to the imputation of Christ's righteousness given in justifi-cation. The reformed view conceives of union and imputation as distinct, inseparable, and simultaneous realities. The Lutheran view construes union and imputation as distinct but separable realities. The so-called New Perspective formulation of N. T. Wright suggests that union and imputation are functionally equivalent with one another (i.e., inseparable and indistinct). Let us examine each in turn.

Union and Imputation in Reformed Theology: Distinct, Inseparable, and Simultaneous

It is critical to note by way of summary that there is good reason to affirm that a significant strand of the reformed tradition construes the imputation of Christ's righteousness as distinct-yet-inseparable from union with Christ. The imputation of Christ's righteousness, the reckoning of Christ's righteousness as the believer's own, occurs simultaneously with union, but can be distinguished from union with Christ, given its uniquely forensic and judicial nature.

Regarding the structural soteric significance of union with Christ, Calvin offers a classic formulation. He says, "First, we must understand that as long as Christ remains outside of us, and we are separated from him, all that he has suffered and done for the salvation of the human race remains useless and of no value to us."[28] This means simply that it is "by faith ... we come to enjoy Christ and all his benefits."[29] Apart from union with Christ, there are no benefits of redemption for sinners. Union with Christ therefore organizes the core of Calvin's soteriology and supplies the nuclear theological structure for the application of redemption to the believer.

Calvin elaborates on the fundamental structure of union with Christ, which he terms the "two-fold grace of God." He says,

---

[28]Calvin, *Institutes*, III.1.1, 537.

[29]Calvin, *Institutes.*

> By partaking of him, we principally receive a double grace (*duplex gratia*), namely, that being reconciled to God through Christ's blamelessness, we may have in heaven instead of a Judge a gracious Father; and secondly, that sanctified by Christ's Spirit we may cultivate blamelessness and purity of life.'[30]

However, the question still remains: how are these blessings *related* to one another? Calvin argues that these two basic classes of redemptive benefits are distinct-yet-inseparable realities, which are received simultaneously in the believer's union with Christ. He reasons that just "(a)s Christ cannot be torn into parts, so these two which we perceive in him together and conjointly are inseparable – namely, righteousness and sanctification."[31] Calvin continues, "It is indeed true, that we are justified in Christ through the mercy of God alone, but it is equally true and certain, that all who are justified are called by the Lord, that they may live worthy of their vocation." And he therefore concludes, "Let then the faithful learn to embrace him, not only for justification, but also for sanctification, as *he has been given to us for both these purposes*, lest they render *him asunder* by their mutilated faith."[32] In other words, the benefits of justification and sanctification remain distinct in the application of redemption in Christ.

But while distinct from one another, they are *inseparably related* and *simultaneously received* though faith union with Christ.[33] Commenting on 1 Corinthians 1:30, Calvin reasons as follows,

> But since the question concerns only righteousness and sanctification, let us dwell upon these. Although we may distinguish them, Christ contains both of them inseparably in himself. Do you wish, then to attain righteousness in Christ? You must first possess Christ; but you cannot possess him without being made partaker in his sanctification, because he cannot be divided into pieces. Since, therefore, it is solely by expending himself that the Lord gives us these benefits to enjoy, he bestows both of them at

[30]Calvin, *Institutes*, III.11.1, 725.

[31]Calvin, *Institutes*, III.11.6, 732.

[32]John Calvin, *Calvin's Commentaries*, vol. XIX, (Grand Rapids, Michigan: Baker, 1996), 294.

[33]Cf. Peter Lillback, *The Binding of God: Calvin's Role in the Development of Covenant Theology* (Grand Rapids, Michigan: Baker, 2001), 183.

> the same time, the one never without the other. Thus it is clear how true it is that we are justified not without works yet not through works, since in our sharing in Christ, which justifies us, sanctification is just as much included as righteousness.[34]

Another way of putting the matter is that incorporation into Christ by faith includes within it the possession of Christ's own righteousness, which is reckoned to the believer by virtue of solidarity with the obedient, crucified, and resurrected Son of God.[35] Union with Christ in Calvin's soteriology involves within it the notion of the imputation of his righteousness, reckoned as the believer's own. Calvin himself puts it eloquently:

> I confess that we are deprived of this utterly incomparable good [justifying righteousness] *until* Christ is made ours. Therefore, that joining together of Head and members, that indwelling of Christ in our hearts – in short, that mystical union – are accorded by us the *highest degree of importance*, so that Christ, having been made ours, makes us *sharers with him* in the gifts with which he has been endowed. We do not, therefore, contemplate him *outside ourselves* from afar in order that his righteousness may be imputed to us but *because we put on Christ and are engrafted into his body – in short, because he deigns to make us one with him. For this reason*, we glory that we have *fellowship of righteousness with him.*[36]

The only reason anyone would assume an intrinsic conflict between union and imputation as simultaneous realities turns

---

[34]Calvin, Institutes, III.16.1, 797-98.

[35]It should be noted that while Calvin does refer to justification as the "main hinge on which religion turns" and "a foundation ... on which to build piety toward God" (*Institutes*, 3.11.1), the basic structure of his soteriology, as outlined above, demands that union with Christ frame the hinge and supply the bedrock on which the foundation rests. For an excellent discussion regarding why Calvin's theology of union with Christ makes the relative priority of justification and sanctification "indifferent theologically," consult Richard B. Gaffin Jr., "Biblical Theology and the Westminster Standards," *The Practical Calvinist: An Introduction to the Presbyterian and Reformed Heritage*, ed. Peter A. Lillback, (Mentor/Christian Focus Publications, Great Britain: 2002), 430-39.

[36]Calvin, *Institutes*, III.11.10, 737 (italics mine). For an insightful historical and theological treatment of Calvin's theology of union with Christ, consult Mark A. Garcia, *Life in Christ: The Function of Union with Christ in the Unio – Duplex Gratia Structure of Calvin's Soteriology with Special Reference to the Relationship of Justification and Sanctification in Sixteenth-Century Context* (unpublished doctoral dissertation, University of Edinburgh, 2004).

on *a presupposed Lutheran conception of imputation*, which leads us to consider the post-Reformation Lutheran understanding regarding the relationship between union with Christ and imputation.

Union and Imputation in Post-Reformation Lutheran Theology: Distinct, Separable, and Sequential

Post-Reformation conservative Lutheran theology offers a robust theology of justification by grace alone through faith alone in Christ alone. Definitive formulations of post-Reformation Lutheran soteriology appear in the systematics textbooks written by Francis Pieper and John Theodore Müeller, both of which are entitled *Christian Dogmatics*.

Müeller begins in the section entitled "The Doctrine of Soteriology" by recognizing that "the purpose of the doctrine of soteriology is to show how the Holy Spirit applies to the individual sinner the blessed salvation which Christ has secured for all mankind by his vicarious atonement."[37] Müeller observes that

> As soon as the sinner by faith accepts God's general pardon ... he is personally justified ... justification is thus by grace alone without works. It (justification) puts the believer into possession of all the merits or blessings secured by Christ's perfect obedience. The justified sinner has entered into the state of grace and peace, in which he is assured of his present and final salvation.[38]

The first step of salvation consists in receiving the pardon of God for justification, by which the believer comes to possess all the merits secured by Christ's perfect obedience and enters into an estate of grace and peace.

However, it is not yet clear precisely how justification relates to union with Christ. Müeller amplifies his thought along these lines with the following remark. "Justification effects the mystical union by which the Holy Trinity, in particular the Holy Spirit, dwells in the believer ... It (the mystical union) is the result of justification, not the cause of it (Gal. 3:2)."[39] In other words,

---

[37]John Theodore Müeller, *Christian Dogmatics* (St. Louis, Missouri: Concordia, 1934), 319.

[38]John Theodore Müeller, *Christian Dogmatics*, 319.

[39]John Theodore Müeller, *Christian Dogmatics*, 320.

justification is the first in a logical series of blessings of the gospel – the chief blessing from which all other redemptive benefits derive.

Justification stands in a similar causal relationship to sanctification. Müeller reasons that "justification produces sanctification ... sanctification follows justification as its effect."[40] Accordingly, justification supplies the central soteric benefit, from which every other benefit derives, including union with Christ and sanctification.

Betraying the heart of Lutheran soteriology, Müeller entitles the third section of his treatment of the doctrine of Justification by Faith as follows: "The Doctrine of Justification The Central Doctrine of the Christian Religion."[41] According to Müeller, "it requires little proof that the article of justification by faith is the central doctrine of the entire Christian religion."[42]

Complementing Müeller's reflections in a chapter in his *Christian Dogmatics* entitled "Justification the Central Doctrine of the Christian Religion",[43] Francis Pieper adds the following observations. He says, "In Lutheran theology the article of justification is the chief article by which the Christian doctrine and the Christian church stands and falls; it is apex of all Christian teaching."[44] The apex of all *Christian teaching*, not merely Christian *soteriology*, is justification by faith alone. Justification therefore supercedes the importance of *historia salutis*, union with Christ, eschatology, the kingdom of God, and the humiliation and exaltation of Christ.

Pieper makes this explicit when he says, "this doctrine of justification by faith in the crucified Christ is the central article not only in Paul's theology ... but in Scripture all doctrines serve the doctrine of justification."[45] Pieper goes on to say that "Christology serves merely as the substructure of the doctrine of justification."[46] Surpassing his theological progenitor in what must rank as a high

---

[40]John Theodore Müeller, *Christian Dogmatics*.

[41]John Theodore Müeller, *Christian Dogmatics*, 371.

[42]John Theodore Müeller, *Christian Dogmatics*.

[43]Francis Pieper, *Christian Dogmatics*, vol. II (St. Louis, Missouri: Concordia, 1950), 512.

[44]Francis Pieper, *Christian Dogmatics*, vol. II, 520.

[45]Francis Pieper, *Christian Dogmatics*, vol. II, 513.

[46]Francis Pieper, *Christian Dogmatics*, vol. II.

point for Lutheran theological hyperbole, Müeller goes so far as to say, "the doctrine of justification by faith in the crucified and risen Christ is the *entire* Gospel."[47]

To summarize the points made above, post-Reformation conservative Lutheran soteriology, represented ably in the works of Pieper and Müeller, affirms two critical propositions. First, justification logically, if not temporally, precedes union with Christ. justification is the cause of union with Christ; union with Christ is the effect of justification. Second, justification is not only the center of soteriology, but justification supplies the center of the entire Christian religion. Justification is apex of all Christian teaching and forms the entirety of the gospel.

Geerhardus Vos, in *Redemptive History and Biblical Interpretation*, incisively distinguishes the reformed (or covenantal) view from the Lutheran view just surveyed. His observation insightfully uncovers the basic structural differences between reformed and Lutheran soteriology:

> By faith [the Christian] is a member of the covenant [of grace], and that faith has a wide outlook, a comprehensive character, which not only points to justification but also to all the benefits which are in Christ. Whereas the Lutheran tends to view faith one-sidedly – only in its connection with justification – for the reformed Christian it is saving faith in all the magnitude of the word. According to the Lutheran, the Holy Spirit first generates faith in the sinner who temporarily still remains outside of union with Christ; then justification follows faith and only then, in turn, does the mystical union with the Mediator take place ... The covenantal (or reformed) outlook is the *reverse. One is first united to Christ, the Mediator of the covenant, by a mystical union, which finds its conscious recognition by faith. By this union with Christ all that is in Christ is simultaneously given.* Faith embraces all this too; it not only grasps justification, but lays hold of Christ as Prophet, Priest, and King, as his rich and full Messiah.[48]

According to Vos, reformed theology construes union with Christ as the most basic soteric reality of the gospel in terms of which all benefits are given to the believer simultaneously.

---

[47]Francis Pieper, *Christian Dogmatics*, vol. II, 372.

[48]Geerhardus Vos, *Redemptive History and Biblical Interpretation* (Phillipsburg, New Jersey: P&R, 2001), 256 (italics mine).

But for the Lutheran, justification is a bare declarative act of imputation that occurs outside of or prior to union with Christ. Thus, on the Lutheran view, justification remains distinct from union, but they are not inseparable facets of one soteric reality. The Lutheran formulation therefore helpfully accounts for justification and union remaining distinct, but continues on to affirm that justification and union with Christ are *separable*. Justification, on Lutheran premises, is a verdict that occurs outside of and apart from union with Christ, and it is *in this sense* that reformed theology in the tradition of Calvin would not be comfortable with an alien righteousness that is given to the sinner apart from union with Christ (although reformed theology in the tradition of Calvin is comfortable with an alien righteousness in the sense that the believer's righteousness for justification is always and only Christ's righteousness imputed and received by faith alone in union with Christ). Therefore, while the Lutheran successfully maintains the distinct side of the formulation, the inseparable side of the formulation is fatally compromised. An opposite extreme emerges in the formulation of N. T. Wright.

Union with Christ and Imputation: Inseparable and Indistinct (N.T. Wright)

N. T. Wright's reformulation of imputation in relation to union with Christ deserves brief consideration, because his option is neither Lutheran nor reformed. In *What Saint Paul Really Said*, Wright chides the traditional view of imputation as involving the apparently absurd notion of a "substance or gas" passed through a courtroom.[49] Such a view is simply not warranted by texts that refer to the righteousness of the judge in the law court, and it seems clear by implication that similar considerations would apply to the imputation of Christ's righteousness. Wright's comments on Romans 5 offer no additional clarification.[50] Put in summary form,

[49]N. T. Wright, *What Saint Paul Really Said* (Grand Rapids, Michigan: Eerdmans, 1997), 98.

[50]N. T. Wright, *The Letter to the Romans*, The New Interpreter's Bible: A Commentary in Twelve Volumes, vol. 10, ed., Leander E. Keck, (Nashville, Tennessee: Abingdon, 2002), 522-32. It is disappointing that Wright opts to avoid the most important exegetical and theological issues pertaining to imputation in a text that so clearly appears to demand the historic reformed doctrine of imputation.

it seems as though in Wright's estimate the notion of imputation espoused by reformed (and Lutheran) theology is simply not in the purview of Paul's concerns in the fifth chapter of Romans, and we would not expect such a strange notion to appear in Paul's theology in the first place. Does this mean that Wright has no place at all for imputation?

Wright does have a place for imputation, but only if it is redefined in a manner similar to the way righteousness language is redefined. What does imputation look like in Wright's theology? Wright's proposal turns on a fundamental proposition: union with Christ makes imputation, as sketched above in the theology of Calvin, unnecessary or redundant. Wright reasons that if we take seriously the theological function of union with Christ in Pauline soteriology, we ought to understand union with Christ and imputation as functional equivalents. He says,

> Paul's doctrine of what is true of those who are in the Messiah *does the job*, within the scheme of *his* thought, that the *traditional protestant emphasis on the imputation of Christ's righteousness did within that scheme*. In other words, that which imputed righteousness was trying to insist upon is, I think, fully taken care of in Romans 6, where Paul declares that what is true of the Messiah is true of all his people.[51]

Wright's point is simply that *union with Christ in Paul's thought* does the job of *imputation in traditional Protestant theology*. While his intentions are laudable, his formulation raises serious problems from both biblico-systematic and historical-theological perspectives.

First, Wright seems to assume that a fundamental disjunction exists between the thought of Paul, on the one hand, and traditional Protestant theology,[52] on the other hand. However, as

---

[51]N. T. Wright, "New Perspectives on Paul," paper presented at the 10th Edinburgh Dogmatics Conference at Rutherford House, Edinburgh, 25-28 August 2003, 13.

[52]Given the radical differences turned up between the Calvinist and post-Reformation Lutheran positions, it would serve us better to avoid such generalizations as "traditional Protestant" theology and speak with greater historical nuance and precision.

we have seen in the previous sections, there is a deep convergence between Pauline and reformed soteriology, precisely on the point of union with Christ and the imputation of righteousness. One easily gets the impression from Wright's language that "the traditional protestant emphasis" is merely a "scheme" that has nothing substantially in common with Paul's theology. But, as we have seen, this simply is not the case.

Second, Wright's appeal to Romans 6 is not sensitive to Paul's actual concern in that passage. Notice that Romans 6 is not about justification, but definitive sanctification, which is the aspect of union with Christ focused on the *enslaving power* of sin, as opposed to the judicial guilt of sin.[53] Union with Christ effects a principial breach with the enslaving *dominion* of sin (Rom. 6:4, 9-11). By virtue of union with Christ, the believer has died to sin (vv. 2, 7) with reference to its controlling power (vv. 8-14). Just as Christ has died to sin once for all and is alive to God (v. 10), so also the believer should consider himself dead to sin and alive to God in Christ Jesus (v. 11). Hence, the believer is no longer a slave to sin but to righteousness (v. 18), so that he must now present his bodily members "as slaves of righteousness unto holiness" (v. 19). Paul's focus in Romans 6 is the definitive and renovative aspect of union with Christ. To appeal to Romans 6 and claim that it does in Paul's thought what imputation handled in "the traditional protestant scheme" involves a category confusion. The guilt of sin is taken care of by imputation, but the *power* of sin by definitive (and progressive) sanctification, and imputation and

---

[53]For an outstanding treatment of this topic, consult John Murray's "Definitive Sanctification" and "The Agency in Definitive Sanctification" in The Collected Writings of John Murray, vol. II (Carlisle, Pennsylvania: Banner of Truth, 1977), 277-93. He says, "just because we cannot allow for any reversal or repetition of Christ's death on the tree we cannot allow for any compromise on the doctrine that every believer has died to sin and *no longer lives under its dominion* ... Hence, the decisive and definitive entrance upon newness of life in the case of every believer is required by the fact that the resurrection of Christ was decisive and definitive. Just as we cannot allow for any reversal or repetition of the resurrection, so we cannot allow for any compromise on the doctrine that every believer is a new man, the old man crucified, that the body of sin has been destroyed, and that, as a new man in Christ Jesus, he serves God in the newness which is none other than that of the Holy Spirit of whom he has become the habitation and his body the temple" ("The Agency of Definitive Sanctification", 293).

renovation have distinct functions in both Pauline and Calvinistic formulations.

Third, and expanding the previous criticism, it is simply not historically accurate to say that union with Christ, especially in light of Romans 6, does the same job that Protestant theologians (e.g. Calvin) had in view when speaking of imputation. In Calvin's soteriology there is a clear and non-negotiable distinction between forensic and renovative benefits given in union with Christ. Union with Christ is a multi-faceted reality that includes within it distinct-yet-inseparable benefits that fall out in two basic classes: forensic/imputative and renovative/transformative. Union with Christ *per se*, is neither imputation nor renewal, but includes both within its compass – distinctly, inseparably, simultaneously, and eschatologically. Hence, it is neither historically accurate in terms of Calvin's theology, nor exegetically tenable in terms of Pauline theology, to claim that union in Pauline theology "does the job" of imputation in Calvin's "older protestant" theology.

Wright's proposal proceeds on the mistaken assumption that a renovative category in Pauline soteriology is functionally equivalent to imputation in traditional Protestant soteriology. The consequence of this mistaken assumption is that Wright winds up fusing soteric benefits that ought to remain distinct. Wright enlists a renovative category in Pauline soteriology to serve the foreign task of imputation, which in the final analysis engenders all sorts of confusion.

The problem with Wright's formulation therefore amounts to the opposite error of the post-Reformation Lutherans. He so stresses the inseparability of blessings that are given in union that he allows their inseparability to undermine the *distinction* in view between union with Christ and imputation. This error is as equally problematic and theologically unhelpful as the Lutheran formulation. We cannot allow soteric inseparability to eclipse meaningful distinctions (NPP extreme), and we cannot allow meaningful distinctions to imply separability (Lutheran extreme).

Summary and Conclusion

To summarize, then, the reformed conception of union with Christ and justification is not (a) the Lutheran option, nor (b) the NPP version advocated by N. T. Wright. The reformed position is a *tertium quid*, a third thing, which stands out as a unique and clearly defined option that avoids the problematic aspects of both Lutheranism and N. T. Wright. And what this means when we relate union with Christ to justification is simple. For the believer to participate in Christ by faith (union with Christ) and to have his righteousness and meritorious obedience reckoned as his own (imputation) are distinct-yet-inseparable soteric realities. To separate the two is the problem that emerges in Lutheran theology. To fail to distinguish the two by making the one functionally equivalent with the other appears in Wright's formulation. To insist that union with Christ and imputation of righteousness are distinct-yet-inseparable benefits given simultaneously and eschatologically in the *ordo salutis* is the reformed (and biblical) position outlined above.

Reformed theology, in seeking to be faithful to Scripture, cannot rest easily with either extreme. Union with Christ involves the imputation of Christ's righteousness, and the imputation of Christ's righteousness requires union with Christ. There need be no intrinsic incompatibility, in terms of reformed soteriology, between union with Christ and the imputation of righteousness. Imputation and union are distinct-yet-inseparable realities of our eschatological salvation in Christ, and this distinctive theological formulation is a fruit of a consistently biblical and Calvinistic soteriology.

Calvin's Development of The Doctrine of Forensic Justification: Calvin And the Early Lutherans On The Relationship of Justification And Renewal

Peter A. Lillback

Introduction

In spite of the obvious disagreements between Lutherans and reformed, many are unaware that the two bodies that are the primary heirs of Luther's and Calvin's theologies had a distinctive approach to the cardinal doctrine of justification. This lack of awareness is due in part to the substantial agreement between the Reformers on many aspects of their views on justification. Among these, the most obvious is their mutual attack on the Roman conception of justification. Luther asserts, "The popish sophisters do spoil us of this knowledge of Christ and most heavenly comfort...."[1] Likewise Calvin writes, "Thus the schools of the Sorbonne, mothers of all errors, have taken away from us justification by faith, which is the sum of all piety."[2] The Protestant Reformers believed that Rome had corrupted free grace with human works of merit, and had compromised Christ's satisfaction of divine wrath for sin by intruding the human invention of penance.

The common elements of Luther and Calvin in their teaching on justification are substantial. Each rejects human merit in favor of divine grace. Both see the centrality of Christ's death in satisfying the justice of God. Both argue strongly for the "exclusive particle" – by faith *alone*. Both intimately connect the imputation of Christ's righteousness, forgiveness of sins, reconciliation, acceptance, and

---

[1]Martin Luther, *Martin Luther, Selections from His Writings*, ed. John Dillenberger (Garden City, N.Y.: Doubleday, 1961), 135.

[2]John Calvin, *Institutes of the Christian Religion*, vol. 20 of *Library of Christian Classics*, ed. John T. McNeill, trans. Ford Lewis Battles, Library of Christian Classics (London: SCM Press, 1960), III.15.7.

eternal life with justification. Both insist that justifying faith is a living faith.

Moreover, the unity of the Reformers' mutual opposition to Rome and their similarity in their discussion of justification is augmented by Luther's and Calvin's contemporaneousness:

> Moreover, that he [Calvin] was a contemporary of Martin Luther and knew exactly what Luther was teaching helps us to understand whether or not he was in favor of Luther's formulation of the doctrine of justification by faith. If he disagreed, he would certainly have said so, while on the other hand, if he agreed there would also be a clear indication of this fact.[3]

This is relevant because Calvin was a keen student of the theological literature of his day.

Further, both Luther and Calvin emphasized the importance of justification. For Luther it was the article of the standing and falling church, which if lost would amount to losing Christ himself.[4] Calvin declared that justification was the hinge on which the whole doctrine of salvation turns.[5] The sheer proportion of space allotted to the doctrine in his *Institutes* indicates Calvin's esteem for this biblical truth.[6]

Nevertheless, there are no direct quotations from Calvin that prove his complete agreement with Luther's doctrine of justification. Generally, Calvin avoided mentioning Luther by name in his writings. Thus when he rejects Luther's doctrine, as in his discussion of the Lord's Supper, or fully agrees with him, as in his acceptance of Luther's condemnation of the Bishop of Rome, Calvin does not explicitly state his relationship to Luther. So Calvin's agreement or disagreement with Luther must be developed from specific comparisons made from texts from each of the Reformers.

Calvin's position in the reformed tradition was as a second generation reformer. He became the leader of the reformed

---

[3]W. Stanford Reid, "Justification by Faith According to John Calvin," *Westminster Theological Journal* 42, no. 2 (Spring 1980), 290.

[4]Luther, *Martin Luther, Selections from His Writings*, 100, 106.

[5]Calvin, *Institutes*, III.11.1.

[6]Reid, "Justification," 291.

movement that had developed from such men as Zwingli, Bullinger, Oecolampadius, and Bucer. Since Calvin identified himself with the Swiss reformed of Zurich through his own subscription to the *Consensus Tigurinus* in 1549, it is not inconsequential to recall Luther's remarks concerning the reformed theologians' doctrine of justification. In his 1531 *Commentary on Galatians*, Luther rejected the doctrine of the Swiss, including their doctrine "about the righteousness of Christ". Luther contemptuously called those in the Zwinglian tradition "fanatical spirits" and "sectarians".[7]

Moreover, it has been easy to assume after the lapse of five centuries since the Protestant Reformation that the final dogmatic formulations of Lutheran and reformed orthodoxy were identical with the initial Reformers. But such is not the case. Instead, a gradual development and at times a differing expression of elements of the doctrine of justification can be seen in the maturation of the early Reformers' doctrines.

The purpose of this study, then, is to identify a specific example of the distinctive understandings of justification in Calvin and in the early Lutherans. In particular, we will consider how Luther and the early Lutherans included regeneration in their doctrine of justification, seeking to harmonize it with the forensic idea of justification. But we shall also see that Calvin's teaching on forensic justification emphasizes that the sinner is declared to be legally righteous before God as the Judge of sinners by faith. In Calvin's forensic view he insists on defining justification with the sense of "declared righteous." He thereby rejects the meanings of "becoming righteous" or being "made righteous", phrases which emphasize the idea of man's renewed nature before God. We shall also see that Calvin came to view the merging of forensic justification with renewal, as found in the early Lutheran theologians, as a generally non-biblical way of describing the doctrine. Calvin instead emphasizes the declarative or forensic nature of justification. He will consider the view of justification held by Luther, Melanchthon, and Chemnitz as largely inconsistent with the forensic nature of justification. And most intriguingly, Lutheran orthodoxy – mature Lutheran theology – will ultimately agree with Calvin, in defining

[7]See Peter Lillback, *The Binding of God: Calvin's Role in the Development of Covenant Theology* (Grand Rapids, Michigan: Baker Book House, 2001), 78-80.

justification in a forensic manner. This raises the fascinating question of whether Lutheran orthodoxy ultimately agrees more with Calvin than with Luther on this foundational question of the Protestant doctrine of justification.

Calvin's final expression of justification is in a covenantal context that declares that renewal or regeneration is the beginning of the Holy Spirit's work of sanctification and is thus not part of justification. Instead, it is a distinguishable benefit of the covenant, a covenantal benefit that is simultaneous and inseparable with forensic justification although clearly distinct from it and logically subordinated to it. Luther's emphasis on the connection of renewal with justification requires that he sever all discussion of obedience from justification. Moreover, the blending of justification with renewal also makes forensic justification difficult for Luther to express clearly. Calvin, by teaching an explicit forensic justification that excludes renewal, is able to give renewal its full expression of the new nature's new obedience, since it is a necessary yet distinguishable accompaniment of God's covenant of grace. In Calvin's mind renewal is a completely distinct benefit of the covenant in relationship to forensic justification.

Putting the thesis of this article aside for the moment, let us begin our study by simply underscoring the importance of the doctrine of justification and its theological complexity in Luther's mind. Luther declared:

> As you have often heard, most excellent brothers, because that one article concerning justification even by itself creates true theologians, therefore it is indispensable in the church and just as we must often recall it, so we must frequently work on it ... Although we say we know, when we occupy ourselves with justification, nevertheless, it is not so, as some people think, that when they have heard the Word once or twice, they believe they have consequently become theologians. They are badly mistaken ... So great and so difficult a thing is faith and so sharp is the debate about faith! Therefore, this teaching is essential and of great use, and the better it is understood the more it pleases.[8]

---

[8]*The Disputation Concerning Justification* in Martin Luther, *Luther's Works*, eds Helmut T. Lehmann and Jaroslav Jan Pelikan (St. Louis, Philadelphia: Concordia Publishing House Fortress Press, 1955), 34:157.

With Luther's blessing, then, let us begin a comparison of the doctrine of forensic justification and its relationship with the doctrine of renewal as seen in Calvin and the Reformational era Lutheran theologians Martin Chemnitz, Philip Melanchthon, and Martin Luther.

The Classic Pattern of the Reformational Debate: The Reformers' Definition of Justification Contrasted With Roman Catholicism

The Protestant definition of justification overtly differs from that of Rome, as officially expressed at the Council of Trent. The Tridentine definition governing Catholicism states,

> This preparation or disposition is followed by justification, which is not the mere forgiveness of sins, but also Sanctification, and the renewal of the inner man, by the voluntary reception of grace and gifts: whence the man from unrighteous becomes righteous, from an enemy becomes a friend, so as to be heir according to the hope of eternal life.[9]

Accordingly, historians and theologians have distinguished Rome from Protestantism in terms of the Catholic merging of justification (forgiveness of sins) with sanctification and renewal while Lutheran and reformed theology insisted upon the forensic or legal declaration of righteousness *coram deo*. Thus an editorial note in Calvin's *Commentary on Epistle to the Romans* says:

> It never was the doctrine of the Reformation, or of the Lutheran and Calvinistic divines, that the imputation of righteousness affected the moral character of those concerned. It is true, whom God justifies he also sanctifies: but justification is not sanctification, and the imputation of righteousness is not the infusion of righteousness.[10]

---

[9]*Acts of the Council of Trent*, 6th Session, VIII in Jean Calvin, *Selected Works of John Calvin: Tracts and Letters*, ed. Jules Bonnet and Henry Beveridge (Grand Rapids, MI: Baker Book House, 1983), III.95.

[10]Calvin, *Romans 3:21*, in John Calvin, *Calvin's Commentaries: Calvin Translation Society* (Grand Rapids, Michigan: Baker Book House, 1979), 135, n.1. (All references to Calvin's commentaries are from the CTS Edition unless otherwise noted.)

Similarly Cunningham writes of Luther and Melanchthon,

> But though their views upon this subject became more clear and enlarged, yet they held in substance from the beginning, and brought out at length, and long before the Council of Trent, most fully and clearly the great doctrine of the Reformation, – viz., that justification in Scripture is properly descriptive only of a change upon men's legal state and condition, and not on their moral character, though a radical change of character invariably accompanies it....[11]

Berkhof states:

> But however Calvin may have differed from Luther as to the order of salvation, he quite agreed with him on the nature and importance of the doctrine of justification by faith. In their common opposition to Rome they both describe it as an act of free grace, and as a forensic act which does not change the inner life of man but only the judicial relationship in which he stands to God.[12]

This construction of the Reformational schism on justification, what we here call "the Classic Pattern of Reformation Debate," has been held not only by English-speaking scholars, but examples of German scholarship can also be cited to the same effect. Accordingly, Baur designates the Evangelical Church's understanding of justification as a forensic act *justificare = justum pronuntiare*, while the Catholic Church's understanding he depicted as a medicinal act, *justificare = justum efficere*.[13]

But is it true that from the very beginning of Luther's Reformation and throughout its entire course the issue separating Rome and Protestantism was a forensic conception of justification (to be declared righteous) vis-à-vis a renewal or moral conception of justification (to be made righteous)? Can this be demonstrated

---

[11]William Cunningham, *Historical Theology* (London: Banner of Truth Trust, 1960), 2:13.

[12]Louis Berkhof, *The History of Christian Doctrines* (Grand Rapids, Michigan: Baker Book House, 1975), 220.

[13]Ferdinand Christian Baur, *Der Gegensatz Des Katholicismus und Protestantismus Nach Den Principien und Hauptdogmen der Beiden Lehrbegriffe* (Tubingen: O. Zeller, 1834), 151, 184.

among the primary Reformers? Or, is this rather the final articulation of the doctrine by Protestant orthodoxy that is being read back into the early Reformers?

Martin Chemnitz: Lutheran Orthodoxy on Forensic Justification and Renewal

An appropriate place to begin this analysis is with Martin Chemnitz, one of the leading theologians in the production of the 1577 *Formula of Concord*, and hence a chief spokesman for Lutheran orthodoxy. In his monumental *Examination of the Council of Trent* written 1566-75. Chemnitz attempts to define the real issue between Rome and Lutheranism on justification. He first denies the charge made by the Tridentine decrees that Lutheranism "... taught that the believers have only the forgiveness of sins but that they are not also renewed by the Holy Spirit; also that Christ earned for us only the reconciliation and not also at the same time the renewal...."[14] His retort is directly to the point, "But these are only shameless and slanderous calumnies, by which they raise a noise in order that inexperienced people may not notice what the controversy is about."[15] The real issue dividing Rome and the Protestants is not the necessity of renewal – which both sides affirm argues Chemnitz but the real question is if this renewal is the ground of the believer's justification before God. This is the gravamine at the heart of the debate.[16]

Chemnitz then proceeds to argue skillfully for the forensic meaning of justification.[17] Thus far he fits the classic pattern of the Reformation debate. But just prior to his extended proof of the forensic meaning of justification, he includes an unexpected and startling paragraph. Instead of entirely censuring the patristic theologians for their failure to teach an unequivocal forensic justification, he allows the admissibility of the patristic definition, namely, renewal! This is unanticipated because this admission seems to weaken his argument concerning the importance of forensic justification. Further, while Lutheranism used patristic

---

[14]Martin Chemnitz, *Examination of the Council of Trent*, ed. Fred Kramer ([St. Louis, Mo.]: Concordia Publishing House, 1971), 465.

[15]Chemnitz, *Examination of the Council of Trent*, 466.

[16]Chemnitz, *Examination of the Council of Trent*, 468.

[17]Chemnitz, *Examination of the Council of Trent*, 469f.

evidence to bolster their case, Lutheran theologians were quite willing to dispense with the fathers' teachings if they were contrary to Scripture. Why then did Chemnitz raise this alternate understanding of justification in his discussion of forensic justification? Providing a significant clue, Chemnitz writes,

> For although the fathers mostly take the word "justify" for the renewal, by which the works of righteousness are wrought in us through the Spirit, we do not start a quarrel with them where they according to the Scripture rightly and appropriately teach the doctrine how and why a person is reconciled to God, receives the remission of sins and the adoption, and is accepted to life eternal. This difference in meaning has often been shown by our teachers and also how the former meaning can be rightly, piously and skillfully understood and admitted according to the analogy of faith and the perpetual sense of the Scripture if it is accepted with the fathers according to the manner of the Latin composition. However, the papalists have not been placated at all. For the dissension and strife in the article of justification is not only about words but chiefly about the matters themselves.[18]

What is observed in Chemnitz's comment, is an effort to allow not only for the "fathers" but his "teachers" as well, to have properly used justification with the sense of renewal, without compromising the forensic sense. Thus Chemnitz could not simply reject all renewal language in justification because he was aware that his "teachers" had expressed themselves in a similar manner as the fathers. By way of concession, Chemnitz admits that the Protestant message on justification was not always exclusively couched in forensic terms, although he insists that this was always the intended meaning.

In agreement with Chemnitz the *Formula of Concord* (1577), which was the work of several leading Lutheran theologians, explains:

> Sometimes, as in the Apology, the words *regeneratio* and *vivificatio* are used in place of justification, and then they mean the same thing, even though otherwise these terms refer to the renovation of man and distinguish it from justification by faith.[19]

---

[18]Chemnitz, *Examination of the Council of Trent*, 468.

Here, Melanchthon's *Apology of the Augsburg Confession* (1531) is cited as an example of the Lutheran teachers who have used non-forensic synonyms for justification. The solution offered by the *Formula* is that when this is done such words are to be understood differently from their normal meanings. Forensic justification in such cases governs the meaning of the intent rather than the renewal language governing the meaning of justification. Is this the intent of Melanchthon's usage of these words, or does this rather indicate a perspective of later Lutheran orthodoxy, that must now come to grips with an earlier and differing initial Lutheran theological tradition?

As we address this question let us again consider *The Formula of Concord*. The *Formula* again refers to the *Apology's* coordinating of regeneration and justification. The explanation advanced by *The Formula* is then further developed. The *Formula* explains that a careful differentiation must be made between these terms to avoid confusion,

> Since the word "regeneration" is sometimes used, in place of "justification," it is necessary to explain the term strictly so that the renewal which follows justification by faith will not be confused with justification and so that in their strict senses the two will be differentiated from one another.[20]

The two senses in which "regeneration" can be employed are then distinguished:

> The word "regeneration" is used, in the first place, to include both the forgiveness of sins solely for Christ's sake and the subsequent renewal which the Holy Spirit works in those who are justified by faith. But this word is also used in the limited sense of the forgiveness of sins and our adoption as God's children. In this latter sense it is frequently used in the Apology, where the statement is made, "justification is regeneration"...[21]

---

[19]*Epitome*, III. 5. in Theodore G. Tappert, "Confessions of the ELC," in *The Book of Concord the Confessions of the Evangelical Lutheran Church*, ed. and trans. Theodore G. Tappert (Philadelphia: Fortress Press, 1959), 474 .

[20]*Solid Declaration*, III. 18 in Tappert, "Confessions of the ELC," 542.

[21]*Solid Declaration*, III. 18 in Tappert, "Confessions of the ELC,".

According to the *Formula*, then, regeneration can be used in a broad sense where both forgiveness of sins and the sanctification of the believer are intended, or in a narrow sense where only the forgiveness of sins and the believer's adoption as God's children are in view. Thus in this way the theologians of the *Formula* sought to defend the forensic sense of justification in light of the problem of explaining what appeared to be ambiguous language on the part of the early Lutheran Reformers. Next, we shall see that this concern of Lutheran orthodoxy to establish the foundational sense of forensic justification comports well with Calvin's teaching on justification.

Calvin on the Relationship Between Renewal and Forensic Justification

Having considered Lutheran orthodoxy's efforts to clarify the Lutheran understanding of forensic justification, prompted by the ambiguity of the earlier Lutheran writings, we may legitimately inquire if Calvin spoke with similar ambiguity. Interestingly, and perhaps surprisingly, a gradual development in Calvin's conception of justification can be discerned as well. In his first edition of the *Institutes*, Calvin not only did not provide a special discussion of justification, he did not even define the term.[22] But in the second edition of 1539, he provides his first definition of justification. Calvin writes: "He is said to be justified in God's sight who is both reckoned righteous in God's judgment and has been accepted on account of his righteousness."[23] The forensic concept is unmistakable here. Thus, Calvin's acceptance of the forensic conception is articulated precisely in the 1539 edition,

> If an innocent accused person be summoned before the judgment seat of a fair judge, where he will be judged according to his innocence, he is said to be "justified" before the judge. Thus, justified before God is the man who, freed from the company of sinners, has God to witness and affirm his righteousness.[24]

---

[22]Cf. Francois Wendel, *Calvin: the Origins and Development of His Religious Thought*, Philip Mairet (London: Fontana, 1965), 257.

[23]Calvin, *Institutes*, III.11.2. All dating given in this study with respect to Calvin's *Institutes* are taken from the textural apparatus of the Battles edition which is based upon the *Opera Selecta* of Barth and Niesel.

[24]Calvin, *Institutes*, III.11.2 .

Thus there is evident development in Calvin from the 1536 to the 1539 edition of the *Institutes* – from no definition of justification at all to a clear forensic definition. Four years later in the third edition of 1543, Calvin adds a clear statement of imputation. He explains, "Therefore, we explain justification simply as the acceptance with which God receives us into his favor as righteous men. And we say that it consists in the remission of sins and the imputation of Christ's righteousness."[25]

Why Calvin did not define justification in his first edition is not clear. But, it is possible he did not define justification in 1536 because he was not yet sure of its exact meaning. Significantly, when Calvin does define justification in the second edition of 1539, this occurs in the same year as the publication of his first biblical commentary on the Epistle to the Romans. This chronological correlation of the two texts suggests that his research for the Romans commentary enabled him to decide between varying alternatives of defining justification in favor of the forensic sense. This account of the historical development of Calvin's thought on justification finds support in his comments on Romans 1:17,

> Of greater moment is what some think, that this righteousness does not only consist in the free remission of sins, but also, in part, includes the grace of regeneration. But I consider, that we are restored to life because God freely reconciles us to himself, as we shall hereafter show in its proper place.[26]

This statement provides a number of important clues. First, Calvin apparently knew of the Melanchthonian usage of regeneration in coordination with justification. In fact, he states that he made special usage of Melanchthon's commentary on Romans along with those of Bullinger and Bucer.[27] Second, contrary to the explanation the *Formula of Concord* would offer some forty years later for this phenomenon, Calvin implies that when regeneration is used in coordination with justification, it does not mean the forgiveness of sins. To place such a meaning on Calvin's statement above would

---

[25]Calvin, *Institutes*, III.11.2.

[26]*Comm. ad Romans* in Calvin, *Calvin's Commentaries: Calvin Translation Society*, 65.

[27]Calvin, *Calvin's Commentaries: Calvin Translation Society*, xxv.

produce the following tautology, "this righteousness does not only consist in the free remission of sins, but also, in part, includes the free remission of sins (i.e. "the grace of regeneration"). So it is clear that Calvin here understands regeneration in the sense that the *Formula* would later deny namely, the "subsequent renewal of the Holy Spirit". Third, it is clear that at this early date, regeneration for Calvin is either subsequent or perhaps contemporaneous with reconciliation. (Reconciliation is a clear Calvinian synonym for justification, "Doubtless he means by the word 'reconciled' nothing but 'justified'."[28]) Fourth, Calvin here opts in favor of defining justification with the sense of righteousness as forgiveness of sins to the exclusion of regeneration. In so doing, he thereby makes regeneration a separate benefit of Christ's redemptive work, which must be distinguished from justification. Finally, that Calvin could begin his remarks with the comment, "Of greater moment is what some think ..." indicates that the explanation of the relationship of justification and renewal had not yet developed into a hard and fast understanding. Thus, Calvin at this point was willing to accept those who in some sense blended justification and renewal as still within the sphere of a biblical view of justification.

But astonishingly, Calvin himself at one point admits the possibility of regeneration being a part of justification! Thus in his exposition of Paul's epistle to Titus published in 1549, nearly two years after his own critique of the Council of Trent, Calvin writes, on Titus 3:7,

> If we understand "regeneration" in its strict and ordinary meaning, it might be thought that the Apostle employs the word "justified" instead of "regenerated;" and this is sometimes the meaning of it, but very seldom; yet there is no necessity which constrains us to depart from its strict and more natural signification. The design of Paul is, to ascribe to the grace of God all that we are, and all that we have, so that we may not exalt ourselves proudly against others. Thus he now extols the mercy of God, by ascribing to it entirely the cause of our salvation. But because he had spoken of the vices of unbelievers, it would have been improper to leave out the grace of regeneration, which is the medicine for curing them.[29]

---

[28]Calvin, *Institutes*, III.11.4 .

Calvin here explains Paul's use of the word "justified". He suggests that it is possible that Paul here uses justification as a synonym for regeneration, with regeneration being understood in "its strict and ordinary meaning." What Calvin means by the "strict and ordinary" sense of regeneration can be seen from the immediate context. Commenting on verse five, he writes: "It is therefore the Spirit of God who regenerates us, and makes us new creatures; but because his grace is invisible and hidden, a visible symbol of it is beheld in baptism." Clearly, the grace of renewal corresponds to Calvin's understanding of regeneration. Further, Calvin also interprets the grace of regeneration as "the medicine for curing" sinners. Yet, Calvin clarifies that "justified" is only seldomly so used and thus it is not necessary to understand it in this sense here. Nevertheless, in this passage in Calvin's mind, "regeneration" may be viewed as a legitimate meaning for justification. So as unlikely as it may seem, Calvin in this instance is willing to assert that justification for Paul can mean, albeit seldom, "the medicine for curing" and the renewal of the Spirit.

But is not Calvin then guilty of potentially mingling together two distinct benefits of Christ's redemptive work? Calvin is conscious of this concern but believes that this is precisely what Paul himself is doing in this text. Calvin explains:

> Still this does not prevent him from returning immediately to praise divine mercy; and he even mingles both blessings together – that our sins have been freely pardoned, and that we have been renewed so as to obey God. This, at least is evident, that Paul maintains that "justification" is the free gift of God; and the only question is, what he means by the word *justified*. The context seems to demand that its meaning shall be extended further than to the imputation of righteousness; and in this larger sense it is seldom (as I have said) employed by Paul; yet there is nothing that hinders the meaning of it from being limited to the forgiveness of sins.[30]

---

[29]*Comm. ad Titus* 3:7, Calvin, *Calvin's Commentaries: Calvin Translation Society*, 335. This dating follows that of T.H.L. Parker.

[30]*Comm. ad Titus* 3:7, Calvin, *Calvin's Commentaries: Calvin Translation Society*, 335.

It is interesting that Calvin here exegetes this text by presenting a merging of justification and renewal when two years earlier he had written in refutation of the German Interim,

> If any one, on the other hand, objects that we are made partakers of Christ only by being renewed by his Spirit unto the obedience of the law, this must be acknowledged to be true; but let Regeneration be what it may, we deny that justification is to be placed in it.[31]

Thus while Calvin allows justification to include on rare occasions the sense of renewal, he refuses to admit that renewal is the basis of justification. In parallel fashion, ten years later in his fifth and final edition of the *Institutes* (1559) Calvin severely criticizes Osiander for doing this very thing,

> To prove the first point – that God justifies not only by pardoning but by regenerating – he asks whether God leaves as they were by nature those whom he justifies, changing none of their vices. This is exceedingly easy to answer: as Christ cannot be torn into parts, so these two which we perceive in him together and conjointly are inseparable – namely, righteousness and sanctification... But if the brightness of the sun cannot be separated from its heat, shall we therefore say that the earth is warmed by its light, or lighted by its heat? ... Here is a mutual and indivisible connection. Yet reason itself forbids us to transfer the peculiar qualities of the one to the other. In this confusion of the two kinds of grace that Osiander forces upon us there is a like absurdity ... Osiander mixes that gift of regeneration with this free acceptance and contends that they are one and the same.[32]

In summary, then, it is evident that Calvin knew of the early debate of whether or not it was legitimate to include regeneration within the Reformational understanding of justification. Calvin clearly advocated a strong forensic conception and refuted both Rome

---

[31]John Calvin, *The True Method of Giving Peace, and of Reforming the Church*, in Jean Calvin, *Tracts Containing Antidote to the Council of Trent German Interim with Refutation: True Method of Reforming the Church: Sinfulness of Outward Conformity Romish Rites: Psychopannyschia; or, The Soul's Imaginary Sleep Between Death and Judgment.*, trans. Henry Beveridge (Edinburgh: Calvin Translation Soc, 1851), III.244.

[32]Calvin, *Institutes*, III.11.6.

and Osiander on this score. Nevertheless, he still was willing to grant that regeneration in some sense could on infrequent occasion be used as the definition of justification in Paul's theology. In the case of Titus 3:7 justification could be joined with a sense of renewal and thus "extended further than to the imputation of righteousness".

The best understanding of Calvin's view here is found in his parallel concepts of the *duplex gratiam* (the double benefits of grace, namely justification and sanctification) of the covenant of grace and his emphasis on the concept of the union with Christ.

> Therefore, that joining together of Head and members, that indwelling of Christ in our heart – in short, that mystical union – are accorded by us the highest degree of importance, so that Christ, having been made ours, makes us sharers with him in the gifts with which he has been endowed. We do not, therefore, contemplate him outside ourselves from afar in order that his righteousness may be imputed to us but because we put on Christ and are engrafted into his body – in short, because he deigns to make us one with him. For this reason, we glory that we have fellowship of righteousness with him. (Calvin, *Institutes*, III.11.10.)[33]

The point made by Calvin here is one of the doctrinal conceptions that distinguishes the reformed and Lutheran understandings of salvation which Berkhof mentioned when he was quoted above ("But however Calvin may have differed from Luther as to the order of salvation, he quite agreed with him on the nature and importance of the doctrine of justification by faith ...").[34]

Once again, it is evident that there was a conscious development in the early Reformation's doctrine of justification in terms of its relationship to renewal. What stands clear at this point is that Calvin was consciously and actively seeking to highlight justification in terms of forensic justification and imputation. In so

[33]See Richard B. Gaffin Jr., "Biblical Theology and the Westminster Standards," in *The Practical Calvinist*, ed. Peter A. Lillback (Mentor/Christian Focus, 2002), 439.

[34]Geerhardus Vos developed the differences between Lutheran and reformed understandings of salvation and justification in the following way:

The covenant is neither a hypothetical relationship, nor a conditional position; rather it is the fresh, living fellowship in which the power of grace

doing he was setting the stage for the mature Protestant doctrine of justification. He was also correcting the earlier Lutheran theologians' general ambiguity at this very point.

Melanchthon's Doctrine of Forensic Justification and Its Relationship to Renewal

With this background of Chemnitz, Lutheran orthodoxy's *Formula of Concord* and Calvin's views of the relationship of justification and renewal, let us now turn our attention to Melanchthon and then to Luther in regard to this question. Above, we saw that the *Formula of Concord* cites Melanchthon as writing, "Justification is Regeneration." Was this Melanchthon's normal usage? Moreover, did Melanchthon simply use regeneration as a synonym for forensic justification as the *Formula* states?

The fact is that Melanchthon uses regeneration in a non-forensic sense as a legitimate definition of justification. Melanchthon's justification doctrine was not simply a declarative righteousness, but encompassed a moral, effective righteousness as well. As we shall now see, Melanchthon does not fit neatly into the classic pattern of the Reformation debate, that is, the

---

is operative. Only by the exercise of faith does it become a reality. It is always believers who act as true covenant partners with God. They who are partners also have the promises in their entirety sealed to them as believers. The covenant is a totality from which no benefit can be excluded.... By faith [the Christian] is a member of the covenant, and that faith has a wide outlook, a comprehensive character, which not only points to justification but also to all the benefits which are in Christ. Whereas the Lutheran tends to view faith one-sidedly – only in its connection with justification – for the reformed Christian it is saving faith in all the magnitude of the word. According to the Lutheran, the Holy Spirit first generates faith in the sinner who temporarily still remains outside of union with Christ; then justification follows faith and only then, in turn, does the mystical union with the Mediator take place. Everything depends on this justification, which is losable, so that the believer only gets to see a little of the glory of grace and lives for the day, so to speak. [That is, the mystical union occurs by the divine act of justification.] The covenantal outlook is the reverse. One is first united to Christ, the Mediator of the covenant, by a mystical union, which finds its conscious recognition in faith. By this union with Christ, all that is in Christ is simultaneously given. Faith embraces all this too; it not only grasps justification, but lays hold of Christ as Prophet, Priest, and King, as his rich and full Messiah (Richard B. Gaffin Jr., ed., *Redemptive History and Biblical Interpretation: The Shorter Writings of Geerhardus Vos* [Phillipsburg, N. J.: Presbyterian and Reformed Publishing Co., 1980], 256).

justification-as-renewal viewpoint versus the justification-as-a forensic-declaration-of-righteousness perspective.

Melanchthon's first edition of the *Loci Communes* published in 1521 consciously includes renewal in its definition of justification. He writes, "Therefore, we are justified when, put to death by the law, we are made alive again by the word of grace promised in Christ; the gospel forgives our sins, and we cling to Christ in faith..."[35] While this citation might be set aside as inconclusive since Melanchthon seems to be simply rehearsing the events that lead up to and follow the acts of justification, there is no mistaking his intention when he writes, "For justification has begun but is not consummated. We have the firstfruits of the Spirit (Rom. 8:23), but not yet the whole harvest."[36] Here justification is not defined as a completed act but conceived of as a process which is clearly united to the benefits associated with the Spirit. And even more clearly, he expresses the renewal aspect of justification when he writes,

> For here our justification is only begun; we have not yet completed it. Thus Paul commands us from time to time to be transformed by the renewal of our mind (Rom. 12:2). And in Phil. 3:12 he says that he has not yet attained, that he is not yet perfect, but that he presses on that he may make it on his own.[37]

For Melanchthon, justification is viewed as a process, not only an act, and thus is defined with a sense that is inclusive of renewal. Thus Melanchthon's early conception of justification was not articulated as an exclusive forensic justification.

Was this a faltering misstep by Melanchthon in his fledgling attempt to state the doctrine? This is not the case for as we saw above, ten years later (1531) in his *Apology*, Melanchthon is still speaking in renewal language. So in the great foundational document of Lutheranism, the *Augsburg Confession* written by Melanchthon and read at the imperial diet of 1530 before Charles V, Melanchthon defines the Lutheran doctrine of justification

---

[35]Philipp Melanchthon, *Loci Communes Theologici*, ed. and trans. Wilhelm Pauck (Westminster, 1969), 88.

[36]Melanchthon, *Loci Communes Theologici*, 106.

[37]Melanchthon, *Loci Communes Theologici*, 125.

in terms of "becoming righteous," rather than of being "declared righteous." He declares:

> It is also taught among us that we cannot obtain forgiveness of sin and righteousness before God by our own merits, works, or satisfactions, but that we receive forgiveness of sin and *become righteous* before God by grace, for Christ's sake, through faith, when we believe that Christ suffered for us and that for his sake our sin is forgiven and righteousness and eternal life are *given* to us. For God will *regard* and *reckon* this faith as righteousness, as Paul says in Romans 3:21-26 and 4:5. (Italics mine.)[38]

Here at the fountainhead of Lutheran confessional theology, justification is defined first in a renewal sense – "become righteous." Then, Melanchthon adds that the faith of the believer is "reckoned" or "regarded" as righteousness. Thus, forensic overtones are present, but in tandem with the concept of "becoming righteous".

The statements made by Melanchthon the following year (1531) to defend the *Confession* against the Catholic refutation entitled the *Confutatio* clarify his understanding of justification as the dual relationship of forensic justification and renewal. Here Melanchthon interprets his own vocabulary:

> And "to be justified" means to make unrighteous men righteous or to *regenerate* them, as well as to be *pronounced or accounted righteous*. For Scripture speaks both ways. Therefore we want to show first that faith alone makes a righteous man out of an unrighteous one, that is, that it receives the forgiveness of sins.[39]

Similarly, he explains, "Therefore we are justified by faith alone, justification being understood as making an unrighteous man righteous or effecting his regeneration."[40] Renewal is an aspect of Melanchthon's conception of justification, and faith is also the means of receiving the Holy Spirit. He writes: "Faith alone justifies because we receive the forgiveness of sins and the Holy Spirit by faith alone."[41] Again he writes "...by faith alone we receive

---

[38]Tappert, "Confessions of the ELC," 32.
[39]Tappert, "Confessions of the ELC," 117.
[40]Tappert, "Confessions of the ELC," 78.

the forgiveness of sins for Christ's sake, and by faith alone are justified, that is, out of unrighteous we are made righteous and regenerated men."[42] Here there are two distinct objects that are received by the instrument of faith. The first is forgiveness of sins, the second, which is specifically designated as justification, is the making of an unrighteous man righteous or regenerating him. Thus Melanchthon does not conform to the classic explanation of what separated Rome and Protestantism. In his view, justification is the divine renewal and moral change from unrighteous to righteous. Yet, also in his view, regeneration does not exhaust the sense of justification, "Justification is reconciliation for Christ's sake ... From what we have said it is clear that justification does not mean merely the beginning of our renewal, but the reconciliation by which we are later accepted."[43] Speaking of the righteousness of the law, Melanchthon can also express these parallel concepts of justification in negative terms, "Therefore it does not justify; that is, it neither reconciles nor regenerates nor of itself makes us acceptable before God."[44] Thus Melanchthon's writings frequently connect these different aspects of his understanding of justification: "Faith alone accepts the forgiveness of sins, justifies, and regenerates."[45] and "...the reasons that compel us to hold that we are justified, reconciled, and reborn by faith."[46]

Yet, with his uniting of these various aspects of justification, Melanchthon seeks to maintain the distinctive sense of those passages of Scripture that can only be understood in a forensic sense. Thus, Melanchthon carefully explains the challenging texts of Romans 2:13 and James 2:22:

> "To be justified" here does not mean that a wicked man is made righteous but that he is pronounced righteous in a forensic way, just as in the passage (Rom. 2:13), "the doers of the law will be justified." As these words, "the doers of the law will be justified," contain nothing contrary to our position, so we maintain the

---

[41]Tappert, "Confessions of the ELC," 119.
[42]Tappert, "Confessions of the ELC," 123.
[43]Tappert, "Confessions of the ELC," 129.
[44]Tappert, "Confessions of the ELC," 132.
[45]Tappert, "Confessions of the ELC," 152.
[46]Tappert, "Confessions of the ELC," 155.

> same about James's words, "A man is justified by works and not by faith alone," for men who have faith and good works are certainly pronounced righteous. As we have said, the good works of the saints are righteous and please God because of faith. James preaches only the works that faith produces, as he shows when he says of Abraham, "Faith was active along with his works" (2:22). In this sense it is said, "The doers of the law will be justified"; that is, God pronounces righteous those who believe him from their heart and then have good fruits, which please him because of faith and therefore are a keeping of the law. These words, spoken so simply, contain no error....[47]

Thus, justification for Melanchthon has more than one nuance. Since he frequently defines justification with renewal ideas, he here indicates that there are passages where the forensic conception must be dominant, or as in these passages, is necessary. To counter the claims of Rome's works righteousness doctrine, Melanchthon here argues that a man is "pronounced righteous" by his doing of the law and by his faith working with his works. This, in Melanchthon's mind of course, is a declarative justification, not of the unbeliever, but of the "saints" whose works are "righteous and please God because of faith". This has been termed by some as the "justification of the just". This conception for Melanchthon "when spoken so simply, contains no error." If Melanchthon had not held to a renewal conception of justification, he would not here have had to distinguish the sense of these passages from others with the introduction, "'To be justified' here does not mean...." Another example of Melanchthon's cautious exegesis in this regard says:

> This is how Scripture uses the word "faith," as this statement of Paul shows, "Since we are justified by faith, we have peace with God" (Rom. 5:1). In this passage "justify" is used in a judicial way [Latin reads "Forensi consuetudine"] to mean "to absolve a guilty man and pronounce him righteous," and to do so on account of someone else's righteousness, namely Christ's, which is communicated to us through faith.[48]

---

[47]Tappert, "Confessions of the ELC," 143.
[48]Tappert, "Confessions of the ELC," 154.

It is evident that Melanchthon's precision here indicated by "In this passage 'justify' is used in a judicial way" would be redundant if he held to the exclusive forensic meaning of "to declare righteous". Given Melanchthon's close working relationship with Luther, we must then also inquire if Luther's teaching on justification incorporated the concept of renewal as well.

Luther's Doctrine of Justification: The Relationship of Renewal to Forensic Justification

Does Luther conceive of justification in a fashion similar to Melanchthon? The presumption at this point must be that Luther himself taught a doctrine of justification that incorporated renewal concepts as well. How could it be otherwise, given Melanchthon's labors under Luther's guidance and Lutheran orthodoxy's desire to systematize Luther's insights and teachings?

Melanchthon's expression of the renewal of the believer in justification was highlighted above from his *Loci Communes*, or *Common Places.* So Luther's unmeasured praise for Melanchthon's classic theological treatise takes on keen significance for our discussion. Luther writes in 1525 four years after the publication of the first edition of the *Loci*, concerning Erasmus' arguments for the freedom of the human will,

> They have been refuted already so often by me, and beaten down and completely pulverized in Philip Melanchthon's *Commonplaces* – an unanswerable little book which in my judgment deserves not only to be immortalized but even canonized. Compared with it, your book struck me as so cheap and paltry that I felt profoundly sorry for you ...[49]

Could Luther have held the *Loci* in such esteem, if Melanchthon's doctrine of justification was not in accord with his own?

Luther also expresses his essential agreement with Melanchthon's *Apology of the Augsburg Confession* although he never lauded it as highly as the *Loci.* Thus Luther writes to the Leipzig Lutherans banished by Duke George in 1533, "There is our Confession and

---

[49]Martin Luther and Desiderius Erasmus, *Luther and Erasmus: Free Will and Salvation*, trans. E. Gordon Rupp and Philip S. Watson (Philadelphia: Westminster Press, 1969), 102.

the Apology ... Adhere to our Confession and Apology."[50] Luther began but never completed his German Apology of the Confession. Melanchthon wrote to Johann Brenz on April 8, 1533, "Luther is now preparing a German Apology."[51] It is not likely that this was simply a translation into German of Melanchthon's work since the Latin term *instituit* seems to indicate an independent work rather than a translation.[52] Early Lutheran Johann Brenz, paid a compliment to the *Apology* in terms similar to that which Luther had given to the *Loci*, "The *Apology*, in my opinion, is worthy of the canon".[53]

In accord with the previous examples, found in Melanchthon, Chemnitz, and the other cited early Lutheran writings, Luther can be seen to have also held to renewal concepts in this doctrine of justification. There is, of course, no lack of forensic oriented terminology in Luther's writings, although rather surprisingly, Luther himself never actually used the term "forensic". The use of the word forensic is thus a distinctive contribution of Melanchthon himself.[54] Thus Luther says, "But here the question is, by what means we are justified and attain eternal life. To this we answer with Paul, that by faith only in Christ we are pronounced righteous ..."[55] But Luther's full range of expression must be given due consideration. When this is done, there is also a definite renewal aspect to his doctrine of justification. Thus Luther writes in his *Preface to the New Testament* (1522), "...that whoever believed on the seed of Abraham should be blessed, i.e. delivered from sin, death, and hell. Thus *made righteous*, he would live in eternal bliss."[56] Again he writes, "Thus it is not by our own works, but by His work, His passion and death, that He *makes us righteous*, and gives us life and salvation."[57] Paraphrasing 1 Timothy 1:9 he

[50]Cited in Friedrich Bente, *Historical Introductions to the Book of Concord* (St. Louis: Concordia Publishing House, 1965), 47.

[51]Bente, *Historical Introductions to the Book of Concord*, 43.

[52]Bente, *Historical Introductions to the Book of Concord*, 43.

[53]Philipp Melanchthon et al., *Corpus Reformatorum.* (Halis Saxonum: Schwetschke, 1911), II.510, my translation.

[54]*Cf.* Friedrich Loofs, "Die Rechfertigung Nach Den Lutherschen Gedanken in Den Bekenntnisschriften Des Konkordienbuches," *Theologische Studien und Kritiken* 94 (1922): 317.

[55]Galatians in Luther, *Martin Luther, Selections from His Writings*, 116.

[56]Luther, *Martin Luther, Selections from His Writings*, 16. *The emphases in these following citations are mine.*

[57]Luther, *Martin Luther, Selections from His Writings*, 17.

states, "...understand this, that a man is *given righteousness*, life, and salvation by faith; and nought is required of him to give proof of this faith."[58] In his *Freedom of a Christian* written in 1520, he expresses himself, "To preach Christ means to feed the soul, *make it righteous*, set it free, and save it, provided it believes the preaching."[59] And most clearly, he says, "This is as though he said, 'Faith, which is a small and perfect fulfilment of the law, will fill believers with so great a righteousness that they will need nothing more to *become righteous*.'"[60] While these expressions come from his earlier writings in the 1520s, Luther expresses himself similarly in his *Galatians Commentary* of 1531, "Because thou hast laid hold upon Christ by faith, through whom thou *art made righteous*, begin now to work well."[61] That Luther develops his doctrine of justification with the phrase "art made righteous" in 1531 is important, for this is his mature reflection on the matter of justification. He had lectured on the epistle of Galatians twice before, in 1519 and 1523, but he considered only the lectures of 1531 to have been of enough value to save for future generations.[62] It is unlikely that he inserted an accidental renewal element into his exclusively forensic conception of justification.

Beyond these citations, however, other pertinent passages establish the renewal element in Luther's teaching on justification. Loofs has helpfully summarized Luther's terms for justification in his German translation of the Bible. Luther's justification terminology in his translation of the New Testament includes: *Rechtfertigen, gerecht werden, gerecht machen,* and *gerecht sein.*[63] Luther continued to edit and rework his translation to the very end of his life with a band of notable Lutheran theologians. That these terms remain in the Luther Bible attests to Luther's willingness to speak both in terms of renewal as well as forensic language.

Luther's conception of the parallel between Adam and Christ is instructive at this point. In his *Preface to Romans*, he writes,

---

[58]Luther, *Martin Luther, Selections from His Writings*, 17-18.
[59]Luther, *Martin Luther, Selections from His Writings*, 55.
[60]Luther, *Martin Luther, Selections from His Writings*, 56.
[61]Luther, *Martin Luther, Selections from His Writings*, 111.
[62]*Cf.* Luther, *Martin Luther, Selections from His Writings*, 99.
[63]Loofs, p. 320. Loofs gives a lengthy list of scriptural citations.

> Paul now makes an interesting digression, and discusses the origin of both sin and righteousness, of death and life. He shows how Adam and Christ represent two contrary types, and says, in effect, that Christ had to come as a second Adam and to transmit His righteousness by virtue of a new, spiritual birth in faith. This is the counterpoise to what Adam did when he transmitted sin to us through our earlier, physical birth.[64]

Here Luther asserts that Christ's righteousness is transmitted to the believer in the new birth in faith. It is regeneration that conveys Christ's righteousness just as real sin is present in all men by virtue of their birth in flesh tainted by Adam's sin. Again, Luther says,

> As sin has been inherited by us from Adam, and has now become our own, so must also Christ's righteousness and life become our own, in such a way that the same power of righteousness and life may work in us, just as though they had also been inherited by us from him. For there is in him not a merely personal, but an actual and powerful righteousness and life – yea, a fountain which gushes and flows forth into all who become partakers of himself, just as from Adam sin and death have flowed into man's whole nature. And it is therefore now declared that men become righteous and alive from sin and death, not from themselves or through themselves, but through the alien righteousness and life of this Lord Christ, namely, when he touches them with his hand and imparts to them through the word his work and power to blot out sin and death, and they believe the same.[65]

Here the righteousness of Christ is compared to a flowing fountain that fills the partaker of Christ. Thereby he *becomes* righteous. It is the alien righteousness – alien to the sinner since it is really Christ's – that by faith blots out sin and death when Christ touches them in his word. Thus "medicinal" language is coupled with imputation (alien righteousness). Here Luther sees this renewal in terms of Christ and the believer's faith without direct reference to the Holy Spirit. Christ himself is the sanctifier.

---

[64]Luther, *Martin Luther, Selections from His Writings.*, 28.

[65]Cited in R. Seeburg, *Textbook of the History of Doctrines* (Philadelphia, 1905), II.262, n.1.

Yet Luther also sees the Holy Spirit as a real agent in the forgiveness of sins. What would normally be considered justification terminology, Luther also employs in the domain of sanctification. He states in his *Large Catechism* (1529),

> As the Father is called Creator and the Son is called Redeemer, so on account of his work the Holy Spirit must be called Sanctifier, the One who makes holy. How does this sanctifying take place? Answer: Just as the Son obtains dominion by purchasing us through his birth, death, and resurrection, etc., so the Holy Spirit effects our sanctification through the following: the communion of saints or Christian church, *the forgiveness of sins*, the resurrection of the body, and the life everlasting. (Italics mine.)[66]

In this quotation of the *Large Catechism*, Luther understands that part of sanctification is the forgiveness of sins, which is the normal definition of justification. Further, the distinction he makes seems to imply that justification was made possible by Christ's redemption while the application of this redemption, namely, forgiveness of sins, is made by the Holy Spirit. Thus the Holy Spirit sanctifies in part by forgiving sins. And lastly, it is important to notice that Luther bypasses the believer's works of new obedience in his statement on sanctification by the Holy Spirit. Luther again explains,

> If you are asked, What do you mean by the words, "I believe in the Holy Spirit"? you can answer, "I believe that the Holy Spirit makes me holy, as his name implies." How does he do this? By what means? Answer: "Through the Christian church, *the forgiveness of sins ...*" (Italics mine.)[67]

Even the sacraments, the means of grace in the believer's sanctification participate in the forgiveness of sins,

> Further we believe that in this Christian church we have the forgiveness of sins, which is granted through the holy sacraments

---

[66]Martin Luther, *Large Cathechism*, in Martin Luther, *Selected Writings of Martin Luther*, ed. Theodore G. Tappert (Philadelphia: Fortress Press, 1967), 415.

[67]Luther, *Selected Writings of Martin Luther*, 416.

> and absolution as well as through all the comforting words of the entire Gospel.[68]

Further, Luther conceives of this forgiveness as an ongoing process to remedy the partial holiness of the believer,

> Now we are only halfway pure and holy. The Holy Spirit must continue to work in us through the Word, daily granting forgiveness until we attain to that life where there will be no more forgiveness. In that life are only perfectly pure and holy people, full of goodness and righteousness, completely freed from sin, death, and all evil, living in new, immortal and glorified bodies.[69]

Thus the Holy Spirit "grants forgiveness" daily in the growth of the believer's holiness enroute to the celestial perfection. This work of the Holy Spirit will continue even to the last day, "For he has not yet gathered together all his Christian people, nor has he completed the granting of forgiveness."[70] For Luther, then, Christ can be described as the source of the believer's renewal through his alien righteousness and the Holy Spirit can be called the Sanctifier because he forgives sins. Thus Luther's theology of justification does not neatly fit the classic pattern of the Reformational debate.

Was Luther conscious of speaking in both forensic as well as effective or renewal language in his doctrinal formulations? This appears to be the case as can be seen when he expressed his dual conception of justification in 1532.

> These are the *two parts of justification*. The *former* is the grace revealed through Christ, that through Christ we have a God appeased, so that sin is no longer able to accuse us, but the confidence of conscience in the mercy of God is reduced to certainty. The *latter* is the bestowal of the Spirit with his gifts, who illuminates against the pollution of the spirit and the flesh. (Italics mine.)[71]

Luther's justification teaching thus possessed a bipartite structure.

---

[68]Luther, *Selected Writings of Martin Luther*, 417.

[69]Luther, *Selected Writings of Martin Luther*, 418.

[70]Luther, *Selected Writings of Martin Luther*, 419.

[71]Cited in Seeburg, *Textbook of the History of Doctrines*, II.263, n.1.

And this viewpoint was in his mind non-negotiable. Luther had an opportunity presented to him when he was asked to prepare two lists of articles. The first was to declare those doctrinal points that were negotiable, the second list was to be those doctrinal matters that were beyond reconsideration. The articles that Luther thus prepared were destined to become symbolical for Lutheranism in the *Book of Concord*. They were entitled *The Smalcald Articles*, and were written in 1537. They were intended to be the Protestant negotiation instrument at the long-awaited ecclesiastical council that was to settle the Protestant-Rome schism, which had finally been called by Pope Paul III. The council had been originally scheduled for 1537 in Mantua. But it was not convened until 1546, the year of Luther's death, and became instead the Council of Trent, since the location had changed.

So Luther had a historic opportunity to articulate his doctrine of justification over against what he saw as the errors of Rome, at the beginning of the final decade of his illustrious career. His resolution to remain unmoved, on the doctrine of justification as if at a second Diet of Worms, is seen under the thirteenth heading of Part III. It is entitled, "How Man is Justified Before God, And His Good Works," and declares:

> I do not know how I can change what I have heretofore constantly taught on this subject, namely, that by faith (as St. Peter says) we get a new and clean heart and that God will and does account us altogether righteous and holy for the sake of Christ, our mediator. Although the sin in our flesh has not been completely removed or eradicated, he will not count or consider it.
>
> Good works follow such faith, renewal, and forgiveness.[72]

Luther's determined answer here underscores his view that renewal is an aspect of justification. Justification is thus getting a new and clean heart, as well as being accounted as righteous, and experiencing the non-imputation of sins. Instead of insisting upon forensic justification as the core of his doctrine that was at the heart of his dispute with Rome, he refused to budge from his belief that justification was the union of a new heart, an accounting

[72]Theodore G. Tappert, ed., *The Book of Concord: the Confessions of the Evangelical Lutheran Church* (Philadelphia: Fortress Press, 1959), 315.

as righteous, the forgiveness of sins as well as renewal, under the heading of the Reformational doctrine of justification.

Conclusion

As we conclude our reflection on the classic Reformational debate on justification from the earliest Lutheran Reformers in terms of how they related renewal and forensic concepts in their doctrine of justification would it not have been most helpful had Melanchthon actually asked Luther of his view of the relationship of justification and renewal? The fact is, that he did. Because of the profound appreciation of Luther's students for his every word, a most pertinent dialogue has been preserved for the students of the theology of the Reformers in *Luther's Tabletalk*:

> Philip Melanchthon said to Luther, the opinion of St. Austin of justification (as it seemeth) was more pertinent, fit and convenient, when he disputed not, than it was when he used to speak and dispute; for this he saith: "We ought to censure and hold that we are justified by faith, that is *by our regeneration*, or *being made new creatures*" Now if it be so, then we are *not justified only by faith*, but by all the gifts and virtues of God given to us. Now what is your opinion, sir? Do you hold that a man is *justified by this regeneration* as St. Austin's opinion? Luther answered and said, *I hold this*, and am certain that the true meaning of the gospel and of the apostle is, that we are justified before God *gratis*, for nothing, only by God's mere mercy wherewith and by reason whereof he imputeth righteousness unto us in Christ. (Italics mine.)[73]

Luther's answer preserved here not only unmistakably includes regeneration, but goes on to join it with a parallel clause of imputing righteousness. It should be seen that Luther here is not affirming what Melanchthon terms the "disputing" opinion of Augustine. Augustine often argued that it was the works of regeneration that served as the ground of the believer's justification.[74] Much better than this, Luther affirms echoing Melanchthon's words, is Augustine's teaching that one is justified by faith which is also inclusive of one's regeneration. Thus Luther and early Lutheranism

---

[73]Bell's trans. Ed. 1652, p. 208, cited in William G. T. Shedd, *A History of Christian Doctrine* (Minneapolis: Klock and Klock, 1978), II.258.

[74]*Cf.* Seeburg, *Textbook of the History of Doctrines*, I.349.

affirmed the connection and identification of justification with regeneration or renewal.

In view of the early Lutheran Reformers' conception of both a renewal as well as a forensic conception of justification, we must highlight the distinctiveness of Calvin's doctrine of forensic justification. Luther, Melanchthon, Chemnitz, and the confessions of early Lutheranism strikingly differ from Calvin with respect to the concept of an exclusive forensic justification. The early Lutherans insisted upon the centrality of both renewal and forensic concepts as parts of their justification teachings. Calvin, however, allowed the non-forensic idea only as a rare unnecessary possibility in the writings of Paul.

This difference then between Calvin and Luther as well as the early Lutherans suggests a remarkable conclusion. If it is true that forensic justification without concomitant elements of renewal came to be the distinctive Protestant perspective, so much so that it is often today viewed as the classic pattern of the Reformational debate, then the evidence presented here argues that this was due much more to Calvin's influence rather than that of Luther. For it was Calvin who blazed the trail for the ultimate triumph of the primacy and exclusivity of forensic justification in Protestant theology.

Calvin's basic thesis argues for the believer's union with Christ, which through the covenant of grace, offers the dual, distinct yet inseparable covenant benefits of justification and sanctification, a sanctification that begins with and encompasses regeneration or renewal by the Holy Spirit. This solution that Calvin posits enables and ensures a distinctive forensic justification. Yet, it does not dismiss nor diminish the necessity of moral renewal. Thus in this way, Calvin can give full weight to the importance of the Lordship of Christ in the believer's life that is manifested by good works in covenantal obedience. Accordingly, Calvin left an indelible mark on Protestantism. His insistence on forensic justification and his emphasis on a renewal that manifested itself in a life empowered by the Holy Spirit and evidenced by the new obedience of faith became the core understanding of reformed theology. His doctrine of forensic justification also became the standard for both Reformed and Lutheran orthodoxy. Perhaps the true surprise here is that the reason that Reformed and

Lutheran expressions of justification appear so much alike is because Lutheran orthodoxy – whether consciously or unaware – ultimately adopted Calvin's view of forensic justification.

John Owen on Justification

Carl R. Trueman

Introduction[1]

The doctrine of justification, famously dubbed by Luther as "the article by which the church stands or falls," was no less a controversial doctrine in Owen's time than it had been at the inception of the Reformation.[2] It is of course necessary at the outset to acknowledge the fact that Owen's context for his discussion of justification is a complex one.

For a start, the basic significance of the doctrine as one of the key theological distinctives which marked Protestantism off from Roman Catholicism meant that discussion of justification was always going to be profoundly political, both ecclesiastically and in the more general social sense. There were, by Owen's time, well-established polemical lines of debate between Protestants and Catholics into which his own exposition of the doctrine needs to be fitted.

Second, the wider Western trajectories of doctrinal discussion within which the Reformed orthodox stood also need to be taken into account: for all of the radical differences between Protestant and Catholic theologians on this issue, particularly as these

---

[1]This is an abridged version of a longer discussion of the topic in Carl R. Trueman, *John Owen* (Aldershot: Ashgate, 2007).

[2]Owen quotes Luther (without giving a specific textual reference) as saying "Amisso articulo justificationis, simul amissa est tota doctrina Christiana" ("When the article of justification is lost, the whole of Christian teaching is lost at the same time"), John Owen, *The Works of John Owen*, ed. W. H. Gould (Edinburgh: The Banner of Truth Trust, 1977), V.57. Standard histories of the doctrine are: Albrecht Ritschl, *The Christian Doctrine of Justification and Reconciliation: the Positive Development of the Doctrine*, trans. H. R. Mackintosh, Macaulay (Edinburgh: T.&T. Clark, 1900); Alister E. McGrath, *Iustitia Dei: A History of the Christian Doctrine of Justification*, 3rd (Cambridge: Cambridge University Press, 2005).

positions received confessional codification at the Council of Trent and then in subsequent Protestant creeds, both Catholics and Protestants conducted their discussions in terms which one might characterize in broad terms as Augustinian, being rooted in the anti-Pelagian writings of the Bishop of Hippo and in the understandings of righteousness, divine and human, and other corollary doctrines which were developed in its aftermath. Once again, we need to remember Owen was not just a reformed, or even Protestant, theologian; we also need to keep in mind that he was an *Augustinian* theologian.[3]

Third, Owen wrote on justification in the context of an England where specific local difficulties had imposed peculiar requirements on theologians dealing specifically with this doctrine: antinomianism and neonomianism both arose in specific social contexts and were symbiotic in an antagonistic way; Owen needed to bear the Scylla of one and the Charybdis of the other in mind as he penned his great treatise on the topic.[4]

Owen on Imputation of Active and Passive Righteousness

When Owen comes to write on justification in 1677, then, the debate about justification, specifically with reference to imputation and Christology, was considerably more elaborate

---

[3]I am aware of the problematic nature of this term; I use it to refer to a theologian who stands within the broad, anti-Pelagian tradition of Western theology, and who has a high regard for the authority of Augustine's writings. The problem with the term is not, of course, simply that which typically affects any broad tradition or collection of traditions which take their name from an individual and thus raise complex question about fidelity, continuity, etc. with the conceptual content of the work of the original writer. For example, theologian Daphne Hampson has raised the significant question of whether the underlying notions of humanity and personhood in Catholicism and Protestantism are not fundamentally different, the former being primarily substantial, the latter more relational. From this, she has argued that Protestantism deviates significantly from Augustine in a manner which has decisive impact on the notion of justification: see her *Christ Contradictions: The Structure of Lutheran and Catholic Thought* (Cambridge: Cambridge University Press, 2001).

[4]Two recent studies on the subject of the context of antinomianism which are worth consulting are David R. Como, *Blown by the Spirit: Puritanism and the Emergence of an Antinomian Underground in Pre-Civil War England* (Stanford: Stanford University Press, 2004); and Theodore Dwight Bozeman, *The Precisianist Strain: Disciplinary Religion and Antinomian Backlash in Puritanism to 1638* (Chapel Hill: University of North Carolina Press, 2003).

than it had been in the sixteenth century. In fact, Owen's commitment to imputation of both Christ's active and passive obedience is evident from the *Savoy Declaration* of 1658 which was essentially a modification of the *Westminster Confession*. Most of the modifications involve the teaching on church polity, but the article on justification is expanded from the WCF to include specific reference to the imputation of both the active and passive righteousness of Christ. Owen, along with Thomas Goodwin, was one of the principal architects of the document, and thus the document can be assumed to reflect his theology and his view of the inadequacy or ambiguity of the original WCF formulation.[5]

Owen's major discussion of justification is *The Doctrine of Justification by Faith, through the Imputation of the Righteousness of Christ; Explained, Confirmed, and Vindicated* (London, 1677), although some of the issues had been touched on numerous occasions in previous works, most notably those in the exchange with Baxter surrounding the latter's *Aphorisms of Justification*. In *The Doctrine of Justification*, Owen makes the claim in the preliminary chapter that he does not intend to deal with the passive/active distinction at any length.[6] Nevertheless, he then proceeds in the treatise itself to tackle the issue head on, as it lies very much at the heart of the debates in which he was engaged.

As one would expect, particularly in light of the *Savoy Declaration*, Owen maintains the standard orthodox position of the imputation of both Christ's active and his passive obedience; and he articulates this position through polemical examination of the arguments against this point. As far as his opponents go, he divides them into three groups regarding the

---

[5]Savoy XI.i reads as follows: "Those whom God effectually calleth, he also freely justifieth, not by infusing righteousness into them, but by pardoning their sins, and by accounting and accepting their persons as righteous, nor for any thing wrought in them, or done by them, but for Christ's sake alone; nor by imputing Faith itself, the act of believing, or any other Evangelical obedience to them, as their righteousness, but by imputing Christ's active obedience unto the whole Law, and passive obedience in his death for their whole and sole righteousness, they receiving and resting on him and his righteousness by Faith; which Faith they have not of themselves, it is the gift of God." "Savoy Declaration," in *A Declaration of the Faith and Order Owned and Practised in the Congregational Churches in England/ Agreed Upoin and Consented Unto by Their Elders and Messengers in Their Meeting at the Savoy, October 12, 1658* (London, 1658), 20-21.

[6]Owen, *Works*, V.63.

role of Christ's active obedience in the work of justification: those who see it as impossible; those who see it as useless; and those who see it as pernicious.[7] In the first group, he cites Socinus, *De Jesu Christo Servatore* 3.5, as arguing that Christ's obedience was necessary for his own salvation, and that even his death was an offering on behalf of himself, which God then rewarded with adoption.[8]

This is clearly consistent with Socinian soteriology, rejecting as it does the vicarious nature of Christ's work and insisting instead upon its paradigmatic significance. Thus, Smalcius' *Racovian Catechism*, Chapter 8, "Of Christ's Death," makes it clear that the death is purely an example and an encouragement to believers, and that any notion of vicarious sacrifice or satisfaction is "fallacious, erroneous, and very pernicious," a point which has obvious significance for the nature of justification.[9]

It is worth remembering, however, that, although Owen chooses to focus on the Socinians in refuting this position, it is not entirely different to that articulated by Piscator and Gataker who regarded Christ's positive obedience to the law as being part of his obligation as rational creature, although the teleological significance is clearly very different. Indeed, the connection between Socinianism and those who were "soft" on the imputation of Christ's active obedience was already well established in the controversial rhetoric of the time, and not entirely without some historical foundation. For example, Piscator's *Profitable Treatise* was, the author tells us, written at the request of his friend, Conrad Vorstius who wished him to refute Bellarmine on justification. The preface is dated 18 December 1593, some time before Vorstius became Public Enemy No. 1 in the reformed world; but the connection was surely not insignificant, either theologically or in terms of public association.[10]

Further, Anthony Wotton, a leading English proponent of something akin to Piscator's position, was subject to a decades-

[7]Owen, *Works*, V.262.

[8]Owen, *Works*, V.253.

[9]*The Racovian Catechism* (Amsterdam, 1652), 122-39, esp. 126; cf. the comments of Francis Cheynell, *The Rise, Growth, and Danger of Socinianisme* (London, 1643), 24.

[10]Johannes Piscator, *A Learned and Profitable Treatise of Man's Justification* (London, 1599), Preface.

long campaign accusing him of being a Socinian, a campaign mounted by the vigorously orthodox George Walker. Walker himself was to be a delegate at the Westminster Assembly, and was to target Gataker also as a Socinian.[11] We should note, however, that the notion that Christ's obedience to the law was an essential component of fitting him to offer his death as a satisfaction on behalf of others had a long pedigree in Western theology and lay very much at the heart of Anselm's rationale for incarnation in *Cur Deus Homo*.

In opposition to this rejection of the imputation of both active and passive righteousness, Owen argues from the integrity of the person and work of the mediator to the necessity for seeing both active and passive righteousness imputed to the believer. Central to this is the typical orthodox primary emphasis upon the *person* of the mediator, not the *natures* of the mediator:

> If the obedience that Christ yielded unto the law were for himself, whereas it was the act of his person, *his whole person*, and the divine nature therein, were 'made under the law;' which cannot be. For although it is acknowledged that, in the ordination of God, his exinanition was to precede his glorious, majestical exaltation, as the Scripture witnesseth, Phil. 2:19; Luke 24:26; Rom. 14:9; yet absolutely his glory was an immediate consequent of the hypostatical union, Heb. 1:6; Matt. 2:11.[12]

---

[11]Walker pursued Wotton with an obsessive commitment which can only lead later observers of his campaign to speculate about what personal issues lay beneath the surface. He even kept up the campaign after Wotton's death in 1626. Walker's account of the dispute, which began in 1611, can be found in his *A True Relation of the chiefe passages betweene Mr Anthony Wotton, and Mr George Walker* (London, 1642). Wotton's position can be found in the work which his son published posthumously, *Mr Anthony Wotton's Defence Against Mr George Walker's Charge, Accusing him of Socinian Heresie and Blasphemie (Cambridge, 1641)*, itself a response to Walker's *Socinianisme in the Fundamentall point of Justification discovered and confuted* (1641). Wotton's work contained a preface and postscript by Gataker. Gataker himself had to go into print to defend himself against the charge of Socinianism made against him by Walker: *An Answer to Mr George Walker's Vindication or rather Fresh Accusation* (London, 1642).

[12]Owen, *Works*, XII.256. Cf. the similar argument of George Downame: "But these men shold have remembred, that the person, who ... did obey the Law, was and is not onely man but God also, and therefore, as his bloud was Gods bloud, so his obedience was the obedience of God, and consequently was performed not of duty, nor for himselfe. For if of duty, then God had been a debtor to the

Of course, such an argument is scarcely likely to persuade any Socinian because they would reject the major presupposition, the Chalcedonian definition of Christ's person. Nevertheless, within a Reformed orthodox framework, the argument is clearly a coherent one, pointing back to the establishment of Christ as mediator under the terms of the covenant of redemption, and assuming mediation according to both natures and the anhypostatic nature of Christ's humanity. The union of natures in the incarnation is what qualifies Christ as capable of acting as mediator, and this is because that union is determined by the voluntary covenant of redemption, the doctrinal context for understanding the incarnate mediator.[13] Owen accepts the medieval Scotist terminology of *viator* and *possessor* as applied to Christ, to distinguish his earthly sojourn from his later glory, but sees the historical movement contained therein as reflecting the voluntarily established terms of the covenant, and not as indicating any initial deficiency in his qualifications as mediator.[14]

The importance of federalism is also clear in several of Owen's other arguments on this issue. For Owen, it is crucial that Christ's appointment as mediator in the covenant of redemption means that

---

Law: Neither needed the humane nature, being by personall union united to the divine, to obey, or to merit for it selfe; seeing from the first moment of the conception therof, it was personally united to the Deity of the Sonne of God, in whose person it subsisting was, from the beginning of the being therof, most happy, and enjoying the beatificall vision, being at that time, as the Schoolemen speake both viator et comprehensor. Neither did the humane nature, which doth not subsist by it selfe, work any thing by it selfe in the work of our redemption, but God manifested in the flesh, did in and by it both obey and suffer for us." *A Treatise of Justification* (London, 1634), 29. Cf. the argument of Featley to the Westminster Assembly, *Daniel Featley, Dippers Dipt*, 5th (London, 1647), 196; also James Ussher, *Immanuel, or, the Mystery of the Incarnation of the Son of God* (London, 1653), 11.

[13]"The Lord Christ was every way meet for the whole work of mediation, by the ineffable union of the human nature with the divine, which exalted it in dignity, honour, and worth, above any thing or all things that ensued thereon. Again, that which is an effect of the person of the Mediator, as constituted such, is not a qualification necessary unto its constitution; that is, what he did as mediator did not concur in the making of him meet so to be." Owen, *Works*, V.258. "[T]he compact between the Father and the Son as unto his undertaking for us undeniably proves all that he did in the pursuit of them to be done for us, and not for himself." Owen, *Works*, V.258-59.

[14]Owen, *Works*, V.259.

all his works are those of voluntary condescension in the ordained economy of salvation, not necessary to his being, and as such their significance and value is determined by the covenant which is the defining ground of the work of incarnation.[15] In addition, the position of Christ as federal sponsor means that he always acts in a public, not a private or personal, capacity, and that strict comparison with any other individual is not legitimate. His whole life, having its causal ground in the covenant of redemption, is that of the sponsor of the covenant of grace, and thus in its entirety it has a significance which embraces all of the objects of the covenant of grace. The theology of federal headship, rooted in the covenant of redemption between Father and Son, thus repeatedly connects to the debate on justification and allows for conceptual precision in clarifying the status and role of Christ as mediator.[16]

In this context, Owen engages both in his treatise on justification and in his commentary on Hebrews in an extended refutation of the notion that Christ's sponsorship, as mentioned in Heb. 7:22, refers to his sponsorship on behalf of God, whereby the covenant is shown to human beings to be sound. This was the exegesis favored by Socinians such as Schlichtingius, Remonstrans, such as Grotius, and the influential seventeenth-century English commentator, Bishop Hammond, all of whose works are explicitly mentioned by Owen in this context.[17] Owen, standing within an established and respectable exegetical tradition at this point, argues rather that

---

[15]Owen, *Works*, V.257-58.

[16]Owen, *Works*, V.260-61; also Owen, *Works*, X.174-77; Owen, *Works*, XII.502-3; cf. David Dickson, *The Summe of Saving Knowledge* (Edinburgh, 1671), Head II; also Patrick Gillespie, *The Ark of the Covenant Opened* (London, 1677). In this context, it is interesting to note that the Savoy Declaration modifies Chapter 8 of the WCF by explicitly using covenantal language to describe the appointment of Christ as mediator by the Father. As the specific conceptual terminology of the covenant of redemption did not start to become commonplace in reformed theology until the late 1640s, it is not significant that it is absent from the WCF.

[17]Owen, *Works*, V.182-83, 22, 599-600. Hammond's comment reads as follows: "Christ was Sponsor and Surety [of that covenant] for God, that it should be made good to us on God's part (on condition we performed that which was required of us) viz. the Covenant confirmed to us by Christ in the Gospel, a better Covenant then the Covenant of the Law, wherein Moses undertook for God to us." Henry Hammond, *A Paraphrase, and Annotations Upon All the Books of the New Testament, Breifly Explaining All the Difficult Places Thereof* (London, 1659), 741.

the sponsorship is on behalf of men and women and directed to God, not on behalf of God and directed to men and women.[18]

What this does, of course, is secure the priesthood, and thus the sacrifice, of Christ as something which is offered to God, and which thus refuses to reduce the significance of the incarnation simply to revealing something of God. Again, the roots of Owen's argument in this context lie theologically with his understanding of the covenant of redemption, but, as noted, his exegesis is not exceptional.[19] Further, his understanding of the etymology of the Greek word itself leads him to argue that sponsorship presupposes inadequacy or defect on behalf of the party being represented by the sponsor; and this cannot apply to God but only to the sons and daughters of Adam. Here, his thinking connects with Roman law: Owen translates the Greek as *surety*, as do the Geneva Bible and the Authorized Version, and states that this is the equivalent of *fideiussor*.[20] This is a term drawn from Roman law to refer to a guarantor of a debt or obligation who acts voluntarily and on behalf of the one in debt.[21] In all of this, particularly in his use of the language of *sponsor* (the term used in the Vulgate) and *fideiussor*, he stands within typical Reformed orthodox treatments of Christology in the context of the covenant of redemption.[22]

The final argument Owen offers in this refutation of the Socinian claims concerning the impossibility of imputation of

---

[18]Owen, *Works*, V.184-96, 22, 501-12.

[19]See especially Owen, *Works*, V.191, 22, 505. Cf. William Gouge, *A Learned and Very Useful Commentary on the Whole Epistle to the Hebrewes* [London, 1655], 193-94; David Dickson, *An Exposition of All St Paul's Epistles* [London, 1659], 196; Edward Leigh, *A Systeme or Body of Divinity* [London, 1657], 575; see also the definition in Thomas Wilson, *A Christian Dictionary* [London, 1647], n.p.: "Surety 1. One that undertaketh for the debt of another man. Prov. 6.1 ... 2. Christ, who undertooke to answer the debt of our sins to God's justice, by his obedience to death. Heb. 7.22." While this particular point is not a matter of comment in either the Dutch Annotations or the various editions of the Westminster Annotations, Giovanni Diodati does do so, and offers something of a mediating position, whereby Christ is surety for the elect in satisfying God's wrath, and for God by assuring believers of the Father's favor through the Spirit: Giovanni Diodati, *Pious and Learned Annotations Upon the Whole Bible* (London, 1648), 375 (New Testament).

[20]Owen, *Works*, V.184, 187.

[21]E.g. Justinian, *The Institutes of Justinian*, 7th, trans. Thomas Collett Sandars (London: Longmans, Green, 1941), III.xx.

[22]See the entries under *fideiussio* and *sponsio* in Richard A. Muller, *Dictionary of Latin and Greek Theological Terms: Drawn Principally from Protestant Scholastic Theology* (Grand Rapids, Michigan: Baker Book House, 1985).

active obedience relates to the meaning of the term *under law*, which he reads his opponents as meaning "obliged to obey God by virtue of the relationship that necessarily exists between the Creator and all rational creatures." Owen accepts that this is indeed the case, but then pushes the argument forward into the eschatological realm: Christ's human nature, as a creature, will be obliged to God as creator even in the eschaton, a point he supports with reference to the communication of properties which will never involve the direct communication of self-existent deity to Christ's humanity; but, argues Owen, to claim that this involves the heavenly Christ being *under law* in the Pauline sense of *obliged to fulfill it on his own account* is clearly absurd in such a context.

Further, the notion of the law as specially imposed by God with a view to reward also points to the absurdity of seeing Christ as *under law* for his own sake: again, the hypostatic union itself was quite sufficient to make Christ's human nature worthy of eternal life for itself. Here we see the obvious doctrinal intersection of the covenant of works and that of redemption in the context of Christology and mediation.[23]

Indeed, as Owen elaborates upon the saving efficacy of Christ's mediation, he is very clear that the terms of Christ's penal work on the cross are set by the Creator–creature framework as covenantally established in Genesis 1–3. Working against the background of reformed exegesis of Romans 5, with its parallel of Adam and Christ, Owen argues in *Of the Death of Christ* (his 1650 response to Baxter's *Aphorisms*) that the penalty which Christ underwent as federal sponsor on behalf of the elect was death; and in so doing, he connects Galatians 3:13, Romans 8:3, and Genesis 2:17.[24] Thus, as representative human being, Christ must both fulfill the law positively on behalf of humanity because of Adam's abject failure so to do, and he must undergo punishment of death because of Adam's breaking of the original covenant. It is not Christ's ontology as the Divine–human person which requires this, but his covenantal status as representative which demands it.

The presence of these three types of argument (from hypostatic union; from condescension; and from federal headship) at least

---

[23]Owen, *Works*, V.261-62.
[24]Owen, *Works*, X.448.

in a very brief form in earlier works by Downame and Featley suggests that, by the time he writes in the 1670s, Owen is working within an established framework of standard orthodox responses to criticisms of the mainstream position.[25]

As is typical of Owen, however, this lack of originality in the basic trajectories of argument does not prevent him from engaging in significant theological elaboration, of a kind which lays bare the sophisticated underlying structure of the reformed orthodox theology to which he is committed, particularly as it finds its ground in the doctrine of the Trinity, specifically the covenant of redemption and its determinative impact upon both the history and the order of salvation. Having highlighted this, it is now necessary to turn to one of the implications which his opponents saw in the connection he drew between atonement and justification: the problems of eternal justification, with its connotations of antinomianism.[26]

Owen and Eternal Justification

The primary criticism of Owen on atonement and justification came from Richard Baxter, for whom the issues of antinomianism and its perceived conceptual foundation, eternal justification, were more than just theological games. His experience in the

---

[25]See Daniel Featley, *Dippers Dipt*, 5th (London, 1647), the appendix of which contains Featley's speeches on the issue of twofold imputation to the early sessions of the Westminster Assembly; see esp. 196-97; also Downame, *A Treatise of Justification*.

[26]It is worth mentioning one final argument used by Owen's contemporaries to deny the imputation of Christ's double righteousness to the believer is a more straightforwardly exegetical one, and this again serves to bring out the importance of federalism to Owen's own theological position. Gataker is a good example of this: in his *Antidote*, he argues that Scripture never associates the life of Christ with the works of redemption, remission, and justification; rather, the textual evidence points squarely towards the suffering and death of Christ as being the grounds for this: see Thomas Gataker, *An Antidote Against Errour, Concerning Justification*, (London, 1670), 5, 28-31. Featley himself responded to such arguments as proposed by Tilenus and Piscator in his second speech on Article 11 to the Westminster Assembly: *Dippers Dipt*, 196-97. By Owen's day, then, the standard response to this was to argue that references in the New Testament to the blood of Christ etc. are to be taken synecdochically, and that they simply subsume both active and passive obedience under the one term; it is thus hardly surprising that we should find Owen making this conventional case: Owen, *Works*, V.271.

Civil War as an army chaplain left a lasting impression on him: the impact and influence of radical sectarianism and its frequent connection to what Baxter regarded as moral anarchy left Baxter with a lasting fear of anything which might disrupt the smooth running of the godly commonwealth, be it antinomianism or pedantic doctrinal militancy.[27]

It should be noted at the outset that the Protestant doctrine of justification by imputation was always going to be vulnerable to criticisms of tending towards eternal justification. Late medieval theologians had used the distinction between God's absolute power and his ordained power, along with that between congruent and condign merit, to break the necessary connection between the logical priority of actual righteousness in a real sense, and God's declaration that a particular person was justified. Thus, in placing the declaration in God's will, not the intrinsic qualities of the one justified, it is arguable that the necessary connection not only between ontological factors and justification but also between chronological factors and justification had been decisively abolished. Given that Protestantism actually intensified this medieval emphasis, it is not surprising that some reformed theologians, including Owen, should find themselves under suspicion of holding to eternal justification.

The name perhaps most associated with sophisticated expressions of the doctrine of eternal justification in Owen's day was that of Tobias Crisp. Indeed, the republication of his works in 1690 was to bring the elderly Baxter out of retirement on the grounds that he needed to refute the dangerous tenets of "Crispianism."[28] In the 1640s, however, the posthumous publication of his sermons occasioned vigorous opposition not simply from the likes of Baxter, but also from orthodox figures such as Samuel Rutherford, who, in the wake of the debates at the Westminster Assembly, saw Crisp's work as part and parcel of a dangerously

[27]See Carl R. Trueman, "Richard Baxter on Christian Unity: A Chapter in the Enlightening of English Reformed Orthodoxy," *Westminster Theological Journal* 61 (1999): 53-71; on the question of Baxter and the church in general, of particular note is the work of Paul C. –H. Lim, *In Pursuit of Purity, Unity and Liberty: Richard Baxter's Puritan Ecclesiology in Its Seventeenth-Century Context* (Leiden: Brill, 2004).

[28]Crisp's works were published posthumously, in three volumes, in the 1640s.

antinomian trajectory in English Puritan thought which was also connected to the sinister calls for that most un-Presbyterian tenet, liberty of conscience in religious matters.[29] Others, such as Stephen Geree and John Benrigge were also quick to respond, concerned that Crisp's teaching on eternal justification subverted the need for the moral imperatives of Christian sanctification.[30]

In fact, an examination of Crisp's writings reveal that his position on the timing of justification was somewhat more sophisticated than the bald characterization implied by the term "eternal justification." First, it is important (particularly for our subsequent discussion of Owen and Baxter) to note the covenantal/Christological context of Crisp's understanding of justification. For Crisp, the covenant of grace is, in a threefold sense, to be identified with Christ: fundamentally, in the sense that he is the one who establishes the covenant with God the Father (Crisp here anticipating the development of the covenant of redemption); materially, as he both represents God to the people and the people to God; and equivalently, in the sense that once the believer has Christ as an earnest of salvation, then he or she has the equivalent of the whole covenant, even though there will be progress in the Christian life.[31]

This latter point is particularly significant as it points towards the problems inherent in dismissing Crisp as antinomian *tout court*: if there is progress in the Christian life, then there is need for nuance in understanding how time and eternity are connected. It does, however, point to the strong Christological federal representation which underlies Crisp's scheme and which thus parallels that of Owen. As the covenant is objectively fulfilled in Christ, what significance can history have?

Crisp is very clear that justification does precede faith. In this context, faith serves to manifest that which is already true, i.e. one believes that one is already justified and this act of belief makes manifest that which was before hidden. This is rooted in the objectivity of Christ's work in the covenant of grace.[32] Yet, even as

---

[29]Samuel Rutherford, *A Survery of the Spirituall Antichrist* (London, 1648).

[30]Stephen Geree, *The Doctrine of the Antinomians by Evidence of Gods Truth Plainely Confuted* (London, 1644); John Benrigge, *Christ Above All Exalted as in Justification So in Sanctification* (London, 1645).

[31]Tobias Crisp, *Christ Alone Exalted* (London, 1643), 171-77.

he is emphatic in teaching that reconciliation was effected in Christ and thus completed on Calvary, Crisp sets God's eternal justifying love, the atonement, and the life of the individual elect, in the context of a basic distinction between God in eternity, conceived of in Boethian terms of simultaneous access to all points in time, and the sequential nature of time as experienced by creatures.

Thus, from all eternity God knows who are his, and he knows that Christ has made satisfaction for them; yet, given the fact that human beings experience life sequentially, it can be really said that, considered in themselves, men and women do actions that are at enmity with God.[33] The solution, therefore, lies in the logical problems generated by language which reflects human experience of time rather than the divine relationship to time in eternity. It is arguable that the solution is unsatisfactory, but it highlights the complexity of argument with which the reformed orthodox addressed such issues and once again indicates the need to avoid simplistic categorical arguments which seek to reduce Reformed orthodoxy to systems of logical deduction from single axioms. Further, anticipating a point which connects directly to the problem which Baxter sees in Owen's theology of justification because of the latter's understanding of atonement, Crisp makes it clear that his view assumes the identity of Christ's punishment with that which elect sinners deserve.[34]

It is this point on which Baxter focuses in the appendix to *Aphorismes of Justification*: presupposing the force of the Socinian critique of reformed atonement theory, and the usefulness of the Grotian response, Baxter claims that if Christ has paid the actual price for our sins, as Owen argues in his 1647 work, *The Death of Death*, then this payment is not refusable by God; nor is it possible that there be a chronological delay between payment and dissolution of the personal debt, since it is either paid or not paid; thus, the elect are justified in Christ, and faith must fulfill a mere epistemological function whereby the members of the elect come to acknowledge that which they are already, namely, justified. In other words, justification by faith is justification in the forum of the conscience, not in the forum of God himself.[35]

---

[32]Crisp, *Christ Alone Exalted*, 168, 198-99.

[33]Crisp, *Christ Alone Exalted*, 393-97; cf. 328-30.

[34]Crisp, *Christ Alone Exalted*, 398-401.

Baxter is particularly upset with the implications of a passage in Owen's work which he sees as clearly reducing faith to acknowledgment of prior justification and thus of laying the groundwork for a radical antinomianism.[36] While he gives no precise reference, the passage in Owen to which he appears to be objecting occurs in Book III of *The Death of Death*. Here, Owen declares that Christ, by his death, did, "*ipso facto*, deliver us from the curse, by being made a curse for us". He then proceeds to explain why this did not mean that all the elect were not immediately justified from that moment by drawing an analogy with a prisoner detained in a foreign country: though he has a right to liberty from the moment the ransom is paid, yet he does not enjoy possession of that liberty until such time as the news of his delivery is brought to him.[37] The analogy is weak and unfortunate because it really does play to the notion that faith is a merely epistemological tool whereby those of the elect come to realization that they are what they always, in fact, have been; and the only movement from wrath to grace in history is in the forum of the individual conscience. This point is not lost on Baxter, who hits Owen hard at this point.[38]

---

[35]Richard Baxter, *Aphorismes of Justification: With Their Explication Annexed* (London, 1649), Appendix, 146-59. Owen responded to *Aphorismes of Justification* in *Of the Death of Christ, the Price He Paid, and the Purchase He Made* (London, 1650), though Baxter, never one to allow others to have the last word, kept up the polemic in *Rich. Baxter's Confession of His Faith* (London, 1655). Owen, himself no slouch in the matter of controversy, then responded to this work in the appendix to his long treatise on Socinianism, *Vindiciae Evangelicae* (London, 1655), entitled, "Of the Death of Christ, and of Justification."

[36]*Aphorismes of Justification: With Their Explication Annexed*, Appendix, 155-57.

[37]Owen, *Works*, X.268.

[38]"1. Whether a man may fitly be said actually, and ipso facto, to be delivered and discharged, who is not at all delivered, but onely hath right to deliverance, I doubt. 2. Knowledge and possession of a deliverance, are farre different things: A man may have possession and no knowledge in some cases; or if he have both, yet the procuring of knowledge is a small matter, in comparison of possession. 3. Our knowledge therefore doth not give us possession; so that the similitude failes; for it is the Creditor's knowledge and satisfaction that is requisite to deliverance. And our creditour was not in a farre and strange countrey, but knew immediately and could either have made us quickly know, or turned us free before we had knowne the cause. 4. Nor can it easily be understood, how God can so long deny us the possession of Heaven, if wee had such absolute actuall Right (as he speaketh) so long ago." Baxter, *Aphorismes of Justification: With Their Explication Annexed*, 156-57.

Of course, Owen's analogy, and indeed, the language which he uses, do tend when taken in isolation to lend themselves to the kind of reading (and criticism) offered by Baxter; and it would seem that, under such pungent polemical pressure, Owen is forced to elaborate his position in the two later treatises which give a much clearer grounding and articulation of his point than the rather unfortunate prisoner passage of 1647. At the heart of his mature argument is the covenantal structure of salvation. In this context, he argues, it is crucial to understand that God's desire to save is prior to the establishment of the covenant of redemption between Father and Son, and thus to any consideration of Christ's satisfaction. Thus, he precludes at the outset any crude notion that Christ's death in any way changes the Father's mind or somehow buys his favor in a crude, commercial sense.[39]

The power of this argument is reinforced when Owen draws attention to the fact that Christ's death, considered in abstraction from its covenantal context, has no meaning or significance as a payment because, considered as such, it is no payment.[40] If, however, the death is considered as a covenantal action, then it does have meaning as a payment; but the force of this is to focus attention on the will of God as the determining factor in the economy of salvation. The positive relationship of Owen's theology to the more voluntarist/Scotist trajectories of late medieval thought is here evident and allows him to argue that the economy of salvation, of which Christ's sacrifice is a part, is to be understood as an act of God's sovereign will and not to be subjected to the narrow canons of particular human logic.[41]

---

[39]Owen, *Works*, X.455-56. This point is simply a clarification of Owen's position as laid out at length in Book I of *The Death of Death*.

[40]"The suffering of Christ may be considered ... [a]bsolutely, as in itself, abstracting from the consideration of any covenant or compact thereabout; and so it cannot be said to be a refusable payment; not because not refusable, but because no payment." Owen, *Works*, X.458.

[41]In discussing the distinction between the death of Christ considered abstractly and covenantally, Owen concludes: "This distinction is not accommodate to this difficulty [of the non-refusability of payment]; the sole reason thereof being what was held out before, of the interest of God's sovereign right to the bestowing of purposed, purchased, promised blessings, as to times and seasons, according to the free counsel of his own will." Owen, *Works*, X.458.

It might be argued, of course, that Owen's shift on divine justice in the early 1650s would render this argument somewhat weaker, given that he adopts a position whereby atonement is necessary if God is to forgive sin.[42] Yet this is not the case: the question of necessity of atonement vis-à-vis God's attributes and his intention to save is a determining factor in the nature of the atonement, covenantally considered, but in itself exerts no decisive influence on the overall structure and disbursement of covenant blessings. As the death of Christ purchases all benefits for the elect, including faith (which is, in a sense, a condition of the covenant of grace). So even after 1653 Owen sees that the atonement needs to be understood within the broad contours of the covenant and of the order of salvation; and he regards faith as given at a point in time determined by the will of the Father, with the voluntarist accent still strongly evident. This tracks to the second covenantal strand of Owen's thinking on justification which defuses the issue of eternal justification: if the covenant of redemption establishes the nature of Christ's death as satisfaction, then the covenant of grace, made by God the Father with Christ on behalf of the elect, embodies within itself not only the election of individuals to salvation, but also the times, circumstances, and means by which the elect will come to enjoy salvation and all its benefits.[43]

In fact, Owen regards Baxter's claims that his (Owen's) theology requires that the elect be justified from the moment of Christ's death as resting upon a misconstruction of the union of the elect with Christ.[44] What Owen does claim is that the union of Christ with the elect in his atonement is not a real union in the sense of some form of actual, direct participation but that it must be understood in terms of federal representation, again with the whole context of covenant and covenantal terms being crucial. The imputation of sin to Christ is thus not strictly parallel

---

[42]See "A Dissertation on Divine Justice," in Owen, *Works*, X; also Carl R. Trueman, "John Owen's Dissertation on Divine Justice: An Exercise in Christocentric Scholasticism," *Calvin Theological Journal* 33 (1998): 87-103.

[43]"This is that I say, Christ hath purchased all good things for us; these things are actually to be conferred upon us in the time and order by God's sovereign will determined and disposed. This order, as revealed in the gospel, is, that we believe and be justified, etc." Owen, *Works*, XII.608. Cf. Owen, *Works*, V.216-18.

[44]Owen, *Works*, XII.606.

to the imputation of Christ's righteousness to sinners because it is not simply incarnation, absolutely considered, which is the foundation of the salvific scheme, but the covenant which lies behind the incarnation and which gives the incarnation meaning for salvation. Thus, imputation of sin to Christ and imputation of righteousness to the elect both need to be set against the background of covenant terms; and the covenant terms are such that union with Christ by faith is necessary in order for the imputation of righteousness to take place.[45]

Conclusion

John Owen's treatment of justification is a classic example of Reformed orthodoxy at its best: rooted in the ongoing anti-Pelagian trajectory of Western theology and operating within the established Protestant consensus, Owen yet demonstrates the ways in which that consensus was itself under strain, exegetically, theologically, and socially, in the seventeenth century, and how it was necessary for doctrinal formulation of the doctrine to undergo careful elaboration in order to respond to such. In particular, his defence of the imputation of Christ's active and passive righteousness and his vigorous rejection of Baxter's accusations that his theology was antinomian and demanded a doctrine of eternal justification points towards the covenantal/Christological heart of his theology.

As such, he is an example of how federal theology could be deployed to set the Protestant confessional consensus on a much firmer conceptual foundation than was the case in the early Reformation; and also how Reformed orthodoxy's theological structure is highly elaborate and irreducible to soundbites about dogmatizing; rather, Owen's treatment exhibits the typical Reformed attention to the exegesis, doctrinal synthesis, and church consensus and is one more piece of evidence as to how and why

[45]"God hath appointed that there shall be an immediate foundation of the imputation of the satisfaction and righteousness of Christ unto us; whereon we may be said to have done and suffered in him what he did and suffered in our stead, by that grant, donation, and imputation of it unto us; or that we may be interested in it, that it may be made ours: which is all we contend for. And this is our actual coalescency into one mystical person with him by faith." Owen, *Works*, V.217-18; cf. Owen, *Works*, V.353-54; also Owen, *Works*, XII.606-607.

the reformed faith became more elaborate in its argumentation during the course of the seventeenth century.

The Active Obedience of Christ and the Theology of the Westminster Standards: A Historical Investigation

Jeffrey K. Jue

In the present discussions over the doctrine of justification there has been a growing opinion that the traditional reformed orthodox formulation needs to be revised. One significant point of revision is the rejection of the active obedience of Christ as the meritorious righteousness imputed to the believer. Proponents of the so-called New Perspective on Paul and Federal Vision Theology have reconstructed their doctrine of justification with this modification in mind.[1] While much of the debate focuses on exegetical considerations, advocates for change are now claiming that historically there was tolerance on this specific point within reformed orthodoxy.[2]

The *Westminster Confession* (WCF) 11:1 states:

> Those whom God effectually calleth he also freely justifieth; not by infusing righteousness into them, but by pardoning their sins,

---

[1]For advocates of the New Perspective see James D. G. Dunn and Alan M. Suggate, *A Fresh Look at the Old Doctrine of Justification by Faith* (Cumbria: Paternoster Press, 1993), 27-28; N. T. Wright, *What Saint Paul Really Said* (Grand Rapids, Michigan: William B. Eerdmans Publishing Company, 1997), 96-103, 131-33. For Federal Vision theologians, see Rich Lusk, "A Response to 'The Biblical Plan of Salvation'," in *The Auburn Avenue Theology, Pros and Cons: Debating the Federal Vision*, ed. E. Calvin Beisner (Fort Lauderdale: Knox Theological Seminary, 2004), 139-43; James B. Jordan, "Merit Versus Maturity," in *The Federal Vision*, eds. Steve Wilkins and Garner Duane (Monroe: Athanasius Press, 2004), 194-95; Andrew P. Sandlin, "Covenant in Redemptive History: 'Gospel and Law' or 'Trust and Obey'," in *Backbone of the Bible: Covenant in Contemporary Perspective*, ed. Andrew P. Sandlin (Nacogdoches: Covenant Media Foundation, 2004), 69-70. It should be noted that advocates of the Federal Vision Theology affirm active obedience only as that which qualifies Christ to be the sinless sacrifice.

[2]James R. Daniel Kirk, "The Sufficiency of the Cross," *Scottish Bulletin of Evangelical Theology* (2006): 36-64.

> and by accounting and accepting their persons as righteous: not for any thing wrought in them, or done by them, but for Christ's sake alone: not by imputing faith itself, the act of believing, or any other evangelical obedience, to them as their righteousness; but by imputing the obedience and satisfaction of Christ unto them ... [3]

The Confession refers to the imputation of the obedience and satisfaction of Christ, but what is the nature of the obedience that is imputed? Chapter 11 does not distinguish between the active and passive obedience of Christ. Why not? The recent recovery of vital historical sources reveals that there was substantive debate on this issue at the Assembly.[4] In September of 1643 the Assembly discussed revisions for Article Eleven, on the doctrine of justification, of the Thirty-Nine Articles.[5] Robert Paul writes,

> One of the major issues discussed at this time was the Article on justification ... Thomas Gataker and Richard Vines argued learnedly that only the passive obedience and suffering of Christ were imputed to the believer, while Dr. Daniel Featley argued just as strongly (and apparently more persuasively) that both the passive and active obedience to the Law were to be imputed to the believer. This was the view that prevailed at the Assembly, and it was in line with the position taken by Archbishop Ussher in drafting the Irish Articles.[6]

As Paul indicates, after lengthy debate, the Assembly agreed to revise the eleventh Article and they included the statement that Christ's "whole obedience and satisfaction being by God imputed to us."[7] The "whole obedience" specifically referred to

---

[3]All citations from the Westminster Standards are from: *Westminster Confession of Faith* (Glasgow, 1990, 6th edition).

[4]Chad B. Van Dixhoorn, "Reforming the Reformation: Theological Debate at the Westminster Assembly 1643–1652, Volumes 1–7" (Cambridge: University of Cambridge, 2004). The appendices of this dissertation (volumes 3-7) contain a full transcript of the minutes of the Assembly.

[5]Van Dixhoorn, "Reforming the Reformation," I.270ff.

[6]Robert Paul, *The Assembly of the Lord: Politics and Religion in the Westminster Assembly and the 'Grand Debate'* (Edinburgh: T&T Clark, 1985), 84-85. Paul argues that William Twisse also supported the passive obedience only position, but Van Dixhoorn has found very little evidence for this. Van Dixhoorn, "Reforming the Reformation," I.335.

[7]Van Dixhoorn, "Reforming the Reformation," I.293.

Christ's active and passive obedience.[8] Yet, after what seemed like a conclusive decision, the word "whole" was surprisingly omitted in chapter eleven of the *Westminster Confession of Faith*. Does the Confession reflect a change within the Assembly that altered their earlier resolution?

In an attempt to explain the omission, J. R. Daniel Kirk notes that the word "whole" was struck in the final form in order to compromise with those who held to a passive righteousness only position.[9] Kirk assumes that the omission of the word "whole" demonstrates that the Confession was a consensus document and allowed for "a range of views with respect to the precise nature of Christ's righteousness."[10] Precedence for Kirk's conclusions can be found in William Barker's study of the Westminster divines. He affirms the same reading of the Assembly's debates over the doctrine of justification. Barker writes, "[t]he Westminster divines, in such controversies, sought to be clear and faithful to Scriptural language, yet to allow for shades of difference within a generic Calvinism."[11] Likewise in their introduction to the minutes of the Assembly, Alex Mitchell and John Struthers give the impression that the language of Chapter 11 was the result of intense theological brokering, where both sides conceded various points in order to reach a consensus.[12]

While these previous studies rightly draw our attention to an important theological debate, more thorough historical investigation is required in order to substantiate such a bold

---

[8]Van Dixhoorn writes, "Active obedience was termed whole obedience in the debate and by the committee since those whose [*sic*] held to the active obedience thought that only the active and passive obedience together comprised the whole obedience of Christ." Van Dixhoorn, "Reforming the Reformation," I.293.

[9]Kirk, "The Sufficiency of the Cross," 37-38.

[10]Kirk, "The Sufficiency of the Cross," 37-38.

[11]William S. Barker, *Puritan Profiles: 54 Influential Puritans at the Time When the Westminster Confession Was Written* (Fearn, Scotland: Mentor/Christian Focus Publications, 1996), 176.

[12]Mitchell and Struthers write, "This was probably the reason, that though most of them [the divines] favoured the views of Ussher and Featley [which included the active obedience of Christ], they were content with a more general expression than they at first used, and that in return Gataker agreed to abstain from further controversy about the matter," Alex F. Mitchell and John Struthers, eds., *Minutes of the Sessions of the Westminster Assembly of Divines* (Edinburgh, 1874, reprinted 1991), lxvi-lxvii.

conclusion regarding the intentions and theology of the Westminster divines. This essay will begin such an investigation in order to determine historically if indeed there was latitude on this point in the reformed orthodox doctrine of justification represented by the Westminster Assembly. What is necessary is an assessment of the historical context, doctrinal debates, and theological constructions of the seventeenth-century Stuart church. Only then can we gain a more accurate understanding of the work of the Assembly and their historic doctrine of justification.

I. The Historical-Theological Context of the Stuart Church

Any understanding of the Westminster Assembly's doctrine of justification must take into account the historical-theological context of the early seventeenth century. Theological construction in the post-Reformation era was distinguished for its detailed precision and systematic codification. Protestant universities required comprehensive theological curriculums, while churches composed confessions to guard against the growing challenges of aberrant teachers.[13] In England this process emerged in the context of intense political and ecclesiastical turmoil. Theology and politics were intertwined. Consequently theological divisions within the church impacted the nation as a whole and ultimately contributed to the outbreak of civil war.[14] Earlier Whig and Marxist historians generally reduced the factionalism of revolutionary England to two

---

[13]Richard Muller writes, "The early orthodox ... shared the desire to create a theological system suited to the successful establishment of Protestantism as a church in its own right, catholic in its teaching, capable of being sustained intellectually against its adversaries, and sufficiently technical and methodologically consistent to stand among the other disciplines in the university." Richard A. Muller, *Prolegomena to Theology*, vol. One of *Post-Reformation Reformed Dogmatics : The Rise and Development of Reformed Orthodoxy, Ca. 1520 to Ca. 1725* (Grand Rapids, Mich.: Baker Books, 1987), 62. Also see Richard A. Muller, *After Calvin: Studies in the Development of a Theological Tradition* (Oxford: Oxford University Press, 2003), 130-36, 144-45.

[14]For studies on the religious roots of the English Civil War, see John Morrill, "The Religious Context of the English Civil War," *Transactions of the Royal Historical Society* 34 (1984): 155-78; Nicholas Tyacke, *Anti-Calvinists: The Rise of English Arminianism c. 1590–1640* (Oxford: Oxford University Press, 1987); Anthony Milton, *Catholic Reformed: The Roman and Protestant Churches in English Protestant Thought, 1600–1640* (Cambridge: Cambridge University Press, 1995); David Como, "Puritans, Predestination and the Construction of 'Orthodoxy'

parties: conservative Anglicans versus radical puritans.[15] However more recent studies demonstrate the multi-variegated theological landscape of early Stuart England.[16] Anthony Milton argues that there was a "broad spectrum of views running from crypto-popish 'Arminian' zealots on the one hand, through to die-hard puritan nonconformists on the other."[17] Thus, any seventeenth-century doctrine must be examined within a nexus of theological opinions and articulations (and doctrinal solidarity may vary from issue to issue) in order to understand the motivations and intentions of various English divines.

Discussions of the doctrine of justification in seventeenth-century England likewise must be placed within the context of multiple distinctive parties. Doctrinal formulations were shaped by political, pastoral, and exegetical concerns specific to England, yet reflective of similar trends in the broader international reformed community. These concerns provide the background in which to locate the Westminster Assembly's doctrine of justification and to understand its position in reformed orthodoxy.

A. Anti-Popery

The vitriolic attacks between Protestants and Roman Catholics did not end with the sixteenth-century Reformation. In fact, in the early seventeenth century most of Western Europe was engaged in the Thirty Years War where religion played a significant role.[18] Protestants fought Roman Catholics on the battlefield and in print; and, since the time of Martin Luther, the doctrine of justification featured as a central point of contention. The Roman Catholic Church continued to be viewed as deficient in teaching

---

in Early Seventeenth Century England," in *Conformity and Orthodoxy in the English Church, c. 1560–1642*, eds. P. Lake and M. Questier (Woodbridge: Boydell Press, 2000), 64-87.

[15]See Christopher Hill, *Society and Puritanism in Pre-Revolutionary England* (London: Secker and Warburg, 1964); S. R. Gardiner, *The First Two Stuarts and the Puritan Revolution* (London: Longmans, Green & Co., 1876).

[16]See Milton, *Catholic and Reformed*; Kenneth Fincham, ed., *The Early Stuart Church, 1603–1642* (Stanford: Stanford University Press, 1993).

[17]Milton, *Catholic and Reformed*, 5.

[18]See Klaus Bussman and Hans Schilling, eds., *1648: War and Peace in Europe* (Münster and Osnabrück: Westfälische Landesmuseum für Kunst und Kulturgeschichte, 1998).

that righteousness was infused into the believer in order for the believer's works to be included as the grounds of justification.[19] In contrast, in its most basic form, all Protestants insisted that the believer's justification before God was by grace alone, through faith alone, in Christ alone.

In early seventeenth-century England, "anti-popery" reached a fevered pitch. Milton writes, "hatred of popery was seen as a manifestation of true religion, a testimony of the individual's commitment to God. This was not just the view of extreme puritans, but was also strongly maintained by establishment divines."[20] Roman Catholics were perceived as a looming threat both at home and abroad. England watched with great anxiety the progress of the Thirty Years War, especially with the marriage of King James' daughter to the Elector Palatine. But at home in England, there was a constant fear of plots and conspiracies allegedly designed by Roman Catholic priests and Jesuits. The Gunpowder Plot confirmed these fears, along with England's wars with Spain and France in the 1620s.[21]

Another dimension of anti-popery in the British Isles was the growing interest in apocalyptic thought. Since Luther's first identification of the papacy as the prophetic Antichrist, Protestants framed their struggle against Rome within a grand apocalyptic drama.[22] Biblical books like Daniel and Revelation were exegetically mined to explain the cosmic battle between Christ and Antichrist, which many apocalypticists believed was observable in the geopolitical events of the seventeenth century. This interest

---

[19] The Council of Trent, Canons 9 and 11.

[20] Milton, *Catholic and Reformed*, 35.

[21] Milton, *Catholic and Reformed*, 42-43.

[22] Helpful studies include Peter Toon, ed., *Puritans, the Millennium and the Future of Israel* (Cambridge and London: Clarke & Co. Ltd, 1970); Bryan W. Ball, *A Great Expectation: Eschatological Thought in English Protestantism to 1660* (Leiden: Brill Academic Publishers, 1975); Richard Bauckham, *Tudor Apocalypse: Sixteenth Century Apocalypticism, Millenarianism, and the English Reformation* (Oxford: Sutton Courtney Press, 1978); Paul Christianson, *Reformers in Babylon: English Apocalyptic Visions From the Reformation to the Eve of the Civil War* (Toronto: University of Toronto Press, 1978); Katherine R. Firth, *The Apocalyptic Tradition in Reformation Britain, 1530–1643* (Oxford: Oxford University Press, 1979); Robin B. Barnes, *Prophecy and Gnosis: Apocalypticism in the Wake of the Lutheran Reformation* (Stanford: Stanford University Press, 1988); Heiko Oberman, *Luther: Man Between God and the Devil* (New Haven: Yale University Press, 1989); Irena Backus, *Reformation Readings of the Apocalypse; Geneva, Zurich, and Wittenberg* (Oxford: Oxford University Press, 2000).

was heightened by the birth of millenarianism in 1627. In that year, the publication of Joseph Mede's *Clavis Apolcalyptica* (and the simultaneous publication on the continent of Johann Heinrich Alsted's *Diatribe de mille annis apocalypticis*) introduced a millenarian eschatology that was well received on the continent, in England, and as far as colonial North America.[23] Mede supported the identification of the papacy as Antichrist and argued that the practice of adoring and venerating saints in the Roman Catholic Church was the fulfillment of the "doctrine of demons" prophesied in 1 Timothy 4:1, and marked the great apostasy of the latter times.[24] Millenarians, following Mede's exegesis of Revelation 20, anticipated Christ's defeat of Antichrist, followed by the establishment of a terrestrial Kingdom of Christ on earth extending for 1,000 years.[25]

The anti-Roman Catholic and apocalyptic climate sets the broadest backdrop for the divines at Westminster. Political events between Protestant and Roman Catholic nations were watched by all with great interest, while the depth and scholarly weight of Mede's writings were attractive for many, including William Twisse, Thomas Goodwin, Jeremiah Burroughs, and John Dury.[26] In the preface to the English edition of Mede's *Clavis*, Twisse wrote: "for may it be said of Mr Mede in reference to his Expositions of the Revelation, Many Interpreters have done excellently, but he surmounteth them all."[27] In fact, divines at the Assembly were so enamored with millenarianism that the Scottish delegate, Robert Baillie, wrote home complaining about the number of "chiliasts" in attendance.[28] With these prevailing

---

[23]For more on Mede see Jeffrey K. Jue, *Heaven Upon Earth: Joseph Mede (1586–1638) and the Legacy of Millenarianism* (Dordrecht: Springer, 2006). And for Alsted see Howard B. Hotson, *Johann Heinrich Alsted 1588–1638: Between Renaissance, Reformation, and Universal Reform* (Oxford: Oxford University Press, 2000) and *Paradise Postponed: Johann Heinrich Alsted and the Birth of Calvinist Millenarianism* (Dordrecht: Kluwer Academic Press, 2001).

[24]Joseph Mede, *The Apostasy of the Latter Times* (London, 1641); Jue, *Heaven Upon Earth*, 95-100.

[25]Jue, *Heaven Upon Earth*, 141-244.

[26]Jue, *Heaven Upon Earth*, 141-244.

[27]William Twisse, "A Preface Written by *Doctor Twisse* Shewing the Methode and Excellency of *Mr Mede's* Interpretation of This Mysterious Book of the Revelation of Saint John," in *The Key to the Revelation*, Joseph Mede (London, 1643).

[28]Chiliasm (derived from the Greek word meaning 1000) is the patristic term for millenarianism (derived from the same word in Latin). Robert Baillie,

twin concerns, it is easy to see the influence of apocalypticism and anti-popery on the theology of the Westminster Standards. The original version explicitly states that the pope is Antichrist, and the Standards exclude Roman Catholic views on the sacraments, forms of worship, and on the doctrine of justification.[29] Whatever theological disagreements emerged during the Assembly's debates on justification, no one wanted to return to Rome.

B. Arminianism

The ascendancy of Charles I to the throne in 1625 altered the theological climate in Stuart England. With the appointment of William Laud to the Archbishop of Canterbury, Nicholas Tyacke argues that a Calvinist consensus was disrupted by ecclesiastical prelates with "anti-Calvinist" sympathies.[30] David Como writes, "[w]hether Arminian in the strict theological sense, however, there seems little doubt that the late 1620s saw the ascendance of a new and in many ways distinctive ideological group to power within the church."[31] While the dividing lines may not have been so neat, it is clear that the Church of England was not unified on issues pertaining to predestination and by implication the doctrine of

---

The Letters and Journals of Robert Baillie, ed. David Laing (Edinburgh: Robert Ogle, 1841), 88.313.

[29]WCF 11, 25, 27-29, and the Directory of Worship. WCF 25:6, in the original version states: "There is no other head of the church but the Lord Jesus Christ: nor can the Pope of Rome in any sense be head thereof; but is that antichrist, that man of sin, and son of perdition, that exalteth himself in the church against Christ, and all that is called God." In 1903 the Presbyterian Church U.S.A. adopted a revised version of the Confession that removed this section.

[30]Tyacke, *Anti-Calvinists: The Rise of English Arminianism c. 1590–1640*. It is important to note that Tyacke's original thesis has been challenged and modified in subsequent studies. For challenges, see Peter White, *Predestination, Policy and Polemic: Conflict and Consensus in the English Church from the Reformation to the Civil War* (Cambridge: Cambridge University Press, 1993); White, *Predestination*; Kevin Sharpe, *The Personal Rule of Charles I* (New Haven: Yale University Press, 1993). For modifications see Milton, *Catholic and Reformed*; Seán F. Hughes, "The Problem of 'Calvinism': English Theologies of Predestination c. 1580–1630," in *Belief and Practice in Reformation England: A Tribute to Patrick Collinson By His Students*, eds. S. Waduba and C. Litzenberger (Aldershot: Ashgate, 1998), 229-49; David Como, "Puritans, Predestination and the Construction of 'Orthodoxy' in Early Seventeenth Century England".

[31]David R. Como, *Blown by the Spirit: Puritanism and the Emergence of an Antinomian Underground in Pre-Civil-War England* (Stanford: Stanford University Press, 2004), 75.

justification. It is important to note that the rise of Arminianism in England was not isolated from the anti-Roman Catholic and apocalyptic concerns previously discussed. Charles' wife, Henrietta Maria, was the daughter of France's King Henry IV. There was great fear that she would advocate for a stronger Roman Catholic presence in England. Likewise Archbishop Laud introduced forms of worship, which were similar to certain practices in the Church of Rome (genuflecting during the worship service, calling the communion table an altar, etc.)[32] Puritans accused Laudians of being crypto-papists, and the most compelling evidence was Laud's ban in 1633 of all publications that identified the papacy as Antichrist.[33] Following Tyacke's basic thesis, this was a major contributing cause which led to the outbreak of civil war.

In this context we would expect the rejection of Arminian theology by the Calvinist divines at Westminster. While predestination was vigorously debated, the Arminian doctrine of justification introduced significant differences as well. Of course Arminians were quick to assert that they did not hold to the Roman Catholic doctrine of justification, nevertheless they desired to re-examine the necessity for works in relation to the believer's justification. Alister McGrath describes competing English traditions where the "formal cause of justification is held to be either imputed righteousness or inherent and imputed righteousness – but not inherent righteousness alone."[34] The doctrine of justification took an interesting form for Arminians who held that inherent righteousness was included. Justification was described as having both a beginning and an end. The beginning was limited to the acquittal of the guilt of sin and the cleansing of our sinfulness through the imputation of Christ's righteousness. The merit of Christ provided this beginning for the individual who received this justification by faith. Again, Joseph Mede illustrates this well; he wrote:

---

[32]Milton, *Catholic and Reformed*, 494-503.

[33]Milton, *Catholic and Reformed*, 120.

[34]Alister McGrath, *Justitia Dei: A History of the Christian Doctrine of Justification* (Cambridge: Cambridge University Press, 1988), 286.

> And this is what we call justification of a Sinner, which is an Absolution or remission of Sins by the onley merits and satisfaction of Christ accepted for us and imputed to us[.][35]

What was conspicuously missing in Mede's description was the positive benefit of Christ's merit which was the reward of eternal life. Mede further argued:

> the bloud and suffering of Jesus Christ, imputed to us by Faith, cleanseth and aquitteth us of all the sins whereof we stood guilty ... so the imputed righteousness ... makes our works (though of themselves far short of what they should be, yet) to be acceptable and just in the eyes of the Almighty.[36]

Essentially what Mede did was to place sanctification within the "end" of justification. According to Mede, in addition to cleansing and acquitting the believer, the imputed righteousness of Christ made the believer's own works acceptable before God. These works then would be accounted in the believer's justification in the end. Mede continued, "but besides justification, there is a sanctification with the works of piety towards God and righteousness towards men, as the Fruits, yea as the End of our justification, required to eternal life."[37] Thus the believer's works of piety, made acceptable by Christ's righteousness, would contribute to the end of justification required for eternal life.[38] The English Arminian doctrine of justification, as illustrated by Mede, indeed differed from the teaching of the Westminster Standards.

Clear antagonism existed between the Arminian Laudians and the divines at Westminster.[39] After all, the Assembly was

---

[35]Joseph Mede, *The Works of the Pious and Profoundly-Learned Joseph Mede*, 4th (London, 1677), 155. It is worth noting that Mede is a good example of how each individual theological issue must be accessed properly within the nexus of varying opinions. Mede's apocalyptic writings were so popular amongst the puritans, that they overlooked his loyalty to the Laudian establishment and his anti-Calvinist views. Jeffrey K. Jue, *"Heaven Upon Earth": Joseph Mede (1586–1638) and the Legacy of Millenarianism* (Dordtrecht: Springer, 2006), 19-35.

[36]Mede, *Works*, 156.

[37]Mede, *Works*, 156.

[38]Also see Milton, *Catholic and Reformed*, 72-77.

[39]One example is the debate between William Twisse and Thomas Jackson. See William Twisse, *A Discovery of d. Jackson's Vanitie* (Amsterdam, 1631); also see

convened for the purpose of constructing a confessional standard for a new church to replace the one headed by Archbishop Laud. The polity, forms of worship, and doctrines of the Anglican order were abolished and replaced with a reformed Presbyterian Calvinism – although these changes were essentially aborted during the Interregnum and Restoration periods.[40]

Nevertheless the Arminian articulation of the doctrine of justification was another seventeenth-century option, one that the divines were careful to exclude from their position. But what accounts for the willingness of certain theologians, in the context of pervasive anti-popery and apocalyptic interest, to move seemingly towards a quasi-Roman Catholic position by incorporating inherent righteousness and works in the doctrine of justification? Another theological movement was surfacing from beneath the myriad ecclesiastical debates of the time.

C. Antinomianism

Recent studies have uncovered what is being called an "underground" antinomian movement, specifically in London (although having broader geographical implications) during the years preceding the Civil War.[41] First, it is important to define antinomianism in the context of seventeenth-century England. Como and Lake write,

> Antinomianism is perhaps best described as a rooted propensity to exalt the transformative power of God's free grace and to play

---

Sarah Hutton, "Thomas Jackson, Oxford Platonist and William Twisse, Aristotelian," *Journal of the History of Ideas* 29 (1978): 635-52; White, *Predestination*, 256-71.

[40]See G. E. Aylmer, *The Interregnum: The Quest for Settlement* (London: Macmillan Publishing, 1972); Robert S. Bosher, *The Making of the Restoration Settlement: The Influence of the Laudians, 1649–1662* (London: Dacre Press, 1951); Martin I. J. Griffin Jr., *Latitudinarianism in the Seventeenth Century Church of England* (Leiden: Brill Academic Press, 1992).

[41]David Como and Peter Lake, "Puritans, Antinomians and Laudians in Caroline London: The Strange Case of Peter Shaw and Its Contexts," *Journal of Ecclesiastical History* 50, no. 4 (October 1999): 684-715; Peter Lake, *The Boxer's Revenge: 'Orthodoxy,' 'Heterodoxy,' and the Politics of the Parish in Early Stuart London* (Stanford: Stanford University Press, 2001); Theodore Dwight Bozeman, *The Precisionist Strain: Disciplinary Religion & Antinomian Backlash in Purtanism to 1638* (Chapel Hill: University of North Carolina Press, 2004); David R. Como, *Blown by the Spirit*.

> down, even to deny, the role and use of the moral law in the lives of justified Christians.[42]

Next, it is necessary to examine the motivations for constructing a theology that denied the obligation to the moral law for Christians. David Como and Theodore Bozeman both argue that a certain disciplinary emphasis developed in puritan practical theology.[43] This emphasis was seen most in the local parishes, where puritan ministers exhorted their congregations to live a precise and disciplined life of godliness. This "precisionist" practice was not intended to subvert the reformed doctrine of justification, since justification was based on the merit of Christ alone, but it was believed that persistent ungodly living would result in divine chastisement. The nation of Israel in the Old Testament was a case in point for many puritan ministers.[44] Likewise, there was the prolific production of practical divinity manuals like Richard Rogers, *Seaven Treatises Containing such Direction as is Gathered out of the Holie Scriptures* (1604) and Christopher Dow, *A Discourse of the Sabbath and the Lord's Day* (1636). In addition to living a precise godly life, puritan ministers encouraged their congregations to examine their own consciences in relation to their individual salvation and to demonstrate evidence for conversion in their daily lives.[45]

What this practical divinity amounted to for some was essentially an antinomian backlash. Como explains,

> Although [the] mainstream mode of piety seems to have proved sufficient for the large majority of godly people, there can be little question that for some men and women, the disciplines, demands, and general tenor of normative puritanism proved to be a passageway into despair and insecurity. For such people ... antinomianism provided a ray of hope, a profoundly attractive alternative religiosity equally rooted in scripture ... eminently more assuring than its mainstream counterpart.[46]

---

[42]Como and Lake, "Puritans," 695.

[43]Bozeman, *The Precisionist Strain*, 29-60; David R. Como, *Blown by the Spirit*, 37.

[44]Bozeman, *The Precisionist Strain*, 32-39.

[45]Bozeman, *The Precisionist Strain*, 105-20, 129-36.

[46]David R. Como, *Blown by the Spirit*, 37.

Antinomians offered a relief from the perceived tyranny of puritan practical divinity. Instead of focusing on the oppression of the moral law, antinomians emphasized the grace of God. How this concern manifested itself was most evident in their doctrine of justification. What lay at the heart of antinomian interests was the issue of assurance. Because of this, antinomians, like John Eaton, vehemently rejected Roman Catholicism and the Arminianism of Archbishop Laud.[47] Neither Roman Catholicism nor Arminianism, with their inclusion of inherent righteousness in justification, provided full assurance for the troubled believer. Moreover, the practical divinity of mainstream puritans seemed to introduce an essential element of examination for the purpose of discerning works of sanctification, which would attest then to one's justification. For antinomians, such a model was deficient as well, because they believed that it overemphasized sanctification as a barometer for justification.

The antinomian solution for the doctrine of justification drew heavily on the Protestant reformed tradition. John Eaton wrote,

> the perfect holinesse and righteousness, not of the Godhead, but of the humane nature of Christ wherein he performed perfect obedience, both active and passive in fulfilling the whole law of God, is the formal cause of our justification, which only after the nature of the forme ... giveth unto us not only the name, but also the true being of righteous men in the sight of God.[48]

In line with the reformed orthodoxy, Eaton affirmed both the active and passive obedience of Christ as the grounds for the believer's justification. Likewise he taught that the imputation of Christ's righteousness rendered the believer holy, perfect and free from sin in the sight of God.[49] Eaton stated,

> the Wedding garments of Christs perfect righteousnesse, by which the justified person is made so truly, and so perfectly holy and righteous from all spot of sinne in the sight of God, that God

---

[47]David R. Como, *Blown by the Spirit*, 188.

[48]John Eaton, *The Honey-Combe of Free Justification by Christ Alone* (London, 1642), 262-63.

[49]David R. Como, *Blown by the Spirit*, 182.

> doth, and (by his actuall power) can see no sin in his justified children freely by faith onely, without workes, Rev. 3:18.[50]

Thus far, it would seem that Eaton was within the bounds of the standard Protestant position. But Como points out a repeated phrase in Eaton's writings, the notion of "free justification."[51] This phrase was intended to highlight the fact that God saw absolutely no sin in the justified individual. Eaton was not stating that justification rendered the individual inherently perfect, as some antinomians asserted, but it supposedly freed the individual from the enslavement of meeting the requirements of the law either as the cause or evidence of justification.[52] Moreover "free justification" provided the absolute assurance central to Eaton's concerns.

Still, the antinomian doctrine of justification had other theological implications. By emphasizing the complete removal of sin in free justification, Eaton de-emphasized the importance of accompanying works of obedience in sanctification. He encouraged believers to look to their faith and free justification for assurance and not to the evidential work of sanctification – this he regarded as puritan legalism.[53] Antinomians wanted to minimize all aspects of human participation in salvation. Consequently, the instrumental role of faith was diminished in the antinomian soteriology. Free justification was no longer described in terms of that which was received by faith, but instead that which was completed in the work of Christ and in eternity.[54] Many antinomians affirmed the

---

[50]John Eaton, *The Discovery of the Most Dangerous Dead Faith* (London, 1642), 182.

[51]Eaton, *Dead Faith*, 183.

[52]Como and Lake, "Puritans," 698. Como writes, "This in a nutshell was Eaton's analysis of English puritan theology: while outwardly paying tribute to the principle of justification by the imputation of Christ's perfect righteousness, English puritans ... in practice maintained the belief that sin remained visible to God after justification. From Eaton's standpoint this was equivalent to the claim that Christ had not fully satisfied God's wrath, and that some legal work therefore remained necessary to purge sin or earn salvation." David R. Como, *Blown by the Spirit*, 189-90.

[53]David R. Como, *Blown by the Spirit*, 193.

[54]Como writes, "In their efforts to transfer all saving merit from human beings to Christ, the antinomians thus from a certain perspective devalued faith itself, emptying it of its instrumentality. Faith, on their view, did not really justify;

notion of eternal justification for the elect. The intention was to safeguard any inclination to view faith as a meritorious work, by asserting that the Christian's justification actually preceded faith as an eternal act of God comparable to election.[55]

Now it was not the case that antinomians unilaterally opposed good works, or even works of the law, but they argued that such works ought not to be done out of fear or spiritual self-gain.[56] Instead the true believer should seek to do good and obey God out of joy and thanksgiving.[57] The law was not to be used as an oppressive standard, but as a reminder of God's grace in freeing the Christian from the law's obligations. Eaton wrote,

> And the more this faith of free justification ... encreaseth; the more this peace and joy in the holy Ghost encreaseth... And the more this peace and joy encreaseth, the more the foresaid love encreaseth, and enflameth the heart to walk freely, cheerfully, and zealously in all Gods will and commandments declaratively to manward, and to doe our vocations, and all good workes freely, of mere love, without hope of reward or fear of punishment, which is true sanctification.[58]

Ultimately antinomians believed this addressed better the pastoral concern to encourage individuals struggling with the issue of assurance and magnify the grace of God.

For both puritans and Laudians, antinomianism was detested. Antinomians were considered not only theologically heretical, but politically subversive. They were a threat to the practical theology of the puritan mainstream and the established order of the Anglican Church. Theologically, for reformed puritans and Arminian Laudians the believer's works, although functioning very differently, retained an important role in their soteriologies. Antinomianism was viewed as a categorical rejection of the

---

rather, it recognized and apprehended a prior justification which had already been effected by Christ's death." David R. Como, *Blown by the Spirit*, 201.

[55]David R. Como, *Blown by the Spirit*, 203. It is important to note that eternal justification was not exclusively held by antinomians in the seventeenth century.

[56]David R. Como, *Blown by the Spirit*, 199.

[57]David R. Como, *Blown by the Spirit*, 214.

[58]Eaton, *Dead Faith*, 76-77.

necessity for good works and thus would lead to unrestrained licentious and ungodly behavior. Politically, antinomians were also seen as an underground movement that was critical of the established religious authorities, whether Laudian or mainstream puritans. In the late 1620s, persecution of antinomians ultimately resulted in legal action and the suppression of antinomianism, with puritans and Laudians emerging as strange bedfellows when cooperating to bring charges against antinomians in the Court of High Commission.[59] Thus, for the Westminster divines, antinomianism presented a third position to navigate in the turbulent theological waters of seventeenth-century England.

II. The Justification Debate at the Westminster Assembly

With the historical-theological context summarized, a more accurate assessment is possible of the issues and concerns of various divines. As mentioned earlier, in 1643 the Westminster Assembly debated specific revisions to the Eleventh Article on justification. Chad Van Dixhoorn's recent work provides an excellent narrative of the debate.[60] Van Dixhoorn notes that from the outset the Assembly was careful to exclude all positions that presented inherent righteousness as a cause of justification.[61] This obviously excluded the Roman Catholics. The minutes record Henry Wilkenson, Sr.'s comments against the "papists,"

> 2 places I would lay together that may conduce to the conclusion in hand. Rom. [3:23], "we all fall short of the glory of God." If ther be a deficit in the best, then ther can be noe supererogation; one defect makes the worke evil ... All men & all means excluded from matter of merit.[62]

Wilkenson was simply reaffirming the doctrine of total depravity and the need for Christ's imputed righteousness. Thus, one intention of the revisions was to uphold an explicit anti-Roman Catholic doctrine of justification, so "a papist that lookes upon this article might see their doctrine condemned."[63] After all, this

[59]Como and Lake, "Puritans," 686-92; David R. Como, *Blown by the Spirit*, 73ff.
[60]Van Dixhoorn, "Reforming the Reformation," 1.270-344.
[61]Van Dixhoorn, "Reforming the Reformation," 1.275.
[62]Van Dixhoorn, "Reforming the Reformation," 3.9.
[63]Van Dixhoorn, "Reforming the Reformation," 3.11.

was a Protestant assembly with a puritan majority intent on bringing a long-awaited thorough Reformation to England.

Following their condemnation of popery, the divines quickly moved to discussing the antinomian views. Specifically, they first discussed the antinomian understanding of eternal justification.[64] An overwhelming majority of divines agreed that justification was "actual," meaning that it occurred in time, and was not eternal.[65] In the course of continual discussion, however, a significant division emerged. A proposal came regarding the grounds of justification which added the phrase Christ's "whole obedience & satisfaction being by God imputed to us."[66] The understanding was that the "whole obedience" referred to Christ's active and passive obedience.[67] This proposal was met with strong opposition from Richard Vines and Thomas Gataker. Vines argued that it was only Christ's passive obedience that was imputed to the believer. He stated,

> I confesse I sticke at this, whether the active obedience of Christ be imputed to us to justification. I have never delivered it in publique because I thought there might be something in it, soe many learned men of that mind ... but when we inquire what is that obedience imputed as the matter of his righteousnesse, it seemes to me to be his passive, his poenall, formall sufferings, the accomplishment whereof is in his death ... That which the legall purgings & expiations in the time of the law did foresignify was bloud & that was necessary to be. That which purgeth all sin & leaves none, that is our righteousness, [nothing] but the bloud of Christ.[68]

For Vines, justification consisted only of the remission of sins according to the sacrificial death of Christ on the cross. He argued that Romans 5 spoke of only one act of disobedience done by Adam, and subsequently only one act of obedience by Christ, his death on the cross.[69]

---

[64]Van Dixhoorn, "Reforming the Reformation," 1.277-78.
[65]Van Dixhoorn, "Reforming the Reformation," 3.14.
[66]Van Dixhoorn, "Reforming the Reformation," 1.293.
[67]Van Dixhoorn, "Reforming the Reformation," 1.293.
[68]Van Dixhoorn, "Reforming the Reformation," 3.31.
[69]Van Dixhoorn, "Reforming the Reformation," 1.293-94.

Thomas Gataker likewise objected to the language of "whole obedience," but for slightly different reasons and with greater depth. Gataker also limited justification to the passive obedience of Christ, because he argued that justification only acquitted the believer from the guilt of sin. He maintained that "the bloud of Christ doth purge me from all iniquity & soe the Jury cannot find me and the Judge must aquit me."[70] Yet, Gataker differed from Vines because he did not view the remission of sins as an aspect of justification. For Gataker, forgiveness was an act of grace, while justification was an act of justice based upon the work of Christ in receiving the condemnation for sin in the believer's place and satisfying the wrath of God.[71] Moreover Gataker's denial of active obedience was effected by his reconstruction of the two-Adam Christology.

The classic biblical passage for understanding the two-Adam Christology is Romans 5:12-21. There the apostle Paul draws a comparison between two federal heads, and he explains what was lost in the first Adam, and what was recovered in the second, Jesus Christ. Vines argued that the "one act of righteousness which resulted in justification" (v. 18) and the "obedience of the One" (v. 19) referred to Christ's passive obedience only. Gataker agreed with Vine's interpretation but drew out the Christological implications. No one was denying that Christ had lived a perfect life, but Gataker rejected the understanding that Christ's perfect and righteous life added a positive benefit to the believer's justification. For Gataker, the reward of eternal life was not the result of Christ's active obedience to the law imputed by faith in justification. He insisted, "By justification we are raised to noe higher estate than Adam before the fall".[72] In other words, for Gataker, eschatological reward was not included in justification. Gataker's short treatise on justification sheds more light on this point. He insisted that all human beings were in one of two states: justified or unjustified. The justified person was guiltless and innocent, the unjustified was condemned and at fault. He wrote,

---

[70]Van Dixhoorn, "Reforming the Reformation," 3.37.

[71]Van Dixhoorn, "Reforming the Reformation," 1.282-87; Thomas Gataker, *An Antidote Against Errour, Concerning Justification* (London, 1679), 19, 23.

[72]Van Dixhoorn, "Reforming the Reformation," 3.29.

> he must of necessity be deemed or doomed just or righteous; there being no medium or middle state between a delinquent or a guiltie person and one guiltless or just. He that can proov himself no delinquent, but free from fault must of necessity be justified, acquitted and assoiled as just... If nothing but sin can make a man unjust, then surely the utter absence of sinne can make a man just.[73]

What was implied in Gataker's theology of justification was the denial of a probationary state for Adam. In a speech at the Assembly, Gataker was explicit:

> Justification is in common sence an assoyling of a man from the guilt of sin; against this objected the example of Adam: he could not be Justifyed in this maner because Adam was created Innocent but not Just. A[nswer]: I cannot find a medium betwixt these 2. To say that Adam was not made Just but innocent is directly against scripture: created in righteousnesse & true holynesse.[74]

Gataker's definition proposed that Adam's original sinless condition placed him in the category of justified prior to the Fall and the initiation of God's redemptive work.

Nevertheless it was not the case that Gataker considered the active obedience of Christ meaningless. According to Gataker, the active obedience of Christ was necessary to demonstrate that in his human nature he was obligated to keep God's law. He explained, "To say that Christ being as man inferior to God did in that regard owe duty to God, I see not why erroneous."[75] Likewise his active obedience was necessary to insure a perfect sacrifice.[76] Vines stated,

> We doe not exclude the merit of Christ ... I doe not deny that any personall act of Christs did goe to make his doings meritorious: the personal dignity of Christ was sufficient for that. If Christ doe live on earth & ther is another use why he should perfourme obedience

---

[73]Gataker, *An Antidote*, 19-20.
[74]Van Dixhoorn, "Reforming the Reformation," 3.70.
[75]Van Dixhoorn, "Reforming the Reformation," 3.28.
[76]Van Dixhoorn, "Reforming the Reformation," 1.297.

> in the time before his apearing in his office & in this time he must obay & he could not have sinned, yet he might be a fit sacrifise.[77]

Van Dixhoorn concludes that behind this formulation was the theology of Anselm of Canterbury. Summarizing Anselm, Van Dixhoorn writes,

> Christ could make satisfaction only by doing something above and beyond the call of duty. And that was to die. Because death is debt that humans owe to God as a result of sin, and since the God-man was sinless, Christ's death was supererogatory, something "above God's requirement of him" that gave it its "value as satisfaction. And the value of Christ's death is infinite because of the infinite worth of his person, and therefore is superabundant to make satisfaction for sins."[78]

No doubt that the Anselmian precedence carried significant weight, and Gataker, along with Vines, insisted that Christ's obedience must be understood as his duty according to the *pactum salutis*, whereby he was to accomplish salvation by suffering and dying for his people.[79] Gataker claimed that the "dignity of Christ's person adds to the merit of Christ's person: the bloud of God."[80]

In addition, although Gataker's doctrine of justification did not include eternal life, he did discuss it elsewhere. The doctrine of adoption provided the believer with the "right to the heavenly inheritance."[81] And this right was given as a "free gift" from God,

---

77 Van Dixhoorn, "Reforming the Reformation," 3.46.

78 Van Dixhoorn, "Reforming the Reformation," 1.298. Van Dixhoorn is quoting Robert Strimple, "St. Anselm's Cur Deus Homo and John Calvin's Doctrine of the Atonement," in *Anselm: Aosta, Bec and Canterbury*, eds. D. E. Luscombe and G. R. Evans (Sheffield: Sheffield Academic Press, 1996), 350-51.

79 Van Dixhoorn, "Reforming the Reformation," 1.298. Gataker wrote, "I conceiv, that keeping our selves within the bounds of Christian sobriety in this profound mysterie, we may safely say, that Christ's humiliation through the whole cours of his life, and his sufferings as wel in Soul as in Bodie, in his whole humane nature consisting of both neer upon his death, together with his death in that manner inflicted and sustained, the eminence of the person being even God as wel as Man, that was content to expose and abase himself unto al this ... being duelie weighted, was such and so great as God deemed in Justice eqivalent unto, and wel worthie to weigh down, whatsoever was requisite to the discharge of the debt of all those that had interest therein." Gataker, *An Antidote*, 29.

80 Van Dixhoorn, "Reforming the Reformation," 3.27.

81 Gataker, *An Antidote*, 3.

something that individuals could never earn on their own.[82] Old Testament typology was cited by Gataker to support his view. He viewed Noah's deliverance from the flood and Abraham's promise of the land of Canaan as temporal types of God's favor and grace, now given in Christ who delivered his people and gave them a heavenly inheritance.[83] What was conspicuously missing in Gataker's formulation was any concept of merit in relation to heavenly reward.

It is somewhat surprising to see differences at the Westminster Assembly on the doctrine of justification. Moreover Richard Vines and Thomas Gataker were well-known theologians and churchmen with strong credentials.[84] What would influence them to depart from the mainstream reformed view of justification? Were they simply crypto-Arminians or was there something of more significant theological and pastoral concern? Van Dixhoorn notes,

> For some divines it appears that the antinomians in London loomed larger than papists in Madrid. It is not unimportant that the minutes of the Assembly record more than twice as many references to antinomians as to papists. It is certainly significant that the divines never petitioned Parliament to pass tough measures against recusants, but it frequently petitioned against antinomianism and the synod's antinomianism committee was one of its most active.[85]

Antinomianism was considered a greater threat to orthodoxy than other theological deviances. For Vines and Gataker, this was a major theological error from which they sought to guard the church. In fact, Gataker was involved in a number of acrimonious debates with antinomians and wrote an entire treatise refuting antinomianism.[86] At the Assembly, their great concern was that a construction of justification that included the active obedience of Christ both resembled and would lead to antinomianism. Vines

---

[82]Gataker, *An Antidote*, 29.

[83]Gataker, *An Antidote*, 57.

[84]See Barker, *Puritan Profiles*, 132-35, 154-61.

[85]Van Dixhoorn, "Reforming the Reformation," 1.28.

[86]Thomas Gataker, *Antinomianism Discovered and Confuted: And Free-Grace As It is Held Forth in Gods Word* (London, 1652). Also see David R. Como, *Blown by the Spirit*, 93f.

and Gataker feared that upholding the imputation of Christ's perfect obedience to the law resulting in the just reward of eternal inheritance, would excuse believers from any obligation to the moral law. Francis Taylor stated this well: "this seemes to give a great bent to the Antinomians. If it be granted that Christ hath performed the law for me, then it will follow I am not bound to keepe this lawe myselfe."[87] This was precisely Gataker's concern,

> Christ did keepe the precepts of the law for our good, but if therefor in our stead, then it will follow that we are not bound to keepe it. That which another man performed in my stead, that I am not bound to doe. It is answered by Gomarus: obey in way of thankefullnesse unto God, & soe Christ. A[nswer]: those are noe sufficient answer to what aleadged, for if true that Christ hath freed me from the obedience by keeping it in my stead, then I doe not stand bound to it by virtue of the obligation of a creature.[88]

As a veteran of antinomian debates, this was a serious issue for Gataker. He considered the active obedience position potentially amenable to a heterodox theology. Consequently the fear of antinomianism was directly tied to the issue of the active obedience of Christ in justification.

The antinomian threat placed many divines in a reactionary theological position. Gataker was not the only one to depart from a more traditional view of justification because of this threat. Even Richard Baxter's controversial doctrine of justification was shaped by his anti-antinomian concerns.[89] However, theologians like Vines and Gataker were not enticed by the Arminian solution. Again, Arminians were concerned with antinomianism as well. Joseph Mede likewise denied the imputation of the active obedience of Christ, fearing that the active obedience position

---

[87] Van Dixhoorn, "Reforming the Reformation," 3.39-40.

[88] Van Dixhoorn, "Reforming the Reformation," 3.61. Franciscus Gomarus (1563–1641) was appointed Professor of Theology at the University of Leiden in 1594. He opposed Jacobus Arminius and was very active at the Synod of Dordt. See Muller, *PRRD I*, 1.31.

[89] See Hans Boersma, *A Hot Pepper Corn: Richard Baxter's Doctrine of Justification in Its Seventeenth-Century Context of Controversy* (Zoetermeer: Boekencentrum, 1993), 220-28; Paul Chang-Ha Lim, *In Pursuit of Purity, Unity, and Liberty: Richard Baxter's Puritan Ecclesiology in Its Seventeenth-Century Context* (Leiden: Brill Academic Press, 2004), 182-83.

would lead some to be "idle and doe nothing."[90] While Arminians, Vines, and Gataker all denied active obedience, their theological similarities went no further. Arminians incorporated inherent righteousness and the works which follow as the grounds of justification. Gataker had no sympathy for this position. He insisted, "no man ... if he come to be araigned, as a sinner at Gods Tribunal, and there tried by Gods Law, whither written or inbred, can be justified by his works."[91] Likewise justification, for Gataker, was a judicial and not renovative act. Gataker was careful to distinguish between justification and sanctification; justification addressed the problem of sin's guilt, while sanctification dealt with sin's corruption.[92] Therefore denying the active obedience of Christ in justification, in the context of the seventeenth century, did not result necessarily in a form of semi-Pelagian soteriology.

III. Active Obedience and the Westminster Standards

The response to Vines and Gataker at the Assembly was equally passionate and theologically rigorous. Arguments were made that defended the position that justification included both the active and passive obedience of Christ. Wilkenson stated, "For my part I doe excedingly aprove of those arguments brought to magnify the passive righteousnesse of Christ, yet I cannot exclude the active obedience."[93] He pointed to the offices of Christ as prophet, priest, and king, and concluded "now ther are points of active righteousnesse in all those three offices which more surely concurre to the salvation of a sinner."[94] Lazarus Seaman added, "In the same sence that the passive obedience of Christ is imputed, the active must be imputed."[95] Seaman further asserted that the grounds of justification is "Christ, the whole Christ, his righteousness: habituall yet essentiall. His whole obedience & satisfaction: all

[90]Joseph Mede, *The Works of the Pious and Profoundly-Learned Joseph Mede, B.D. Sometime Fellow of Christ's Colledge in Cambridge.*, ed. John Worthington (London: Printed by Roger Norton, for Richard Royston, bookseller to His Most Sacred Majesty, 1677), 215. Jue, *Heaven Upon Earth*, 55.

[91]Gataker, *An Antidote*, 5.

[92]Gataker, *An Antidote*, 10, 11, 35.

[93]Van Dixhoorn, "Reforming the Reformation," 3.33.

[94]Van Dixhoorn, "Reforming the Reformation," 3.33.

[95]Van Dixhoorn, "Reforming the Reformation," 3.42.

this come into the ground."[96] Opponents of Vines and Gataker were convinced that in justification, Christ's active and passive obedience could not be separated. George Walker stated, "To make me without sin is noe thing except also made righteous; you cannot separate Christs active and passive obedience."[97]

In regards to the exegesis of Romans 5, Peter Smith offered a first reply.

> By "the righteousnesse of one" must be understood the active obedience of Christ, & the reason is because the word is frequently taken, especially in the Ould Testament, for the morrall law, & soe 1 Luk. 6. Ther is a communication in the workes of Christ, his active and passive obedience.[98]

Thomas Goodwin provided an additional substantial response. He gave two reasons for why active obedience was taught in this scriptural passage. The first reason was, "From the opposition betweene Adam's sin & Jesus Christ's obedience," because the "gift of righteousness" did not refer to the passive obedience alone. For Goodwin, the "gift of righteousness" according to "grace" (v. 17) was not simply the satisfaction of God's justice in Christ's death on the cross.[99] In addition, Goodwin's second reason was found in verse 18. "In 18 v. it is called a justification of life ... the right to eternall life."[100] For Goodwin, this was what was offered in justification, not simply the satisfaction of God's justice, but the positive reward of eternal life. Goodwin did not deny that the blood sacrifice of Christ was essential, in fact "the active obedience would not save without this," but there was likewise a "righteousnesse of the law" that must be fulfilled.[101] Thomas Wilson also concurred with Goodwin's interpretation: "Adams obedience without limitation was Imputed, therfore Christs obedience without restriction."[102]

---

[96]Van Dixhoorn, "Reforming the Reformation," 3.42. By "habituall," Seaman was referring to the active righteousness of Christ demonstrated in his active obedience.

[97]Van Dixhoorn, "Reforming the Reformation," 3.35.

[98]Van Dixhoorn, "Reforming the Reformation," 3.28.

[99]Van Dixhoorn, "Reforming the Reformation," 3.28.

[100]Van Dixhoorn, "Reforming the Reformation," 3.28.

[101]Van Dixhoorn, "Reforming the Reformation," 3.28.

Likewise the Christological issues were addressed. Daniel Featly spoke directly to these concerns. He rejected the idea that Christ, in his human nature, was obligated to keep the law for himself. Featly stated:

> if Christ not bound to fulfill the law for himselfe, then his fulfilling the law is to be imputed to us; but he is not bound, for he is lord of the law, king of the church. There is emphasis in that son of man is lord of the Sabbath. If this be not true we are at a great losse; we loose all Christs workes. Whatsoever is *debitum* is not *meritum*.[103]

Additionally, Charles Herle was unconvinced as to how Christ's active obedience demonstrated his dignity and made him the perfect sacrifice. Herle questioned,

> It was said Christ obedience was naturall, & soe he might actually obey, & yet be obliged to it too. I doe not well see how this obligent can stand with the dignity of his nature. Though the human nature of Christ be a creature, yet it is not a person. The obligation is a personall thing, the terminus of this obligation must be the person of the son.[104]

Herle believed that it was inappropriate to speak about Christ's obligations according to his human nature alone. He considered this tantamount to Christological heresy since it separated Christ's humanity from his divinity. As such, any obligation ascribed to Christ must be directed to the person and not one of the two natures. Featly, Herle, and Goodwin were careful to distinguish the obligations of Christ on earth versus the ascended

---

[102]Van Dixhoorn, "Reforming the Reformation," 3.45. William Gouge added, "It hath been proved out of the Scripture, Rom. 5:19; 2 Cor. 5:21. In the 2 texts an opposition paralell Adam & Christ in one. Adams transgression imputed to us & Christs obedience imputed to us; in the other, our sins & Christs righteousnesse imputed. Wher many simples come to an antidote, every one hath their virtue to a speciall use; soe the particulars of the lord Jesus, their speciall use in us. Heb 7, wher Christ is named a suerty, it is set downe. Holy, harmelesse: all this as our suerty." Van Dixhoorn, "Reforming the Reformation," 3.63.

[103]Van Dixhoorn, "Reforming the Reformation," 3.65. Featly's speeches at the Assembly were later published in *The Dippers dipt or The Anabaptists Duck'd and Plung'd over Head and Eares, at a Disputation in Southwark* (London, 1651).

[104]Van Dixhoorn, "Reforming the Reformation," 3.75.

Christ in heaven. They explained that obedience only applied to Christ on earth for the purpose of salvation.[105] Consequently, for those denying the position of Anselm, active and passive obedience were both part of the *pactum salutis*.

Furthermore, an integral part of the debates over a two-Adam Christology was the refutation of Gataker's position that justification did not include the inheritance of heaven. Featly argued that in justification, eternal life (given in Christ) follows salvation from eternal death (brought forth by Adam).[106] Goodwin commented, "justification of life: I did not meane of Christ's life, but this: whereas eminently our title to eternall life is found upon the active because suited to the law which runs upon doing [an]d not suffering, by his doing properly this law is fullfilled."[107] Herle also described active obedience as the "distinct ground of title to life & how by scripture it apeares in that of 'doe this & live'."[108] Walker went on to refute Gataker's specific comments denying a middle state between unjustified and justified. He stated,

> It was said ther is noe medium betwixt pardon of sin & righteousnesse. If pardon of sin makes a man righteous with Adams righteousnesse, whether doth it put him into a heavenly state? 1 Cor: 15:47. Take Adam in his pure naturales & injoying that righteousnesse in Paradise; this would not raise him. The rule by which he comes unto it is the law, & power is by Jesus Christ.[109]

Walker was convinced that Gataker's two-Adam Christology was inconsistent, since Adam was righteous but not justified, and he believed Gataker ultimately denied a probationary state for Adam. Finally, Theodore Backhurst agreed that adoption gave the believer "a title to heaven," but he maintained that this was not without a "positive righteousnesse" according to Galatians 4:26-27.[110]

In the course of this vigorous debate the proponents of the active obedience position were careful to respond to the charge of

[105]Van Dixhoorn, "Reforming the Reformation," 1.300-01.
[106]Van Dixhoorn, "Reforming the Reformation," 3.43.
[107]Van Dixhoorn, "Reforming the Reformation," 3.48.
[108]Van Dixhoorn, "Reforming the Reformation," 3.50.
[109]Van Dixhoorn, "Reforming the Reformation," 3.29.
[110]Van Dixhoorn, "Reforming the Reformation," 3.39.

antinomianism. They were intent on demonstrating that holding to the imputation of Christ's perfect righteousness according to his active obedience did not provide a free license to live without obligation to God's moral law. Thomas Goodwin was clear in his rejection of antinomianism:

> For that of the Antinomians, If looke out to Christ fulfilling the law the end that they say, then it ware good. We meane it only to justification ... We are to be conformable to Christ, though he did fullfill the law for us, & he is a patterne set up by God in his active obedience.[111]

Goodwin argued that the justified person now sought to conform his or her life to Christ and in so doing desired to live as Christ did, in obedience to God's law. Likewise Goodwin distinguished between two obligations that human beings have to the law. First, there was an obligation with the promise of life; second, there was an obligation because they are creatures. Christ fulfilled the first obligation, but the second still functioned.[112] Herle, however, approached this from a slightly different theological angle. He could not see how the active obedience position led "to the necessity of the Antinomian doctrine?"[113] For Herle, under the covenant of works human beings, "through the flesh," were unable to keep the law of God. Only Christ possessed the "value & the virtue" and "the price & power" to attain the required holiness. Herle concluded that Christ accomplished this "in our stead," and now freed the believer from this original covenant. This freedom was not for the purpose of abandoning the law, but it was a true freedom to obey the law; again, this freedom was in contrast to the bondage of sin that made all obedience impossible.[114]

Finally, the Assembly concluded its discussions with a vote on September 12, 1643. The vote was overwhelmingly in favor of the "whole obedience" language, or active obedience position, and the minutes record at least three dissenting votes, with Thomas Gataker's dissent noted.[115] However, as we provocatively

---

[111]Van Dixhoorn, "Reforming the Reformation," 3.41.
[112]Van Dixhoorn, "Reforming the Reformation," 3.66.
[113]Van Dixhoorn, "Reforming the Reformation," 3.64.
[114]Van Dixhoorn, "Reforming the Reformation," 3.64.
[115]Van Dixhoorn, "Reforming the Reformation," 3.77, 1.321.

introduced at the beginning of this essay, the word "whole" does not appear in chapter eleven of the Westminster Confession. This leads to the obvious question: why did the divines omit this word in their major confessional statement? Could it be that during the intervening two years, between the debates on Article 11 in 1643 and the writing of the Confession in 1645, that many of the divines changed their minds on what they consider to be an allowable position on justification for the sake of a consensus? Ultimately, to the disappointment of historians and theologians alike, these questions cannot be answered with clear historical evidence. The minutes record that reports were presented to the Assembly on the doctrine of justification from the committee, and that the Assembly debated these reports, but nothing is included about the substance of the reports or the debates.[116] Disappointingly, the minutes do not contain any discussion on why the word "whole" was omitted. Thus, any explanations for why the word "whole" does not appear in the Confession are simply tentative suggestions or at best provisional possibilities, and must be qualified as such.[117] Van Dixhoorn offers the best analysis of the "plausible interpretations," and he suggests "there must have been a range of postures toward these statements, and motives for voting the wording they now contain."[118]

Instead of rehearsing again the possible explanations for the omission and creating even more speculation, it may be more useful to examine this issue in relation to the fuller system of theology presented in the Westminster Standards. Specifically it is important to delineate the relation between justification and Westminster's two-Adam Christology. From the outset it is clear that the WCF teaches that the first Adam was under a covenant of works in which "life was promised ... upon the condition of

---

[116]Van Dixhoorn, "Reforming the Reformation," 3.27. Likewise there is no information on the committee meetings on justification. Van Dixhoorn, "Reforming the Reformation," 3.324.

[117]The Orthodox Presbyterian Church's report on justification reaches this same conclusion: "[a]ny argument that the Westminster Assembly of Divines cast its teaching on justification to allow room for those who would deny the imputation of Christ's active obedience is, at best, speculative," *Report on Justification Presented to the Seventy-third General Assembly of the Orthodox Presbyterian Church* (2006), p. 73.

[118]Van Dixhoorn, "Reforming the Reformation," 3.328. Van Dixhoorn presents possibilities pro and con for the omission being a step toward consensus.

perfect and personal obedience" (WCF 7:2). Adam's fall resulted in the imputation of the guilt of his sin and the conveyance of the corruption of sin to all humankind (WCF 7:3). Thus, the promise of life was no longer possible under the covenant of works (WCF 7:3). But the Lord was pleased to make a second covenant, "commonly called the Covenant of Grace: whereby he freely offereth unto sinners life and salvation by Jesus Christ" (WCF 7:3). Subsequently, salvation was offered in Christ according to the covenant of grace. How did Christ accomplish salvation in this covenant? WCF 8:5 states,

> The Lord Jesus, by his perfect obedience and sacrifice of himself, which he through the eternal Spirit once offered up unto God, hath satisfied the justice of his Father; and purchased not only reconciliation, but an everlasting inheritance in the kingdom of heaven, for all those whom the Father hath given unto him.

The parallels between the first Adam and Christ, the second Adam, are obvious. Christ's "obedience" accomplished the "personal obedience" that Adam failed to render in order to receive "life" or "everlasting inheritance."

Yet what is the nature of Christ's "perfect obedience?" First, it is important to remember that Larger Catechism Question & Answer (LC Q & A) 92 and 93 teaches that the obedience required of Adam was to the moral law, and that the moral law promised "life upon the fulfilling, and [threatened] death upon the breach of it." Likewise, according to the covenant of grace, the Confession teaches that Jesus Christ "was made under the law, and did perfectly fulfil it" (WCF 8:4). By fulfilling or perfectly obeying the law, Christ achieved what Adam failed to do. Therefore, Christ's obedience along with his suffering and death on the cross accomplished redemption.

Moving from the accomplishment of redemption, to the application of redemption, the LC Q & A 70 states:

> Justification is an act of God's free grace unto sinners, in which he pardoneth all their sins, accepteth and accounteth their persons righteous in his sight; not for any thing wrought in them, or done by them, but only for the *perfect obedience* and full satisfaction of Christ, by God imputed to them, and received by faith alone.[119]

WCF 11:1 concurs in teaching that justification includes the imputation of the "obedience and satisfaction of Christ." According to the Westminster Standards, the grounds of justification include the imputation of the perfect obedience of Christ, that is his obedience to the law, which merits or purchases (the language of WCF 8:5) everlasting life. Thus, the promise of life lost in the first Adam's disobedience was recovered in the second Adam's perfect obedience, and this is imputed to the believer by faith.

The two-Adam Christology set forth in the Westminster Standards, in comparison, is not consistent with what Vines and Gataker advocated at the Assembly. Essentially, the two-Adam Christological structure in the Standards supports a doctrine of justification that includes, in substance, the active obedience of Christ. In the Standards, Christ's obedience to the law was not for the purpose of demonstrating his own dignity and worthiness to be the sacrificial lamb, nor because his human nature was obligated to the law, as Vines and Gataker argued. Christ's perfect obedience to the law earned exactly what was lost in Adam's disobedience to the law. In addition, while Gataker taught that justification did not include eternal life, the Standards affirm that the eschatological reward for Christ's positive perfect obedience was the promise of eternal life (8:5); and since the perfect obedience of Christ is imputed to the believer in justification (LC Q & A 70), subsequently justification includes the promise of eternal life.

Although primary sources do not shed additional light on why the Assembly in WCF 11:3 chose to omit the word "whole," and this question probably will go down as a tantalizing unsolved historical mystery, the Westminster system of doctrine as a whole does provide more specific details. Placing the doctrine of justification within the Westminster Standards as a whole reveals a distinct and consistent theological system that does not comport with the system of theology presented by Vines and Gataker, which includes their "passive obedience only" doctrine of justification. This should not come as a surprise. The position of Vines and Gataker was demonstratively voted down. We should expect that decision to be exhibited in the theology of the Westminster Standards.

---

[119]Italics mine.

IV. Final Thought

We began this essay describing the contemporary discussions regarding the doctrine of justification. In ecclesiastical and academic institutions that subscribe to the Westminster Standards, proponents of the New Perspective on Paul within these institutions claim that the passive obedience only position on justification was historically permitted, given Vines and Gataker's positions at the Assembly and the apparent omission made in chapter eleven of the Confession itself. In essence this is an attempt to build an argument on historical precedence. However, if we grant that the positions of men like Vines and Gataker are acceptable and within the bounds of the Standards, it is not the case that proponents of the New Perspective are simply modern-day versions of Vines and Gataker. One very significant illustration will suffice.

Neither Vines nor Gataker considered the believer's works of obedience as the grounds of justification. We have outlined already Vines and Gataker's differences with their contemporary seventeenth-century semi-Pelagian opponents (i.e. Arminians and Roman Catholics). However, in their redefining of the doctrine of justification, advocates for the New Perspective view justification no longer as how one enters the covenant, but how one stays in the covenant.[120] Consequently, New Perspective supporters argue that there is a present as well as a future justification, with the future justification grounded in the Christian's "Spirit-led" works of obedience.[121] This construction is nearly identical to what

[120]E. P. Sanders, *Paul and Palestinian Judaism* (Philadelphia: S.C.M., 1977), 543; Wright, *What Saint Paul Really Said*, 119, 122 and N. T. Wright, *Paul in Fresh Perspective* (Minneapolis: Fortress Press, 2005), 119.

[121]See Don B. Garlington, *Faith, Obedience, and Perseverance: Aspects of Paul's Letter to the Romans* (Tübingen: J.C.B. Mohr, 1994), 152-55; Wright, *What Saint Paul Really Said*, 118, 129; Wright, *Paul in Fresh Perspective*, 57, 148. It is important to clarify that formulating a future aspect of justification is not inherently Arminian or New Perspective. The language of open acquittal in LC Q & A 90 and Shorter Catechism Q & A 38 suggests a future forensic or legal aspect of justification for the believer on the Day of Judgment. Moreover, following the Westminster Standards, there is one act of justification with present and future aspects and the one act (with its present and future aspects) is grounded in the work of Christ alone. See Richard B Gaffin Jr., *By Faith, Not By Sight: Paul and the Order of Salvation* (Milton Keynes: Paternoster Press, 2006), 81-84; and Lane G. Tipton, "Union with Christ and Justification," in this volume.

Arminians, like Joseph Mede, were advocating. In contrast, Vines and Gataker did not ground any part of the believer's justification in human works (whether Spirit-led or not). The seventeenth-century English context of anti-popery and Arminian/Calvinist tension demonstrates the historical impossibility of this being acceptable to any of the divines, including Vines and Gataker. Modern-day revisionists should be cautioned against committing historical anachronisms.[122]

[122]In addition, Richard Gaffin notes another semi-Pelagian element in James Dunn's, and perhaps also N. T. Wright's, doctrine of original sin, in which they deny the imputation of Adam's first sin; obviously, this also conflicts with the teachings of the Westminster Standards (WCF 6: 3, 6). See Richard B. Gaffin Jr., "Paul the Theologian," *Westminster Theological Journal* 62 (2000): 135.

Justification and Violence Reflections on Atonement and Contemporary Apologetics

William Edgar

> And, in fact, we believe that in falling away from this foundation [of justification by the imputation to us of Christ's obedience], however slightly, we could not find rest elsewhere, but should always be troubled. Forasmuch as we are never at peace with God till we resolve to be loved in Jesus Christ, for of ourselves we are worthy of hatred. (*Gallican Confession* of 1559, article XVIII)

Has not the doctrine of justification been established, and the attending issues settled? Did not the sixteenth-century Reformers exhaust the subject and establish it for the future, at least in the Protestant heritage? It would seem not, at least to certain quarters in the church today. Various scholars in our times are, indeed, revisiting the whole question of justification. Some argue that "Paul was not a Lutheran," and thus we need to redefine the whole matter and come to a new understanding of what the New Testament actually meant as it defined justification in the setting of Second Temple Judaism.

Our interest here is not in that question, important as it may be for current discussions.[1] Rather, we are concerned to address justification as a fundamental element in Christian apologetics. A first concern is to locate the reality of justification in human experience. It is our contention that when classic justification, based on the propitiatory work of Christ, is absent, human beings will grasp for substitutes, often grotesque ones. A few historical examples will be entered in evidence. A second concern is to take issue with certain recent theologians who attempt to redefine justification so as to accommodate revisionist views of theology.

[1]For discussions of the New Testament and its interpreters, see chapters 1, 2, and 5 in the present volume.

To that end we will interact with some modern systematic theologians, as well as with more ancient authors. Finally, we want to argue that the true meaning of justification is still, indeed, more than ever, foundational for the Christian worldview. And thus we will argue that the atonement, which is the center of redemption-accomplished, and justification, which is the crucial entry point for redemption-applied, continue to function as the architectural foundation for the Christian message, and thus the apologetic for its truth, over against various forms of contemporary unbelief.

Perverted Atonement

The French Revolution officially began July 14, 1789, with the storming of the Bastille. From the term "bastide" (fortress) the structure was originally built to protect the eastern wall of the city of Paris. But it soon became a dreaded place for the incarceration of political prisoners, usually enemies of the monarchy. Now a prison, it was only defended by a number of aging veterans and a handful of Swiss mercenaries. They were no match for the thousands of attackers on that fateful day. As well, the moment was charged with symbolism. Indeed, much of the French Revolution, real enough in itself, was nothing if not high and bloody drama, even a ritual of atonement.

At three thirty, Sunday afternoon, the 12th of July, 1789, a young journalist from Picardie stood up on a table inside the *Palais Royal* and gave an impassioned speech. The radical Camille Desmoulins, coiffed with a green leaf in his beret, came to the end of his speech and shouted, "to arms." Mobilized, the group descended into the streets. The immediate cause of their unrest was the dismissal of the Minister of Finance, Jacques Necker, to them a clear provocation of the ordinary French civilian. This crowd of rebels selected an unusual first target: forcing the closing of all the theaters in Paris, symbolically implying that no drama should rival their own.[2] Things snowballed. The group became larger and angrier. It tumbled onto the *Place Louis XV* (which would be renamed *Place de la Révolution*, and, after Napoleon, *Place de la Concorde*). Unfortunately a couple of

[2]James H. Billington, *Fire in the Minds of Men* (New York: Basic Books, 1980), 31ff.

stray bullets from the royal guard killed a few people. More provocation ensued. Two days later, the now massive crowd converged on the Bastille and liberated the incarcerated from their prison. The subsequent story is well known: successive revolutionary governments, regicide, foreign wars, the reign of terror, and, finally, Napoleon's rule.

We have here, among much else, a case of secular atonement. One of the central rituals within the drama of the French Revolution was meant to achieve expiation. It was important to be cleansed from the past, while at the same time holding up revolutionary ideals. A so-called humane execution device, the guillotine, was authorized. This instrument had a long prehistory, dating back to the Middle Ages. But now, Dr. Joseph Ignace Guillotin, a Deputy to the Assembly, proposed the City use it for all criminals. In March of 1791, the Assembly declared the guillotine to be the only instrument of execution. The justification? All offenders were treated equally, replacing the previous discrimination between the highborn and lowborn, the latter being subject in those times to particularly cruel forms of execution. After consultation with the renowned surgeon, Dr. Antoine Louis (it was originally to be called the "Louisette" – but to his relief they decided on the Deputy's name), the government was assured this was a clean and efficient method of execution. The revolutionary Parisian version was constructed by Tobias Schmidt, a German engineer and piano-builder. It was first used in April, 1792 at the *Place de Greve* (now *Place de l'Hôtel de Ville*). When the victim was high-placed, the machine was moved to the *Place de la Révolution*. Louis XVI was executed there on January 21, 1793. Many other notables perished by the blade. Thousands of victims were killed per year until more peaceful times could arrive.

The Guillotine was the centerpiece of the revolutionary drama.[3] Other aspects could be mentioned as well. The *Palais Royal* from which Desmoulins launched his appeal was a sort of arcade, with several cafés, symbolically named according to Enlightenment principles. The *Caveau* was underground, literally and metaphorically; it was the meeting place for the Girondins as they plotted the toppling of the monarchy and the establishment

---

[3]Strange and sordid aspects of this ritual could be mentioned. Small models were used for women's earrings. It was used in numerous countries around Europe right up until the late twentieth century. Hitler and the Nazis used the guillotine far more extensively than the French.

of the First Republic in 1792. The *Mécanique* was full of robots and celebrated modern science. The *Foy*, symbolizing the new faith in egalitarianism and reason, was the place where the first crowd was mobilized. Desmoulins actually jumped up on a table there called *table magique*, which stood for the "magic" of utopia. In these cafés politics were discussed, words were invented, or given new meaning (democracy, communism, nationhood, liberty).[4] Though secular in one sense, the parallels with religion are astonishing, especially given the purported anti-Catholicism of the French Revolution. The Bastille was Babylon. Destroying the prison was a *tabula rasa*, even a new birth (the word "nation" means just that). The term Enlightenment was a parody of Jesus Christ, "Light of the World." At the Cathedral of Notre Dame, the central altar was replaced by a mound of dirt with a tree planted in it, representing the new *earth* of the new heavens and earth. Processionals used a local prostitute instead of Mary on the stand, and sang hymns to the glory of the Supreme Being and of human reason by the composer François Joseph Gossec. The calendar was changed from Gregory's, with the birth of Christ as year one, to the revolution's beginning with the First Republic. Days had ten hours, months were "decades" of ten days, with rhyming names from plants, animals or tools, all of which was meant to appeal to human reason.[5]

Thus, the guillotine was a counterfeit for Calvary. The proffered death was certainly far less agonizing for victims than that of the gibbet, but intended all the same as a symbol of blood ritual. The guilty, those who refused the new birth, were expiated for the good of the citizens of the new "church," the citizens of the Republic. There was high ceremony, including a processional to the square, where victims were transported in humility, not on a donkey, but on a mule-drawn cart. Their last words were recorded and published throughout France.

Purging for Honor

The French Revolution is a particularly modern example of atonement rituals meant to cleanse the world from past evils and

[4]See François Fosca, "Histoire," in *Histoire Des Cafés de Paris* (Paris: Firmin-Didot, 1934).

[5]Jean Favier, ed., *Chronique de la Révolution 1788–1799* (Paris: Larousse, 1988).

open up new paths to freedom. There are many others. They vary greatly depending on the time, the culture, and the location. Yet, although the particular diagnosis of the social ill and the particular hope for a better future may vary, the patterns are similar. Consider another example, that of lynching in the American South.

Sociologist Orlando Patterson has made important contributions to "rituals of blood," particularly in racial relations in North America. He has studied the gruesome phenomenon of lynching in the post-bellum South, and connects it to structural and cultural factors.[6] Between 1882 and 1968, 80 percent of lynchings took place in the South (by far the greatest number in the Deep South), where 72 percent of the victims were African-American.[7] Psychological and economic factors certainly existed, but Patterson argues that at the heart of the matter was ritual killing and blood sacrifice. The practice has existed well beyond the American South, especially among the more "advanced" pre-modern peoples. Often it was connected with slave holding.

Patterson asks what sacrifice represents, and why it is one of mankind's most sacred rituals. His first answer, following Henri Hubert and Marcel Mauss, is that sacrifice represents the unusual combination of celebration and the purging of evil.[8] Then, he follows René Girard, whose life's work has been on the nearly universal phenomenon of displacing violence on to victims, or a victim, as a fundamental way to hold a society together.[9] Girard insists that more attention needs be given to the quasi-religious nature of sacrifice. In the case of human sacrifice, he argues, the historical and cultural factors provide the explanation for the tendency of ritual cleansing in so many parts of the world, at so many times.

With these conceptual frameworks in mind, Patterson examines the culture of honor in the Celtic layer behind the American

---

[6]Orlando Patterson, "Feast of Blood: 'Race,' Religion, and Human Sacrifice in the Postbellum South," in *Rituals of Blood: Consequences of Slavery in Two American Centuries* (Washington, D.C.: Civitas/CounterPoint, 1998), 169-232.

[7]Patterson, "Feast," 176.

[8]Patterson, "Feast," 182-83. See Henri Hubert and Marcel Mauss, *Sacrifice: Its Nature and Function*, trans. W. D. Halls (Chicago: University of Chicago Press, 1964).

[9]Patterson, "Feast," 184. See René Girard, "La violence et le vrai savior de l'homme," *Corporation Canadienne Des Sciences Religieuses* 10 (1981): 1.

South. Stressing the frontier mentality which characterized much of white America in the nineteenth century, he looks closely at the obstacle of slavery and the consequences of emancipation. To explain the phenomenon of lynching in the South, he argues that a mechanism was needed to safeguard *honor*. "What both the transmitted Celtic herding culture of honor and the frontier environment initiated, the institution of slavery and the secular religion of racism institutionalized."[10] Slaves had been considered the "domestic enemy." But what kind of tactics did they use? They were reckoned to be subversive, wanting to infiltrate by tactics such as intermarriage and usurpation. Interestingly, and linking this to the French Revolution, Patterson cites newspaper articles in which African-Americans were identified with the *Jacobins*, and other destroyers of the white race.[11] During Reconstruction and beyond, honor was lost, and the sense of the domestic enmity of African Americans only increased, since for the first time blacks had legal opportunities similar to whites. And so, in this setting, ritual sacrifice, complete with sermons, a carefully chosen site, a symbolic tree (for the Klu Klux Klan it became a burning cross), all of them, combined in a complex "religion of the Lost Cause."[12]

Cleansing, True and False

The main point we are making is that human beings in a variety of settings where some serious threat to justice is perceived will be driven to resort to some sort of substitute propitiatory atonement. From the Nazi-perpetrated Holocaust (*the Shoah*) to the killing fields of Cambodia, Rwanda, or the Ukraine, we witness the horrors of human attempts at mass-level atonement. The parallels are clear. Of course, from the perception to the unspeakable cure, we have a wildly perverted counterfeit of divine judgment. My thesis, hardly original, is that, in the absence of a true understanding of justice, and of justification, inevitable damage will be done. Without the full recognition of the comprehensive and final nature of Christ's atonement at Calvary, to the end of

---

[10]Patterson, "Feast," 191.

[11]Patterson, "Feast," 191-92. See John Hope Franklin, *The Militant South* (Boston: Beacon Press, 1964).

[12]Patterson, "Feast," 208.

justification, counterfeits will be invented. Purging a people from enemies, celebrating the end of evil, these are the central longings of human existence. They twist the truth of God's true justice and his true justification. Because without Christ, because of whose death and resurrection the world will be judged (Acts 17:31) and because of whose death his people's guilt is removed, and whose resurrection is for their justification (Rom. 4:24), human beings will resort to devilish deviations.

Not every sham variety of atonement is so horrendous as these examples. In our contemporary therapeutic culture we find aspirations toward purging that are less destructive of human life, though no less serious as departures from the truth. Consider how much advertising is connected to the need for reparation. From the perfumes and deodorants, which make us feel cleaner, to the vacations in exotic places, which make us feel renewed, Madison Avenue promotes products and schemes that appeal to the human psychological need for redemption, all in a consumerist guise. Perverted atonements come in all kinds of shapes and forms. They appeal to our most basic needs.

May we say this boldly? Justification, founded on atonement, is the central apologetic issue of our time, or of any time. No wonder! In the absence of true justification we remain not only enemies of one another, but enemies of God (Rom. 5:10). And so, without a clear articulation of this doctrine, we are bound to fall into desperate versions like these. Without fully understanding that God is the only one who can justify, we invent every possible kind of substitute. Indeed, without understanding that it is God who is offended, our methods of reparation will always fall far short.

Justice, and its active form, justification, are at the center of biblical religion. Because God cannot but require perfect justice, it should be no surprise that the issues of injury, offense, righteousness, integrity, and redemption are woven into the warp and woof of the way the world is, and the way we think about it. It is no surprise that so many philosophers and thinkers, not to mention ordinary people, devise hundreds of ways to remedy the problems of injustice in human existence. Let us consider only two such reflections. Significantly, a good deal of modern theology is reassessing these doctrines in the light of our contemporary awareness of injustice.

Warm Embrace Is Not Justification

So, then, what kind of issue is justification? How should theologians evaluate it? Today we are confronted with a number of voices which plead for a reconsideration of the classic Reformation position, in favor of new emphases. They often interact with issues such as violence, ethnic cleansing, oppression of women, in ways that the Reformation fathers did not, at least on the surface. And they are often full of insights, making poignant applications. What can we learn from them? What are the attendant dangers? Let us briefly examine two such voices.

Miroslav Volf has written a powerful account of the human condition and its remedy, using the categories of *exclusion* and *embrace* as his central paradigm.[13] He argues that if we are to find justice, it will have to be in a struggle against exclusion and in a march toward embrace. Volf defines exclusion not as differentiation, which is potentially a good thing, but as separation pure and simple. The Genesis account praises "separating-and-binding," but not simple otherness, he notes. This is because it is perfectly normal and healthy to define our identities in relation to other people. What we should not do is "exclude" others from the possibility of such good separation and good binding.[14] Exclusion shuts people out in a cruel way. Having been raised in Croatia, Volf is particularly sensitive to the pernicious idea of ethnic cleansing. He describes first hand the typical moves toward exclusion which tend toward such unholy purging. They involve renaming people "unclean," and then abandoning them, either passively or actively. He insists, though that we should not attempt to neatly divide the world into guilty perpetrators and innocent victims. In reality things are more messy. No one has clean hands, he asserts. His arguments surely draw on his Lutheran background. For example, he argues that "the very act of mapping the world of noninnocence into the exclusive categories of "pure" vs. "corrupt" entails corruption."

---

[13]Miroslav Volf, *Exclusion and Embrace: A Theological Exploration of Identity, Otherness and Reconciliation* (Nashville: Abingdon Press, 1996).

[14]Volf, *Exclusion*, 65ff.

This is because "there is no absolute standpoint from which relative human beings can make pure judgments about purity and corruption."[15] The remedy for this problem thus diagnosed is that God will receive hostile humanity into divine communion, and that this reception in turn becomes the model for human embrace of others.

In passing, Volf argues that the popular categories of "oppression" and "liberation" are of limited value. The reason is that the modern ideal of freedom tends to mean only the absence of interference from outside, but not the desperately needed power to live with dignity. These categories thus feed the crusading tendency of those who claim the higher ground. One of the most harmful legacies of modernity is the cruel grand narrative which seeks justice, in the name of freedom, without God. Rather than freedom, love should be the goal.[16]

Where is the pivot point for love for him? It is in the transformed heart. The heart must learn to forgive. It must learn to repent. And where do we find the resources for this change of heart? By placing "both our unjust enemy and our own vengeful self face to face with a God who loves and does justice." It is only when we are in the presence of the God of the crucified Messiah that we can overcome exclusion.[17]

But here is a serious problem in Volf's construction. It is one thing to be in the presence of such a receptive God, a God who, as he puts it, will not be God without humanity, a God who empties himself in order to show what the Trinity really is. It is quite another, in our view, to have a God who so loved the world that he provided true atonement, in history, for his people. Is it not the very nature of love not to be driven by necessity (as in this God who will not be without humanity)? Furthermore, does God really empty himself? Does he not humble himself by adding humanity on to his deity, not by subtracting from it? But most seriously, Volf's construct omits, or at least dramatically downplays, the idea of a God whose justice needs to be satisfied, and whose wrath needs to be deflected onto Christ if righteousness is to be imputed to his people. Is not the love of God displayed precisely in this,

---

[15]Volf, *Exclusion*, 83.
[16]Volf, *Exclusion*, 105.
[17]Volf, *Exclusion*, 124.

that while needing to be satisfied, he found a marvelous way to do so, while not *excluding* his people in hell?

Unless we are seriously misreading what this brilliant, engaging theologian is saying, it appears he cannot bring himself to speak of a real sacrifice for sins. Indeed, for him, the cross of Christ, which he praises as being the end of violence, emerges merely as an example, albeit the ultimate example, of God's command to replace the *lex talionis* with the principle of nonresistance.[18] At best, the cross "lays bare the mechanism of scapegoating," because in his truthfulness and justice he showed vengefulness for what it was. The cross thus becomes a part of the struggle for God's truth and justice, but not the end of the matter.[19] In short, there is no substitutionary atonement in his scheme. As a consequence, one has to ask, can true and lasting social justice possibly follow? Can there be this embrace he so longs for?

In a fascinating section on the affliction of memory, Volf argues that one cannot and should not forget the past. Yet somehow memories of past horrors should not serve to keep hatreds alive, but to shield against the guilty past and to build a more hopeful future. As a shield against evil, memory is a kind of active energy only, because, "complete restitution of the past is not only impossible; its very thought is terrifying."[20] But is this true? Of course, the Jew will not forget the cruel Nazi, nor will the mother forget the kidnapper of her child. And yet, forgetting is at the heart of the gospel, is it not?

Does not the God of the Bible truly and radically "forgive and forget"? So much so, that he requires the same of us: "forgive us our trespasses as we forgive those who trespass against us." For Volf the only forgiving and forgetting is achieved by reaching deep stages of "nonremembering – in the arms of God." But how deep is a deep stage? Will there not always be a deeper stage to haunt the forgiver? Further, what kind of God is this one who helps us to forget, within his bosom? In parentheses, I am using the masculine pronoun here, which Volf will not do.[21] He is a nonremembering

---

[18]Volf, *Exclusion*, 291.

[19]Volf, *Exclusion*, 292-93.

[20]Volf, *Exclusion*, 132.

[21]I cannot resist making the observation that many contemporary theologians, out of a correct desire to stress that God has no gender, incorrectly refuse masculine pronouns or the label of Father or Son. Revelation is telling us

God, one who engages in "eschatological forgetting" because of the "paradoxical monument" of the cross. At best, this is vague terminology meant to signify that God can put human sins behind him. As we come into his presence, we may do the same, without for a moment forgetting the horrors of past evils. But this falls far short of the radical biblical declaration that God actually remembers our sins no more, because they have been imputed to the Son, as he suffered on the cross (Rom. 3:25-26; Heb. 10:14)! I don't want my sins put behind, I want them eradicated.

So, we doubt that this approach really and truly may lead to peace and love. The best we can do, according to Volf, is to break the cycle of violence, and when we do the effect is "to plant a seed from which the fragile fruit of Pentecostal peace grows." Volf agrees that at times some violence may be required to prevent greater violence. So he is not a complete pacifist. And yet he says, if anyone puts on the soldier's gear, not the cross, then he cannot claim to worship the Messiah who proclaims blessing not to the violent but to the meek.[22] This view lacks the crucial distinction Protestants have always made between rejecting personal vengeance and accepting public justice. In the end, Volf succumbs to the rather emotional argument that says there can never be a just war, because everyone fighting a war will claim his side to be just, which cannot be true.

The Bible's approach to the subject is entirely different. It is the same Christ who atoned for the sins of his people at Calvary who also rules the nations and opens the seven seals of judgment on them. It is the same God whose righteousness was revealed so that he may be just-and-justifier who also rules the world through magistrates who are a terror to bad conduct (Rom. 3:26; 13:3). If we are to present a compelling apologetic to the world, with the claim that violence will be ended, it cannot be by a cross that is only an example. There must be atonement for sin, and, first, the imputation of Christ's righteousness to the account of his people, and, second, the certainty of judgment for those who refuse to receive the free gift. Without this, there can be no guarantee against bloody revolutions and evil lynchings.

---

something essential about the divine economy, and about begetting, not about a gendered God.

[22]Volf, *Exclusion*, 306.

It is certainly true that exclusion and embrace have their place. And it seems convincing to argue that they are superior as paradigms to oppression and liberation. But unless the fundamental paradigms of transgression and forgiveness, sin and expiation are there, then how may humans be released?

But the deepest question, the one contemporaries often shy away from, is nevertheless the only question that really matters: how may God be satisfied? What is at stake in the human predicament is not first and foremost how we may become free. It is how God may be satisfied, how his standards may be met, how his wrath may be reversed. That is the great problem of history. That is the central dilemma in the human condition. If God can save us, because he loves us, how can he remain just, and yet the justifier of the ungodly? Unless justification begins with God's own requirements for justice, or, to use the older word, with satisfaction, then everything is lost, and no amount of pleading for forgiving and forgetting, or for "divine embrace" can really help us at all. Because, what is at stake in the quest for justice, must begin and end with divine satisfaction. Of course, justification is about the standing of human beings before a righteous God. But the truly central issue is how God can be satisfied, and yet justify sinful people. How can he remain just in the face of evil? How may he be just and yet the justifier of the ungodly who are being redeemed?

Truly, the gospel of justification by faith provides the answer. And there can be no such justification without the atonement of Christ. There is indeed reconciliation in his sacrifice, but not without both expiation and propitiation. In the biblical revelation, we learn that expiation has a primary reference to our liability arising from God's holiness. Christ gave himself as a sin-offering to God, for the sake of sinners who are guilty before him. It is a penal and substitutionary sacrifice. We also learn that propitiation is a covering of God's anger so that it is turned away. In a word, we have the substitutionary atonement. "If we are to believe that the atonement is God's vicarious dealing with the judgment upon sin, it is absolutely necessary to hold that it is the vicarious endurance of that in which this judgment is epitomized."[23] Only when God's

---

[23]John Murray, *Redemption Accomplished and Applied* (Edinburgh: Banner of Truth Trust, 1961), 32.

just fury against sin is a part of the finished work of Christ can it also be said that reconciliation occurs. And reconciliation is the mending of an enmity, or, rather, the peace treaty between God and his people. Only then can we have the desired nonremembering God, one who engages in "eschatological forgetting." Even here, though, the cross is so much more than a "paradoxical monument." It is redemption accomplished.

Feminist Concerns

Another type of interaction with the classic Reformation position comes from the halls of feminist theology. Of course we could find hundreds of different examples with differing kinds of concerns. One of the most articulate feminist theologians, also an expert on the Protestant Reformation, is Serene Jones, the thoughtful author of *Feminist Theory and Christian Theology*.[24] Jones' stated purpose is to press feminist theory over the terrain or landscape of Christian doctrine as she understands it, in hopes of "remapping" the main theological loci, especially justification and sanctification. As an expert on Luther and Calvin she interacts with the classic sixteenth-century view, attempting to amend it with awareness from a contemporary feminist consciousness.[25] Without pausing over the many insights Jones brings to the discussion, let us begin with her basic view of the female condition. She represents *strategic essentialism*, a position she explains and defends. *Simple* essentialism claims women are fundamentally different from men, both biologically and psychologically. To cite the usual attributes, for some, women are more nurturing than men, while for others, they have more power to bring peace and reconciliation than the naturally more aggressive male. Jones takes the point, but only so far. She believes that women's nature is constructed as well.

Constructivism argues that gender is determined by language and culture, not biology. Our conventions expect women to behave in a certain manner, and thus pressure is applied for them to fit in. Clothes, children's toys, roles played in institutions, these indicators send signals to girls about their sexual identity

[24]Serene Jones, *Feminist Theory and Christian Theology: Cartographies of Grace* (Minneapolis: Fortress Press, 2000).

[25]Her previous works include *Calvin and the Rhetoric of Piety* (Louisville: Westminster/John Knox Press, 2005).

which then become self-fulfilling as they grow into womanhood. As expected, constructivists argue that essentialism throws up a dangerous "wall of inevitability," and locks women in to preset roles which then become impossible to change.

Jones rejects *simple* constructivism, though, because it tends toward cultural determinism, which can end up being even more oppressive than essentialism. Further, she worries that in this view women emerge as mere victims of a sexist culture. Most of all, it provides no basis for morals: "If no single description of women's lives is correct and all are equally valid, what standards are available for assessing harm or the nature of justice and injustice in women's lives?"[26] So, in the end, she argues for *strategic essentialism.* Her fundamental reason for adopting this "in between" position is that it allows her to be pragmatic, to move from theory to action. Because strategic essentialism gives no single, definitive answer for an action plan, it is more flexible. For example, the answer to the question whether women are by nature more "nurturing" than men varies. In some circumstances, such essentialism is oppressive, restricting tough jobs such as politics to men. In others, however, it is a helpful corrective to patriarchal views of power, hierarchy, and control.[27]

The conceptual framework for this in-between position is hard to find. Perhaps there isn't one. Jones engages in a kind of search for norms which can never quite be universal. She claims that language systems and social organizations contain certain conceptual rules in order to make sense of the world. But one cannot make them into absolutes or universals. So, where does this leave us? And, specifically, where does this leave women? By which values will she be guided when deciding what is oppressive and what is corrective?

Here, Jones turns to theology. While she is in agreement with some of the "basics" of Christian theology, such as God's love, the goodness of creation, the power of grace, etc., at the same time she believes that various theological formulations as they have come down to us have been harmful to women. Because of a theological discourse that is patriarchal women's humanity has been diminished. How does this work? She argues, for example,

26. Jones, *Feminist Theory and Christian Theology: Cartographies of Grace*, 41.
27. Jones, *Feminist Theory and Christian Theology: Cartographies of Grace*, 45.

that Martin Luther's use of a "courtroom drama" for the purpose of explaining justification is tacitly exclusive of women. Luther's divine Judge is like the tribunal patriarch of Roman law, which she takes to be masculine. The Judge declares mankind guilty, which is helpful when it comes to proud, aggressive males, but not helpful for women, who feel guilty enough because of their subordinate place in society. Furthermore, as Luther's God wrathfully "undoes" the subject by having it crucified in Christ, women, who are already undone and whose lives are already fragmented, are simply confirmed in their sense of guilt, not encouraged. Because in Western culture women are "always receiving," always there to please men, Luther's construction simply adds insult to the injury.[28]

Jones uses the strongest language to reinforce her view. Relying on French feminist Luce Irigaray, she diagnoses the woman's condition as having no "skin," lacking an "envelope of her own."[29] She has been "constructed by Western discourse to be radically fluid, to be a space that is always receiving – she is *in* her relationship, to a fault" Thus, she is merely an extension of male arrogance, her clothes becoming "garments for his pleasure."[30] Again, of course, these sorts of emotional descriptions are remarkably imprecise. Who are these victims? How does Western discourse become fluid, whatever that may mean? But, for whatever reason, a woman comes "not with a robust self that needs to be dismantled by the wrath of the Law but as a de-natured subject whose lack of self is her prison."[31]

As a remedy to this problem, Jones suggests several things. First, she would reverse the traditional order in the application of redemption, putting sanctification first, then justification. When sanctification comes first a woman is met not with undoing but is given "the center and the substance she needs to become the subject then judged and graciously forgiven." This would send women the signal that God wishes to empower and liberate them rather than "break what little self-confidence they have."[32]

---

[28]Jones, *Feminist Theory and Christian Theology: Cartographies of Grace*, 62.

[29]Luce Irigaray, *An Ethics of Sexual Difference*, trans. Gillian C. Gill (Ithaca: Cornell University Press, 1993), *ad loc.*

[30]Jones, *Feminist Theory and Christian Theology: Cartographies of Grace*, 62.

[31]Jones, *Feminist Theory and Christian Theology: Cartographies of Grace*, 63.

[32]Jones, *Feminist Theory and Christian Theology: Cartographies of Grace*, 63.

Second, justification itself she redefines in order to deconstruct the way traditional culture has defined women. Coming second, justification becomes a way of "forgiving the sins of constructions that bind us, so that, through God's mercy, we may be opened to the crafting work of the Holy Spirit." For women, this person-crafting liberates from restrictive conceptions of gender.[33]

It is always important to listen to such arguments before finding fault with them. Serene Jones reminds us, as do many other feminists, that the oppression of women is a reality. All too often, their humanity has indeed been diminished. Often, women's identity has been defined exclusively in relation to men, and thus in a co-dependent manner. To put it in Volf's terms, it has lacked separation-and-binding. Women's status before God has been justified only through men, rather than on its own.

And yet! Surely to reverse the order of the application of redemption, putting sanctification first, is not salutary. In fact, it is to return to the very kind of corruption that led the Reformers to react. Because if we start with "person-crafting," we cannot really take human sin and guilt before God seriously. To put it another way, unless we can be acquitted before an angry God, no amount of sanctification, albeit by God's grace, can make us right before God. Unless justification is first, then we are again under bondage. For who can find a place in communion with God by being transformed? Even if the transformation is by grace, which it is for Jones, as it was for the medieval church, it cannot satisfy the requirements of a holy God. We are back to the problem we saw in Miroslav Volf's construction. If redemption is first and foremost an embrace, not the propitiation for sins, then all is lost (1 John 2:2). Further, if justification is only a way of forgiving the sins of constructions that bind us, what happens to the primary problem: our enmity with God? For that matter, how can we know which of these binding constructions are sinful, and which may not be? Here, constructive essentialism does not tell us anything specific.

While Jones' arguments are subtle and nuanced, there is no question that she denies the equal opportunity condition of human sinfulness. In her construct, even though she recognizes male pride,

[33]Jones, *Feminist Theory and Christian Theology: Cartographies of Grace*, 66.

women are considered more oppressed than men, because they are co-dependent on men. How can she avoid characterizing them as somewhat less guilty before a holy God than are men. But the heart of Paul's defense of justification is that all have sinned, and thus no one is less sinful. By the same token God brings the same free gift of righteousness to all his people, which thus excludes any claims to innocence or merit (Rom. 3:23-7). Only with this gospel of justification can we then find true liberation and true equality before God (Gal. 3:28). Only by beginning with justification, can we then move on to the work of sanctification, with all the requirements for social justice that entails. Sadly and ironically, without these biblical priorities, there can be no real hope. For how can we ever really work ourselves free of the prison of lack of self? No gospel can effectively do this. But if true, objective guilt is the universal problem, then justification sweeps it all clean, giving real hope for a truly fresh start and a substantial liberation from prisons of all kinds. The Reformers well understood that if you begin with moral reform you will end, not with liberation, but with despair.[34]

Prophetic Untimeliness

This is the title of a book by Os Guinness which forcefully reminds us that the true voice of prophecy should not accommodate to the world's toning down of Christian doctrine.[35] So, how may we listen to the concerns of those who suffer, without giving them answers they may want, but which won't help them? And how may we be true reformers in our day, without forgetting that the greatest deformation is in God's relationship to us? For example, it is certainly true that where there are victims, the justice and compassion of the kingdom of God are called to the fore. Perhaps

---

[34]In his thoughtful critique of Eberhard Jüngel, Wolfhart Pannenberg, and Jürgen Moltmann, Mark Mattes underscores the dangers exhibited by each of these theologians of making ethics the initial focus, rather than the gospel of justification. When law becomes the form of the gospel, then the gospel is lost. "Driving these theologies is an apologetic: the gospel itself will be justified to (Schleiermacher's) cultured despisers of religion when it delivers the new moral world." See Mark C. Mattes, *The Role of Justification in Contemporary Theology* (Grand Rapids: Eerdmans, 2004), 98.

[35]Os Guinness, *Prophetic Untimeliness: A Challenge to the Idol of Relevance* (Grand Rapids: Baker/Hourglass, 2003).

our society fosters too much whining about victimization. At the same time, this should not blind us to the reality of real victims where they do exist, nor excuse us from helping them. Thus we must hear the concerns of Miroslav Volf and of Serene Jones, and must take care not to throw out the baby of social justice with the bathwater of distorted theology. But we want to argue that it is precisely the classical model of justification which can give us true zeal for social action.

Because, in addition to not issuing in social justice, things will go seriously awry when the fundamentals of the atonement and justification are not understood. Indeed, without this clear, robust articulation of the finished work of Christ and the imputation of his righteousness to believers, the world will inevitably stray into violence. As we have seen, the French Revolution, the Jim Crow lynchings, and so much of the brutality of the previous 200 years, are no mere coincidence. What was slowly but surely diminished in the West was the theological worldview which asserted the end of violence God's way.

It is important to note that various voices in the nineteenth century already had spoken out against giving up the full, robust idea of atonement and justification. But most did not listen. No one was more clairvoyant than the great Russian novelist Fyodor Dostoevsky. Telling is the famous quip spoken by Ivan, one of the four sons in *The Brothers Karamazov*, to wit, "If there is no immortality then everything is permitted."

This astonishing novel is the story of patricide, the murder of a father. Fyodor Karamazov was a despicable character. Each of his sons had reasons to kill this evil man. He abused other people, produced a child through the village madwoman, and made a considerable fortune by ravishing his competitors. Although his actual murderer was Smerdyakov, the motive was shared. Ivan was the one who justified it philosophically. Here is his argument. Though not a moral relativist, he strongly held that God was unjust. Because there is widespread cruelty and injustice, it is God who must be sentenced. In the famous "Grand Inquisitor" chapter, he argues that *two* fathers ought to die, father Karamazov and God himself. They both had created life with unfairness, both were the authors of suffering. If innocent people must suffer, Ivan tells his brother Alyosha, then, "I cannot accept God's world." He relates that awful story of the general who sends his dogs to tear up a little peasant child. Even the righteous Alyosha agrees that such a man ought to be shot.

So the problem centrally put in the novel is that God seems unable to vindicate his justice. In Ivan's imaginative account, God sends his son back into the world in the middle of the Spanish Inquisition, to preach compassion and liberty. But the local Cardinal arrests him, saying, in effect, we've got a good thing going here, by using raw power, so don't ruin it. What does Ivan's Christ do? He forgives the Cardinal with a kiss. This God and his Christ are powerless to prevent the cruelties of the Inquisition. In fact, the Grand Inquisitor believes the church must correct God's approach, which is ineffective because it offers love to bad people and good people alike. At last, the chapter tells us, the church can vanquish freedom in order to make men happy! Instead of freedom, which people cannot support, there will be "miracle, mystery, and authority," and, just as significant, there will be bread. Christ in this account made an enormous mistake in refusing to change stones into bread.

Of course, this is not the author's point of view, though one can sense how much he struggled with the problem. Indeed, for Dostoevsky, this "bread" which Christ avoided giving out is the seduction of material prosperity, made possible by technology and industry, symbolized again and again by the Tower of Babel.

The novel is a study on the problem of evil, and on the problem of justice. If God is good, then why can he not correct the injustices of the world? Smerdyakov, the ugly, illegitimate perpetrator, is really the true face of Ivan, who is cultured and civilized on the surface, but discovers his true character throughout, and eventually goes mad. But the Russian liberals, the intellectuals who want to do away with the Tsar and with all paternal authority, even God's, are no less cruel, in their true face. As Thomas G. West puts it, "The crude and smirking Smerdyakov, consumed by hate, is the genuine expression of the liberal intelligentsia's revolt against the authority of the biological father, the father Tsar, the fathers of the Church, and God the Father."[36]

---

[36]"Sin of the Fathers," a book review of Joseph Frank: *Dostoevsky: The Mantle of the Prophet, 1871-1881*, vol 5 in the series on Fyodor Dostoevsky, Princeton: Princeton University Press, 2002, in *Claremont Review of Books* II/4, Fall, 2002, p. 29.

Dostoevsky did believe in God's justice. He was vehemently against patricide. He thought God was both good and powerful, though he struggled along with Ivan to see it clearly. Thus he could not accept the secular liberal dream of his time. He believed there must be a real Father, and that life made no sense without him. In *The Devils*, we see what happens to a small town when the liberals take over. Though leftist, they are cruel and willing to do anything at all to achieve their goals. They preach equality, but are capable of mass murder. They are in fact tyrants.

Dostoevsky was particularly clairvoyant about the future. His prophetic counterparts, Alexis de Tocqueville and Friedrich Nietzsche believed something quite different about the twentieth century. They thought that mankind would become bland, tame, soft, as sheep without a shepherd. For Tocqueville, this would become a bureaucratic despotism, a moderate, American-style democracy, founded on Christian religion. For Nietzsche, there would be the death of God, followed by the end of all human striving. The only remedy is to have tyranny, the superman who could pull us out of our torpor. If this occurred, perhaps evil would go away. Of course, Nietzsche hoped for a salvation through aesthetics, and was highly skeptical about the Christian doctrine of the atonement because it was "flattering" to humankind. So his vision was a strange mixture of recognizing raw power and yet hoping for the success of beauty.

But Dostoevsky saw it altogether differently. We don't need to find tyrants, he would predict. They are readily available in the race itself. If we give up on God, then anything can and will happen. After the death of God, some might still talk of equality and Enlightenment values, but the seething reality underneath would be the evil of the human heart. Who was right? Tocqueville? Nietzsche? An honest recall of Stalin, Hitler, Chairman Mao, Ho Chi Min, and Osama Bin Laden brings the answer. Dostoevsky saw it. His reasoning was solid: without faith in an atoning, justifying God, however difficult to believe at times, we are prone to cruelty. Patricide might be understandable, but it is wrong. Perhaps his modern day equivalent, Alexandr Solzhenitsyn, saw it clearly as well. He did not have Dostoevsky's nostalgia for the older regime. But he saw that without the courage to begin with God, anything can and does happen.

May we dare to be untimely prophets? May we be bold enough to declare the full council of God, whether it be convenient or popular, or not? Has the hour ever been more primed for preaching and exhibiting the full, vigorous affirmation of the classical biblical doctrine of justification? May we be so bold as to declare the greatness of God, his love, yes, but his holiness as well, and thus the need for justification based on the gospel of divine satisfaction? Unless our God be transcendent enough, unless he be holy and glorious enough, we will never appreciate the first and foremost reason for the atonement. Christ's death for our sins, and his resurrection for our justification: this is the gospel! For it is the only way God may remain just, and yet justify the ungodly. Further, unless we sense the true agony of the cross, but also the powerful victory of the resurrection, we will never understand how costly, and thus how unique is that atonement which leads to justification. Failing that, we will find hundreds of devilish justifications of our own. And we will never find rest, nor be at peace with God. Indeed, "We believe that in falling away from this foundation [of justification by the imputation to us of Christ's obedience], however slightly, we could not find rest elsewhere, but should always be troubled."

Covenant Faith

K. Scott Oliphint

The title of this chapter is meant to point to the fact that faith itself is, intrinsically, a human condition which issues forth in the context of our relationship to God. Because all of God's human creatures are covenantally qualified creatures – that is, we all are in a relationship to God – what we are, do, and become takes place *coram deo*; it takes place in the presence of, and in the context of, responsibility to God himself. For those who are covenantally in Adam, all that is done *coram deo* is condemnable (see, for example, Rom. 3:10-18). For those who are covenantally in Christ, all that is done *coram deo* is done in the context of our ultimate acceptance, precisely because we are in Christ (see, for example, Rom. 8:29-39). The point, however, is that man is, intrinsically and eternally, a covenant creature. This means that man is defined, essentially, in terms of his relationship to God.

In that context, therefore, we would like to set forth a view of "covenant faith." This covenant faith has two primary aspects – *original* faith and *saving, justifying* faith. Both of these aspects depend on the revelation of God, are directed toward that revelation, and "determine" God's attitude toward us.[1] So, while the first aspect of faith that we will discuss is not directly relevant to the biblical doctrine of justification, it *is* relevant to the faith that justifies. It is our hope, therefore, that a discussion of covenant faith will shed helpful light (1) on our "original faith" and thus our covenantal status as human beings before God and (2) on justifying faith.

[1] "Determine" God's attitude toward us, not in the sense of placing demands on God, but in the sense of evoking a certain action of God toward us as a response to the faith that we exercise.

Original Faith: A Universal Condition

As we will see below, much that is necessary for a biblical understanding of saving, justifying faith is readily available in the literature. We will highlight some of the main elements for such an understanding in our next section. Before looking specifically at *saving* and *justifying* faith, it seems there is one aspect of faith that is rarely discussed. This aspect of faith is that which provides for continuity (though there are significant *discontinuities* as well) between life in Adam and life in Christ. As such, it might best be labelled *original* faith. As we will see, covenant faith embraces both *saving* faith *and* (what is called) "*original*" faith. It is this non-saving, non-justifying "original" aspect of covenant faith that we would like to explain here, in order in the next section to show its relationship to saving, justifying faith.

Admittedly, the discussion that follows in this section has embedded within it a specifically apologetic concern. There is thought to be, generally, a divide between faith and reason such that faith has its exercise and application within a specific *religion*, while reason is reserved for that which is outside of a specific religious context. Putting the matter in its most general terms, there is thought to be a division, perhaps even a separation, between faith and reason. Without hoping even to scratch the surface of the age-old debate between faith and reason, we should be aware that in the vast majority of those debates, the context itself seems to be wide of the mark with respect to the proper setting for such a debate.

One example should suffice. Perhaps the most common, and commonly adapted, notion of the relationship of faith and reason comes from the quintessential Enlightenment philosopher, Immanuel Kant. In Kant's *Critique of Pure Reason*, he notes, "I have therefore found it necessary to deny knowledge in order to make room for faith."[2]

What might Kant mean by this? At least part of what he means is that those things that require faith – things, for Kant, that are consigned to the *noumena* – are things to which "pure reason" cannot apply. The very fact that they are "noumenal" requires that

[2]Immanuel Kant, *Critique of Pure Reason*, trans. Norman Kemp Smith (New York: St. Martin's Press, 1958), 29: "*Ich mußte also das Wissen aufheben, um zum Glauben Platz.*"

they be divorced from the categories and contexts that allow for pure knowledge itself. On this scheme – and we should not have to argue here of its vast and continuing influence – there is a divorce, or at least a radical separation, between that which pertains to knowledge and that which pertains to faith.

Whenever faith and reason are discussed, by and large (though not in every case), what is meant is that there are those things that we can know, things perhaps which are a result of science, or of evidence, or of some kind of reasoning process, and then there are those "other" things, things in which we must exercise faith. The exercise of faith, in this context, is difficult precisely to define, but it seems to mean something like the notion that we should instill in ourselves an attitude that, though contrary to reason, evidence or any kind of reasoning process, nevertheless gives us some kind of positive perspective in the midst of that toward which our faith is exercised.

This view, however, no matter how predominant, has a ring of inauthenticity to it. In a discussion of the differences and similarities between faith and reason, the Princetonian theologian B. B. Warfield critiques the common, Kantian, notions of the two:

> "Faith," "belief," it is said (e.g. by Kant), is conviction founded on evidence which is subjectively adequate. "Knowledge" is conviction founded on evidence which is objectively adequate ... Are all "beliefs," "faiths," specifically such, in their very nature inadequately established convictions; convictions, indeed – matters of which we feel sure – but of which we feel sure on inadequate grounds – grounds either consciously recognized by us as inadequate, or, if supposed by us to be adequate, yet really inadequate?[3]

Warfield is skeptical of the Kantian thesis, since it suggests a great divide between objectively adequate grounds, which would result in knowledge, and subjectively adequate grounds, which would result in faith. Warfield goes on to say:

---

[3]B. B. Warfield, "On Faith in Its Psychological Aspects," in *Biblical and Theological Studies*, B. B. Warfield (Philadelphia, Pennsylvania: Presbyterian and Reformed Publishing Co., 1952), 380-81.

> To believe on grounds of the inadequacy of which we are conscious, is on the face of it an impossibility. The moment we perceive the objective inadequacy of the grounds on which we pronounce the reality of anything, they become subjectively inadequate also. And so long as they appear to us subjectively adequate, the resulting conviction will be indistinguishable from "knowledge."[4]

Typically, then, faith is thought to be opposed to reason, in the sense that its exercise is in no way dependent on reason. This has had the deleterious effect of separating those who are "of faith" from those who are "of fact" in such a way that faith has been segmented off to the outer "religious" margins of society. But, as James says (though admittedly in a different context), "My brothers, these things ought not to be so" (James 3:10). It ought not to be the case that Christians allow a discussion of faith to proceed in such a way that it is divorced from knowledge, or science, or fact.

One way to begin to address such a problem is to recognize the universality of faith. What seems to have escaped the notice of most, and perhaps of most Christians, in this regard, is that faith is that which any and every exercise of reason presupposes, and on which all exercises of reason depend. One of the ablest and most helpful discussions of this aspect of faith, *with an important qualification that will be addressed below*, comes to us from Abraham Kuyper.

In his *Encyclopædie der Heilige Godgeleerdheid*,[5] Kuyper argues, rightly for the most part, that faith is a universal, human condition. He offers something of a transcendental argument, in that he seems to argue from the impossibility of the contrary. Or, to put it in the language of scholastic theology, he argues that faith is a universal *principium* from which *all* reasoning and demonstration proceed.[6]

---

[4]B. B. Warfield, "On Faith in Its Psychological Aspects," in *Biblical and Theological Studies*, B. B. Warfield (Philadelphia, Pennsylvania: Presbyterian and Reformed Publishing Co., 1952), 381.

[5]Abraham Kuyper, *Encyclopædie der Heilige Godgeleerdheid, 3 Vols.* (Amsterdam: J. A. Wormser, 1894). Part of Volume I and all of Volume II is translated into English in Abraham Kuyper, *Principles of Sacred Theology*, J. Hendrik De Vries, trans. (Grand Rapids, MI: Baker Book House, 1980). The material on faith is in Volume II.

[6]This idea that one must always have a non-demonstrable starting point is nothing new; it goes back at least to Aristotle. See, for example, Aristotle, *The Basic Works of Aristotle*, ed. Richard McKeon (New York: Random House,

There is no objection, therefore, to the use of the term *faith for that function of the soul* (ψυχή) by which it obtains certainty directly and immediately, without the aid of discursive demonstration. This places faith over against "demonstration;" but *not* of itself over against *knowing*.[7] That which we know, in a general sense, according to Kuyper, we know because we have faith. This faith involves our cleaving to something, holding fast to it, leaning upon and trusting it.[8]

Without moving too far afield from our topic, it should not escape our notice that Kuyper's notion of faith as that which supports knowledge, but which itself is not subject to demonstration or discursive reasoning, is a notion that has taken center stage in discussions epistemological in the last few decades. Beginning, for the most part, with the work of Alvin Plantinga, many philosophers have concluded that, due to the paucity of options available to epistemologists, there must be something deeply and inherently flawed about previous received epistemological traditions. Central to much of the received tradition is that one is allowed rationally to believe only that which can be evidentially supported, or supported by way of demonstration.[9] Plantinga, following (to some extent) Thomas Reid, has attempted to show how it can be that one can be rational and warranted in one's beliefs, and thus have knowledge, even in such cases where there is no evidential or demonstrative support.[10]

1968), Metaphysics, Book IV, in which he states, "For it is impossible that there should be demonstration of absolutely everything (there would be an infinite regress, so that there would still be no demonstration) ... "

[7]Kuyper, *Principles*, 128-29.

[8]Kuyper, *Principles*, 128.

[9]Plantinga's first concerted effort that began to question the standard understanding of rationality and knowledge was *God and Other Minds; a Study of the Rational Justification of Belief in God* (Ithaca, N.Y.: Cornell University Press, 1972). His initial position in that book, now modified and more developed, is set forth in his trilogy on warrant – *Warrant: The Current Debate* (New York, etc.: Oxford University Press, 1993); Alvin Plantinga, *Warrant and Proper Function* (New York, etc.: Oxford University Press, 1993); Alvin Plantinga, *Warranted Christian Belief* (New York, etc.: Oxford University Press, 2000).

[10]For a critical assessment of Plantinga's application of his epistemology to Christian belief, see K. Scott Oliphint, "Epistemology and Christian Belief," *Westminster Theological Journal* 63, no. 1 (Spring 2001): 151-82. For an attempt at

Kuyper is not following Reid, and for good reason. Rather, he is arguing that the application of faith is an inescapable human condition. It is, therefore, indispensable for human knowledge.

> But the indispensableness of faith goes much farther, and it may safely be said that with the so-called exact sciences there is no investigation, nor any conclusion conceivable except in so far as the observation in the investigation and the reasoning in the conclusion are grounded in faith.[11]

This point bears emphasis, especially with respect to a defense of Christianity. Perhaps an example would be helpful here. A group of university students met one evening to discuss the defense of Christianity. The argument given to them was that unless Christianity is true, there can be no way to justify, for example, the fact of an orderly universe. After the presentation, the speaker was met by one of the physics professors at the university. The professor approached the speaker, introduced himself as an atheist and then noted, in a moment of existential honesty, that there was no way he could justify his own profession on a daily basis, given that he had no way to account for the orderly universe that he had to presuppose every day. How then does one account for such a lack of justification? At minimum, the professor was acknowledging that he had simply accepted certain facts as facts, without reckoning with the incoherence of that acceptance vis-à-vis his own worldview (atheism). This is, in part, what Kuyper means by faith.[12] Properly used or misused, faith is and always will be a means of becoming firmly convinced of a thing, and of making this conviction the starting-point of conduct, while for this conviction no empirical or demonstrative proof is offered or found.[13]

---

a positive approach toward a Christian epistemology, see K. Scott Oliphint, *Reasons for Faith: Philosophy in the Service of Theology* (Phillipsburg, N. J.: Presbyterian and Reformed Publishing Company, 2006), Part 2, chs. 5-8.

[11]Kuyper, *Principles*, 131.

[12]There is more to the story, of course. It is not the case that all that the atheist needed to justify his profession was original faith. Rather, in his admission, he noted that there were certain things that he simply had to accept. This "acceptance" is a part of original faith. In order, further, to be able to account for the things accepted, one must have saving, justifying faith.

[13]Kuyper, *Principles*, 131.

But it is just at this point that Kuyper may have a problem. The problem seems to be that he tends toward a notion of faith that is, in and of itself, without content. His notion of faith is merely formal.[14] By "formal" Kuyper seems to indicate that faith *qua* faith is merely a human *capacity* into which is poured differing *content*.[15] This, however, can hardly be the case.

Think again of the physics professor mentioned above. Suppose he came to the conclusion that his problem was a lack of recognition of the faith that he was exercising as a physicist. What would that faith, then, *be*? At best it would be a subjective property which was meant to provide the foundation for that which is objective. In that sense, it would be no more helpful to the knowledge situation than was Descartes' *cogito ergo sum*. Granted that Descartes' starting point was supposed to be indubitable, it was, nevertheless, a subjective property that proved, by way of his own methodology, to be deficient for knowledge.[16] Thus, Descartes' rationalism led to skepticism.

But it is just *skepticism* that is the catalyst for Kuyper's discussion of faith, and which Kuyper wants to avoid; it is skepticism that motivates his discussion of formal faith in the first place. Void of content, however, it will not be possible to save Kuyper's formal faith from the fate of Descartes' disastrous dictum. One man's indubitable *cogito* is another man's formal faith. Each and every subjective property disintegrates with any attempt to pour objective content into it. Fortunately for Kuyper, the resolution to his own dilemma is found in the very tradition which Kuyper sought to follow.

In his brief critique of Kuyper with respect to apologetics, Cornelius Van Til argues, as we have said, that Kuyper's view of formal faith would itself lead to the very skepticism that Kuyper seeks to avoid. This is the case, we should remember, because the

---

[14]Kuyper, *Principles*, 125.

[15]This is further confirmed in Kuyper's notion that "The formal process of thought has *not* been attacked by sin, and for this reason palingenesis works no change in this mental task," Kuyper, *Principles*, 159.

[16]Thus, the "Cartesian circle" in which, in Descartes' *Meditations*, he argues from the trustworthiness of clear and distinct ideas, to the existence of God, which existence, then, is meant to be the foundation of the trustworthiness of clear and distinct ideas. From ideas to belief to the same ideas – one is never able to escape the subjective.

notion of formal faith as presented in Kuyper is a strictly *subjective* notion; it does not have an objective corollary that would allow, so to speak, a "bridge" from subject to object.[17]

The needed "bridge," however, is, as a matter of fact, the *content* of the faith that is universally had by us. The content of that faith, as it comes to expression by way of the *sensus divinitatis*, is the knowledge of God that all men have by virtue of their creation in the image of God. According to Van Til:

> All this [i.e. Kuyper's notion of "formal faith"] is at variance with what Kuyper, following Calvin, has taught with respect to the sense of deity. Again and again Kuyper has insisted that man always confronts God in every fact that he meets. There is no such thing as formal faith. To be sure, all men have faith. Unbelievers have faith as well as believers. But that is due to the fact that they too are creatures of God. Faith therefore always has content. It is against the content of faith as belief in God that man has become an unbeliever. As such he tries to suppress the content of his original faith.[18]

The "original faith" of which Van Til speaks here is the knowledge of God implanted in all human beings by virtue of our being created in God's image. Thus, as is the case with saving faith, "original faith" includes, and is not antithetical to, *knowledge*; it is knowledge of God. Further on, Van Til notes of Kuyper's view of formal faith:

> Then its content can take any form he wants it to have. Then its content is actually indeterminate. And thus there is no foundation for man's knowledge of himself or of the world at all. Identification of himself as the subject of knowledge is possible to man only in terms of the fact that in his very act of self-identification he identifies himself as the creature of God. If one allows that

[17]Despite current, postmodern, attempts to dismiss it, it is not an overstatement to say that *the* problem of epistemology remains to find an explanation for the connection that must obtain between subject and object. Kuyper thought his notion of faith *would* provide the necessary bridge: "Without faith you can never go from your *ego* to the *non-ego*; there is no other bridge to be constructed from the phenomenal to noumena; and scientifically all the results of observation hang in air," Kuyper, *Principles*, 131.

[18]Cornelius Van Til, *The Defense of the Faith* (Philadelphia: Presbyterian and Reformed Publishing Co., 1955), 385.

> identification of the human self as the subject of knowledge is possible without God's identifying himself to man as his Creator and judge in the same act, there is no basis for knowledge.[19]

The implications of this statement for epistemology are radical, vast and far-reaching, though Van Til does not pursue them here. The point he is making is one Calvin makes in the first statement of his *Institutes*, i.e. that knowledge of ourselves is coterminous with knowledge of God the Creator. There can be no such thing, therefore, as true knowledge of the self without at the same time being a knowledge of God the Creator. Kuyper believes this, and makes this point himself. What he seems not to realize is that the *content* of this faith that is universal is, in fact, the knowledge of the living and true God.

If we begin to think in these terms, then we should be able to see that knowledge, both in terms of that which is had by the unregenerate, as well as that which is had by the regenerate, can only be knowledge in the context of one's relationship to God. That is, *all* knowledge, is, first and foremost, *covenant* knowledge. It presupposes that one knows God and that the knowledge of God, as it is given in his revelation (both natural and special) provides the "connection" that is needed for knowledge in general. The "connection" is provided because the revelation of God gets through to us, both in its natural mode and its special mode, when it does, in such a way as to *be* knowledge.

Fundamental to the *sensus divinitatis*, therefore, is the fact that this knowledge of God, given that all people have it, and given that it is had by virtue of our being made in the image of God, means that it is a knowledge that is both *universal* and *immediate*. The fact that it is universal is a part of Paul's point in Romans 1:18ff. As Paul explains the condition of mankind in Adam, he notes that we all are without excuse by virtue of God's revelation in nature (v. 20).[20]

The "immediacy" of the knowledge of God that we all have does not mean that this knowledge is not mediated through

---

[19] Van Til, *The Defense of the Faith*, 385.

[20] Or is Romans 1:18ff. meant specifically for Gentiles? In any case, the point is that no one can escape God's judgment because he has made himself universally known to all.

anything. For surely it is mediated, as Paul says, "through the things that are made." Rather, it is immediate knowledge because it is not gained by way of inference. There is nothing that we do – no demonstration, no syllogism – that is the ground for the acquisition of this knowledge. It is, as our Christian forefathers would say, *cognitio insita*; it is *implanted* (or inserted) knowledge of God, that is given to us, through the things that are made, by God himself.

It is knowledge, therefore, that comes to us through the things that are made. It is knowledge that requires that the nature of the world be such that God is always and everywhere revealing himself through it, and that this revelation is not something that is resisted, or even resist*able*, by us, but is rather something that we do indeed receive, accept and thus *know*.

If it is the case, therefore, that all of us know God, and we know him by virtue of being created in his image (itself a metaphysical notion), then there is a universal, metaphysical ground for anything, and everything, else that we can and do know. Given that all of us begin our cognitive awareness with sure and certain knowledge (of God), all else that we know will have that knowledge as its anchor. All else that we know, if we know it, will be consistent with that knowledge. It would be impossible for us to know something, therefore, that in any way contradicted or contravened that essential, fundamental, metaphysical knowledge of God. Since God is *the* immediate, metaphysical fact *par excellence*, anything else that comes to us as knowledge will have that knowledge as its Archimedean point.

What might this mean for non-inferential knowledge or faith? We know immediately, when we do, because of the nature of the world and its constituent parts. That is, knowledge is inextricably linked with the way things really are. As we have seen, we first and foremost know God. And, as Paul says, we know him "through the things that are made." Entailed, therefore, in our knowledge of God is a knowledge of the thing, or things, made through which we know God. It is not the case, we should note, that Paul is arguing that knowledge of God comes through the things that are made, without at the same time knowing the thing itself. Thus, it seems, the way in which we begin with respect to knowledge is by being confronted with the reality of God's creation, in all its splendor, and, because of sin's effects, in all its ugliness as well.

Now that which is indubitably, relentlessly, clearly, and comprehensively "present" to and in all of us is the revelation of God. We know him by virtue of his presence.[21] But we also know the things made, the things of this world – including, at least, other people, the world around us, the testimony of others, our own memories – because, as present to us, these things are the conduits through which God himself is revealed and known.

It is not the case, therefore, that "common-sense" beliefs, or non-inferential beliefs (or knowledge) must be universal in order to be justified. Rather, what *is* universal is the knowledge of God. And it is universally the case that this knowledge comes through all that God has made, including we ourselves. It will be expected, therefore, that, included in being the image of God is the fact that we are, as image, covenantally bound to the rest of creation such that our knowledge of it and interaction with it is an essential aspect of who we are as image. The "connection," therefore, between our own knowledge and the world as known is made by God himself, who always and everywhere is revealing himself to his covenant creatures (creatures made in his image) such that, in knowing what he has made, we know him. What is "common sense" to us all, therefore, is not necessarily a specific set of non-inferred beliefs, but rather the knowledge of God which all of us have, and the concomitant knowledge of the created world which brings that knowledge of God to us.

Faith, then, at its core, is a surrender. We surrender ourselves to that which is presented to us in order to begin to know what it is.[22] In his clear and helpful "reconnoitering" of Van Til's epistemology, Hendrik Stoker notes:

> Man ... *meets* knowingly the knowable by *trusting* it. In order to know, *faith* in the knowable ... is an indispensable necessity ... Faith, too, is an act of knowing, without which man, the knower, does not really meet the knowable. Faith is, in a specific sense,

---

[21]Note the covenantal implications that are central to this kind of knowledge.

[22]Without attempting to detail the complexities of this "surrendering," we should note that it is, in some of its aspects, voluntary, and in some, involuntary.

> a surrender; only by surrendering himself to the knowable, i.e. by accepting it, can man responsibly fulfill his task of knowing.[23]

At least one of the implications of this for epistemology is this: just as in theology there must be a *principium essendi* (an essential principle) that grounds our *principium cognoscendi* (cognitive principle), i.e. just as the existence and character of God grounds our knowledge of him, since that knowledge presupposes his existence and character (as given to us in Scripture), so also in epistemology generally. That is, with respect to knowledge in general, it must be the case that the existence and character of God ground our knowledge of him *as given to all through all that is made*. All knowledge, therefore, if it *is* knowledge, presupposes, first, the knowledge of God (the universal *principium cognoscendi)*, and, second, his existence (the universal *principium essendi)*.

As Kuyper argues, therefore, original faith is that which moves us to receive, to lean upon, to trust that which is given. And that which is given is, fundamentally, the revelation of God. Covenant faith, then, in its original form, is that which binds us to the revelation of God such that we receive it and accept it, in order, from that faith, to know the world and its characteristics.

Saving, Justifying Faith: Continuity and Discontinuity

It remains for us to explain the more specific element of saving, justifying faith, and to show (some of) its connections to the above. So, our topic for this section is, in the main, saving faith. Specifically, our topic is the faith that justifies.

What we must remember first (though we will not detail it here) and what remains a crucial focus of our entire discussion is expressed well by Calvin:

> ... we must understand that as long as Christ remains outside of us, and we are separated from him, all that he has suffered and done for the salvation of the human race remains useless and of no value for us. Therefore, to share with us what he has received from the Father, he had to become ours and to dwell within us.[24]

[23]Hendrik G. Stoker, "Reconnoitering the Theory of Knowledge of Professor Dr. Cornelius Van Til," in *Jerusalem and Athens: Critical Discussions on the Philosophy and Apologetics of Cornelius Van Til*, ed. E. R. Geehan (New Jersey: Presbyterian and Reformed Publishing Co., 1977), 28.

This is, it should be noted, a striking statement. In a discussion concerned with the way in which we receive the grace of Christ, Calvin wants initially to make plain in the starkest possible language that the very work of Christ itself is empty and void of any application whatsoever "as long as Christ remains outside of us." Calvin continues:

> Therefore, to share with us what he has received from the Father, he had to become ours and to dwell within us. For this reason, he is called "our Head" (Eph. 4:15), and "the first-born among many brethren" (Rom. 8:29). We also, in turn, are said to be "engrafted into him" (Rom. 11:17), and to "put on Christ" (Gal. 3:27); for, as I have said, all that he possesses is nothing to us until we grow into one body with him. *It is true that we obtain this by faith.*[25]

It would be difficult to argue, given Calvin's emphasis at the beginning of this, third, book of the *Institutes* that the notion of union with Christ was not central in his own soteriology.[26] Calvin is here setting the theological stage for the other, crucial and necessary, elements of salvation that he will discuss in the rest of the book. Whatever else he has to say, therefore, (and there is much else that he wants to say) he says with this foundation firmly set in place.

But just what is this faith that unites us to Christ? To use categories familiar in theological discussions of this sort, it is a *saving* faith and a *justifying* faith. These two "faiths" are not different, but are two, and two primary, aspects of the one faith that is ours in Christ.[27] There are, of course, other aspects to

---

[24]John Calvin, *Institutes of the Christian Religion*, vol. 20 of *Library of Christian Classics*, ed. John T. McNeill, trans. Ford Lewis Battles, Library of Christian Classics (London: SCM Press, 1960), III.1.

[25]Calvin, *Institutes*, III.1, emphasis mine.

[26]For a current historical treatment of Calvin's notion of union with Christ as it relates to justification and sanctification, see Mark A. Garcia, "Life in Christ: The Function of Union with Christ in the *Unio-Duplex Gratia* Structure of Calvin's Soteriology with Special Reference to the Relationship of Justification and Sanctification in Sixteenth-Century Context" (Edinburgh: University of Edinburgh, 2004).

[27]Note John Owen on the identity of saving and justifying faith: "Saving faith and justifying faith, in any believer, are one and the same; and the adjuncts of saving and justifying are but external denominations, from its distinct operations

this faith, but these two are typically highlighted, and for good reason. In Scripture's use of the words associated with faith, it connects faith primarily with salvation and with justification. In proceeding from the more general to the specific, we hope to establish a continuity with respect to faith in its various exercises that would provide an apologetic context for biblical faith itself.

In order to note the relationship of original faith to saving faith, it should be helpful to note the way in which the *Westminster Confession of Faith* describes justifying faith:

> **WCF 11:1** Those whom God effectually calleth He also freely justifieth; not by infusing righteousness into them, but by pardoning their sins, and by accounting and accepting their persons as righteous: not for anything wrought in them, or done by them, but for Christ's sake alone: nor by imputing faith itself, *the act of believing*, or any other evangelical obedience, to them as their righteousness; but by imputing the obedience and satisfaction of Christ unto them, they *receiving and resting on Him* and His righteousness, by faith: which faith they have *not of themselves*; it is *the gift of God*.

Note well first of all, that faith is an "act." It is not, as the Confession makes plain, a work wrought by us; but it *is* an act. It is something *we* do, not something God does. Notice also that faith is that which "receives and rests on" Christ. Saving, justifying faith, therefore, is, we could say, a "state of mind," or an "attitude," or perhaps a "posture." But it is also, we should add, a state of mind not unfamiliar to those who do not have saving faith. According to Warfield:

> Religious belief may differ from other belief only in the nature of its objects; religious beliefs are beliefs which have religious conceptions as their content. ... What is prominent in this state of mind is precisely trust. ... Thus in its higher applications the element of trust which is present in faith in all its applications, grows more and more prominent until it finishes by becoming

---

and effects. But yet saving faith does act in a peculiar manner, and is of peculiar use in justification, such as it is not of under any other consideration whatever." John Owen, *The Works of John Owen*, ed. W. H. Gould (Edinburgh: The Banner of Truth Trust, 1977), V p .122.

> well-nigh the entire connotation of the term; and "to believe in," "to have faith in" comes to mean simply "entrust yourself to."[28]

So, let us call this general attitude of "accepting and receiving" the "pistic posture" ("pistic" from the Greek word for faith, πίστίς). The "pistic posture" is a state of mind in which one accepts and receives the revelation of God – in its various modes, forms and contexts.

If we think of the original aspect of this covenant faith, we can readily see that, in that faith, there is a "receiving and accepting" of the revelation of God that is essentially, initially at least, *in*voluntary. As we noted above (and without working through the exegetical details of Romans 1:18f.) it is clear that Paul is describing a universal situation.[29] The situation is such, for all who are made in God's image, that we inevitably and necessarily have the knowledge of God. We have this knowledge because God makes it evident to us through the entirety of his creation. This knowledge includes God's power and divinity (v. 20), but it also includes a knowledge of God's requirements (v. 31; 2:14-16).

Original faith, therefore, has the revelation of God as its object, and it includes our "receiving and accepting" that revelation in such a way that we are, by virtue of being his image, those who know the God who made us and who rules over us. The "pistic posture" of all men is such that they receive and accept the revelation of God.

As Paul goes on to note, however, this knowledge that God gives to us through creation is not something, since the fall, that we love and acknowledge. Rather, in Adam, we seek to hold this knowledge down (κατεχόντων). That suppression is evidenced in our complete lack of thankfulness (v. 21), in our exchanging the knowledge that we have for a lie (v. 25), and for images and idols of creation (v. 23). In other words, though it is true that we receive and accept the revelation of God involuntarily, in that we do not choose to do so, nor

---

[28]B. B. Warfield, "Psychological," 392-94.

[29]Paul's language of that which is revealed "from heaven," and "since the creation of the world," such that men are 'without excuse' serves to underscore the fact that what he is describing is not something peculiar to some but not other individuals. Rather, he is describing certain aspects of the image of God in it post-fall function. Thus, it applies to all of humanity.

do we have the knowledge of God by way of our own processes of inference, it is, nevertheless, the case that, once received and accepted, we work tirelessly and persistently to keep this knowledge of God from rising to the surface of our consciousness.[30] We perpetually, so to speak, swim against the current of God's revelation to us.

It seems fair to say, therefore, that the continuity between original faith and saving, justifying faith is found in two ways. Both aspects of this covenant faith have God's revelation as their object. In original faith it is God's general revelation that is its object; in saving faith it is God's special revelation. But just as the two modes of revelation have always, even before the fall, been mutually given and dependent,[31] so also are the two modes of covenant faith – original and saving – meant to be together. To have original faith without saving faith is as "unnatural" and confused as having general revelation without special revelation. Such is the case only because of the fall.

What is lacking, therefore, in original faith is, in some ways, that which makes saving faith saving, i.e. *resting*. In the reformed conception of saving, justifying faith, three primary elements were distinguished. The first was knowledge (*notitia*). This vitally important aspect should not be understated or underestimated as a necessary aspect of faith (original and saving). Faith, then, as we said above, is in no way opposed to knowledge, but must necessarily include it. The second aspect was assent (*assensus*). In the application of assent, we deem to be true that which we claim to know. The application of assent moves us from mere propositional knowledge – for example, "I know *that* the Scriptures teach that Christ died on the cross," – to the affirmation that such knowledge is true – "I know *that* the Scriptures teach that Christ died on the cross, and this teaching is true."

The final aspect, however, is the core of saving, justifying faith. It is the aspect of trust (*fiducia*). John Murray explains the relationship between these aspects this way:

---

[30]In other words, *once received and accepted* involuntarily, the knowledge and truth that we have is *voluntarily*, in differing ways and stages, perverted, subverted and undermined until and unless we are restored and regenerated in Christ.

[31]For a helpful analysis of the relationship of special and general revelation, see Cornelius Van Til, "Nature and Scripture," in *The Infallible Word: A Symposium by the Members of the Faculty of Westminster Theological Seminary* (Phillipsburg, N. J.: Presbyterian and Reformed Publishing Co., 1978), 263-301.

> Saving faith is not simply assent to propositions of truth respecting Christ, and defining the person that he is, nor simply assent to a proposition respecting his sufficiency to meet and satisfy our deepest needs. Faith must rise to trust, and to trust that consists in entrustment to him. In faith there is the engagement of person to person in the inner movement of the whole man to receive and rest upon Christ alone for salvation. It means the abandonment of confidence in our own or any human resources in a total act of self-commitment to Christ. As *assensus* is cognition passed into conviction, so *fiducia* is conviction passed into confidence. Herein resides the unique and distinguishing character of this faith. It is abandonment to Christ against all issues, the deepest and most ultimate.[32]

Justified By Faith

With respect to this justifying faith, therefore, we should be clear that it is an *act* – it is exercised, not by God but by us – and that it is the *cause* of our justification. The history of theology with respect to justification, especially since the Reformation, is replete with discussions of just *how* or in what way faith is the cause of our justification. We cannot hope to bring that debate to an end here. A couple of points, however, should be noted.

First of all, the construction of *believing into* (πιστεύω with εἰς) is unique to the New Testament[33] and is central to the "in Christ"

---

[32]John Murray, *Collected Writings of John Murray* (Edinburgh: Banner of Truth Trust, 1977), II.258.

[33]The New Testament construction has its conceptual equivalent in the Old Testament as well. According to Warfield:

> "In the Greek of the Septuagint πιστεύειν takes its place as the regular rendering of הֶאֱמִין and is very rarely set aside in favour of another word expressing trust (Prov. xxvi.25 πείθεσθαι). In a few cases, however it is strengthened by composition with a preposition (Deut. i.32, Judg. xi.20, 2 Chron. xx.20, cf. Sir. i.15, ii.10 etc., I Macc. i.30, vii.16, etc., ἐμπιστεύειν; Mic. vii.5, καταπιστεύειν); and in a few others it is construed with prepositions (ἔν τινι, Jer. xii.6, Ps. lxxvii.22, Dan. vi.23, 1 Sam. xxvii.12, 2 Chron. xx.20, Mic. vii.5, Sir xxxv.21; ἐπὶ τινα, Isa. xxvii.16 (?), III Macc. ii.7; ἐπὶ τινι, Wis. xii.2; εἰς τινα, Sir. xxxvii.31; κατά τινα, Job iv.18, xv.15, xxiv.22).
>
> It was by being thus made the vehicle for expressing the high religious faith of the Old Testament that the word was prepared for the New Testament. (Benjamin Breckinridge Warfield, "Faith," in *Biblical and*

function of faith.[34] It is central to the "in Christ" function of faith, not because the function of faith is to unite us to Christ – that is the work of the Spirit in regeneration – but rather because it is the grace gift of faith, as exercised, that motivates us to affirm such a union. The "pistic posture" relative to saving faith is that we acknowledge that which we have come to see, i.e. that Christ has saved me from my sins.

Second, in much of the current literature, the notion of faith (πίστις) as it is often used in Scripture, has been thought to refer, not to *our* faith in which we are justified, but rather the faithfulness of Christ.[35] Put simply, one of the reasons for arguing this way is due to the fact that many want to show the Reformation doctrine of justification by faith alone to be an invention of Luther rather than a proper reading of Paul.[36] If the "faith" language of Paul is referring primarily to Christ's acts rather than to ours, then it would be necessary for us to understand Paul's notion of justification in a far different light than what the Reformation has given to us.

> *Theological Studies*, ed. Samuel G. Craig [Philadelphia, Pa.: Presbyterian and Reformed Publishing, 1968], 432-33.)

[34]Note Warfield again:

> The special New Testament construction, however, is that with εἰς, which occurs some forty-nine times, about four-fifths of which are Johannine and the remainder more or less Pauline. The object towards which faith is thus said to be reliantly directed is in one unique instance 'the witness which God hath witnessed concerning his Son' (1 John v.10), where we may well believe that "belief in the truth of the witness, that is, the Incarnate Son Himself." Elsewhere the object believed on, in this construction, is always a person, and that very rarely God ... and most commonly Christ ... (Benjamin Breckinridge Warfield, "Faith," 438).

For examples of this construction in the New Testament, see Matt. 18:6; Mark 9:42; John 1:12; 3:16, 18, 36; 6:29, 35, 40; 7:38f; 9:35f; 11:25f, 48; 12:36, 44, 46; 14:1, 12; 16:9; Acts 10:43; 20:20; 20:21; Rom. 4:9; 5:2; 1 John 5:10, 13.

[35]This argument has been (to my mind) definitively decimated by Moisés Silva in "Faith Versus Works of Law in Galatians," in *Justification and Variegated Nomism: Volume 2 – The Paradoxes of Paul*, eds. D. A. Carson, Peter T. O'Brien, and Mark A. Seifrid (Grand Rapids, Michigan: Baker Academic, 2004), 217-48. Readers interested in the current debates of the so-called "New Perspective" should consult the entirety of Silva's article. The material below will follow that article.

[36]Admittedly, this grossly oversimplifies the matter, but it doesn't thereby misconstrue it.

A couple of points should suffice here to call this "New Perspective" understanding of faith seriously into question.[37] First of all, the sheer weight of concern in the New Testament on the act of faith significantly tilts the balance toward the traditional understanding of faith as our act, not Christ's. According to Silva, " ... the constitutive writings of Christianity (including the Pauline Corpus) give so much prominence to human faith, that their authors would surely expect readers to understand πιστίς in this sense unless contextual factors excluded such a meaning ... "[38] That is, the notion of faith, *our* faith, is so prominent in Scripture generally that one would expect it to be the predominant use in each case individually until or unless the context determined otherwise (as it does, for example, in Romans 3:3 where τὴν πίστιν του Θεου refers, not to faith in God, but to God's faithfulness). Second, the apostle Paul, who, in terms of the inspired authors of Scripture, is the most prolific exponent of the doctrine of justification, repeatedly uses the verb πιστεύω in such a way that must refer to *our* faith, not to Christ's faithfulness.[39]

> In conspicuous contrast, we cannot find even one *unambiguous* reference to the πιστίς that belongs to Christ. To put it differently but more concretely, Paul never uses πιστιεύω with χριστός as its subject, nor does he explicitly use πιστός as a predicate of χριστός. The point here ... is not that Paul *was incapable* of using such language or that the concepts behind such language were foreign to him. All that needs to be recognized is that those linguistic combinations, to say the least, *were not characteristic of the apostle.*[40]

The biblical references, therefore, to the act of faith as *our* act – an act which brings about the declaration from God of our righteousness in Christ – have not been convincingly redefined in such a way that would necessitate in us a new understanding of our justification.[41] Finally, and perhaps most importantly, we

---

[37]Owing, here, solely to Silva's article mentioned above.

[38]Silva, "Faith Versus Works," 230-31.

[39]Silva, "Faith Versus Works," 231.

[40]Silva, "Faith Versus Works," 231-32.

[41]There are other arguments set forth by Silva that seem to be incontrovertible, two of which are worth mentioning here. (1) The notion that the genitival

must be careful to note that the biblical, reformed understanding of justification by faith alone is never meant to communicate that it is faith that saves us. Here it may be helpful to think of the notion of justification in light of the standard, Aristotelian framework of causality.[42]

The philosophers postulate four kinds of causes to be observed in the outworking of things. If we look at these, however, we will find that, as far as the establishment of our salvation is concerned, none of them has anything to do with works.

> For Scripture everywhere proclaims that the efficient cause of our obtaining eternal life is the mercy of the Heavenly Father and his freely given love toward us. Surely the material cause is Christ, with his obedience, through which he acquired righteousness for us. What shall we say is the formal or instrumental cause but faith?[43]

The central and important point to be made here is that it is not our faith that saves us, neither is it faith in Christ that saves us. Rather, it is *Christ* that saves us, and he does so through the instrumentality of faith, and of faith alone. This is not to say, as historic reformed theology has sought to make clear, that the faith that saves us is *itself* alone. It is to say that the faith that is not alone, is the alone instrument through which our justification comes to us.[44] Neither is faith the ground of our justification. Calvin's causal framework above notes Christ's obedience as the material cause of our justification, since it is Christ's righteousness (in his perfect life and obedient death) that is imputed to our account.

---

construction of πίστις Ἰησοῦ Χριστοῦ is meant to be objective rather than subjective is linguistically untenable. The artificiality of the labels themselves leaves a position based on such labels weak at best. (2) The way in which many of the church fathers, whose native language was Greek, understood such a construction leaves little question as to how the genitival construction is to be understood. See Silva, "Faith Versus Works," 230f.

[42]For an analysis of Calvin's use of causal language with reference to faith and justification, see Paul Helm, *John Calvin's Ideas* (Oxford: Oxford University Press, 2004), 399ff.

[43]Calvin, *Institutes*, III.14.17.

[44]Negatively, *any* view that proposes to add another instrumentality to justification than that of faith, or which proposes another ground of justification than the work of Christ is outside of the context of classic reformed theology.

The "matter" of our justification, therefore, is in Christ and his work. The faith that we are given, and which we exercise, is the "tool" that God ordains in order to credit Christ's righteousness to our account. We are counted righteous, therefore, (according to Calvin's notion of the causal framework) *because* we have faith, *because* Christ obeyed his Father, in life and in death, *because* of the Father's mercy toward us, freely given to us.

What, then, does saving, justifying faith *do*? In bringing together that which is original (though perverted after the fall) in us, in uniting the revelation of God (general and special), it is the channel through which we, for the first time, are able rightly to know (Col. 3:10). Not only so, it is the channel through which we are made righteous. And, inextricably linked to these, it is the channel by which we are declared to be, and thus are becoming, holy (Eph. 4:24).

Saving, justifying faith does not, therefore, supplement original faith, as if original faith is half the puzzle, to which is added saving faith to complete it. Rather, it subdues and transforms original faith in such a way that, because God has given us life, brings about the necessary response of obedience – an obedience that, in faith, bows to the revelation of God in the world, in his word, and in his Word.

All men are creatures of faith. The faith that we all have has been given to us, it is a gift, and it has as its object the clear revelation of God. Saving, justifying faith is, after the fall, sanctified covenant faith, because of which we acknowledge the God who is revealed, as we come to rest in his Son.

The Pastoral Implications of the Doctrine of Justification

J. Stafford Carson

The task of the preacher and pastor is not only to explain and expound the great doctrines of the Christian faith, but to repeatedly put himself in the shoes of his listeners by asking the question, "So what?" A sensitive and effective preacher will imagine a recalcitrant listener sitting in the back pew during a worship service asking what the cash value is of the doctrine or truth that the preacher is expounding. If the preacher is to be faithful to his task, then he must give clear, practical application. It is the same for theologians. If theology is the application of the Word of God to all of life, then in any theological debate or discussion, we need to be able to flesh out the practical implications of what we profess to believe. The pastoral implications and applications of the doctrine of justification are numerous and crucial to the life and well-being of the church. Theologians know that the doctrine of justification addresses questions which lie at the very heart of the Christian life, and that is why it is critical that such doctrines are not only stated clearly and accurately, but that their pastoral implications are also spelt out.

The doctrine of justification has obvious application in evangelism, preaching, and the personal counseling of individuals. As John Owen put it, justification is "the proper relief of the conscience of a sinner pressed and perplexed with a sense of the guilt of sin. For justification is the way and means whereby such a person doth obtain acceptance before God, with a right and title unto a heavenly inheritance."[1] It is critical that every pastor has a clear and unambiguous response to those who, under a stricken

[1]John Owen, *The Works of John Owen*, ed. W. H. Gould (Edinburgh: The Banner of Truth Trust, 1977), V.7.

conscience, seek pardon from their sin and the assurance that they are right with God. The answer and antidote is found in the exposition and explanation of the substitutionary atonement of Christ, and how that the benefits of the atonement are received by faith and are based on grace. It is the doctrine of justification by faith which brings the light, the relief, and the acceptance that sinners crave and need. It results in people being "accepted and forgiven".

The substitutionary atonement is the very heart of the gospel and the basis on which we can provide an answer to the problems of guilt, brokenness, bondage, and alienation from God. Central to all our evangelism and the nurture of new believers in the faith is the explanation of what God was doing in Christ as he took our place and died our death on the cross. John Stott says that the doctrine of substitution affirms not only a fact, namely that God in Christ substituted himself for us, but its necessity, namely that there was no other way by which God's holy love could be satisfied and rebellious human beings could be saved.[2] Professor Cranfield's comments on Romans 3:25 are a wonderfully concise statement of orthodox belief:

> God, because in his mercy he willed to forgive sinful men, and, being truly merciful, willed to forgive them righteously, that is, without in any way condoning their sin, purposed to direct against his own self in the person of his Son the full weight of that righteous wrath which they deserved.[3]

True spiritual life is apparent in the lives of men and women only when they see that the problem of their sin and alienation before a holy God is answered in the work of Jesus Christ. The darkness of sin, and the sadness caused by the consequences of sin, begins to dissolve when people step out into the light of fellowship with God and his Son. So it is critical that pastors, preachers, elders, and all those who have responsibility for the cure of souls are able to simply and clearly explain the doctrine of justification in terms of its origin, its ground, and its means. In the current atmosphere of debate that surrounds the doctrine, we must be sure that we

---

[2]John R. W. Stott, *The Cross of Christ* (Leicester: IVP, 1986), 161.

[3]C. E. B. Cranfield, *The Epistle to the Romans*, International Critical Commentary (Edinburgh: T&T Clark, 1975–79), 217.

understand and state what the Scriptures teach in the matter of our salvation.

However it would appear that as preachers we have not done a good job in what we might think was a central part of the content of our preaching and teaching ministry. It seems that many Christian people in the evangelical and Reformed churches have not grasped the personal implications of the doctrine of justification by faith. Richard Lovelace made the point some years ago:

> Only a fraction of the present body of professing Christians are solidly appropriating the justifying work of Christ in their lives. Many have so light an apprehension of God's holiness and of the extent and guilt of their sin that consciously they see little need for justification, although below the surface of their lives they are deeply guilt-ridden and insecure. Many others have a theoretical commitment to this doctrine, but in their day-to-day existence they rely on their sanctification for justification, in the Augustinian manner, drawing their assurance of acceptance with God from their sincerity, their past experience of conversion, their recent religious performance or the relative infrequency of their conscious, wilful disobedience. Few know enough to start each day with a thoroughgoing stand upon Luther's platform: *you are accepted*, looking outward in faith and claiming the wholly alien righteousness of Christ as the only ground for acceptance, relaxing in that quality of trust which will produce increasing sanctification as faith is active in love and gratitude.[4]

This devastating analysis actually comes as no surprise to many pastors who deal with people regularly. So many Christians seem to understand how that the righteousness of Christ imputed to them gives them a standing before God, but revert quickly to a works-based salvation as they live their Christian lives. Without a clear grasp of the doctrine of justification by faith through grace, and its distinction from the work of sanctification, they easily fall into one of two errors. On the one hand, they focus almost exclusively on their own performance and because they manage to get a few things right in their lives, they develop a Pharisee-like

[4]Richard F. Lovelace, *Dynamics of Spiritual Renewal* (Downers Grove: IVP, 1979), 101.

pride. They begin to despise others who have not achieved the same degree of spiritual success in their lives or who have not kept to the spiritual disciplines with the same degree of rigor as they have done. Inevitably a sense of spiritual superiority develops, and with it comes all the attendant tensions and stresses that pride produces within a body of Christians.

The opposite error is a feeling of guilt. Some people understand clearly that the Christian life is a call to obedience, service, and devotion but they have not managed the same level of performance in these areas as others. Alternatively, they are aware of the sins of their heart and they are struggling to deal with such issues as impurity, impatience, anger, or a judgmental attitude, but have known only limited success in applying the gospel to their own hearts. The result is a sense of failure and guilt, and the belief that God, as a result, is displeased and unhappy with them. Because of their failure to deal with sin, they don't really believe that they deserve his blessing and favor.

As soon as we focus on our achievements and our performance, we forget the meaning of grace and the blessings which God's grace brings to those who deserve only his wrath. Adopting the mindset of the Pharisee, Christian believers unconsciously think that they have earned God's blessing through what they do. On the other hand, guilty believers are convinced that they have forfeited God's favor and blessing because of their lack of discipline or because of their disobedience. What the two groups have in common is that they have forgotten, if they ever knew, the basic truth of the doctrine of justification by faith based on grace.

It is only by carefully and clearly explaining the truth that sinners are accepted and forgiven by God because of the obedience and death of Jesus Christ, and not by our own works or efforts, that people in our churches and fellowships will be able to avoid the twin dangers of pride and guilt. This explanation of the gospel of grace must permeate all our preaching and counseling and must be the basis on which we call on people to live their Christian lives. They must be told regularly that the only way we can relate to God is through the blood and righteousness of Jesus Christ. It is only Christ's blood, not our good efforts, which will open the way into God's presence and will cleanse us from a guilty conscience (Heb. 10:19-21). That means that we have no need to try to deceive ourselves about our sin or to think that we can somehow pretend that it does not exist or that it is not important. The fact that God promises to forgive sins means that we can call on people to be open and transparent before God, no matter how horrible or nasty their sins are. At the cross, Christ dealt with sin perfectly and completely, and because of him sinners do not have to rationalize or excuse their sinful thoughts, attitudes, and behaviors.

Some may object that this emphasis on grace may encourage licentiousness or apathy. In view of the fact that they will be forgiven, what incentive is there for people to struggle with sinful patterns in their lives? Will not those who are spiritually lethargic and lacking in commitment to Christ's work be reinforced in their abuse of God's grace? Will they not say, "God loves me unconditionally; it doesn't matter how I live"?

It was precisely this abuse of grace that Paul anticipated and dealt with in Romans 6 and Galatians 5. Such a misunderstanding of the doctrine should not deprive us of its essential truth and should actually be an encouragement to be more fulsome and direct in our application. As for those who struggle with guilt, the antidote is certainly not additional guilt resulting from making further demands and laying more burdens on their backs. Their position will be relieved as they realize that forgiveness is theirs in Christ, and the outcome will be a strengthening, not a weakening, of their desire to honor Christ in their lives.

> What is it, then, that sparks the desire in our hearts to lead a disciplined, godly life? It is the joy of knowing that our sins are forgiven, that no matter how much we've stumbled and fallen today, God does not count our sins against us (Rom. 4:8)[5]

In Jack Millar's words, we should preach the gospel to ourselves everyday, and should teach those under our care to do the same. By doing that, says Jerry Bridges, we will address both the self-righteous Pharisee and the guilt-laden sinner who dwells in all our hearts. The application of the gospel of grace to our lives enables us to renounce any confidence in our own goodness as a means of meriting God's blessing on our lives.

---

[5]Jerry Bridges, *The Discipline of Grace* (Colorado Springs: NavPress, 1994), 24.

But there are associated blessings that come to those who live in the atmosphere of the gospel of grace. The sunshine of God's grace ripens some sweet-tasting fruits in the gardens of our lives. Our hearts are filled with joy in the knowledge that our sins are forgiven because of Christ and we are genuinely filled with hope in the knowledge that we are accepted by God and that his benediction will rest upon us at the last, not because of our own efforts, but because we are united to Christ. We can then live our lives courageously, confidently, and freely.

It is, however, in this area of assurance of salvation, that critics of the so-called New Perspective on Paul find it wanting. The conclusion which they come to is that the believer's assurance is grounded essentially in his covenant faithfulness. Such an understanding of assurance differs radically from the traditional Reformed affirmations, that, accepting the necessity of the Christian's obedience, still grounds the believer's assurance in God's promises of salvation to all who believe in Christ. Those promises arise not only from who Jesus is, but also from what he has accomplished.

> Justification without works as a basis is no cheap forgiveness; it is grounded in the full payment of the ransom that justice claimed, the perfect settlement by the sinner's representative and substitute of all legal debts.[6]

There is, however, some necessary foundation-laying that needs to be completed so that the superstructure of the gospel of grace will stand firm. The biblical emphasis is that the glory and majesty of what God has done for sinners in Christ can only be seen against the background of who God is and who we are before him. Conviction of sin and the need for the grace of Christ become real when the truth about God and about us is clearly stated. Isaiah's vision of the holiness and power of God had a major impact on his own understanding of who he was.

---

[6]Henri Blocher, "Justification of the Ungodly (*Sola Fide*): Theological Reflections," in *Justification and Variegated Nomism: Volume 2 – The Paradoxes of Paul*, D. A. Carson, Peter T. O'Brien, and Mark A. Seifrid (Grand Rapids, Michigan: Baker Academic, 2004), 497.

> "Woe to me!" I cried. "I am ruined! For I am a man of unclean lips and I live among a people of unclean lips, and my eyes have seen the King, the Lord Almighty" (Isa. 6:5).

In the tradition that stretches back to the Reformation, preachers must place the doctrine of God and the doctrine of human depravity clearly on the agenda. The holiness of God demands that we sinners become holy if we are to be received by God and made right with him. But that goal of personal righteousness and holiness is beyond us. All our best efforts fall short of God's standards. When we try to analyze the cause of our problem we discover that it lies deep in our own hearts. So the task of preaching and counseling is to present the glory and majesty of God in all its magnificent brightness and luminosity, and to expose the darkness of sin that has enveloped and filled our human hearts, and our spiritual inability.

Professor John Murray observed that in the early 1950s certain key doctrines were missing from contemporary preaching. Among them was what he called "the ministry of judgment" or the proclamation of the demands and sanctions of the law of God.

> When the proclamation of God's law is neglected, the significance of the gospel is correspondingly reduced in our presentation and in the apprehension of men. The gospel is the gospel of salvation, and salvation is, first of all, salvation from sin in its guilt, defilement and power.[7]

The doctrine of justification through faith in Christ cannot be presented in a vacuum. It only makes sense in the context of a deep conviction of sin, and we will never know that we are sinners until the righteousness and holiness of God and his law are clearly expounded. With that truth established, faith in Christ is not just one option which is open to us; it is the only option which we have. Before the awesome majesty and holiness of God, and his relentless opposition to sin, the gospel of a righteousness received by faith alone takes on a new meaning and relevance. Christ is the only answer to our desperate situation, and he becomes ours only through faith and repentance.

---

[7]John Murray, "Some Necessary Emphases in Preaching," in *Collected Writings of John Murray*, vol. 2 (Carlisle, Pennsylvania: The Banner of Truth Trust, 1976), 144.

In applying the truths about God's holiness and human sinfulness, preachers must not sidestep the issue of human guilt before God. When guilt is pushed into the background, and the sense of guilt becomes extinct, then Murray says "the grand article of the gospel becomes correspondingly meaningless"[8] That "grand article" is, of course, the doctrine of justification by grace through faith. Murray observed that at the time of his writing in the early 1950s there was an amazing and distressing paucity of the agonizing question which is the basic religious question: How can a person be right with God? And there was, likewise, a paucity of the exultant joy which comes with the realization that a complete and irrevocable justification is possible by free grace through faith. But the root from which all this impoverishment originates is the absence in our thinking and in our preaching of divine judgment upon human sin. Without that emphasis on the judgment of God against sin and condemnation, the basis is not laid which gives meaning and appeal to the gospel of free and sovereign grace.

Over fifty years later, we could say that the presenting problems of sinners seeking spiritual counsel and comfort is not primarily a sense of guilt before God. People express their experience of sin and the brokenness that it brings in a variety of ways; in terms of alienation, insignificance, loneliness, and emptiness. Some are aware of the pointlessness of so much of their activity while others feel cut off from God. Few understand that their sin renders them guilty and accountable to God. They do not see that they are inveterate idolaters and that because their hearts are "idol factories" they continuously displace God from his rightful place by worshiping their idols. But until there is a deep awareness that one is personally accountable to a perfectly holy God and guilty of rebelling against his authority, there is no appreciation of the necessity and the wonder of what God has done for sinners in Christ.

Busy pastors may think that the insistence on a strictly forensic meaning for justification is a secondary issue. It is possible for people to be saved and justified without a clear notion of the accurate theological sense of the word and of the doctrine. Yet we need to remember that the Reformers worked strenuously to

---

[8]Murray, "Some Necessary Emphases in Preaching," 144.

maintain the forensic understanding because they understood that if any compromise were accepted there was much to be lost. The demands of God's law are absolute. Whatever righteousness that is achieved in us will fall far short of the standards of divine holiness. If our case before God's judgment seat depends in any way on our righteousness we are condemned. Even if we were able to reach a stage where we were obedient to the law, we still have not solved the problem of our past sins and we would be unable to repay that debt. The Bible says that guilt remains when sins have not been atoned for (Rom. 3:25; Heb. 9:15). Only if an alien righteousness is credited to us can we be accepted by God. In other words, only if justification is forensic can we have real hope of salvation.

Those of us who have lived through the second half of the twentieth century have been helped in our preaching and evangelism by the renewed availability of the theological writings and sermons of the Puritans. In reading them, we discovered that the great Reformation themes of the holiness of God and the depth of human depravity were articulated by them in vigorous and heart-searching preaching. The Reformers and the Puritans have taught us that fallen human nature was touched in every area by the deforming presence of original sin. They preached the clear message that even though human beings have the will to do as they please, without the renewing work of the Holy Spirit, they are incapable of seeking and serving God. The best efforts of people are built on the foundation of unbelief, and they have a natural distaste for the rule of God in their lives. They are enemies of God, ready on a daily basis to re-enact the crucifixion as they oppose God's will and his ways in the world. In the light of this analysis, "what is remarkable is not the intensity of God's wrath against sin, but the magnitude of his patience and compassion in sparing and redeeming those who are his enemies."[9] It is in preaching these themes that we set the background which magnifies the beauty and the splendor of justification by grace.

But we need to be renewed in that commitment with regard to our preaching particularly. Many of us began our ministries as we came to communities and congregations where, in the past,

---

[9]Lovelace, *Dynamics of Spiritual Renewal*, 87.

it seems that ministers had been paid by their congregations to protect them from the real God of the Bible by preaching about a God who was only winsome and kind and loving. We knew that, if we were to be faithful preachers of the gospel, what was needed was a full-orbed presentation of the doctrines that centered on a holy and sovereign God who called on sinners to repent and to seek the mercy of God which was found in Christ the Redeemer.

It is in the preaching of the cross that we make the link between God's wrath against sin and the depth of his love and mercy for sinners. Certainly God's mercy, grace, and love must be front and center in our presentation of the doctrine of justification, but those attributes are not credible unless they are set in the context of God's power, sovereignty, holiness, and righteousness. The tension between God's holiness and love is not irreconcilable. God is not at odds with himself. At the cross his justice and love are revealed simultaneously so that Calvin writes of God that "in a marvellous and divine way he loved us even when he hated us".[10] It was P.T. Forsyth who used the expression "the holy love of God" and who wrote that Christianity

> ...is concerned with God's holiness before all else, which issues to man as love ... This starting-point of the supreme holiness of God's love, rather than its pity, sympathy or affection, is the watershed between the Gospel and ... theological liberalism ... My point of departure is that Christ's first concern and revelation was not simply the forgiving love of God, but the holiness of such love.

Again, he wrote,

> If we spoke less about God's love and more about his holiness, more about his judgement, we should say much more when we did speak of his love.[11]

As we review the situation today we believe that we need to be renewed in that emphasis, for not only the doctrine of justification by faith, but also the doctrines of God and man, are being radically

---

[10]*John Calvin, Institutes of the Christian Religion*, vol. 20 of *Library of Christian Classics*, ed. John T. McNeill, trans. Ford Lewis Battles, Library of Christian Classics (London: SCM Press, 1960), II.16.4; *cf.* II.17.2

[11]P. T. Forsyth, *The Cruciality of the Cross* (Hodder & Stoughton, 1909), 5, 6, 73.

re-evaluated. In his book, *Becoming Conversant with the Emerging Church*,[12] Don Carson discusses significant departures from the orthodox understanding of the atonement and justification by faith which he believes are apparent in the writings of Brian McLaren and Steve Chalke, leaders in the emerging church in the US and the UK.

McLaren's fictional character, Neo, he claims, is not very good at handling such biblical themes as idolatry and the wrath of God. For him, the theme of judgment is not tied to the cross in any biblically faithful way. Although McLaren assures us that salvation is by grace and through faith, God's final judgment, however, does not depend on Christ's work on the cross but on "how well individuals have lived up to God's hopes and dreams for our world and for life in it."[13] Carson reckons that to cast the final judgment in this way does not sound like "good news" at all, but simply "like a popularisation of one strand of the so-called 'new perspective' on Paul".[14] Carson's conclusion is that in *The Story We Find Ourselves In*, McLaren almost entirely loses sight of the gospel.

In a similar way, Steve Chalke's *The Lost Message of Jesus*[15] defines God in terms of one controlling attribute: love. Chalke claims that the Bible never makes assertions about God's anger, power or judgment independently of his love. While theologians have spent centuries arguing over the doctrine of original sin, they have missed a startling point: Jesus believed in original goodness. Chalke misses the point that God's declaration with regard to the goodness of creation was made prior to the fall into sin, as well as the explicit statements of Jesus that people are evil and that every sinful behavior has its origin in the human heart (Matt. 7:11; Mark 7:21-23). By failing to do justice to the biblical view of God and sinful humanity, Chalke proceeds to take the next step and states that any notion of penal substitution is offensive and a contradiction of his understanding of God as a god of love.

---

[12]D. A. Carson, *Becoming Conversant With the Emergent Church* (Grand Rapids: Zondervan, 2005).

[13]Brian D. McLaren, *The Story We Find Ourselves In: Further Adventures of a New Kind of Christian* (San Francisco: Jossey-Bass, 2003), 166-67.

[14]Carson, *Becoming Conversant With the Emergent Church*, 181.

[15]*The Lost Message of Jesus* (Grand Rapids: Zondervan, 2003).

> The fact is that the cross isn't a form of cosmic child abuse – a vengeful Father, punishing his Son for an offence he has not even committed. Understandably, both people inside and outside of the Church have found this twisted version of events morally dubious and a huge barrier to faith. Deeper than that, however, is that such a concept stands in total contradiction to the statement "God is love". If the cross is a personal act of violence perpetrated by God towards humankind but borne by his Son, then it makes a mockery of Jesus' own teaching to love your enemies and to refuse to repay evil with evil.[16]

This representation of the cross of Christ is a far cry from traditional orthodox understandings of the atonement and the death of Christ. Evangelical and Reformed theologians have described how the Father and Son concurred in the plan of salvation that centers on the cross. They describe how the Son is determined to do his Father's will, and how that both the Father and the Son suffer in the accomplishment of redemption. They certainly do not understand it in the terms used by such writers as McLaren and Chalke when they use the phrase "a form of cosmic child abuse". Carson concludes, "I have to say, as kindly but as forcefully as I can, that to my mind, if words mean anything, both McLaren and Chalke have largely abandoned the gospel."[17]

It becomes clear that if we are going to be preachers who clearly expound the doctrine of justification by faith, then we must place that doctrine in its proper biblical context. We must also recognize that there are "other gospels" that are being preached and believed, and it is crucial that our presentation of the gospel is controlled by the emphases and contours of Scripture itself. It seems easy to become confused. Anything other than a fulsomely biblical formulation will not be good news for sinners who need to be right with God, and who need to know that they are accepted and forgiven.

But the benefits of a fully rounded explanation of the doctrine of justification by faith do not end with the spiritual benefits that accrue to believers. This doctrine renews us psychologically, corporately, and socially.

---

[16]Chalke, *The Lost Message of Jesus*, 182-83.

[17]Carson, *Becoming Conversant With the Emergent Church*, 186.

The root cause of many problems that people face is the fact that some other idol or god other than Christ is ruling in the heart. Despair, guilt, fear, and anger all come to the degree that something or someone other than Christ is our savior. Functionally, these alternate gods are expected to deliver the security, significance and identity that only Christ can bring. So worshiping and serving one's career, or family, or charitable works, or romantic relationship rather than God ultimately causes a range of psychological imbalances and difficulties.

These problems are addressed and corrected when the gospel of justification is clearly understood. Our relationship to God is transformed from one that is based on fear and our personal performance in order to gain acceptance, to one that is based on love and a desire to please and honor the Lord. In terms of our own identity, we no longer take our cue from what others think about us, or even what we think about ourselves. The critical matter is how God views us in Christ (1 Cor. 4:3, 4). We no longer suffer from an inferiority complex since we know that we are received and embraced by Christ. Neither do we suffer from a superiority complex since we know that we are only sinners saved by grace. By appropriating this doctrine of justification we come to have a unique combination of boldness and humility, and that itself is a sign that we have understood and are living by this doctrine.

This gospel of grace also cuts across the other commonly accepted ways of dealing with problems. A moralistic approach to personal sin says that we must repent and begin to live right. A relativistic approach says that we must just accept ourselves as we are. But the gospel says we are worshiping the wrong god, and only when Christ becomes central in our affections will we be changed and transformed.

Thus pastors must be able to describe the deep and indissoluble connection between embracing the doctrine of justification and the experience of sanctification. It seems all too easy to transform the biblical doctrine of justification by allowing some aberrant forms of the doctrine to go unchecked. Lovelace warns about cheap grace, legalism, and moralism.[18]

---

[18]Lovelace, *Dynamics of Spiritual Renewal*, chapter 4.

By simply divorcing justification and sanctification we can easily arrive at what Bonhoeffer called "cheap grace". The New Testament makes it clear that the attempt to be justified through faith in Christ without a commitment to sanctification is impossible. Since the ground of our justification is our union with Christ, we cannot appropriate his perfect righteousness to cover our sin without also receiving his resurrection power to transform our lives. This attempt to be in union with half a Christ, as the Puritans described it, is precisely the abuse of grace that Paul addresses in Romans 6. The ground of sanctification is our union with Christ in his death and resurrection. Thus, faith and repentance are not separable, so that the condition of justification is not faith plus repentance, but repentant faith. That is why pastors, preachers, and counselors must be careful to show that while James does not add works and human effort to the means of justification, he does make the point that living faith which produces works is true faith.

The attempt to claim justification without a commitment to sanctification can result in all kinds of sinful behavior patterns, and especially what Lovelace identifies as "compulsive egocentric drives which aggravate the flesh instead of mortifying it." Many pastors will instinctively smile inwardly as they recognize personalities that are living evidence of his assertion that "the Protestant disease of cheap grace can produce some of the most selfish and contentious leaders and lay people on earth, more difficult to bear in a state of grace than they would be in a state of nature."[19]

Yet in making this connection between justification and sanctification, we must also be exceedingly careful not to confuse the two categories. Professor Murray has a helpful analogy which explains clearly the difference. It is the difference between the act of a judge and the act of a surgeon. A judge gives a verdict regarding our judicial status. A surgeon, when he removes an internal cancer, does something in us. "The purity of the gospel is bound up with the recognition of this distinction", says Murray. "If justification is confused with regeneration or sanctification, then the door is opened for the perversion of the gospel at its

---

[19]Lovelace, *Dynamics of Spiritual Renewal*, 103-04.

centre."[20] He correctly maintained that justification is still the article by which the church stands or falls.

In addition to cheap grace, we must also avoid on the other hand the danger of legalism. The Puritans and pietists who were eager to guard against the danger of cheap grace were sometimes led to propose an unhealthy and destructive legalism in the area of the spiritual disciplines. By stressing the necessity of testing one's life by the inspection of works or by searching for the internal witness of the Spirit, they actually diverted attention from the central importance of relying on the work of Christ for assurance. Most pastors recognize that legalism can hide itself very well under the guise of pious language. Believing the right doctrines, reading the right books, practicing the right disciplines and involvement with the right ministries can all be used to foster a sense of pride and self-satisfaction. The evils of the society in which we live with its immorality, dishonesty, greed, and violence, and the fact that they can distance themselves from such gross sin, results in people feeling rather good about themselves. The Pharisee in the parable who did not go home justified still managed to offer a prayer of thanks to God! (Luke 18:11).

Believers need to see that they are still guilty of a range of sins which we might consider more refined sins, and which may pass under the radar of the legalism which defines acceptable behavior within many church fellowships, but which still attract the anger and wrath of God. Our irritability, our critical spirit, our censoriousness, our gossiping, our resentment, and our bitterness are sins which God regards as serious. Our best works cannot earn us favor with God; they are just filthy rags. So rather than focusing on our own performance, whether it seems good or bad to us, we look to the grace of Christ which is God's provision for our sin. We trust in the righteousness of Christ from the first day of our Christian walk to the last.

We must also avoid moralism. So much pious advice proffered from our pulpits and in personal counsel is unrelated to Christ and his grace. And since it ignores Christ it often results in either guilt or an awareness of sin on the one hand, or what Paul Tripp calls "fruit-stapling"[21] on the other, reproducing a virtue that is built

---

[20]John Murray, *Redemption Accomplished and Applied* (Edinburgh: Banner of Truth Trust, 1961), 121.

purely on personal will-power without a change of heart. Ministry which brings about real change in people's lives makes clear that the problem of sin is rooted deeply in the human heart and that every victory over that sin is won through faith in Christ, in appropriating our union with Christ, and in relying on the power of the Holy Spirit.

One final area where the doctrine of justification has major implications is with regard to our corporate identity as the people of God within the fellowship of the church. In the gospel of grace, Christians become a new people of God, united to Christ and to each other. Since the doctrine of justification both humbles us, and at the same time assures us that we are loved and accepted by God, we are free from both envy and pride, from both a sense of inferiority and superiority. Our sense of worth is not dependent on receiving approval from others nor through exercising controlling power over others. As a result of understanding who we are in Christ, we can relate to one another with love and compassion. We are also free, when it is appropriate, to confront one another and to speak the truth in love.

More than this, the gospel removes all pride that we might have in our cultures, or in our racial identity, or even in our gender. We do not trust in any of these identities; we trust in Christ alone. In Galatians 3:28 Paul says, "There is neither Jew nor Greek, slave nor free, male nor female, for you are all one in Christ Jesus." The three pairs of opposites which Paul lists in this text describe the three basic fault-lines that run through humanity: ethnicity, economic capacity, and sexuality. Each of these three spheres has been corrupted by sin and as a result they have created wide and deep divisions in our world. But all those who have become children of God through faith in Jesus Christ, those who are no longer under the supervision of the law but have been justified by faith, have been liberated from these identity indicators. Even though the big walls of division like ethnicity, money, and gender remain in place in our world, there is a new standard and a new way of living for those who belong to the kingdom of grace.

The gospel of God's grace has created a new humanity, a community of what Harvie Conn calls "institutionalised righteousness".

---

[21]Paul David Tripp, *Instruments in the Redeemer's Hands* (Phillipsburg: Presbyterian and Reformed Publishing Co., 2002), 63.

> The shape of the church and its calling in the city as "firstfruits" is the shape of the present, proleptic beginning of the end. It is an institution that has identified by faith the coming of the kingdom of God in Christ. In his redeeming work, it has seen the "eruption of an overwhelming and just power" that will, with his return, reconstitute human societies as the single society of the divine warrior through the agency of his triumphant Son.[22]

This new community will only exist to the degree that the gospel is understood and people are taught to live out its implications in their relationship to God and to one another. Many members of our churches are insecure in their relationship to Christ so that they are not free to cut loose from cultural support. It is only when the grace of God in Christ is made real to them, that they are accepted by God, not because of their achievements or their spirituality, but because God has accounted to them the perfect righteousness of Christ. Rather than focusing on the adequacy of their own obedience, they need to focus their attention on Christ. Rather than beginning each day depending on their feelings or their recent performance, they need to be taught to rest in the love of God and the sacrifice of Christ on their behalf. Without that focus, people will be discouraged or apathetic or self-righteous or proud. "Much that we have interpreted as a defect of sanctification in church people is really an outgrowth of their loss of bearing with respect to justification."[23]

If our churches are going to be renewed and become what God has called them to be, then individual members of the church must be taught to build their lives on the foundation of the truth that they are justified before God by faith, not on the basis of their own performance, but by claiming the righteousness of Christ as the only ground for acceptance. That means that they must see clearly the holiness of God, the depth of their sin, and the sufficiency of the atoning sacrifice of Christ. It is this doctrine of justification by faith through grace which must be embraced, not just at the beginning of the Christian life, but every day we live.

---

[22]Harvie M. Conn, *A Clarified Vision for Urban Mission* (Grand Rapids: Zondervan, 1987), 146-47.

[23]*Lovelace, Dynamics of Spiritual Renewal*, 211.

Bibliography[1]

Alexander Finlayson

The purpose of this bibliography is to bring together the key works that have been consulted by the contributors to this volume so that the interested reader may pursue them for further study. The bibliography includes both scholarly and more popular approaches and the reader will find representative works from various periods of church history and from differing theological perspectives. While the main focus of this bibliography is works on justification, the reader will also find exegetical works and works on historical theology, apologetics, ethics, and philosophy.

Almyer, G. E. *The Interregnum: The Quest for Settlement*. London: Macmillan Publishing, 1972

Aristotle. *The Basic Works of Aristotle*. Edited by Richard McKeon. New York: Random House, 1968.

Backus, Irena. *Reformation Readings of the Apocalypse; Geneva, Zurich, and Wittenberg*. Oxford: Oxford University Press, 2000.

Baillie, Robert. *The Letters and Journals of Robert Baillie*. Edited by David Laing. Edinburgh: Robert Ogle, 1841.

Ball, Bryan W. *A Great Expectation: Eschatological Thought in English Protestantism to 1660*. Leiden: Brill Academic Publishers, 1975.

Barker, William S. *Puritan Profiles: 54 Influential Puritans at the Time When the Westminster Confession Was Written*. Fearn, Scotland: Mentor/Christian Focus Publications, 1996.

Barnes, Robin B. *Prophecy and Gnosis: Apocalypticism in the Wake of the Lutheran Reformation*. Stanford: Stanford University Press, 1988.

Baur, Ferdinand Christian. *Der Gegensatz Des Katholicismus und Protestantismus Nach Den Principien und Hauptdogmen der Beiden Lehrbegriffe*. Tubingen: O. Zeller, 1834.

Baxter, Richard. *Aphorismes of Justification: With Their Explication Annexed*. London, 1649.

------. *Richard Baxter's Confession of His Faith*. London, 1655.
Bavinck, Herman. *Our Reasonable Faith*. Grand Rapids, Mich.,: W. B. Eerdmans Publishing Co., 1956.
Benrigge, John. *Christ Above All Exalted as in Justification So in Sanctification*. London, 1645.
Bente, Friedrich. *Historical Introductions to the Book of Concord*. St. Louis: Concordia Publishing House, 1965.
Berkhof, Louis. *The History of Christian Doctrines*. Grand Rapids, Michigan: Baker Book House, 1975.
Billington, James H. *Fire in the Minds of Men*, New York: Basic Books, 1980
Blocher, Henri. "Justification of the Ungodly (*Sola Fide*): Theological Reflections." In *Justification and Variegated Nomism: Volume 2 - The Paradoxes of Paul*, D. A. Carson, Peter T. O'Brien, and Mark A. Seifrid, 465-500. Grand Rapids, Michigan: Baker Academic, 2004.
Boersma, Hans. *A Hot Pepper Corn: Richard Baxter's Doctrine of Justification in Its Seventeenth-Century Context of Controversy*. Zoetermeer: Boekencentrum, 1993.
Bosher, Robert S. *The Making of the Restoration Settlement: The Influence of the Laudians, 1649–1662*. London: Dacre Press, 1951.
Bozeman, Theodore Dwight. *The Precisionist Strain: Disciplinary Religion & Antinomian Backlash in Purtanism to 1638*. Chapel Hill: University of North Carolina Press, 2004.
Bridges, Jerry. *The Discipline of Grace*. Colorado Springs: NavPress, 1994.
Bussman, Klaus, and Hans Schilling, eds. *1648: War and Peace in Europe*. Münster and Osnabrück: Westfälische Landesmuseum für Kunst und Kulturgeschichte, 1998.
Calvin, John. *Calvin's Commentaries*. Grand Rapids, Michigan: Baker Book House, 1979.
-----. *Institutes of the Christian Religion*. Vol. 20 of *Library of Christian Classics*. Edited by John T. McNeill. Translated by Ford Lewis Battles. Library of Christian Classics. London: SCM Press, 1960.
Carson, D. A. *Becoming Conversant With the Emergent Church*. Grand Rapids: Zondervan, 2005.
Chalke, Steve. *The Lost Message of Jesus*. Grand Rapids: Zondervan, 2003.
Chemnitz, Martin. *Examination of the Council of Trent*. Edited by Fred Kramer. St. Louis, Missouri: Concordia Publishing House, 1971.
Cheynell, Francis. *The Rise, Growth, and Danger of Socinianisme*. London, 1643.
Christianson, Paul. *Reformers in Babylon: English Apocalyptic Visions From the Reformation to The Eve of the Civil War*. Toronto: University of Toronto Press, 1978.
Como, David R. *Blown by the Spirit: Puritanism and the Emergence of an Antinomian Underground in Pre-Civil War England*. Stanford: Stanford University Press, 2004.

------. "Puritans, Predestination and the Construction of 'Orthodoxy' in Early Seventeenth Century England." *In Conformity and Orthodoxy in the English Church, c. 1560–1642*. Editors P. Lake and M. Questier. 64–87. Woodbridge: Boydell Press, 2000.

Como, David R., and Peter Lake. "Puritans, Antinomians and Laudians in Caroline London: The Strange Case of Peter Shaw and Its Contexts." *Journal of Ecclesiastical History* 50, no. 4 (October 1999): 684–715.

Conn, Harvie M. *A Clarified Vision for Urban Mission*. Grand Rapids: Zondervan, 1987.

Cranfield, C. E. B. *The Epistle to the Romans*. International Critical Commentary. Edinburgh: T&T Clark, 1975-79.

Crisp, Tobias. *Christ Alone Exalted*. London, 1643.

Cunningham, William. *Historical Theology*. London: Banner of Truth Trust, 1960.

Dickson, David. *An Exposition of All St Pauls Epistles*. London, 1659.

------. *The Summe of Saving Knowledge*. Edinburgh, 1671.

Diodati, Giovanni. *Pious and Learned Annotations Upon the Whole Bible*. London, 1648.

Downame, George. *A Treatise of Justification*. London, 1634.

Dunn, James D. G., and Alan M. Suggate. *A Fresh Look at the Old Doctrine of Justifica-tion by Faith*. Cumbria: Paternoster Press, 1993.

Eaton, John. *The Discovery of the Most Dangerous Dead Faith*. London, 1642.

------. *The Honey-Combe of Free Justification by Christ Alone*. London, 1642.

Fee, Gordon D. *The First Epistle to the Corinthians*. Grand Rapids: Eerdmans, 1987.

Fincham, Kenneth, ed. *The Early Stuart Church, 1603–1642*. Stanford: Stanford University Press, 1993.

Firth, Katherine R. *The Apocalyptic Tradition in Reformation Britain, 1530–1643*. Oxford: Oxford University Press, 1979.

Forsyth, P. T. *The Cruciality of the Cross*. Hodder & Stoughton, 1909.

Gaffin Jr., Richard B., "Biblical Theology and the Westminster Standards." In *The Practical Calvinist*, edited by Peter A. Lillback. Fearn: Mentor/ Christian Focus, 2002.

-----. *By Faith, Not By Sight: Paul and the Order of Salvation*. Milton Keynes: Paternoster Press, 2006.

-----. "Paul the Theologian". *Westminster Theological Journal* 62 (2000).

-----. *Resurrection and Redemption*. Phillipsburg, New Jersey: Presbyterian and Reformed Publishing Co., 1987.

Garcia, Mark A. "Life in Christ: The Function of Union with Christ in the *Unio-Duplex Gratia* Sctructure of Calvin's Soteriology with Special Reference to the Relationship of Justification and Sanctification in Sixteenth-Century Context." Edinburgh: University of Edinburgh, 2004.

Gardiner, S. R. *The First Two Stuarts and the Puritan Revolution*. London: Long-mans, Green & Co., 1876.

Garlington, Don B. *Faith, Obedience, and Perseverance: Aspects of Paul's Letter to the Romans*. Tübingen: J.C.B. Mohr, 1994.

Gataker, Thomas. *An Antidote Against Errour, Concerning Justification;*. London, 1670.

------. *Antinomianism Discovered and Confuted: And Free-Grace As It is Helf Forth in Gods Word*. London, 1652.

Geree, Stephen. *The Doctrine of the Antinomians by Evidence of Gods Truth Plainely Confuted*. London, 1644.

Gillespie, Patrick. *The Ark of the Covenant Opened*. London, 1677.

Gouge, William. *A Learned and Very Useful Commentary on the Whole Epistle to the Hebrewes*. London, 1655.

Griffin Jr., Martin I. J. *Latitudinarianism in the Seventeenth Century Church of England*. Leiden: Brill Academic Press, 1992.

Guinness, Os. *Prophetic Untimeliness: A Challenge to the Idol of Relevance*, Grand Rapids: Baker/Hourglass, 2003

Hammond, Henry. *A Paraphrase, and Annotations Upon All the Books of the New Testament, Breifly Explaining All the Difficult Places Thereof*. London, 1659.

Hampson, Daphne. *Christ Contradictions: The Structure of Lutheran and Catholic Thought*. Cambridge: Cambridge University Press, 2001.

Helm, Paul. *John Calvin's Ideas*. Oxford: Oxford University Press, 2004.

Hill, Christopher. *Society and Puritanism in Pre-Revolutionary England*. London: Secker and Warburg, 1964.

Hotson, Howard B. *Johann Heinrich Alsted 1588–1638: Between Renaissance, Reformation, And the Universal Reform*. Oxford: Oxford University Press, 2000.

------. *Paradise Postponed: Johann Heinrich Alsted and the Birth of Calvinist Millenarianism*. Dordrecht: Kluwer Academic Press, 2001.

Hubert, Henri and Marcel Mauss. *Sacrifice: Its Nature and Function*. Translated by W. D. Halls. Chicago: University of Chicago Press, 1964.

Hughes, Seán F. "*The Problem of 'Calvinism': English Theologies of Predestination c. 1580–1630.*" *In Belief and Practice in Reformation England: A Tribute to Patrick Collinson By His Students*, eds S. Waduba and C. Litzenberger. 229–49. Aldershot: Ashgate, 1998.

Hutton, Sarah. "Thomas Jackson, Oxford Platonist and William Twisse, Aristotelian." *Journal of the History of Ideas* 29 (1978): 635–52.

Irigaray, Luce: *An Ethics of Sexual Difference*, translated by Gillian C. Gill. Ithaca: Cornell University Press, 1993.

Jones, Serene. *Calvin and the Rhetoric of Piety*, Louisville: Westminster/John Knox Press, 2005.

Jordan, James B. "Merit Versus Maturity." In *The Federal Vision*, eds Steve Wilkins and Garner Duane. Monroe: Athanasius Press, 2004.

Jue, Jeffrey K. *Heaven Upon Earth: Joseph Mede (1586–1638) and the Legacy of Millenarianism.* Dordrecht: Springer, 2006.

Justinian. *The Institutes of Justinian.* 7th. Translated by Thomas Collett Sandars. London: Longmans, Green, 1941.

Kant, Immanuel. *Critique of Pure Reason.* Translated by Norman Kemp Smith. New York: St. Martin's Press, 1958.

Kirk, James R. Daniel. "The Sufficiency of the Cross." *Scottish Bulletin of Evangelical Theology* (2006), 36–64.

Kline, Meredith G. *Kingdom Prologue: Genesis Foundations for a Covenantal Worldview.* Overland Park: Two Age Press, 2000.

Knight, George. *The Pastoral Epistles.* Grand Rapids: Eerdmans, 1992.

Kuyper, Abraham. *Encyclopædie der Heilige Godgeleerdheid, 3 Vols.* Amsterdam: J. A. Wormser, 1894.

------. *Principles of Sacred Theology.* J. Hendrik De Vries, trans.. Grand Rapids, MI: Baker Book House, 1980.

Lake, Peter. *The Boxer's Revenge: 'Orthodoxy,' 'Heterodoxy,' and the Politics of the Parish in Early Stuart London.* Stanford: Stanford University Press, 2001.

Leigh, Edward. *A Systeme or Body of Divinity.* London, 1657.

Lillback, Peter. *The Binding of God: Calvin's Role in the Development of Covenant Theology.* Grand Rapids, Michigan: Baker Book House, 2001.

Lim, Paul C. -H. *In Pursuit of Purity, Unity and Liberty: Richard Baxter's Puritan Ecclesiology in Its Seventeenth-Century Context.* Leiden: Brill, 2004.

Loofs, Friedrich. "Die Rechfertigung Nach Den Lutherschen Gedanken in Den Bekenntnisschriften Des Konkordienbuches." *Theologische Studien und Kritiken* 94 (1922); 307–82.

Lovelace, Richard F. *Dynamics of Spiritual Renewal.* Downers Grove: IVP, 1979.

Lusk, Rich. "A Response to 'The Biblical Plan of Salvation'." In *The Auburn Avenue Theology, Pros and Cons: Debating the Federal Vision*, edited by E. Calvin Beisner. Fort Lauderdale: Knox Theological Seminary, 2004.

Luther, Martin. *Luther's Works.* Editors, Helmut T. Lehmann and Jaroslav Jan Pelikan. St. Louis, Philadelphia: Concordia Publishing House Fortress Press, 1955. V.

------. *Martin Luther, Selections from His Writings.* Edited by John Dillenberger. Garden City, N.Y.: Doubleday, 1961. Xxxiii, 526 p.

------. *Selected Writings of Martin Luther.* Edited by Theodore G. Tappert. Philadelphia: Fortress Press, 1967.

Luther, Martin, and Desiderius Erasmus. *Luther and Erasmus: Free Will and Salvation.* Translated by E. Gordon Rupp and Philip S. Watson. Philadelphia: Westminster Press, 1969.

McGrath, Alister E. *Iustitia Dei: A History of the Christian Doctrine of Justification.* Cambridge: Cambridge University Press, 2005.

McLaren, Brian D. *The Story We Find Ourselves In: Further Adventures of a New Kind of Christian.* San Francisco: Jossey-Bass, 2003.

Mattes, Mark C. *The Role of Justification in Contemporary Theology*, Grand Rapids: Eerdmans, 2004

Mede, Joseph. *The Apostasy of the Latter Times.* London, 1641.

------. This Mysterious Book of the Revelation of Saint John. In *The Key to the Revelation, Joseph Mede. London, 1643.*

------. *The Works of the Pious and Profoundly-Learned Joseph Mede.* London, 1677.

Melanchthon, Philipp. *Loci Communes Theologici.* Ed and trans Wilhelm Pauck. Westminster, 1969.

Melanchthon, Philipp, Jean Calvin, Ulrich Zwingli, and Karl Gottlieb Bretschneider. *Corpus Reformatorum.* Halis Saxonum: Schwetschke, 1911.

Milton, Anthony. *Catholic Reformed: The Roman and Protestant Churches in English Protestant Thought, 1600–1640.* Cambridge: Cambridge University Press, 1995.

Mitchell, Alex F., and John Struthers, eds. *Minutes of the Sessions of the Westminster Assembly of Divines.* Edinburgh, 1874, reprinted 1991.

Morrill, John. "The Religious Context of the English Civil War." *Transactions of the Royal Historical Society* 34 (1984): 155–78.

Mounce, William. *Pastoral Epistles.* Nashville: Thomas Nelson Publishers, 2005.

Müeller, John Theodore. *Christian Dogmatics.* St. Louis, Missouri: Concordia, 1934.

Muller, Richard A. *After Calvin: Studies in the Development of a Theological Tradition.* Oxford: Oxford University Press, 2003.

------. *Dictionary of Latin and Greek Theological Terms: Drawn Principally from Protestant Scholastic Theology.* Grand Rapids, Michigan: Baker Book House, 1985.

------. *Prolegomena to Theology.* Vol. One of *Post-Reformation Reformed Dogmatics : The Rise and Development of Reformed Orthodoxy, Ca. 1520 to Ca. 1725.* Grand Rapids, Mich.: Baker Books, 1987.

Murray, John. *Collected Writings of John Murray.* Banner of Truth Trust, 1977. 4 vols.

------. *Redemption Accomplished and Applied.* Edinburgh: Banner of Truth Trust, 1961.

Oberman, Heiko. *Luther: Man Between God and the Devil.* New Haven: Yale University Press, 1989.

Oliphint, K. Scott. "Epistemology and Christian Belief." *Westminster Theological Journal* 63, no. 1 (Spring 2001): 151–82.

------. *Reasons for Faith: Philosophy in the Service of Theology*. Phillipsburg, N.J.: Presbyterian and Reformed Publishing Company, 2006.

Owen, John. *Of the Death of Christ, the Price He Paid, and the Purchase He Made*. London, 1650.

------. *Vindiciae Evangelicae*. London, 1655.

------. *The Works of John Owen*. Edited by W. H. Gould. Edinburgh: The Banner of Truth Trust, 1977.

Patterson, Orlando. *Rituals of Blood*, New York: Basic Civitas, 1998

Paul, Robert. *The Assembly of the Lord: Politics and Religion in the Westminster Assembly Adn the 'Grand Debate'*. Edinburgh: T&T Clark, 1985.

Pieper, Francis. *Christian Dogmatics*. St Louis, Missouri: Concordia, 1950.

Piscator, Johannes. *A Learned and Profitable Treatise of Mans Justification*. London, 1599.

Plantinga, Alvin. *God and Other Minds; a Study of the Rational Justification of Belief in God*. Ithaca, N.Y.: Cornell University Press, 1972.

------. *Warrant and Proper Function*. New York: Oxford University Press, 1993.

------. *Warrant: The Current Debate*. New York: Oxford University Press, 1993.

------. *Warranted Christian Belief*. New York, etc.: Oxford University Press, 2000.

Reid, W. Stanford. "Justification by Faith According to John Calvin." *Westminster Theological Journal* 42, no. 2 (Spring 1980): 290–307.

Ritschl, Albrecht. *The Christian Doctrine of Justification and Reconciliation the Positive Development of the Doctrine*. Translated by H. R. Mackintosh, Macaulay. Edinburgh: T.&T. Clark, 1900.

Rutherford, Samuel. *A Survery of the Spirituall Antichrist*. London, 1648.

"Savoy Declaration." In *A Declaration of the Faith and Order Owned and Practised in the Congregational Churches in England/ Agreed Upoin and Consented Unto by Their Elders and Messengers in Their Meeting at the Savoy, October 12, 1658*. London, 1658.

Sanders, E. P. *Paul and Palestinian Judaism*. Philadelphia: SCM Press, 1977.

Sandlin, Andrew P. "Covenant in Redemptive History: 'Gospel and Law' or 'Trust and Obey'." In *Backbone of the Bible: Covenant in Contemporary Perspective*, edited by Andrew P. Sandlin. Nacogdoches: Covenant Media Foundation, 2004.

Seeburg, R. *Textbook of the History of Doctrines*. Philadelphia, 1905.

Sharpe, Kevin. *The Personal Rule of Charles I*. New Haven: Yale University Press, 1993.

Shedd, William G. T. *A History of Christian Doctrine*. Minneapolis: Klock and Klock, 1978.

Silva, Moisés. "Faith Versus Works of Law in Galatians." In *Justification and Variegated Nomism: Volume 2 - The Paradoxes of Paul*, D. A. Carson,

Peter T. O'Brien, and Mark A. Seifrid, 217–48. Grand Rapids, Michigan: Baker Academic, 2004.

Stoker, Hendrik G. "Reconnoitering the Theory of Knowledge of Professor Dr. Cornelius Van Til." In *Jerusalem and Athens: Critical Discussions on the Philosophy and Apologetics of Cornelius Van Til*, edited by E. R. Geehan. 25–71. New Jersey: Presbyterian and Reformed Publishing Co., 1977.

Stott, John R. W. *The Cross of Christ*. Leicester: IVP, 1986.

Strimple, Robert. "St. Anselm's Cur Deus Homo and John Calvin's Doctrine of the Atonement." In *Anselm: Aosta, Bec and Canterbury*, eds D. E. Luscombe and G. R. Evans. Sheffield: Sheffield Academic Press, 1996.

Smalcius. *The Racovian Catechism*. Amsterdam, 1652.

Tappert, Theodore G., ed. *The Book of Concord the Confessions of the Evangelical Lutheran Church*. Philadelphia: Fortress Press, 1959.

------. *"Confessions of the ELC." In The Book of Concord the Confessions of the Evangelical Lutheran Church*, Edited and translated by Theodore G. Tappert. Philadelphia: Fortress Press, 1959.

Toon, Peter, ed. *Puritans, the Millennium and the Future of Israel*. Cambridge and London: Clarke & Co. Ltd, 1970.

Tripp, Paul David. *Instruments in the Redeemer's Hands*. Phillipsburg: Presbyterian and Reformed Publishing Co., 2002.

Turretin, Francis. *Institutes of Elenctic Theology*. Vol. I. Edited by James T. Dennison Jr. Translated by George Musgrave Giger. Phillipsburg, New Jersey: Presbyterian and Reformed Publishing Company, 1994.

Trueman, Carl R. *John Owen*. Aldershot: Ashgate, 2007.

------. "John Owen's Dissertation on Divine Justice: An Exercise in Christocentric Scholasticism." *Calvin Theological Journal* 33 (1998): 87–103.

------. "Richard Baxter on Christian Unity: A Chapter in the Enlightening of English Reformed Orthodoxy." *Westminster Theological Journal* 61 (1999): 53–71.

Twisse, William. *A Discovery of Jackson's Vanitie*. Amsterdam, 1631.

------. "A Preface Written by *Doctor Twisse* Shewing the Methode and Excellency of *Mr Medes* Interpretation of This Mysterious Book of the Revelation of Saint John" in *The Key to the Revelation*, Joseph Mede (London, 1643).

Tyacke, Nicholas. *Anti-Calvinists: The Rise of English Arminianism c. 1590–1640*. Oxford: Oxford University Press, 1987.

Ussher, James. *Immanuel, or, the Mystery of the Incarnation of the Son of God*. London, 1653.

Van Dixhoorn, Chad B. "Reforming the Reformation: Theological Debate at the Westminster Assembly 1643–1652, Volumes 1–7." Cambridge: University of Cambridge, 2004.

Van Til, Cornelius. *The Defense of the Faith*. Philadelphia: Presbyterian and Reformed Publishing. Co., 1955.

------. "Nature and Scripture." In *The Infallible Word A Symposium by the Members of the Faculty of Westminster Theological Seminary*, 263–301. Phillipsburg, N. J.: Presbyterian and Reformed Publishing Co., 1978.

Volf, Miroslav. *Exclusion and Embrace: A Theological Exploration of Identity, Otherness and Reconciliation*, Nashville: Abingdon Press, 1996

Vos, Geerhardus. *Biblical Theology: Old and New Testaments*. Grand Rapids: Eerdmans, 1948.

------. *Grace and Glory*. Carlisle, Pennsylvania: Banner of Truth Trust, 1995.

------. *The Pauline Eschatology*. Grand Rapids, Mich.,: Baker, 1979.

------. *Redemptive History and Biblical Interpretation : The Shorter Writings of Geerhardus Vos*. Edited by Richard B. Gaffin. Phillipsburg, N.J.: Presbyterian and Reformed Publishing Co. 2001.

Warfield, B. B. *Biblical and Theological Studies*, Philadelphia, Pennsylvania: Presbyterian and Reformed Publishing Co., 1952.

Wendel, Francois. *Calvin the Origins and Development of His Religious Thought*. Philip Mairet. London: Fontana, 1965.

White, Peter. *Predestination, Policy and Polemic: Conflict and Consensus in the English Church from the Reformation to the Civil War*. Cambridge: Cambridge University Press, 1993.

Wilson, Thomas. *A Christian Dictionary*. London, 1647.

Wright, N. T. "New Perspectives on Paul." 10th Edinburgh Dogmatics Conference. Rutherford House, Edinburgh, 2003.

------. *Paul in Fresh Perspective*. Minneapolis: Fortress Press, 2005.

------. *What Saint Paul Really Said*. Grand Rapids, Michigan: William B. Eerdmans Publishing Company, 1997.

The IMPUTATION of ADAM'S SIN

by

JOHN MURRAY

Preface

The material presented in the pages which follow was published in four successive issues of *The Westminster Theological Journal*, XVIII, 2; XIX, 1 and 2; XX, 1. I wish to express my indebtedness to the Editor, the Rev. Professor Ned B. Stonehouse, for his generosity in accepting the articles for publication and for his care in reading and checking the manuscripts. I am likewise indebted to the Managing Editor, the Rev. Professor Paul Woolley, for his labour and care in correcting the proofs. To the Board of Trustees of Westminster Theological Seminary I extend my warm thanks for a leave of absence during 1955 and 1956. It was the leisure granted from other duties during that period that enabled me to undertake some of the research required for the writing of this study.

Grateful acknowledgment is hereby extended to the following publishers for permission to quote from copyrighted books: the Muhlenberg Press, Philadelphia, from Anders Nygren: *Commentary on Romans* (1949); the Lutterworth Press, London, from Emil Brunner: *The Christian Doctrine of Creation and Redemption, Dogmatics* II (1952); the B. Herder Book Co., St. Louis, from H. J. Schroeder: *Canons and Decrees of the Council of Trent* (1941) and from Joseph Pohle, ed. Arthur Preuss: *God the Author of Nature and the Supernatural* (1934); The Macmillan Co., New York, from George D. Smith, ed.: *The Teaching of the Catholic Church* (1949).

JOHN MURRAY

Chapter One

THEOLOGICAL thought of the present day is not only hospitable to the notion of solidarity in sin and guilt; it is keenly sensitive to the fact of such solidarity. Dealing with the Augustinian doctrine of original sin, Emil Brunner can say: "I want to make it clear from the outset that I am in complete agreement with the twofold aim of Augustine: to represent sin as a dominant force, and humanity as bound together in a solidarity of guilt".[1] And C. H. Dodd, commenting on Paul's argument in Romans 5:12-21, says: "What lies behind it is the ancient conception of solidarity. The moral unit was the community ... rather than the individual .... Thus the whole of humanity could be thought of as the tribe of Adam, and Adam's sin was the sin of the race. With the growing appreciation of the ethical significance of the individual, the old idea of solidarity weakened. But it corresponded with real facts. The isolation of the individual is an abstraction."[2] "Adam", he continues, "is a name which stands to him (Paul) for the 'corporate personality' of mankind."[3] Yet of Romans 5:12 Brunner also says: "It does not refer to the transgression of Adam in which all his descendants share; but it states the fact that 'Adam's' descendants are involved in death, because they themselves commit sin".[4] And C. H. Dodd can also say: "Thus Paul's doctrine of Christ as the 'second Adam' is not so bound up with the story of the Fall as a literal happening that it ceases to have meaning when we no longer

---

[1] *The Christian Doctrine of Creation and Redemption. Dogmatics*, Vol. II (London, 1952), p. 103.

[2] *The Epistle of Paul to the Romans* (London, 1934), p. 79.

[3] *Ibid.*, p. 80.

[4] *Op. cit.*, p. 104.

accept the story as such. Indeed, we should not too readily assume that Paul did so accept it."[5] We thus see that the recognition of and the emphasis upon solidaric or corporate sin and guilt in our present-day theology are not to be interpreted as identical with the classic Protestant doctrine of the imputation of Adam's sin. And it does not advance the cause of theology or of exegesis to regard Paul's appeal to the fall of Adam as but the mythical form in which the fact of solidaric unity in sin is expressed. It is not a work of supererogation, therefore, if we address ourselves anew to this question of the imputation of Adam's sin to posterity and to the study of the passage upon which, more than any other, the doctrine is based. It is encouraging to find in so brilliant a scholar as Anders Nygren so appreciative an assessment of the pivotal place which Romans 5:12-19 occupies in this major epistle. "The parallelism which Paul draws between Adam and Christ has seemed so strange and unmanageable that it has made scholars the more willing to treat this section as a parenthesis. More or less consciously interpreters have acted on the assumption that something, which is so foreign to today's thought as to seem unreal, cannot have been of decisive importance to Paul either. To explain how he happened in on the digression, reference has, for instance, been made to the important place which the 'Adam-speculation' came to play in rabbinical thought.... We should not forget that Paul read about Adam on one of the first pages of his Bible; so it is not necessary to look for remoter sources from which the idea might have come.... Paul does not look on Christ as an Adam redivivus. He sets up Adam and Christ in this parallel, not to affirm their identity, but contrariwise to point out the contrast between them. When once one comes to realize what that means to Paul, he forthwith discovers that this passage is by no means a parenthesis or a digression in the apostle's thought. Rather do we here come to the high point of the epistle. This is the point where all the lines of his thinking converge, both those of the preceding chapters and those of the chapters that follow."[6]

In studying Romans 5:12-19 as it bears upon the question of the imputation of Adam's sin to posterity we shall subsume our discussion under the following main subdivisions: I Syntactical

---

[5] *Op. cit.*, p. 80.

[6] Anders Nygren: *Commentary on Romans* (Philadelphia, 1949), pp. 207-209.

Construction; II The Sin Contemplated; III The Union Involved; IV The Nature of the Imputation; V The Sin Imputed.

I. SYNTACTICAL CONSTRUCTION

It is scarcely necessary to argue the fact that verse 12 is an unfinished comparison. Few interpreters dispute this fact. καὶ οὕτως in the middle of the verse does not have the effect of closing the comparison introduced by ὥσπερ. In that event we should have οὕτως καὶ and not καὶ οὕτως (cf. vss. 15, 18, 19, 21 and 6:4, 11). καὶ οὕτως is coordinative or continuative and does not mean "even so" but rather "and so" or "and in like manner" (cf. Acts 7:8; 28:14; 1 Cor. 7:17, 36; 11 :28; Gal. 6:2). Even Pelagius did not suppose anything different as far as the syntax of verse 12 was concerned. The Latin text on which he based his comments was faithful to the Greek in this particular – *et ita in omnes homines* [*mors*]*pertransiit*.[7]

It is not difficult to discover the reason why the comparison introduced in verse 12 had been broken off. The development of Paul's thought required a parenthesis after the concluding clause of verse 12. This parenthesis begins at verse 13 and continues through verse 17. It may well be that we should not regard these five verses as one parenthesis but as two, the first consisting of verses 13 and 14 and the second of verses 15-17.[8] On this construction of the parenthetical portion we should have to say that the thought expressed in verse 12, especially in the last clause, dictated the necessity of appending without delay the data expressed in verses 13 and 14, and then, in turn, the typological datum enunciated at the end of verse 14 – "who is the type of the one to come" – necessitated the setting forth of the series of similitudes,

---

[7]See *Pelagius's Expositions of Thirteen Epistles of St. Paul*, ed. Alexander Souter (Cambridge, 1926), No. 2, p. 45 in *Texts and Studies. Contributions to Biblical and Patristic Literature*, ed. J. Armitage Robinson, Vol. IX, No. 2.

[8]*Cf.* Heinrich A. W. Meyer: *Critical and Exegetical Handbook to the Epistle to the Romans* (E. T., New York, 1884). pp. 193 f. "The illustration, namely, introduced in vv. 13, 14 of the ἐφ' ᾧ πάντες ἥμαρτον now rendered it impossible to add the second half of the comparison *syntactically* belonging to the ὥσπερ, and therefore the Apostle, driven on by the rushing flow of ideas to this point, from which he can no longer revert to the construction with which he started, has no hesitation in dropping the latter ... and in subsequently bringing in *merely* the main tenor of what is wanting by the relative clause attached to 'Αδὰμ: ὅς ἐστιν τύπος τοῦ μέλλοντος in ver. 14."

but particularly of contrasts, instituted in verses 15-17. However we construe these five verses, as one parenthesis or as two, it is quite apparent that Paul does not return to the type of syntax which had been begun in verse 12, but had been broken off, until we arrive at verse 18. Here we have a finished comparison with both protasis and apodosis, the former intimated in ὡς and the latter in οὕτως και. "Consequently then, as through one trespass judgment came upon all men unto condemnation, even so through one righteous act judgment came upon all men unto justification of life."

It is not of much consequence to determine whether verse 18 is resumptive or recapitulatory.[9] It is sufficient for us to know that Paul does not leave us in any doubt as to what the apodosis of verse 12 would have been if it had been completed in terms of the protasis which verse 12 supplies. The completed comparisons of verses 18, 19 place beyond all doubt what the governing thought of this passage is and it is in terms of that governing thought that the comparison of verse 12 would have to be completed.

This parenthesis of verses 13-17, which at first seems to be so awkward and perplexing, proves on closer examination to be eloquent in determining for us the precise import of the clause which, after all, is the most crucial in the exegesis of this whole passage, namely, the last clause in verse 12. The interpretation is established by the eloquent repetitions of the succeeding verses and, as we shall have occasion to note, no consideration is more pertinent to the question than the fact that verses 13-17 are in the form of a parenthesis.

II. THE SIN CONTEMPLATED

The crux of the question in connection with this passage is the reference in the clause ἐφ ᾧ πάντες ἥμαρτον in verse 12. This clause informs us why death passed on to all men and should be rendered "in that all sinned".'[10] Hence the question is: to

[9]Meyer (*ibid.*, p. 194; *cf.* p. 215) argues against other interpreters who hold that in verse 18 the first half of the comparison is resumed and urges in support of his view "not only the unprecedented length, but still more the contents of the supposed parenthesis, which in fact already comprehends in itself the parallel under every aspect" and he concludes: "In ver. 18f. we have *recapitulation*, but not *resumption*".

what does Paul refer when he says "all sinned"? As far as form is concerned the expression itself could refer to the actual sins of men (*cf.* Rom. 3:23). Furthermore, if Paul meant the actual sins of all men, this is without doubt the expression he would have used; no other would have been more suitable to express that thought. The meaning, however, is not to be determined by grammatical possibility but by contextual considerations. There are various views of the force of this expression.

1. The Pelagian view

This view is that the clause in question refers to the actual sins of men.[11] In this event the thought of Paul would be that as Adam sinned and therefore died so in like manner all men die because they sin. Adam is the prototype – he sinned and brought sin and death into the world. Others in like manner sin and they also are afflicted with death. The coordination of sin and death, exemplified in Adam, applies in every case where there is sin.

It needs to be observed that the construction of verse 12 does not disprove this interpretation. Even though on this view we should have expected Paul to use οὕτως καὶ at the middle of the verse rather than και οὕτως, yet it is possible to think of Paul as enunciating the parallelism between the entrance of sin and death through Adam and the passing on of sin and death through all without closing the comparison in terms of the analogy that obtains in the opposite sphere of righteousness and life. In other words, the syntax of verse 12 cannot of itself be pleaded as a conclusive argument against the Pelagian view. There are, however, conclusive objections on factual, exegetical, and theological grounds.

[10]It is unnecessary at this stage in the history of exposition to argue that the Vulgate rendering, *in quo omnes peccaverunt*, though, as we shall see, it is theologically true, is nevertheless grammatically untenable. The force of ἐφ ᾧ is causal and it means "in that", "by the fact that", or simply "because".

[11]*Cf.* Pelagius: *op. cit.* "*Propter ea sicut per unum hominem in hunc mundum peccatum introiit el per peccatum mors*. Exemplo uel forma. quo modo, cum non esset peccatum, per Adam aduenit, ita etiam, cum paene aput nullum iustitia remansisset, per Christum est reuocata ... *Et ita in omnes homines [mors] pertransiit, in quo omnes peccauerunt*. Dum ita peccant, et similiter moriuntur" (p. 45). "*Sicut enim per inoboedientiam unius hominis peccatoris constituti sunt plurimi, ita et per unius oboedientiam iusti constituentur multi*. Sicut exemplo inoboedientiae Adae peccauerunt multi, ita et Christi oboedientia justificantur multi" (p. 48).

(i) The Pelagian view is not actually or historically true. Not all die because they actually and voluntarily sin. Infants die. But they have not actually transgressed after the similitude of Adam's transgression.

(ii) In verses 13, 14 Paul states the opposite of the Pelagian view. For here we are told that death reigned over those who did not sin after the similitude of Adam's transgression. What or whom Paul has in view is difficult to determine, but it is obvious that he is thinking of death as exercising its sway over persons who did not sin as Adam did. It is futile to try to evade the direct bearing of this fact upon the Pelagian interpretation. Paul is saying the opposite, namely, that death reigns universally and therefore reigns over those who are in a different category from that of Adam.[12]

(iii) The most conclusive refutation of the Pelagian interpretation is derived from the repeated and emphatic affirmations of Paul in the immediate context, affirmations to the effect that the universal sway of condemnation and death is to be referred to the *one sin* of the *one man* Adam. On at least five occasions in verses 15-19 this principle is asserted – "by the trespass of the one the many died" (v. 15); "the judgment was from one unto condemnation" (v. 16); "by the trespass of the one death reigned through the one" (v. 17) ; "through one trespass judgment came upon all men unto

---

Cf. also Edouard Reuss: *La Bible: Traduction Nouvelle avec Introductions et Commentaires* (Paris, 1898) ad Romans 5:12-14. "Tous les hommes issus d'Adam péchèrent également .... Il n'y a pas un mot dans le texte qui puisse servir à étayer les thèses scolastiques d'un changement opéré dans la nature de l'homme, de la nécessité de pécher, de l'imputation du péché de tous. Mais it tient aussi a le prouver. Comment le prouve-t-il? Par un autre fait également général et tout à fait incontestable. C'est que tous les hommes issus d'Adam sont morts." Emil Brunner (*op. cit.*, p. 99), while right in recognizing that *in quo omnes peccaverunt* is a mis-translation, puts himself in the Pelagian category as far as interpretation of this text is concerned when he says that "these words mean the exact opposite: namely, that each of us becomes a sinner by his own act".

[12]This consideration that not all men are in the category of Adam militates against Brunner's conception that we are all "Adam". For if we all are "Adam" in respect of Paul's teaching in this passage, then how can Paul speak of some as not sinning after the similitude of Adam's transgression? In other words, in terms of the datum which is the pivotal one in the analogy which Paul is using, namely, the one trespass of the one man Adam, we are not all "Adam". It is to waive exegesis altogether if we do not take account of the uniqueness, the "oneness" of Adam in respect of the position he occupies in this passage.

condemnation" (v. 18); "through the disobedience of the one man the many were constituted sinners" (v. 19). We might think that Paul has needlessly repeated himself, but it is a repetition which establishes beyond dispute that Paul regards condemnation and death as having passed on to all men by the one trespass of the one man Adam. It is quite impossible to construe this emphasis upon the one sin of the one man as equivalent to the actual personal sin of countless individuals. It is indisputable, therefore, that Paul regards the universality of condemnation and death as grounded upon and proceeding from the one trespass of the one man Adam. And the Pelagian insistence that death and condemnation find their ground solely in the personal voluntary sin of the individuals of the race cannot be harmonized with this sustained witness of the apostle.

(iv) The Pelagian exegesis destroys the force of the analogy which Paul institutes in this passage as a whole. The doctrine Paul is illustrating by appeal to the analogy of the condemnation and death proceeding from Adam is the doctrine that men are justified by the free grace of God on the basis of the righteousness and obedience of Christ. What Paul has been controverting in the earlier part of the epistle is that men are justified by their own works. He is establishing the truth that men are justified and attain to life by what another has done, the one man Jesus Christ. How vacuous and contradictory would be any appeal to the parallel obtaining in the relation of Adam to the race if the Pelagian construction were that of Paul, namely, that men die simply because of their own sin and not at all on the ground of Adam's sin! Paul's doctrine of justification would be nullified if, at this point, the parallel he uses to illustrate and confirm it is after the pattern of the Pelagian construction. For it would mean that men are justified by their own voluntary action just as they come under condemnation solely by their own voluntary sin. This is indeed Pelagian doctrine but that it contradicts the teaching of Paul lies on the face of the epistle. The doctrine of justification which this epistle establishes is a doctrine which cannot tolerate as its analogy or parallel a construction of the reign of sin, condemnation, and death which bears any resemblance to the Pelagian. Hence the Pelagian view must be rejected on this ground as well as on that of the others mentioned.

2. The Roman Catholic View

It cannot be maintained that there has been unanimity among Roman Catholic theologians respecting Romans 5:12 or about the clause with which we are more particularly concerned. At the time of the Council of Trent Ambrosius Catharinus held a position similar to that which we shall later on propound as the correct view. He maintained that the sin referred to in the clause, "in that all sinned", is the actual voluntary transgression of Adam imputed to all posterity by reason of the covenant relationship which Adam sustained to the race – when Adam sinned all mankind sinned with him and in him. He insisted that the sin of every one is the act only of the transgression of Adam and not the privation of righteousness or the concupiscence which were the consequences of that sin. It is this sin of Adam imputed to posterity that Catharinus called "original sin" and it is that sin and that alone, he contended, that Paul has in view in Romans 5:12-19.[13] Albertus Pighius, a contemporary of Catharinus held the same position. He is explicit to the effect that the apostle constantly refers the reign of death and the judgment of condemnation, under which we all are concluded, to the one sin of the one man Adam. In him, therefore, not in us, was that sin by which we all have sinned. Even infants are guilty and constituted sinners not on account of their own sin but on account of the sin and disobedience of Adam.[14]

This position is not, however, the official teaching of the Romish Church, and her theologians have followed a different line of thought. The Council of Trent in its "Decretum de Peccato

---

[13]For Catharinus' view see Pietro Soaue Polano: *The Historie of the Councel of Trent* (E. T. by Nathanael Brent, London, 1640), pp. 175 ff.

[14]See Albertus Pighius: *Controversiarum Praecipuarum ... Luculenta Explicatio* (Cologne, 1542). In dealing with Rom. 5:12-19 he says: "Uides, ut Apostolus perpetuo, et constantissime uni peccato unius Adae, acceptum referat mortis regnum, et damnationis, sub quo omnes conclusi sumus, iudicium: unum, et unius peccatum dicit, cuius demerito, omnes mortui sumus .... In illo, non in nobis, peccasse omnes. In illo ergo, non in nobis fuit illud peccatum, quo peccauimus omnes. Unius illius inobedientia, non sua propria, peccatores constitutes multos, qui per aetatem, sub lege nondum existentes, sua inobedientia potuerunt peccatores fieri .... Proinde, quasi interrogares, ob cuius peccatum paruulus, reus, et peccator sit, tibi diserte respondet Apostolus, non ob suum, sed ob Adae peccatum, illum reatu constringi, et peccatorem constitui ..." (Fol. XXIV a). *Cf.* for a succinct statement of Pighius' position Martin Chemnitz: *Examen Concilii Tridentini* (Berlin, 1861), p. 103.

Originali" says: "1. If anyone does not confess that the first man, Adam, when he transgressed the commandment of God in paradise, immediately lost the holiness and justice in which he had been constituted, and through the offense of that prevarication incurred the wrath and indignation of God, and thus death with which God had previously threatened him, and, together with death, captivity under his power who thenceforth *had the empire of death, that is to say, the devil*, and that the entire Adam through that offense of prevarication was changed in body and soul for the worse, let him be anathema.

"2. If anyone asserts that the transgression of Adam injured him alone and not his posterity, and that the holiness and justice which he received from God, which he lost, he lost for himself alone and not for us also; or that he, being defiled by the sin of disobedience, has transfused only death and the pains of the body into the whole human race, but not sin also, which is the death of the soul, let him be anathema."[15] One would gather from these statements that the sin of Adam which is the sin of all is that which by propagation is transfused into all. Obviously this notion is quite distinct from that of the imputation to all of the actual transgression of Adam, as espoused by Catharinus and Pighius.

It is this direction of thought, which appears in the decrees of Trent, that has been characteristic of Romish theologians in the formulation of this doctrine. It is not that Rome in any way denies the fact or the consequences of the actual transgression of Adam. It is simply that in the interpretation of Romans 5:12 and of the sin in which all are implicated by reason of the sin of Adam this sin is conceived of not as the actual sin of Adam imputed but as the habitual sin that is conveyed by natural generation. The matter is stated clearly by Joseph Pohle: "The sin of Adam is original in a twofold sense: (1) As a sinful personal act (*peccatum originale originans*), and (2) as a sinful state (*peccatum originale originatum*). It is the state not the act that is transmitted to Adam's descendants."[16] There are two respects in which the former bears upon the latter. First, the sinful personal act brought the sinful state into existence

---

[15]As translated by H. J. Schroeder: *Canons and Decrees of the Council of Trent* (St. Louis and London, 1941), p. 21.

[16]Joseph Pohle, ed. Arthur Preuss: *God the Author of Nature and the Supernatural* (St. Louis and London, 1934), p. 233.

and, second, the sinful state is truly sinful "only in its logical connexion with Adam's voluntary transgression of the divine command in paradise".[17] But it is only "the habitual sin of Adam (*habitus peccati*), which 'entered into this world' through him, i. e. was by him transmitted to all his progeny".[18]

Rome is reluctant to define precisely that in which this original and habitual sin consists. Insofar as definition is ventured it is conceived of as consisting chiefly in the privation of holiness and justice.'[19] But since man's fall also entailed the loss of integrity, it is hard for Romish theologians to exclude concupiscence from the ambit of original sin. Hence while they are emphatic in maintaining that original sin does not consist in concupiscence,[20] nevertheless they are willing to grant that concupiscence, though it is not itself truly and properly sin, is embraced in the ambit of habitual sin.[21]

After taking all these distinctions and qualifications into account the upshot is that in Romish theology the sin referred to in the last clause of Romans 5:12 is the habitual or original sin which is transmitted to or transfused into Adam's posterity by natural generation and which as to its nature consists essentially in the privation of sanctity, a privation which can be categorized as sinful because of the logical relation it sustains to the 'voluntary' transgression of Adam.[22] In a word, the sin of Romans 5:12 on account of which death passed on to all is transmitted sinfulness.

---

[17]*Ibid.*, p. 246.

[18]*Ibid.*, p. 248.

[19]"Original sin essentially consists in privation of grace, so far as this is voluntary in all men through the will of their progenitor" (*ibid.*, p. 269). *Cf.* also ed. George D. Smith: *The Teaching of the Cutholic Church* (New York, 1949), Vol. I, p. 345.

[20]"Concupiscence as such does not constitute the essence of original sin" (*ibid.*, p. 261).

[21]*Cf.* Ad. Tanquerey: *Synopsis Theologiae Dogmaticae* (New York, 1933), Tom. 11, p. 566. "Ergo peccatum de quo agit S. Paulus non est peccatum actuale; nec aliunde mera poenalitas aut sola concupiscentia, sed peccatum *sui generis*, peccatum *habituale* quod in suo ambitu complectitur *reatum culpae*, *concupiscentiam* seu inclinationem ad peccandum, et utriusque *transmissionem* in omnes homines ob solius Adae culpam."

[22]"Thus original sin, as it is in each one of us, is voluntary, not indeed by any act of our personal will, but through the act of the 'family will,' through our relationship of spiritual dependence upon and solidarity with our first, divinely

It is not our interest at the present time to examine the Romish doctrine of original sin. On this question the battle of the Reformation was closely joined and it would appear that the situation as it exists today does not offer any reason for the abatement of that controversy. But our question at present is not whether Rome's doctrine of original sin is correct but whether it is the notion of *original sin* as distinguished from *imputed sin* that Paul has in mind when he says, "in that all sinned". As far as this question is concerned we are examining the tenability of the interpretation entertained by some Protestants as well as that of Rome. There are decisive objections of an exegetical and theological character to this interpretation.

(i) There is, first of all, a presumptive argument. It would be exceedingly difficult to adjust the notion in question to the thought expressed by the aorist ἥμαρτον. Original sin as construed by Rome or, for that matter, by Protestants is that which is being constantly conveyed by natural generation. As respects conveyance there is a constant process and as respects result there is a constant condition. If the sin alluded to in the clause concerned is original sin, then both the process and the condition are in view as defining the sin. How an historical or indefinite aorist could be used to denote such a sin it is difficult, if not impossible, to conceive. About the only way in which the aorist could be used is by focusing attention on the historical inception of this process and condition. But the Romish interpretation does not thus limit the thought and if original sin is meant it would not be feasible to limit the thought to the once-for-all historical inception. The more we think of this objection the more cogent it becomes. But we are willing to characterize it as presumptive rather than conclusive.

(ii) More cogent is the theological consideration that this view does not accord with the parallel or analogy which Paul institutes in this passage. The validity of this argument rests, of course, upon the outright rejection of the Romish view of justification. Rome regards justification as consisting in regeneration and renovation wrought by the infusion of righteousness and her theologians in

---

appointed, supernatural head and representative Adam" (Geo. D. Smith: *op. cit.*, p. 348).

dealing with Romans 5:12-19 appeal to this concept of justification in support of their interpretation of verse 12, to wit, that there is an obvious parallel between the infusion of righteousness in justification and the transfusion of original sin on account of the sin of Adam. We cannot now digress to refute this doctrine of justification. We must be content with the assertion that it is flatly contradictory of the biblical and Pauline teaching. The doctrine of Paul is that we are justified on the basis of the righteousness of Christ and not by a righteousness infused into us any more than by a righteousness wrought by us. Since this is Paul's doctrine and since he institutes a parallel between the way in which condemnation and death pass on to all men and the way in which justification and life pass on to the justified, the *modus operandi* in the latter case cannot find its analogue in the transfusion or transmission of original sin. The parallel which Paul's doctrine of justification demands must be of a very different sort. So, in brief, the requirements of the analogy instituted are not fulfilled but rather violated by importing into Paul's thought in this passage the notion of transmitted and inherited sin.

(iii) Most conclusive is the objection that the interpretation being debated is inconsistent with the repeated affirmations of Paul in Romans 5:15-19. We have had occasion to refer to these in the refutation of the Pelagian view. But it is well to be reminded that Paul on at least five occasions in successive verses (15, 16, 17, 18, 19) refers the universal reign of condemnation and death to the one trespass of the one man Adam. This sustained emphasis upon the "oneness" of the sin and of the man does not comport with the notion of original sin. Though the Romanist view recognizes that original sin proceeds from the actual transgression of Adam, yet original sin, as that which is transmitted or transfused, is the sin that belongs to all who come by natural generation and cannot be regarded as conforming to such a specification as the one sin of the one man Adam. What is with us habitual, as the Romanist theologians assert, can scarcely be characterized as the one trespass of Adam. For these reasons we shall have to reject this interpretation of the clause, "in that all sinned".

3. Calvin's Interpretation

Calvin's view of original sin is radically different from that of Rome. According to Calvin the original sin which is conveyed by natural generation is itself, intrinsically, radical depravity. The Protestant polemic was directed with vigour against the Romish view that original sin consisted simply in the privation of original righteousness and integrity and that the concupiscence which resulted from the loss of integrity was not itself truly and properly sinful, and the Romish polemic was directed with equal vigour against the Protestant doctrine that original sin involved a radical corruption of our moral and spiritual nature. The respective polemics of these two branches of Christendom must be understood in this light and any agreement there may be respecting the relation of Adam's actual transgression to the original sin with which all are inflicted must not obscure the difference on the nature of original sin itself.

But though Calvin's view of original sin differs so radically from that of Rome his view of the crucial clause in Romans 5:12, "in that all sinned", is, exegetically speaking, similar to that of Rome. For he, in like manner, regards Paul as referring here to original sin. "But Paul distinctly affirms that sin is propagated to all who suffer its punishment. And this he afterwards more expressly declares when a little later he assigns the reason why all of Adam's posterity are subject to the dominion of death, even this, he says, seeing that we all have sinned (*quoniam omnes peccavimus*). But to sin is in this case to be corrupt and vitiated. For that natural depravity which we bring from our mother's womb, though it does not immediately bring forth its fruits, is nevertheless sin in the sight of God and deserves his vengeance. And this is the sin which they call original. For so Adam at his first creation received both for himself and for posterity the gifts of divine favour, so by falling away from the Lord he in himself corrupted, vitiated, depraved, and ruined our nature. Having been divested of God's likeness he could not have begotten seed but like himself. Therefore we all have sinned because we have all been imbued with natural corruption, and so are become wicked and perverse."[23]

---

[23]*Comm. ad* Rom. 5:12; *cf. ad* Rom. 5:15, 17.

The same objections apply to this interpretation as apply to the Romanist position. While it is true that Calvin is not encumbered by the difficulty Romish exegetes encounter when they are faced with the necessity of categorizing as sinful that which does not intrinsically meet the requirements of their own definition of sin and while Calvin's view of original sin is thoroughly Pauline and biblical, yet, exegetically, he has not been successful in analysing the precise thought of the apostle in this passage. In other words, he has not been able to get above the Augustinian tradition in the exposition of Romans 5:12.

4. The Classic Protestant Interpretation

The pivotal question is still before us: what sin does Paul have in view when he says, "in that all sinned"? In order to arrive at what we believe to be the proper view it is necessary to take account of the following considerations.

(i) It is unquestionable that the universal sway of death is represented in verse 12 as resting upon the fact that "all sinned". Whatever the sin contemplated may be, it is the reason why death passed through to all men. And this is simply to say that it is the ground of the universality of death.

(ii) In verses 15-19, however, Paul with unmistakeable clearness asserts that the universal reign of death rests upon the one trespass of the one man Adam. "By the trespass of the one the many died" (v. 15) ; "By the trespass of the one death reigned through the one" (v. 17). And, of course, this relationship in reference to death is coordinate with and parallel to Paul's other statements in reference to condemnation. "The judgment was from one unto condemnation" (v. 16); "Through one trespass judgment came upon all men unto condemnation" (v. 18). Death and condemnation reign over all because of the one trespass of Adam.

(iii) Are we to suppose that Paul is dealing with two different facts when in verse 12 he grounds the death of all in the sin of all and when in verses 15 and 17 he grounds that same death in the one trespass of Adam? Are we to think that in verse 12 Paul is speaking of the sin which is personally and distributively universal either as action or as *habitus* whereas in verses 15-19 he is speaking of sin in its specific singularity as the one trespass of the one man Adam? The conclusion to which the exegetical considerations drive us is that this cannot be the case but rather that Paul must have in view the same sin when in verse 12 he says "all sinned" and when in verses 15-19 he refers to the one sin of the one man. The arguments establishing this conclusion are as follows.

(a) The whole passage (Rom. 5:12-19) is a unit. We cannot fail to see that the central structure is the analogy that obtains between the *modus operandi* of sin, condemnation, death, on the one hand, and of righteousness, justification, life, on the other. In the nature of the case, since the latter complex is for the purpose of negating the first, there are significant and magnificent contrasts, and on these Paul elaborates. But the central strand is the parallelism, and even the contrasts are based upon this substructure. Since this is the case we are forced to conclude that the comparison introduced in verse 12, though broken off and not completed in the express terms which the protasis of verse 12 would suggest and dictate, is in essential thought identical with that which is stated in its completeness in verses 18 and 19. This means that the sin referred to in verse 12, particularly in the last clause, must be that same sin that is defined in verse 18 as "the one trespass" and in verse 19 as "the disobedience of the one man". And when we go back to the three preceding verses (15-17) and bear in mind the closely knit unity of the passage, we must conclude that the same sin is in view in verses 15, 17 where it is called the trespass of the one.

(b) Verse 12 is an unfinished comparison. We only know of its implied apodosis from the following verses. It would be impossible to suppose that Paul, dealing expressly with the subject of the universal reign of death, should so explicitly and repeatedly affirm in the succeeding verses something quite different from that which he affirms in what is the unfinished introduction of his argument. If verse 12 were in a context of its own and if there were some plausible evidence of transition from one phase of teaching to another, then we could say that in verse 12 he deals with one fact and in verses 15-19 with another. But the fact that verse 12 does not complete the comparison and relies upon the succeeding verses to supply this completion makes it totally impossible to posit any transition from one phase of truth to another.

(c) As far as actual personal sin is concerned verse 14 excludes the possibility of interpreting the last clause of verse 12 in such terms. Verse 12 tells us the reason why death passed on to all men. It is that "all sinned". But verse 14 tells us that death reigned over those who did not sin after the similitude of Adam's transgression. The reign of death in verse 14 must have the same import as the passing on of death in verse 12. Hence Paul is saying that death passed on to and reigned over those who did not personally and voluntarily transgress as Adam did, and therefore the "all sinned" of verse 12 cannot refer to individual personal transgression. For these reasons we are compelled to infer that when Paul says "all sinned" (v. 12) and when he speaks of the one trespass of the one man (vv. 15-19) he must be referring to the same fact or event, that the one event or fact can be expressed in terms of both singularity and universality. If this identity confronts us, how are we to explain it? How can Paul say that "all sinned" and then that one sinned and refer to the same fact?

As we attempt to answer this question there is one error we must avoid. We must not tone down the singularity or the universality. Paul's language is eloquent of both. The only solution is that there must be some kind of solidarity existing between the "one" and the "all" with the result that the sin contemplated can be regarded at the same time and with equal relevance as the sin of the "one" or as the sin of "all". What this solidarity is is the subject of the next main subdivision of our discussion.

Chapter Two

III. THE UNION INVOLVED

THE principle of solidarity is embedded in the Scripture and is exemplified in numerous ways. It is not necessary to enumerate the instances in which the principle comes to expression. It is a patent fact that in God's government of men there are the institutions of the family, of the state, and of the church in which solidaric or corporate relationships obtain and are operative. This is simply to say that God's relations to men and the relations of men to one another are not exclusively individualistic; God deals with men in terms of these corporate relationships and men must reckon with their corporate relations and responsibilities.

There is also the institution of the individual, and to discount our individuality is to desecrate our responsible relations to God and to men. The principle of solidarity can be exaggerated; it can become an obsession and lead to fatalistic abuse (*cf.* Ezek. 18:2). All such exaggeration is evil. But it is also evil to conceive of our relations to God and to men atomistically so that we fail to appreciate the corporate entities which to such a large extent condition our life and responsibility. Solidarity works for good and for evil. It is scarcely necessary to be reminded of the beneficent influences which have emanated from its application in the realm of grace. Redemption in its design, accomplishment, application, and consummation is fashioned in terms of this principle. And in the realm of evil it is a fact of revelation and of observation that God visits "the iniquity of the fathers upon the children unto the third and fourth generation of them that hate" him (Exod. 20:5).

It is consonant with these facts of the biblical revelation and of our human experience that the principle of solidarity should come to its broadest and most inclusive expression in racial solidarity and we should not be surprised to find in this case the prototypal solidarity. Racial solidarity is the only possible construction of the various data which the Scripture brings to our attention. Paul bears pointed witness to this fact when he says that "in Adam all die" (1 Cor. 15:22). And it is this same solidaric relationship that forms the background of his thought when he says, "The first man Adam was made a living soul; the last Adam was made a life-giving Spirit" (1 Cor. 15:45).

If we appreciate this fact of racial solidarity and therefore the solidaric relationship which Adam sustains to posterity and posterity to him, we shall be less reluctant, to say the least, to entertain the proposition that the one trespass of Adam can properly be construed as the sin of all.

The fact of solidarity does not, however, determine for us the question of its nature. What is the nature of the union that existed between Adam and posterity? On any biblically oriented view of Adam, it will be granted that from Adam proceeded by way of natural generation all the other members of the human race, that Adam was the natural father of all mankind. It might appear to be an adequate answer to our question to say that the union between Adam and posterity is biological and genealogical and that no more is required to explain the facts. This is to say that Adam was the "natural root" of all mankind. Levi was in the loins of his father Abraham when the latter paid tithes to Melchizedek, and thus it can be said that Levi paid tithes to Melchizedek (Heb. 7:9, 10). In like manner all were in the loins of Adam when he sinned, and so it can be said that they sinned in him and fell with him in his first transgression. It may not be alleged that the fact of seminal relationship is irrelevant in this connection. We may not presume to say that the solidarity of the race with Adam, by reason of which all are involved in his sin, could have been true if he had not been the father of all mankind. Whatever additional principle of solidarity may be posited or established it cannot be abstracted from the fact of biological ancestry.

Exegetes and theologians have not been content to explain the solidarity with Adam in terms simply of our lineage from him. They have been constrained to posit some solidaric relationship other than the genealogical as necessary to a proper grounding of the involvement in Adam's sin, whether this additional relationship is conceived of as coordinate with the genealogical or as in itself the specific ground of the imputation of Adam's first sin. There are two views of this relationship that are worthy of serious consideration. And perhaps they are the only views that can worthily claim consideration. The one is that human nature was numerically and specifically one in Adam and the other that Adam was the appointed head and representative of the whole race.

1. The Realistic View

Perhaps the ablest exponent and defender of the view that human nature was both numerically and specifically one in Adam is William G. T. Shedd. "The doctrine of the specific unity of Adam and his posterity", he says, "removes the great difficulties connected with the imputation of Adam's sin to his posterity, that arise from the injustice of punishing a person for a sin in which he had no kind of participation."[1] And in controverting the representative view he says: "To impute Adam's first sin to his posterity merely, and only, because Adam sinned as a representative in their room and place, makes the imputation an arbitrary act of sovereignty, not a righteous judicial act which carries in it an intrinsic morality and justice".'[2]

In brief, the position is that human nature in its unindividualized unity existed in its entirety in Adam, that, when Adam sinned, not only did he sin but also the common nature which existed in its unity in him, and that, since each person who comes into the world is an individualization of this one human nature, each person as an "individualized portion" of that common nature is both culpable and punishable for the sin committed by that unity.[3] "This unity commits the first sin.... This sin is imputed to the unity that committed it, inheres in the unity, and is propagated out of the unity. Consequently, all the particulars regarding sin that apply to the unity or common nature apply equally and strictly to each individualized portion of it. The individual Socrates was a fractional part of the human nature that 'sinned in, and fell with Adam in his first transgression'.... Consequently, the commission, imputation, inherence, and propagation of original sin cleave

[1]William G. T. Shedd: *Dogmatic Theology* (New York, 1889). Vol. 11, p. 30.
[2]*Ibid.*, p. 36.
[3]*Cf. ibid.*, pp. 43 f.

indissolubly to the individualized part of the common nature, as they did to the unindividualized whole of it. The distribution and propagation of the nature make no alteration in it, except in respect to *form*."[4]

To much the same effect is the view of A. H. Strong. Calling it the Augustinian theory, he says: "It holds that God imputes the sin of Adam immediately to all his posterity, in virtue of that organic unity of mankind by which the whole race at the time of Adam's transgression existed, not individually, but seminally, in him as its head. The total life of humanity was then in Adam; the race as yet had its being only in him. Its essence was not yet individualized; its forces were not yet distributed; the powers which now exist in separate men were then unified and localized in Adam; Adam's will was yet the will of the species. In Adam's free act, the will of the race revolted from God and the nature of the race corrupted itself.... Adam's sin is imputed to us immediately, therefore, not as something foreign to us, but because it is ours – we and all other men having existed as one moral person or one moral whole, in him, and, as the result of that transgression, possessing a nature destitute of love to God and prone to evil."[5] "Adam was once the race; and when he fell, the race fell. Shedd: 'We all existed in Adam in our elementary invisible substance. The *Seyn* of all was there, though the *Daseyn* was not; the *noumenom*, though not the *phenomenom* was in existence.'"[6]

It must be acknowledged that if this view were proven to be correct it would adequately explain the two aspects from which the one fact or event may be viewed, namely, that "one sinned" and "all sinned". The question is whether the relevant evidence supports this construction of the Adamic relation.

---

[4]*Ibid.*, pp. 43 f.

[5]Augustus Hopkins Strong: *Systematic Theology* (Philadelphia, 1907), Vol. 11, pp. 619 f.

[6]*Ibid.*, p. 621; *cf.* Samuel J. Baird: *The Elohim Revealed in the Creation and Redemption of Man* (Philadelphia, 1860), pp. 305-334; Philip Schaff in John Peter Lange: *A Commentary on the Holy Scriptures* (New York, 1915), *The Epistle of Paul to the Romans*, pp. 178 f. A. H. Strong's citation of authorities (*op. cit.*, p. 622) is quite unreliable. His appeal to various theologians in support of the realist position is marked by the lack of discrimination which will be shown later on. For example, an examination of H. Martensen: *Christian Dogmatics*, pp. 173-183 or of C. A. Auberlen: *The Divine Revelation*, pp. 175-180 will not disclose the realist position.

In dealing with this realistic position and the debate between its proponents and the proponents of the representative view of the relation between Adam and his posterity, it is necessary to place in proper perspective what the crux of the debate is. Sometimes the question is confused by failure to recognize that the proponents of representation as over against realism do not deny but rather maintain that Adam is the natural head as well as the representative head of the race. That is to say, they maintain that the race is seminally one in Adam and that representative union is not to be abstracted from seminal union. Francis Turretine, for example, is quite explicit to this effect. For while holding that the foundation of the imputation of Adam's sin is principally "moral and federal" nevertheless he does not leave out of account the natural headship arising from the unity of origin and the fact that all are of one blood. God willed that Adam should be "the stock and Head of the whole human race" and it is for that reason that "all are said to be one man".[7] What the proponents of the representative headship of Adam insist upon is that the natural or seminal union alone is not sufficient to explain the imputation of Adam's sin to posterity. In this particular respect they are at one with the proponents of realistic union, for the latter also insist on the necessity of more than unity of origin.

Furthermore, not only do the proponents of representation hold to seminal union; they also insist on community of nature. In other words, natural union is involved in natural headship and hence they will say that human nature became corrupt in Adam and that this human nature which became corrupt in Adam is transmitted to posterity by natural generation. In respect of the term "human nature", then, the difference is not that the proponents of representation deny community of nature nor do they deny that the human nature which became corrupt in Adam is propagated to the members of the race. The difference is simply that realism maintains the existence in Adam of human nature as an entity that is specifically and numerically one and at this the exponents of representation demur.

Hence the crux of the question is not whether the representative view discounts seminal union or natural headship or community

[7] *Institutio Theologiae Elencticae*. Locus IX, *Quaestio* IX, &&XI, XII.

of nature in that unity which exists between Adam and posterity but simply and solely whether the necessary *plus* which both views posit is to be interpreted in terms of an entity which existed in its totality in Adam and is individualized in the members of the race or in terms of a representation which was established by divine ordination. It is on that restricted question that the debate must turn. Other questions undoubtedly emerge in connection with this restricted question but, relatively, they are subordinate and peripheral. Confusion can be avoided only if the real crux is appreciated and debated on the basis of the pertinent data.

When the distinguishing feature of realism is perceived to be this concept of human nature as *specifically* and *numerically* one in Adam, the appeal on the part of realists to theologians of the past in support of this position is not by any means as valid as it might appear to be. For example, A. H. Strong says that "Calvin was essentially Augustinian and realistic" and appeals, in support of this claim, to the *Institutes*, II, i-iii.[8] Calvin indeed says that all of Adam's posterity became guilty on account of the fault (*culpa*) of one. He speaks of the sin of the one as common.[9] All are dead in Adam, he says, and are therefore implicated in the ruin of his sin. And, if so, he likewise maintains, all must be charged with the blame (*culpa*) of iniquity, for there is no condemnation when there is no blame (*culpa*).[10] Adam plunged all his progeny into the same miseries to which he himself became heir. If we give to such expressions the fullest scope and interpret them as implying that the one sin of Adam is the sin of all, there is no proof that Calvin conceived of the union existing between Adam and posterity in realistic terms. Calvin, however, does not leave us in doubt as to his understanding of the involvement of posterity in the sin of Adam, or, in other words, how the sin of Adam becomes the sin of all. Calvin was not unaware of the objection urged against the doctrine that the sin of Adam involved the race in ruin, namely,

---

[8]*Op. cit.*, p. 621; *cf.* also Shedd: *op. cit.*, p. 44.

[9]*Institutio Christianae Religionis*, II, i, 5: "Qua de re multa fuit illis concertatio, quum a communi sensu nihil magis sit remotum quam ob unius culpam fieri omnes reos, et ita peccatum fieri commune."

[10]*Inst.* II, i, 6: "Qui nos omnes in Adam mortuos esse pronuntiat, jam simul aperte quoque testatur, peccati labe esse implicitos. Neque enim ad eos perveniret damnatio qui nulla iniquitatis culpa attingerentur."

that posterity is charged with the guilt of a sin which is the sin of another and not their own personal transgression.[11] But he did not meet this objection by saying that the sin in question was not only the sin of Adam but also of that human nature, specifically and numerically one, which existed in its undivided totality in Adam and belonged to each member of the race as well as to Adam himself. He did not appeal to the participation of such an entity in the first sin of Adam. And there need not be doubt as to his positive answer to the question how we become involved in the sin of Adam; he does not weary of reiteration. It is to the effect that we derive from Adam by natural generation and propagation a corrupt nature. The key concept is that of hereditary depravity. Adam by his sin corrupted his nature and we all from our birth are infected with that contagion.[12] "We hear that the uncleanness of the parents is transmitted to the children so that all without any exception are defiled from their beginning. But we shall not find the origin of this pollution unless we ascend to the first parent of all, as to the fountain. Thus it is certain that Adam was not only the progenitor of human nature but as it were the root, and therefore the human race was vitiated in his corruption."[13] Adam "infected all his seed with that vitiosity into which he had fallen".[14] "Hence from a rotten root spring rotten branches which transmit their rottenness to other twigs which spring from them."[15] The figure is obviously that of contagion spreading from a corrupted source. And Calvin is even careful to say that Adam's own personal corruption does not pertain to us; it is simply that he infects us with the depravity into which he had lapsed.[16] Indubitably, therefore, according to Calvin, the sin by which posterity is ruined is the depravity which *stems* from the sin of Adam, the corrupted human nature which is the *consequence* of Adam's apostasy and which is communicated to and transfused into us by propagation. And it

---

[11] *Idem*: "Neque id suo unius vitio, quod nihil ad nos pertineat; sed quoniam universum suum semen ea, in quam lapsus erat, vitiositate infecit."

[12] *Ibid.*, II, i, 5: "Omnes ergo qui ab impuro semine descendimus peccati contagione nascimur infecti."

[13] *Ibid.*, II, i, 6.

[14] *Idem.*

[15] *Ibid.*, II, i, 7: "Proinde a radice putrefacta rami putridi prodierunt, qui suam putredinem transmiserunt ad alios ex se nascentes surculas."

[16] *Ibid.*, II, i, 6.

is not without some significance that he appeals to Augustine in support of his contention. "Therefore good men, and above all others Augustine, have laboured on this point to show that we are corrupted not by acquired wickedness but that we bring innate depravity from our mother's womb."[17]

It is not our purpose now to maintain that Calvin has given an adequate account of the relation of the race to the one sin of Adam. Our interest now is merely to show that his emphasis upon hereditary depravity, and the corruption of our nature which emanates from the sin of Adam, is no proof that Calvin held the realist conception of the Adamic union. The representative view of our relation to Adam maintains insistently all that Calvin propounds respecting the propagation of hereditary depravity and does so in Calvinian terms.

Realists also appeal with confidence to Augustine as a proponent of the realist position. It is not our interest or intent to demonstrate that Augustine did not entertain realist conceptions. It is necessary, however, to point out that the statements of Augustine on this subject, quoted or cited by the proponents of realism, are not conclusive in this connection. Augustine does say that "all sinned, since all were that one man".[18] And perhaps the following offers more apparent support than any other to a realist interpretation of Augustine's position. "For God, the author of natures, not of vices, created man upright; but man, being of his own will corrupted, and justly condemned, begat corrupted and condemned children. For we all were in that one man, since we all were that one man, who fell into sin by the woman who was made from him before the sin. For not yet was the particular form created and distributed to us, in which we as individuals were to live, but already the seminal nature was there from which we were to be propagated; and this being vitiated by sin, and bound by the chain of death, and justly condemned, man could not be born of man in another condition. And thus, from the bad use of free will, there arose the train of this calamity which leads the human race by a combination of miseries from its depraved origin, as from

---

[17] *Ibid.*, II, i, 5: "Nos non ascita nequitia corrumpi, sed ingenitam vitiositatem ab utero matris afferre."

[18] *De Peccatorum Meritis et Remissione*, I, x, 11: "in quo omnes peccaverunt; quando omnes ille unus homo fuerunt"; *cf. ibid.*, III, vii, 14.

a corrupt root, to the destruction of the second death, which has no end, those only being excepted who are freed by the grace of God."[19] When, however, the contexts of such quotations as these are examined it will be observed that the paramount interest of Augustine, as of Calvin, is to deny that it is by *imitation* that the one offence of Adam is unto the condemnation of all and to prove that it is by *propagation* that sin was transmitted from the first man to other men.[20] Referring to Paul he writes: " 'By one man', he says, 'sin entered into the world, and death by sin.' This speaks of propagation, not of imitation: for if it were by imitation, he would have said, 'by the devil'."[21] "As therefore, He, in whom all are made alive, besides offering himself as an example of righteousness to those who imitate Him, gives also to those who believe on Him the hidden grace of His Spirit, which He secretly infuses even into infants; so likewise he, in whom all die, besides being an example for imitation to those who wilfully transgress the commandment of the Lord, depraved also in his own person all who come of his stock by the hidden corruption of his own carnal concupiscence. It is entirely on this account, and for no other reason, that the apostle says: 'By one man sin entered into the world, and death by sin, and so passed upon all men; in which all have sinned.'"[22]

Consequently, although Augustine says that all of Adam's posterity were that one man, that the whole human race was in the first man,[23] and that all sinned in Adam when as yet they were that one man,[24] nevertheless when he defines more specifically

---

[19]*De Civitate Dei*, XIII, xiv; *cf. ibid.*, XIII, iii. With slight variation the translation is that of Marcus Dods in *A Select Library of the Nicene and Post-Nicene Fathers* (Buffalo, 1887).

[20]*Cf. De Pec. Mer. et Rem.*, I, ix, 9.

[21]*Ibid.*, I, ix,10.

[22]*Idem*, as translated in *A Select Library of the Nicene and Post-Nicene Fathers* (New York, 1887).

[23]*De Civ. Dei*, XIII, iii: "In primo igitur homine per feminam in progeniem transiturum universum genus humanum fuit, quando illa conjugum copula divinam sententiam suae damnationis excepit."

[24]*De Pec. Mer. et Rem.*, 111, vii, 14: "Unde nec illud liquide dici potest, quod peccatum Adae etiam non peccantibus nocuit, cum Scriptura dicat, *in quo omnes peccaverunt*. Nec sic dicuntur ista aliena peccata, tanquam omnino ad parvulos non pertineant: siquidem in Adam omnes tunc peccaverunt, quando in ejus natura illa insita vi qua eos gignere poterat, adhuc omnes ille unus fuerunt: sed dicuntur aliena, quia nondum ipsi agebant vitas proprias, sed quidquid erat in futura propagine, vita unius hominis continebat."

the sin by which all sinned in Adam and through which death passed to all he does so in terms of original sin or hereditary depravity passed on from Adam to his seed by propagation. The reason why posterity is said to have sinned in Adam is that the "seminal nature",[25] from which all were to be propagated, had been defiled in Adam when as yet it existed only in him. And so, when Augustine exegetes Romans 5:12 and particularly "in whom all sinned", his most defining concept is that Adam "depraved ... in himself by the hidden corruption of his carnal concupiscence all who come of his stock"[26] and that this defilement is propagated by natural generation.

When this is recognized it is not so apparent that Augustine's thought follows the realist pattern. In the last analysis he falls back on the notion of original sin as propagated. And we must bear in mind that the concept of human nature as defiled in Adam and transmitted to posterity by propagation is not the monopoly of the realist. The proponent of representation holds as tenaciously to that doctrine as does the realist. While it is granted that some of Augustine's expressions could readily fall into the realist construction of the Adamic union, there is no clear-cut or conclusive evidence in these quotations that he conceived of the rationale of our involvement in Adam's sin as consisting in the *participation* of human nature, as specifically and numerically one, in the sin of Adam. He conceived indeed of human nature as having become depraved in Adam and as communicated to us. But these two are not identical and to fail to distinguish them leads only to confusion and to misapprehension of the *status quaestionis.*

If the distinguishing feature of realism has been brought into focus and if the question at issue has been placed in proper perspective, we may now address ourselves to the examination of realism as it applies to our topic. It may be repeated that if realism were shown to be correct it would provide an adequate explanation of the two ways in which the one event may be viewed, namely, that "*one* sinned" and yet "*all* sinned". However, is there evidence to support this construction of the relationship of the one to the many?

---

[25]*Cf. De Civ. Dei*, XIII, xiv.

[26]*De Pec. Mer. et Rem.*, I, ix, 10.

(i) W. G. T. Shedd maintains that it is unreasonable to regard representative union of Adam and posterity as a proper basis for the imputation of Adam's sin, because such imputation would be "an arbitrary act of sovereignty". But, we are compelled to ask, does the notion of human nature, specifically and numerically one, human nature as an "elementary invisible substance", in any way relieve the difficulty entailed? For the real question is how the individual members of the race can bear the guilt of a sin in which they did not, *as individuals*, personally and voluntarily participate. And the realist has to admit that the individual members of the race did not *personally* and *voluntarily* participate in the sin of this human nature as it existed in its unity in Adam. The sin of generic humanity is just as far removed from the individual sin of the members of posterity as is the sin of a representative head and that for the simple reason that *as individuals* posterity did not yet exist. In other words, it is as difficult to establish the nexus between the sin of generic humanity and the members of the race as it is to establish the nexus between the sin of Adam as representative head and the members of the race. After all, generic humanity as it existed in Adam is impersonal unindividualized human nature.

(ii) The analogy instituted in Romans 5:12-19 (*cf.* 1 Cor. 15:22) presents a formidable objection to the realist construction. It is admitted by the realist that there is no "realistic" union between Christ and the justified. That is to say, there is no human nature, specifically and numerically one, existing in its unity in Christ, which is individualized in those who are the beneficiaries of Christ's righteousness. On realist premises, therefore, a radical disparity must be posited between the character of the union that exists between Adam and his posterity, on the one hand, and the union that exists between Christ and those who are his, on the other. In Romans 5:15-19 the differences between the reign of sin, condemnation, and death and the reign of righteousness, justification, and life are in the forefront; they are evident from the negations of verses 15-17 and from the emphasis placed upon the superabundance that prevails in the provisions of grace. But there is no hint of the kind of discrepancy that would obtain if the distinction between the nature of the union in the two cases were as radical as realism must suppose. This argument from silence might carry little weight of itself. But the case is not merely that there is no hint of this kind of difference; the sustained parallelism militates against any such supposition. Adam is the type of the one to come (v. 14). Adam as the one is parallel to Jesus Christ as the one (v. 17). The one trespass unto condemnation is parallel to the one righteousness unto justification (v. 18). The disobedience of the one is parallel to the obedience of the one (v. 19). This sustained emphasis not only upon the one man Adam and the one man Christ but also upon the one trespass and the one righteous act points to a basic identity in respect of *modus operandi*. But if, in the one case, we have a oneness that is focused in the unity of the human nature, which realism posits, and, in the other case, a oneness that is focused in the one man Jesus Christ, where no *such* unity exists, it is difficult not to believe that discrepancy enters at the very point where similitude must be maintained. For, after all, on realist assumptions, it is not our union with Adam that is the crucial consideration in our involvement in his sin but our involvement in the sin of that human nature which existed in Adam. And what the parallelism of Romans 5:12-19 would indicate is that the one sin of the one man Adam is analogous on the side of condemnation to the one righteousness of the one man Jesus Christ on the side of justification. The kind of relationship that obtains in the one case obtains in the other. And how can this be if the kind of relationship is so different in respect of the *nature* of the union subsisting?

It is not a valid objection to the foregoing argument drawn from the parallelism in Romans 5:12-19 to say that, since there is an incontestable distinction between the relation of Adam to the race and the relation of Christ to his own, there is no reason why the further distinction which realism posits should be inconsistent with the parallelism of the passage concerned. The distinction which cannot be questioned is that Adam sustains a genetic relation to the whole race and that all are seminally united with and derived from him. This does not hold in the relation of Christ to his people. But the reason why this consideration does not affect the argument is that, in terms of the debate between the realist and the representationist, it is not the fact of seminal, genetic relationship that constitutes the specific ground of our involvement in the one sin of the one man Adam either for the realist or for the exponent of representation. For the realist it is realistic union; for the representationist it is representative union. And in the matter of Romans 5:12-19 it is the question of the ground upon which the one sin of Adam is unto the condemnation of all and the one righteousness of Christ unto the justification of all who are Christ's. Neither the realist nor the representationist holds that the ground in the case of Adam's sin is the fact that Adam is the natural progenitor of the race. Both are concerned with the *specific ground* of the imputation of Adam's sin, and, in respect of the parallel drawn in Romans 5:12-19, the question is whether the *specific ground* posited by the realist for this imputation is compatible with the analogy which is instituted by the apostle between the one sin of the one man unto condemnation and the one righteousness of the one man Jesus Christ unto justification. The specific character of the union which is the specific ground of condemnation and justification is the question at issue.

(iii) When we ask the question as to the evidence provided by Scripture for the existence in Adam of this "elementary invisible substance" called human nature construed as specifically and numerically one, we are at a loss to find it. We are truly one in Adam, in terms of Hebrews 7:9, 10 we were all in the loins of Adam, he is the first parent of all mankind, and seminally there is the unity of Adam and his posterity. Adam was the first endowed with human nature and to all his offspring he has transmitted that human nature by natural procreation. All of this is maintained by representationists as well as by realists and finds support in Scripture. But the additional postulate on the part of the realist, the postulate indispensable to his distinctive position, is not one that can plead the support of biblical evidence. And it is not a postulate that is necessary to explain the facts brought to our attention in the biblical revelation. The union that exists between Adam and posterity is one that can be interpreted in terms for which there is sufficient evidence in the data of revelation available to us.

(iv) The argument of the realist to the effect that only the doctrine of the specific unity of the race in Adam lays a proper basis in justice for the imputation to posterity of the sin of Adam and his contention that the imputation to posterity of the sin of a vicarious representative violates the order of justice[27] do not

---

[27]*Cf.* Shedd: *op. cit.*, p. 36.

take sufficient account of what is involved in our solidaric or corporate relationships. Realists admit that only in the case of Adam and posterity does their postulate of specific unity hold true. And solidaric relationship, they must likewise admit, exists in other institutions where the specific unity exemplified in Adam is not present at all. But, if we analyse the responsibilities entailed in these other solidaric relationships and assess the same in scriptural terms, we shall find that moral responsibility devolves upon the members of a corporate entity by virtue of the actions of the representatives or the representative of that entity.[28] Consequently the denial of the imputation of vicarious sin runs counter to the way in which the principle of solidarity operates in other spheres. And it is not valid to insist that vicarious sin can be imputed only when there is the *voluntary* engagement to undertake such imputation.[29] Corporate relationship exists by divine institution and the corporate responsibilities exist and come to effect apart altogether from voluntary engagement on the part of the persons concerned to assume these responsibilities. It is only because we fail to take account of the pervasiveness of corporate responsibility and think too lightly of the implications of this responsibility that we might be ready to accede to the argument that there cannot be the imputation to us of the sin of a vicarious representative. As the principle applies to Adam it is not difficult to see that imputation of sin on the basis of Adam's representative capacity could operate with unique and universal application. For this would be but the extension to the whole race, in terms of its solidarity in Adam, of a principle which is exemplified constantly in more restricted corporate relationships.

---

[28]It is purely gratuitous to say, as Shedd does, that "representative union requires and supposes the consent of the individuals who are to be represented" (*ibid.*, p. 39). This is not the case in some of the solidaric relationships which exist among men by divine constitution. In the state, for example, it is a fallacy to suppose that the solidarity arises simply and solely from the consent of the citizens or subjects. The state is a divine ordinance and its sanctions and responsibilities do not emanate from voluntary contract on the part of the members.

[29]*Cf.* Shedd: *ibid.*, p. 57.

2. The Representative View

In presenting and defending the representative view it is necessary to relieve it of some misrepresentation on the part of opponents and of certain extravagances on the part of proponents. With reference to the latter, as will be shown later in this series of studies, the representative view is not bound up with the assumption that posterity is involved only in the *poena* of Adam's sin and not in the *culpa*. It is not to be supposed that only realism can hold to the imputation of the *culpa* of Adam's transgression. Furthermore, the representative view is not to be loaded with the distinction between *reatus culpae* and *reatus poenae* which the older reformed theologians rejected and which they characterized and criticized as papistical. With reference to misrepresentation or at least misconception on the part of opponents, it may not be unnecessary to repeat that the representative view does not deny but rather affirms the natural headship of Adam, the seminal union of Adam and posterity, that all derive from Adam by natural generation a corrupt nature, and that therefore original sin is passed on by propagation. W. G. T. Shedd says: "Since the idea of representation by Adam is incompatible with that of specific existence in Adam, the choice must be made between representative union and natural union. A combination of the two views is illogical."[30] It is true that in terms of Shedd's definition of natural union as that of specific existence in Adam there cannot be a combination of the two ideas in the explanation of the imputation of Adam's sin to posterity; to say the least, one idea makes superfluous the other. And it is also true that the representative idea finds in representation rather than in natural headship the *specific* ground of the imputation of Adam's sin. In this respect there is similarity to the realist distinction,

[30]*Ibid.*, p. 39; *cf.* pp. 37 f. It should be noted, however, that realists do not refrain from speaking of Adam as the representative head of the human race. Philip Schaff says: "Adam fell, not as an individual simply, but as the real representative head of the human race" (*op cit.*, p. 179). And A. H. Strong: "Only on this supposition of Natural Headship could God justly constitute Adam our representative, or hold us responsible for the depraved nature we have received from him" (*op. cit.*, p. 623). This use of the word "representative", however, is in their esteem based upon the conception of the specific unity of the race in Adam and does not have associated with it the distinguishing connotation attached to it by those maintaining the representative view in distinction from and opposition to the realist.

because realists find in the specific unity rather than in Adam's parenthood the *specific* ground of the imputation of Adam's sin. But it is quite illogical to maintain that on the representationist view of Adam's natural headship there is any incompatibility between natural headship and representative union. On the representative construction natural headship and representative headship are correlative, and each aspect has its own proper and specific function in the explanation of the status and condition in which the members of the race find themselves in consequence of their relation to Adam. Hence it must be appreciated that emphasis upon the natural headship of Adam and upon the seminal union of Adam and his posterity in reformed theologians is not to be interpreted as vacillation between two incompatible ideas,[31] nor is appeal to natural headship and seminal relationship on the part of such theologians to be regarded as the espousal of the realist construction.[32]

When we come to the question of the evidence in support of the representative view it is necessary to adduce in more positive fashion considerations mentioned already in the criticism of realism.

(i) The natural or seminal union between Adam and posterity is not in question; it is assumed. It might be argued that this is all that is necessary and that Scripture does not clearly establish any additional kind of union, that as Levi paid tithes when he was in the loins of Abraham, so posterity sinned in the loins of Adam.[33] Why postulate more? Some *plus*, however, appears to be demanded. It may not be questioned that there is something severely unique and distinct about our involvement in the sin of Adam. The sin

---

[31]*Cf.* Shedd: *op. cit.*, p. 36.

[32]*Cf.* Shedd's interpretation of Calvin in this regard (*ibid.*, p. 44).

[33]The Westminster Confession of Faith may appear to ground the imputation of Adam's sin upon the seminal relationship in Chapter VI, iii, when, referring to our first parents, it says: "They being the root of all mankind, the guilt of this sin was imputed; and the same death in sin, and corrupted nature, conveyed to all their posterity descending from them by ordinary generation". The Larger Catechism, however, grounds the imputation of Adam's sin upon the covenant institution. "The covenant being made with Adam as a publick person, not for himself only, but for his posterity, all mankind descending from him by ordinary generation, sinned in him, and fell with him in that first transgression" (Q. 22; *cf.* The Shorter Catechism, Q. 16). How the difference is to be explained is another question into which it is not necessary to enter now.

is the *one* sin of Adam. If the relationship to Adam were simply that of seminal union, that of being in his loins, this would not provide any explanation why the sin imputed is the first sin *alone*. We were as much in his loins when he committed other sins and these other sins would be just as applicable to us as his first sin if the whole explanation of the imputation of his first sin resides in the fact that we were in his loins. Hence some additional factor is required to explain the restriction to the one sin of Adam. In the light of the narrative in Genesis 2 and 3 we shall have to infer that the prohibition of the tree of the knowledge of good and evil was associated with and epitomized some special relationship that was constituted by divine institution and by reason of which the trespass or disobedience of Adam in this particular involved not only Adam but all of his posterity by natural generation. In other words, there was a special act of providence by which a special relationship was constituted in terms of which we are to interpret the implications for posterity of that one trespass of Adam in partaking of the forbidden fruit.

(ii) In 1 Corinthians 15:22, 45-49 Paul provides us with what is one of the most striking and significant rubrics in all of Scripture. He comprehends God's dealings with men under the two-fold headship of the two Adams. There is none before Adam; he is the first man. There is none between Adam and Christ, for Christ is the second man. There is none after Christ; he is the last Adam (vv. 45-47). Adam and Christ sustain unique relations to men. And that history and destiny are determined by these relationships is demonstrated by verse 22: "As in Adam all die, even so in Christ all shall be made alive". All who die die in Adam; all who are made alive are made alive in Christ. In view of this comprehensive philosophy of human history and destiny and in view of the pivotal and determinative roles of the first and last Adam, we must posit constitutive ordination on God's part to these unique relationships. And since the analogy instituted between Adam and Christ is so conspicuous, it is surely necessary to assume that the kind of relationship which Adam sustains to men is after the pattern of the relationship which Christ sustains to men. To put the case conversely, surely the kind of relationship that Christ sustains to men is after the pattern which Adam sustains to men (*cf.* Rom. 5:14). But if all that we posit in the case of Adam is simply his natural headship or parenthood, we do not have the kind of relationship that would provide the pattern for the headship of Christ. Hence the analogy would require some community of relationship which the natural headship of Adam does not provide.

(iii) As noted already, Romans 5:12-19 furnishes more evidence relevant to the question at issue than any other passage. The fact that Adam is the type of the one to come (v. 14) and the sustained parallelism throughout the succeeding verses (vv. 15-19) imply some similarity of relationship. And when we ask the question what this common principle is there are three things to be said. (a) In the relation of Adam to posterity we must posit more than natural headship, for the simple reason that, as we found above, this kind of union provides no analogy to the union that exists between Christ and his people. (b) In the case of Christ and the justified we know that the union is that of vicarious representation. In the provisions of grace Christ has been ordained to act for and in the place of those who are the beneficiaries of redemption. His righteousness becomes theirs unto their justification and eternal life. This is a constitution that exists by divine institution, and the whole process which negates the reign of sin, condemnation, and death rests upon the union thereby constituted. (c) The general thrust as well as the details of the passage would indicate that a similar kind of relationship exists in the reign of sin, condemnation, and death. The passage is built upon the contrast between the reign of sin, condemnation, and death, on the one hand, as proceeding from the sin of Adam, and the reign of righteousness, justification, and life, on the other, as proceeding from the righteousness of Christ. We are compelled to recognize an identity of *modus operandi* because Adam is the type of Christ. Why, we may ask, should we seek for any other principle in terms of which the reign of sin, condemnation, and death operates than the principle which is exemplified in the reign of righteousness, justification, and life? We cannot posit less. Why should we posit more when there is no evidence to demand or support it?

We conclude, therefore, that more than natural headship is necessary, that natural headship does not carry with it the notion of "specific unity" in Adam, that the *plus* required to explain the imputation of Adam's *first* sin and no other is not shown by Scripture to be the kind of union which realism postulates, and that when we seek to discover the specific character of the union which will ground the imputation of Adam's first sin we find it to be that same kind of union as is analogous to the union that exists between Christ and his people and on the basis of which his righteousness is theirs unto justification and eternal life. How we should denominate this kind of union is a matter of terminology. If we call it representative union or headship, this will suffice for identification purposes. Solidarity was constituted by divine institution and the solidarity is of such a nature that the sin of Adam devolves upon all naturally procreated posterity.

Chapter Three

IV. THE NATURE OF THE IMPUTATION

IF THE union existing between Adam and his posterity is analogous to that which exists between Christ and his people and may thus be called representative union, the next question that arises is that of the mode by which the sin of Adam comes to be reckoned to the account of posterity. Discussion of this question is required by exegetical and theological considerations, particularly by the data implicit in Romans 5:12-19. But the history of debate on this question compels us to deal with it, even if we were disposed to discount or ignore the exegetical data. And history in this case, as in so many others, dictates the direction in which the discussion must be turned. There are two viewpoints which, in contrast with each other, serve to bring the question into the perspective that throws a flood of light upon the significance of the exegetical data.

1. Mediate Imputation

The name particularly associated with the doctrine of mediate imputation is that of Josua Placaeus (Josué de la Place) of the reformed school at Saumur. He was understood to have taught that original sin consisted simply in the depravity derived from Adam and did not include the imputation of the guilt of Adam's first sin. The Twenty-Eighth Synod of the reformed Churches in France, meeting at Charenton from December 26, 1644 to January 26, 1645, officially condemned this doctrine in the following terms. "There was a report made in the Synod of a certain writing, both printed and manuscript, holding forth this doctrine, that the whole nature of original sin consisted only in that corruption, which is hereditary to all Adam's posterity, and residing originally in all men, and denieth the imputation of his first sin. The Synod condemneth the said doctrine as far as it restraineth the nature of original sin to the sole hereditary corruption of Adam's posterity, to the excluding of the imputation of that first sin by which he fell, and interdicteth on pain of all Church-censures all pastors, professors, and others, who shall treat of this question, to depart from the common received opinion of the Protestant Churches, who (over and besides that corruption) have all acknowledged the imputation of Adam's first sin unto his posterity."[1] Placaeus replied to this decree of the Synod by maintaining that he did not deny the imputation to posterity of Adam's first sin and that therefore he was in entire accord with the Synod's decree in not restricting original sin to hereditary corruption. What he maintained was that the imputation of Adam's first sin was *mediate*, not *immediate*. Immediate and antecedent imputation, he contended, must be distinguished from mediate and consequent. The former takes place immediately and is not mediated by hereditary corruption; the latter takes place mediately and is mediated by this corruption. In the former case the imputation of Adam's first sin precedes corruption in the order of nature and is reckoned to be the cause of corruption; in the latter case the imputation of the first sin follows hereditary corruption and is reckoned to be the effect. Immediate imputation Placaeus rejected and mediate imputation he espoused. In a word his position was that the imputation to posterity of Adam's first sin was mediated through the inheritance from him of a corrupt nature.[2]

---

[1]*Synodicon in Gallia Reformata: or, the Acts, Decisions, Decrees, and Canons of those Famous National Councils of the Reformed Churches in France*, ed. John Quick (London, 1692), vol. II, p. 473.

[2]Placaeus deals with the question in an extensive treatise, *De Imputatione Primi Peccati Adami Disputatio Bipertita* in which he deals with the decree of the Synod of Charenton and with the theologians who had controverted his position as well as with others of the past and contemporary with himself who, he claimed, supported his contentions. This treatise in two parts is found in his *Opera Omnia* (Franeker, 1699), Tom. I, pp. 159-479. The following quotations will serve as examples of his distinction between immediate and mediate imputation. "Sin vero per primum Adae peccatum, primum ejus peccatum actuale intelligitur ... distinguenda est imputatio in imputationem immediatam seu antecedentem, et imputationem mediatam seu consequentem: illa fit immediate, hoc est, non mediante corruptione; haec fit mediate, hoc est, mediante corruptione

It is not surprising that Placaeus should have been understood to deny altogether the imputation of Adam's first sin. For in several places in his works, even subsequent to the decree of the Synod of Charenton, he explicitly contends against the doctrine of the imputation to posterity of the actual first sin of Adam whether this imputation is conceived of as *culpa* or *poena*.[3]

---

haereditaria. Illa ordine naturae corruptionem antecedit; haec sequitur. Illa corruptionis causa censetur esse, haec effectum. Illam Placeus rejicit, hanc admittit" (*Opera Omnia*, I, p. 173).

"Potest enim animo concipi duplex imputatio. *Immediata* et *Mediata*.... Immediatam voco eam, quam solam Theaibus, quas tu refutandas tibi sumpsisti, negare volui; qua putatur *actio* illa Adami, hoc est, vetiti fructus manducatio ejus posteris omnibus (Christo excepto) proxime, immediate, hoc ipso quod filii sunt Adami, imputari ad duas istas poenas proprie dictas, privationem justitiae originalis quam mortem spiritualem appellas, et mortem aeternam. Hanc solam imputationem actionis illius ego negavi, quia non docetur in Sacris literis adequata fidei nostrae norma, quia pugnat cum Sacris literis, quia Deum facit authorem peccati, quia Dei justitiam dehonestat, quia sequitur ex ea Christum esse natura sua peccatorem, quia alia nonnulla trahit secum absurda, mirabilem religionis Christianae puritatem et splendorem obscurantia, quae utinam fratres et conservi nostri a me per theses moniti, aut non prorsus contempsissent, aut non contemptim expendissent!

"Mediatam seu consequentem appello eam, quae haereditariae corruptionis in nos ab Adamo derivatae intuitum consequitur, eaque mediante fit. Hujus enim corruptionis participatione communicamus peccato Adami, eique, ut ita loquar, habitualiter consentimus, ac propterea digni sumus, qui Adamo peccatori annumeremur" (*ibid*., p. 280).

"Quaeritur, *Utrum primum peccatum actuale Adami praecise sumptum, nobis ejus posteris imputetur a Deo justo judice proxime, immediate ac ordine naturae priusquam inhaerenkter corrupti simus?* Tu venerande Frater affirmas: ego nego" (*ibid*., p. 281).

[3]"Quandocunque igitur Deus nobis peccatum originis *imputare* dicatur, sive cum sumus, siue antequam simis, sive in tempore, sive ab aeterno, id peccatum aliud nihil est quam inhaerens illud a nativitate nobis vitium, quod a primo nostro parente non per *imputationem*, sed per carnalem generationem traximus" (*ibid*., p. 442). "Denique de jure non magis ad me *poena* Adami pertinet quam *culpa* (*ibid*., p. 291). "Cum enim affirmo, peccatum actuale Adami nobis non imputari, non hoc volo, peccatum illud non considerari ut peccatum, sed tegi, condonari, et remitti nobis .... Sed, quicquid fit, contendo peccatum illud Adami actuale nostrum peccatum non esse. Itaque nobis jure imputari non posse" (*ibid*., p. 307). "Tribus autem modis communicari potest peccatum, docendo, imputando, et propagando generatione naturali. Non communicavit (Adamus) autem docendo .... Non communicavit etiam imputatione; nam nec imputatio est actio Adami, nec actio justi judicis peccatorem facit .... Communicavit igitur propagatione naturali, transmisso per generationem carnalem semine, quam naturae, tam vitiositatis naturae .... Haec corruptio peccatum est, non quidem

And it is understandable that the critics of Placaeus' position should aver that mediate imputation as propounded by him is tantamount to a denial of the imputation to posterity of Adam's *first* sin.[4]

In the debate that ensued upon the issuance of the decree of the Synod Placaeus was to a very large extent concerned with his opponent Garissolius but also with others, the most notable of whom were Andrew Rivetus and Samuel Maresius. Rivetus wrote a rather lengthy treatise[5] which largely consists of quotations from the creeds of the Protestant Churches and from Protestant theologians. A large number of these quotations do not bear precisely upon the point of the distinction later propounded by Placaeus in his *Disputatio*. Some of them do not even bear upon the question of the imputation of Adam's first sin but are concerned with the doctrine of original sin or inherent depravity. But a considerable number of the quotations are directly germane to the question raised by Placaeus' distinction, in that they expressly assert the priority of the imputation of Adam's first sin. Apparently Rivetus' purpose was not to maintain that *all* these quotations referred to the distinction which the Synod made between the imputation of Adam's first sin and the hereditary depravity derived from him, far less that they all upheld the antecedence of the guilt of Adam's first sin. We can only infer that he set forth a great variety of quotations, many of which supported the distinction which the Synod had formulated and with which Placaeus later professed himself to be in full agreement, and some of which were

actuale, aed habituale, et voluntaria eat, non ut actio, sed ut qualitas, hoc est, non quia est a voluntate, sed quia est in voluntate" (*ibid.*, pp. 708 f.).

[4]*Cf.* Francis Turretine who says of mediate imputation: "Verum si penitus res attendatur, non obscure patebit distinctionem istam ad fucum faciendum esse excogitatam, quae nomen imputationis retinendo, rem ipsam de facto tollit. Nam si ideo tantum Adae peccatum nobis imputari dicitur mediate, quia apud Deum rei constituimur, et obnoxii poenae fimus propter corruptionem haereditariam quam ab Adamo trahimus, nulla erit imputatio proprie peccati Adami, sed tantum labis inhaerentis" (*Institutio Theologiae Elencticae*, Loc. IX, Quaest. IX,8 VI).

[5]*Decretum Synodi Nationalis Ecclesiarum Reformatarum Galliae initio Anni 1645 de Imputatione Primi Peccati Omnibus Adami Posteris* (see *Opera Theologica*, Rotterdam, 1660, Tom. 111, pp. 798-823). See the English translation of some of Rivetus' quotations by Charles Hodge in *Theological Essays: Reprinted from the Princeton Review* (New York, 1846), pp. 196-217.

clearly in conflict with the position later enunciated by Placaeus, namely, that of the consequent or posterior imputation of Adam's first sin.[6] Whatever may be said of the validity of Placaeus' contention in the last two chapters of his *Disputatio* to the effect that the Confessions of the reformed Churches do not favour the doctrine of the immediate imputation of Adam's first sin and that, furthermore, this doctrine is alien to that of the early reformers, it was not difficult for him to show that such creeds as the Gallic, Belgic, Scottish, and Helvetic did not formulate a doctrine of immediate imputation and could not therefore be appealed to in support of the same.[7]

The viewpoint propounded by Placaeus and the debate provoked by it exercised a profound influence upon subsequent thought on the whole question. Theologians like Heidegger and Turretine in the seventeenth century used their polemic talents in opposition to the doctrine of mediate imputation. In the matter of creedal formulation the most significant fact is that the *Formula Consensus Helvetica* (1675) declared explicitly in favor of the doctrine of immediate imputation.[8] Mediate imputation also enlisted its advocates in the centuries that followed. On the continent of Europe the names of Campegius Vitringa, Hermann Venema, and J. F. Stapfer are usually listed as exponents of mediate imputation.[9] In the United States of America mediate

---

[6]The priority of the imputation of Adam's first sin appears quite plainly, for example, in the quotations from William Bucanus, Amandus Polanus, Theodore Beza, Lambertus Danaeus Aureliur, and Robert Rollock. The main thesis of Rivetus' treatise, namely, that the distinction set forth by the Synod of Charenton was the common sentiment of the Protestant Churches, the quotations bear out. With this thesis, of course, Placaeus did not profess to be in disagreement. It has to be borne in mind, however, that it was in support of the Synod's distinction that Rivetus compiled his testimonies, whereas Placaeus' *Disputatio* is devoted to a refutation of *immediate* imputation. But since some of the quotations bear directly upon this latter question Rivetus' treatise is of considerable value in reference to the debate on immediate imputation.

[7]*Cf.* Placaeus: *op. cit.*, pp. 446-459.

[8]*Formula Consensus Helvetica*, Canones X, XI, XII.

[9]With reference to Campegius Vitringa the elder the only reflection on the question that I have been able to find in his published works is that in his *Doctrina Christianae Religionis per Apharismos Summatim Descripta* (Leyden, 1762), edited by Martinus Vitringa, in which he says: "Qui reatus, an a primo Adami peccato *mediate*, an *immediate* pendeat, in scholis subtilius magis, quam utilius disputatur;

imputation was adopted by certain New England theologians of the eighteenth century and was one of the tenets of the new school theology in the Presbyterian Church in the nineteenth century. As representative of the latter, Henry B. Smith vigorously opposed immediate imputation[10] and sets forth mediate imputation as the position which, in his esteem, does more justice to the facts of the case.[11] In dealing with the developments which took place among the New England theologians it is necessary to enter into more detail. For though there is an affinity with the doctrine of mediate imputation as formulated by Placaeus, yet so many marked differences had appeared that the doctrine of mediate imputation, as historically understood, can scarcely be regarded as a proper description of the viewpoint entertained. The case might be more accurately described as one of decided opposition to the doctrine of immediate imputation, an opposition which served as a starting-point for a construction which is in some respects similar to that of mediate imputation but which in the course of development meant the complete abandonment of the notion of the imputation to posterity of Adam's first sin.

Samuel Hopkins is explicit to the effect "that the sin, and the consequent guilt and condemnation of all the human race, were by divine constitution connected with Adam's sinning",[12] that "by virtue of the covenant and constitution made with the father of mankind" all men "fell under condemnation to death" and "are become wholly corrupt and sinful".[13] Hence "the sin and ruin of all mankind was implied and certainly involved in the first act of disobedience of Adam".[14] But, Hopkins continues, "it is not to be

---

cum eadem utrobique res teneatur, et adversus Pelagianizantes asseratur. Id certum, intervenisse hic Dei judicium, et posse proinde hoc consequens peccati protoplastorum, in eorum posteris, hoc sensu appelari peccatum originale imputatum" (Para 11, pp. 347 f.) This would indicate that Vitringa was not very jealous for one position against another in the dispute. The long and informative note by Martinus Vitringa in the same volume (pp. 349-354) provides a survey of the debate in the seventeenth century and of the theologians involved. The English translation of Venema's *Institutes of Theology* by Alex. W. Brown (Andover, 1853) clearly shows that Venema espoused mediate imputation (*cf.* pp. 518 ff.). With Stapfer's position we shall deal later in connection with Jonathan Edwards.

[10]Henry B. Smith: *System of Christian Theology* (New York, 1888), pp. 304-308.

[11]*Ibid.*, pp. 314 ff.

[12]*Works* (Boston, 1854), vol. I, p. 214.

[13]*Ibid.*, pp. 215-217.

supposed that the offence of Adam is imputed to them to their condemnation, while they are considered as in themselves, in their own persons, innocent; or that they are guilty of the sin of their first father, antecedent to their own sinfulness". All that is meant is that by the aforesaid constitution there is "a certain connection between the first sin of Adam and the sinfulness of his posterity" and by this constitution it had been fixed that "all mankind should sin as Adam had done, and fully consent to his transgression".[15] Thus they joined with him in his transgression and made it their own. This conception of divine constitution appears as a refrain in Hopkins' discussion and upon it the connection of the sin of Adam with the sinfulness of all is made to depend. And, although by reason of this constitution all mankind are born in sin and are sinful from the beginning of their existence, Hopkins defends the constitution as just, wise, and good.

On this analysis of the relation of the sin of Adam to the sin of posterity it must be recognized, however, that *the sin* of Adam is not charged to the account of posterity. In reality there is no imputation of Adam's sin to posterity either *mediately* or *immediately*. Hopkins says expressly, "And if the sinfulness of all the posterity of Adam was certainly connected with his sinning, this does not make them sinners before they actually are sinners; and when they actually become sinners, they themselves are the sinners, it is their own sin, and they are as blamable and guilty as if Adam had never sinned, and each one were the first sinner that ever existed. The children of Adam are not answerable for his sin, and it is not their sin any further than they approve of it, by sinning as he did. In this way only they become guilty of his sin, viz., by approving of what he did, and joining with him in rebellion. And it being previously certain, by divine constitution, that all mankind would thus sin and join with their common head in rebellion, renders it no less their own sin and crime than if this certainty had taken place on any other ground, or in any other way; or than if there had been no certainty that they would thus all sin, were this possible."[16] The force of this is that posterity is not involved in the sin of Adam by reason of the divinely constituted relationship

[14] *Ibid.*, p. 216.
[15] *Ibid.*, p. 218.
[16] *Ibid.*, p. 230.

that exists between Adam and posterity; the divine constitution simply insures that posterity will sin as Adam did.

There are two further observations to be made respecting Hopkins' position. First, the doctrine of mediate imputation as originally formulated laid emphasis upon *hereditary* corruption as the medium through which the first sin of Adam was imputed to posterity. Hopkins is clear to the effect that "mankind are born totally corrupt or sinful, in consequence of the apostasy of Adam"[17] and so "a child, an infant, as soon as he exists, may have moral corruption or sin".[18] But, in view of what has been shown already, this native depravity is not to be construed as the medium through which the sin of Adam is imputed even to infants but only as making it certain that all the members of the race will "begin to sin as soon as they begin to act as moral agents".[19] In this respect also Hopkins can scarcely be classified with the earlier exponents of mediate imputation even though there is a genetic relationship. Secondly, when Hopkins says that the sin, which "takes place in the posterity of Adam, is not properly distinguished into original and actual sin, because it is all really actual, and there is, strictly speaking, no other sin but actual sin",[20] he is not to be interpreted as equating the word "actual" with what we call "actual transgressions". What he means is that whenever sin exists, even in an infant, there is a corrupt inclination that is of the same nature with that which is expressed in overt voluntary transgression. What Hopkins is rightly asserting is that evil inclination always precedes overt sin and that this evil inclination is actually sinful and as evil motion exists in infants. In terms of his own principles, therefore, the sin by which posterity becomes sinful and sins as Adam did is predicable of new born infants by reason of the sinful inclination with which they are born, though they do not yet have the capacity or opportunity for voluntary overt transgression.[21]

---

[17]*Ibid.*, p. 226.

[18]*Ibid.*, p. 224.

[19]*Ibid.*, p. 222.

[20]*Ibid.*, p. 224.

[21]*Cf. ibid.*, p. 225. In this respect it appears to me that F. H. Foster's discussion in *A Genetic History of the New England Theology* (Chicago, 1907), pp. 175f. is distinctly misleading. He does not discriminate sufficiently to make clear what Hopkins means by "actual" as distinct from volitional action.

In Nathanael Emmons the development of thought which appears in Hopkins takes on a distinctly more advanced complexion. In dealing with the question how we became sinners by Adam, Emmons maintains that "Adam did not make us sinners, by causing us to commit his first offence",[22] nor did Adam transfer to posterity the guilt of his first transgression,[23] and neither did Adam convey to posterity a morally corrupt nature.[24] The only proper answer, in Emmons' esteem, is that since God made Adam the public head of his posterity he "determined to treat them according to his conduct".[25] God suspended the holiness and sinfulness of posterity upon the conduct of Adam and by this divine constitution the whole human race was rendered unholy and depraved because by his first transgression Adam "proved the occasion of God's bringing all his posterity into the world in a state of moral depravity".[26] In Emmons we find the same principle of divine constitution in terms of which all men become sinners but there is not the semblance of the notion that Adam's sin is reckoned to posterity, not even in the form adopted by Hopkins that "they become guilty of his sin ... by approving of what he did, and joining with him in rebellion". Adam's sin is merely the occasion upon which God acts in accordance with the constitution which he ordained and established.

To much the same effect is the position of Timothy Dwight. "*When I assert, that in consequenence of the Apostacy of Adam all men have sinned; I do not intend, that the posterity of Adam is guilty of his transgression.* Moral actions are not, so far as I can see, transferable from one being to another, The personal act of any agent is, in its very nature, the act of that agent solely; and incapable of being participated by any other agent. Of course, the guilt of such a personal act is equally incapable of being transferred, or participated. The guilt is inherent in the action; and is attributable, therefore, to the Agent only.... *Neither do I intend, that the descendants of Adam are punished for his transgression.*"[27] And Dwight falls back on the same explanation

[22]*Works* (Boston, 1842), vol. IV, p. 487.
[23]*Ibid.*, p. 488.
[24]*Ibid.*, p. 490.
[25]*Idem.*
[26]*Ibid.*, p. 491.
[27]*Theology Explained and Defended* (New York, 1863), vol. I, pp. 478 f.

of the universality of sin, namely, that by the state of things that had been constituted all became sinners in consequence of the transgression of Adam.[28]

Even a brief survey of the New England Theology requires the mention of one other in the genealogy, the name of Nathaniel W. Taylor. Taylor, like his predecessors, maintained that "*the sinfulness of mankind is in consequence of the sin of Adam*".[29] This general proposition, however, does not determine the particular mode of the connection between Adam's sin and the sinfulness of the race. In Taylor's judgment it is in "this general and indefinite manner that the Scriptures exhibit the connection".[30] He protests against what he calls "gratuitous and unauthorized speculation" and proceeds forthwith to two explicit denials: "1. That the posterity of Adam do not become sinners as a consequence of his sin, by being created with a *sinful nature*, or by having such a nature conveyed to them by the laws of propagation.... 2. Adam's posterity do not become sinners as a consequence of his sin, *by being guilty of his sin.*"[31] These quotations illustrate Taylor's frank rejection of the doctrine of inherited depravity, as held by the reformed Churches, and also of the doctrine of the imputation of Adam's sin either in the form of mediate imputation or immediate. Taylor does maintain that "*the constitution or nature*" of mankind is such "*that in all the appropriate or natural circumstances of their existence, thy will uniformly sin from the commencement of moral agency*".[32] In these terms he speaks of total depravity and of mankind as depraved *by nature*. But this is not to be understood in the sense that men are born with a sinful nature or disposition. Nor does it mean that a *sinful* disposition or propensity is the foundation or cause of all sinful volitions. "We mean by depravity", he says, "a sinful volition itself, or rather, a sinful elective preference which becomes predominant in the soul, and comes into existence through that in the physical constitution and in the circumstances of men, which is the ground or reason of the fact...".[33] It is for this reason that depravity is *by nature*.

---

[28]*Cf. ibid.*, p. 480.

[29]*Essays, Lectures, Etc. upon Select Topics in Revealed Theology* (New York, 1859), p. 242.

[30]*Ibid.*, p. 246.

[31]*Idem.*; *cf.* p. 193.

[32]*Ibid.*, p. 192; *cf.* also p. 294.

This development of thought in the New England Theology raises a question on which there has been, and on which there will no doubt continue to be, difference of judgment. It is that of the place that Jonathan Edwards occupies in this area of the history of thought. It has been maintained that in his treatise *The Great Christian Doctrine of Original Sin Defended* he gave expression to the doctrine of the *mediate imputation* of Adam's first sin. In the nineteenth century there were no greater proponents and defenders of the doctrine of immediate imputation than Charles Hodge and William Cunningham and we could scarcely expect any to examine Edwards' discussion with greater care than these two men. Both held that in one chapter of the aforementioned treatise Edwards had given way to the doctrine of mediate imputation. Charles Hodge says: "We think that Edwards here clearly asserts the doctrine of mediate imputation; that is, that the charge of the guilt of Adam's sin is consequent on depravity of heart.... The doctrine of Edwards is precisely that which was so formally rejected when presented by Placaeus."[34] Hodge acknowledges, however, that he is not able to reconcile the view set forth by Edwards in that chapter with several passages which occur elsewhere in the same treatise.[35] And William Cunningham likewise says that mediate imputation "was adopted by Jonathan Edwards in his great work on Original Sin. Edwards' views,

---

[33]*Ibid.*, p. 204; *cf.* also p. 195: "When I say that mankind are depraved *by nature*, I mean that the depravity which I have already described and proved to pertain to mankind, *is truly and properly traced to the physical or constitutional propensities of man for natural good which belong to man, as a man, in the circumstances of his existence as the cause or occasion of it...*".

One further excerpt will help to point up Taylor's position in its divergence from Protestant belief and particularly as it is in conflict with the teaching of Jonathan Edwards, the alleged father of this New England Theology. "Nor does the moral depravity of men consist in a sinful nature, which they have corrupted by being *one* with Adam, and by *acting in his act*. To believe that I am one and the same being with another who existed thousands of years before I was born, and that by virtue of this identity I truly acted in his act, and am therefore as truly guilty of his sin as himself, – to believe this, I must renounce the reason which my Maker has given me; I must believe it also, in face of the oath of God to its falsehood, entered upon the record" [Ezek. 18:3, 4] (*Concio ad Clerum*, New Haven, 1828, pp. 5 f.).

[34]*Op. cit.*, p. 150.

[35]*Ibid.*, p. 151.

however, upon this point do not seem to have been clear or consistent, as he sometimes makes statements which manifestly imply or assume the common Calvinistic doctrine."[36]

If Edwards, in the place concerned, gave expression to mediate imputation it would be at least plausible to argue that the development of the New England Theology on this particular question took its point of departure from Edwards and that, though Edwards would have rejected with all his soul the positions espoused by men like Emmons, Dwight, and Taylor, yet Edwards had provided a direction of thought which in due time culminated in these developments. There need be little doubt that the notion of a divine constitution which, as we have seen, plays so large a part in the formulations of Hopkins, Emmons, and Dwight had been derived, proximately at least, from Edwards, and it became in their hands a convenient rubric by which to eliminate altogether the idea of the imputation to posterity of Adam's first sin.

Edwards' discussion of the question merits close examination. It is surely significant that so erudite and discriminating a theologian as B. B. Warfield should disagree with Hodge and Cunningham in their assessment of Edwards in this regard. Referring to Edwards he says: "In answering objections to the doctrine of Original Sin, he appeals at one point to Stapfer, and speaks, after him, in the language of that form of doctrine known as 'mediate imputation.' But this is only in order to illustrate his own view that all mankind are one as truly as and by the same kind of divine constitution that an individual life is one in its consecutive moments. Even in this immediate context he does not teach the doctrine of 'mediate imputation,' insisting rather that, Adam and his posterity being in the strictest sense one, in them no less than in him 'the guilt arising from the first existing of a depraved disposition' cannot at all be distinguished from 'the guilt of Adam's first sin'; and elsewhere throughout the treatise he speaks in the terms of the common Calvinistic doctrine."[37] It is the judgment of the present writer that Warfield's interpretation is correct. But since Warfield has not demonstrated his thesis and since the subject deserves more extended treatment it is necessary

[36] *The Reformers and the Theology of the Reformation* (Edinburgh, 1866), p. 384.

[37] "Edwards and the New England Theology" in Hastings: *Encyclopaedia of Religion and Ethics* and reprinted in *Studies in Theology* (New York, 1932). p. 530.

to show what Edwards' argument really was and how it need not be identified with mediate imputation. Several observations may help to place the question in clearer light.

(i) There need be no doubt that Edwards taught the imputation of Adam's first sin to all of posterity. Some quotations will bear this out conclusively. "That we may proceed with the greater clearness in considering the main objections against supposing the guilt of Adam's sin to be imputed to his posterity; I would premise some observations with a view to the right stating of the doctrine of the imputation of Adam's first sin, and then show the *reasonableness* of this doctrine, in opposition to the great clamor raised against it on this head. I think it would go far towards directing us to the more clear and distinct conceiving and right stating of this affair, were we steadily to bear this in mind, that God, in each step of his proceeding with Adam, in relation to the covenant or constitution established with him, looked on his posterity as being *one with him*.... And though he dealt more immediately with Adam, yet it was as the *head* of the whole body, and the *root* of the whole tree; and in his proceedings with him, he dealt with all the branches, asif they had been then existing in their root.

"From which it will follow, that both guilt, or exposedness to punishment, and also depravity of heart, came upon Adam's posterity just as they came upon him, as much as if he and they had all coexisted, like a tree with many branches ... it is as if, in every step of proceeding, every alteration in the root had been attended, at the same instant, with the same step and alterations throughout the whole tree, in each individual branch. I think this will naturally follow on the supposition of their being a constituted *oneness* or *identity* of Adam and his posterity in this affair."[38] Again, commenting on Romans 5:12, he says that the latter part of the verse "shows, that in the eye of the Judge of the world, in Adam's first sin, *all* sinned; not only *in some sort*, but all sinned *so* as to be exposed to that *death*, and final destruction, which is the proper *wages of sin*".[39] And referring to the whole passage (Rom. 5:12-19) he says: "As this place in general is very full and plain, so the doctrine of the corruption of nature, as derived from Adam, and

---

[38]*The Great Christian Doctrine of Original Sin Defended* in *Works* (New York, 1855), vol. II, p. 481.

[39]*Ibid.*, p. 459.

also the imputation of his first sin, are *both* clearly taught in it. The *imputation* of Adam's one transgression, is indeed most directly and frequently asserted. We are here assured that *by one man's sin, death passed on all*; all being adjudged to this punishment as having *sinned* (so it is implied) in that one man's sin."[40]

Respecting these quotations two things have to be said. First, the most conclusive evidence in support of a doctrine of mediate imputation would have to be presented if the *prima facie* import of such statements is to be ruled out; the account given is altogether similar to that which we might expect in an exponent of immediate imputation. If, as Edwards says, God looked on posterity as being one with Adam and looked upon their sin as coexisting with Adam's, then the sin is just as directly theirs as it was his. And this is *immediate* imputation.[41] Secondly, Edwards distinguishes between "the corruption of nature, as derived from Adam" and "the imputation of his first sin". The latter is, therefore, a distinct element and does not consist in the corrupt nature with which we are born. Far less may the imputation of the first sin be said to consist in the approval which we give to Adam's sin by sinning as he did. It is readily seen, therefore, how radically Edwards' view of our relation to the first sin of Adam differs from that of Hopkins. The latter was a student of Edwards but it was not from Edwards he learned that "the children of Adam are not answerable for his sin, and it is not their sin any further than they approve of it, by sinning as he did".

(ii) It is here we encounter, however, the analysis propounded by Edwards which has caused so much difficulty and, in our esteem, misunderstanding, namely, his analysis of the first sin of Adam and of our involvement in it which has been construed as a lapse into the doctrine of mediate imputation. Edwards continues: "Therefore I am humbly of opinion, that if any have supposed the children of Adam to come into the world with a *double guilt*, one the guilt of Adam's sin, another the guilt arising from their having a corrupt heart, they have not well conceived of the matter. The *guilt*

---

[40]*Ibid*., p. 461; *cf*. p. 460.

[41]It is not neccasary to discuss the question whether Edwards was a realist in his view of the Adamic union. The realist as well as the federalist holds to *immediate* imputation and the point at issue is not affected by the question of Edwards' affinities on that other issue.

a man has upon his soul at his first existence, is one and simple, viz., the guilt of the original apostasy, the guilt of the sin by which the species first rebelled against God. This, and the guilt arising from the first corruption or depraved disposition of the heart, are not to be looked upon as *two* things, *distinctly* imputed and charged upon men in the sight of God. Indeed the guilt that arises from the corruption of the heart, as it remains a confirmed principle, and appears in its consequent operations, is a *distinct*, and *additional* guilt: but the guilt arising from the first existing of a depraved disposition in Adam's posterity, I apprehend, is *not* distinct from their guilt of Adam's first sin. For so it was not in Adam himself. The first evil disposition or inclination of the heart of Adam to sin, was not properly distinct from his first act of sin, but was included in it. The external act he committed was no otherwise his, than as his heart was in it, or as that action proceeded from the wicked inclination of his heart.... His sin consisted in wickedness of heart, fully sufficient *for*, and entirely amounting *to*, all that appeared in the act he committed."[42] This quotation is pivotal and demands close inspection.

(a) On the face of it this might appear to contradict what has already been maintained that Edwards distinguishes between "the corruption of nature, as derived from Adam" and "the imputation of his first sin". For has he not said that the guilt of Adam's sin and that arising from a corrupt heart are one and not to be looked upon as two things? The solution rests in the distinction which Edwards has been careful to make, namely, the distinction between corruption of the heart as a "confirmed principle" and a corrupt heart as "the first existing of a depraved disposition". If we overlook that distinction and its significance in Edwards' analysis, then we fail to apprehend what is indispensable to a proper understanding of Edwards' position. It is of the latter – "the first existing of a depraved disposition" – and of that *alone* that he speaks when he insists that the first sin of Adam as imputed and the guilt arising from a corrupt heart are one and the same and not two distinct things. To put this beyond dispute we may quote further to show how he labours the distinction. "The depraved disposition of Adam's heart is to be considered two ways. (1) As

---

[42]*Ibid.*, pp. 481 f.

the first rising of an evil inclination in his heart, exerted in his first act of sin, and the ground of the complete transgression. (2) An evil disposition of heart continuing afterwards, as a confirmed principle that came by God's forsaking him; which was a *punishment* of his first transgression. This confirmed corruption, by its remaining and continued operation, brought additional guilt on his soul."[43]

(b) Edwards clearly maintains that the "first existing of a depraved disposition in Adam's posterity", in a word, this "evil disposition" is not a *consequence* of the imputation of the first sin of Adam; it is rather *prior* in the order of nature. "The evil disposition is *first*, and the charge of guilt *consequent*."[44] Now this might appear to be precisely the doctrine of mediate imputation. For is not that doctrine to the effect that the imputation of Adam's sin is mediated through inherited corruption and that the corruption is therefore first in the order of nature and the imputation of Adam's sin the consequence? Verily so. But this latter is not the teaching of Edwards. He says *nothing* of the guilt of Adam's first sin as mediated through hereditary depravity. And this is the all-important difference between Edwards' analysis and that of mediate imputation. When Edwards says that the evil disposition is *first* and the charge of guilt *consequent*, he is not speaking of hereditary depravity and of its relation to the guilt of Adam's first sin. The *evil disposition* which he says is *prior* is that which he constantly insists is *involved in* the first sin of Adam and is really one with it; it is "the guilt of the original apostasy". "The guilt", he says, "arising from the first existing of a depraved disposition in Adam's posterity, I apprehend, is *not* distinct from their guilt of Adam's first sin." This he could not say of *hereditary* depravity. The latter must be identified with what Edwards calls a confirmed and established principle in the heart of posterity and which he says expressly is "a *consequence* and *punishment* of the first apostasy ... and brings new guilt".[45] What then, we must ask, is this first depraved disposition of the heart which is prior in the order of nature to the imputation of Adam's actual transgression and yet is one with the imputed sin? It is here that Edwards' acumen comes to light.

[43]*Ibid.*, p. 482.
[44]*Ibid.*, pp. 482 f.
[45]*Ibid.*, p. 482.

Edwards' own answer is made perspicuous by his appeal to the analogy of Adam himself as an individual. "The first evil disposition or inclination of the heart of Adam to sin, was not properly distinct from his first act of sin, but was included in it." He is here reflecting on the simple fact that on exegetical grounds as well as on sound psychological grounds the overt act of sin on Adam's part cannot be conceived of apart from the evil disposition which the overt act registered. It is the biblical truth that Adam was tempted by being drawn away of his own lust and enticed (*cf.* James 1:14, 15). In the order of nature this sinful inclination is prior to the overt act of sin, yet they are one in that the *sin* cannot be construed except in terms of both aspects. All this is so obvious in the case of Adam's own sin, when biblical principles are applied to its analysis, that it is scarcely necessary to labour the point. But the distinctive feature of Edwards' discussion is that in his exposition of the *imputation to posterity* of this first sin of Adam he considered that the sin as *imputed* must be construed as comprising the same two aspects which apply to Adam's own sin. This is to say that if we are to speak of the imputation of Adam's first sin the imputation must include the evil disposition which gave rise to the act committed as well as the act itself. This is what Edwards means by "the first existing of a depraved disposition in Adam's posterity". "The *first existing* of a corrupt disposition in their hearts", he says expressly, "is not to be looked upon as sin belonging to them, *distinct* from their participation of Adam's first sin."[46] This is quite diverse from the notion of mediate imputation. The first existing of the corrupt disposition is just as direct as the participation in Adam's first sin, for the simple reason that it is involved in that participation. And the only antecedent of this participation is "the *union* that the wise author of the world has established between Adam and his posterity" so that God "looked on his posterity as being *one with him*" and "both guilt ... and also depravity of heart, came upon Adam's posterity just as they came upon him, as much as if he and they had all coexisted, like a tree with many branches".[47]

(c) The evidence would indicate that the depravity remaining as an established and confirmed principle, distinguished by

[46]*Idem.*

[47]*Ibid.*, pp. 481 f.

Edwards from the first existing of a depraved disposition, is to be equated with what has generally been called hereditary depravity. Edwards refers to it in terms of "being born corrupt".[48] He compares this continuance of corruption in the race to the *continued* lack of original righteousness in Adam himself. "But yet, I think it is as truly and in the same manner owing to the course of *nature*, that Adam's posterity came into the world without original righteousness, as that Adam continued without it after he had once lost it."[49] But the most significant observation in this connection is that depravity, viewed in this light, is not only a "*natural* consequence" of the first sin both in Adam and in his posterity but it was also a "*penal* consequence" or punishment of that first sin, a penal consequence or righteous judgment for posterity as it was for Adam himself.[50] This is surely that of which he speaks when he says: "But the depravity of nature remaining an *established principle* in the heart of a child of Adam, and as exhibited in after operations, is a *consequence* and *punishment* of the first apostasy thus participated, and brings new guilt".[51] This is exactly what the proponents of *immediate* imputation have maintained, namely, that hereditary corruption is consequent upon the imputation of the first sin of Adam and is the penal consequence of it. It is only failure to appreciate the distinctions which Edwards makes that will obscure the validity and force of this conclusion. Edwards is plainly on the side of immediate imputation in reference to the relation of hereditary corruption to the first sin of Adam.

(d) When Edwards speaks of "the *derivation of the evil disposition* to the hearts of Adam's posterity" (italics ours)[52] in connection with "the first existing of a depraved disposition", we are not to be misled by the use of the word "derivation" to think that he is referring to derivation by natural generation as in the case of hereditary depravity. After using this term he makes it clear that he prefers to speak of this subject as "the *coexistence* of the

---

[48] *Cf. ibid.*, p. 480.

[49] *Idem.*

[50] And just thus I suppose it to be with every natural branch of mankind: all are looked upon as *sinning* in and with their common root; and God righteously withholds special influences and spiritual communications from all, for this sin" (*idem*).

[51] *Ibid.*, p. 482.

[52] *Idem.*

evil disposition, implied in Adam's first rebellion".[53] Besides, it had been customary for theologians who espoused immediate imputation to speak of the first sin of Adam as *derived*, when they had no thought of derivation by natural propagation but only by imputation. In fact they can speak of the guilt of Adam's first act of sin as "derived down unto us" by way of imputation and as the ground of the corruption propagated.[54]

(iii) There is one other quotation from Edwards that requires comment. It is that from which, without doubt, a great deal of subsequent formulation in the New England theology has sprung. "The first being of an evil disposition in the heart of a child of Adam, whereby he is disposed to *approve* of the sin of his first father, as fully as he himself approved of it when he committed it, or so far as to imply a full and perfect *consent* of heart to it, I think, is not to be looked upon as a consequence of the imputation of that first sin, any more than the full consent of Adam's own heart, in the act of sinning; which was not consequent on the imputation of his sin to himself, but rather *prior* to it in the order of nature."[55] Edwards is here dealing with the same question of "the first existing of a depraved disposition" in the heart of Adam's posterity which, as has been demonstrated above, he insists is involved in the imputation of Adam's first sin. He is not dealing with the voluntary approval and consent which we may be said to render to Adam's sin when we ourselves come to sin as Adam did; he is dealing with "the first being of an evil disposition in the heart of a child of Adam". This, as well as the whole context, demonstrates that he is explicating the meaning of our direct involvement in the first sin of Adam by reason of the *identity* or *oneness* of Adam and his posterity. He is not by any means alluding to the consequence arising from a divinely established constitution that all men will sin as Adam did. He is saying the opposite, that by the divine constitution there is imputed to posterity the sin of Adam *both as evil disposition and overt action.* Edwards' concept is quite alien to that of Hopkins that when the posterity of Adam "actually become sinners, they themselves are the sinners, it is their own sin, and they are as blamable and guilty as if Adam had never sinned, and

---

[53]*Idem.*

[54]*Cf.* Thomas Goodwin: *Works* (Edinburgh, 1865), vol. X, p. 12; vol. V, p. 182.

[55]Edwards: *op. cit.*, p. 482.

each one were the first sinner that ever existed. The children of Adam are not answerable for his sin, and it is not their sin any further than they approve of it, by sinning as he did."[56] Edwards is dealing with *the disposition* which is an integral element of the sin imputed; Hopkins is dealing with the approval which is given by posterity to the sin of Adam when they sin as he did. Edwards finds this disposition to be an integral aspect of the sin imputed by an analysis of what is involved in Adam's first sin; Hopkins finds that the sin of Adam is not imputed to posterity and that the only way in which Adam's sin may be said to be their sin is that they give their consent to it when they sin after the Adamic pattern. And it is scarcely necessary to remark that it is a far cry from Edwards' insistence, that a depraved disposition is the fountain from which the overt act of sin proceeds and for that reason that the first existing of a depraved disposition is involved for posterity in the imputation of Adam's sin, to the frank disavowal by Taylor of the doctrine "that mankind have a sinful nature which they have corrupted by being one in Adam, and by acting in his act, or sinning in his sin".[57]

There are therefore two conclusions with respect to Edwards. First, the allegation that he propounded the doctrine of mediate imputation rests upon failure to appreciate the precise intent of Edwards' analysis of the first sin of Adam as imputed to posterity. Second, though in some respects the terminology of the other New England theologians mentioned is similar to that of Edwards, on this particular doctrine there is a distinct divergence from the position of Edwards, not only on the part of Emmons, Dwight, and Taylor, but also of Hopkins, and it is not warranted to regard Edwards' teaching on the subject of imputation as providing the first step in the relinquishment and denial of the doctrine of the imputation of Adam's first sin, a denial which became unambiguous in the later developments of this New England Theology. It was divergence from Edwards, or at least misunderstanding of his position, that gave birth to this development.[58]

---

[56]Hopkins: *op. cit.*, p. 230.

[57]J Taylor: *Essays* as cited, p. 193.

[58]J. F. Stapfer, as noted above, has been classified as a proponent of mediate imputation, and Edwards, since he quotes Stapfer with approval (*op. cit.*, pp. 483 f.), is alleged to have followed Stapfer in that regard. If Edwards does

It will have become apparent that the question as to the *mode* by which the sin of Adam comes to be reckoned to posterity must be stated and resolved in terms of the antithesis between mediate and immediate imputation as that antithesis had been sharply defined in the Placaean debate of the seventeenth century. The developments of the New England Theology from Samuel Hopkins onwards gave a new direction to thought on the subject of the relation of posterity to the sin of Adam, and so radical was the divergence that this New England Theology cannot properly

---

not set forth mediate imputation, as has been maintained in the preceding discussion, then Edwards' appeal to Stapfer was not in the interest of mediate imputation. It might still be true, however, that Stapfer cast the thought, which Edwards espoused, in the mould of mediate imputation and Edwards took over the former without the latter. But it is not apparent from a study of Stapfer's reflections on this matter in his *Institutiones Theologiae Polemicae Universae* (Zurich, 1743–1750) that he adopted mediate imputation as opposed to immediate. He says: "Et cum omnes posteri ex primo parente ceu ex radice ortum suum trahunt, generis humani universitas cum stirpe non aliter, quam unicum aliquod totum, sive unica massa considerari potest, ut non sit aliquid a stirpe diversum, et non aliter ab ea differunt posteri ac rami ab arbore.

"Ex quibus facile patet, quomodo stirpe peccante omne illud quod ab ea descendit, et cum ea unicum aliquod totum efficit, etiam peccasse judicari possit, cum a stirpe non differat, sed cum ea unum sit.

"Doctrina de peccati primi parentis imputatione immediata tam incredulos, quam alios offendit, si vero ea, quae hactenus ex ipsis rationis principiis deduximus, perpendantur, facile deprehenditur, S. Litteras nihil hic docere, nisi quod ipsa rei ratio postulat, et justo Dei judicio fieri potuisse, ut primus parens dignus non esset, qui susciperet sobolem sanctam, sed pravam et poenae obnoxiam" (Tom. I, p. 236). This is intended to be a defence of immediate imputation. And when, in subsequent sections of his *Institutes*, he enters into more detail (Tom. IV, pp. 513 f.; 561-564) there does not appear to be evidence of mediate imputation. In answer to the objection urged against the imputation of Adam's sin that we never committed the same sin with Adam he draws the distinction between the physical act and the morality of the act and pleads that it is in respect of the latter only that posterity committed the same sin, that is to say, are to be "looked upon as having committed, in a moral estimation, the same sin or transgression of the law in number and in kind" (*ibid.*, p. 514). And when Stapfer contends that the imputation of Adam's first sin must never be conceived of in abstraction from our native corruption and calls the latter *mediate* imputation in distinction from the guilt of Adam's sin as *immediate*, there is no proof of a position identical with or tending to mediate imputation (*ibid.* pp. 562 f.). Stapfer cannot in this case be shown to do more than was characteristic of earlier reformed theologians, namely, to insist that the sin of Adam as imputed and hereditary depravity must not be separated or conceived of in abstraction from each other.

be characterized as a doctrine of *mediate imputation*. However important these developments were and however much they must be taken into account in dealing with the whole question of the effect upon posterity of Adam's sin, yet in a discussion of the precise question as it was formulated in the debates of the seventeenth century the New England Theology does not contribute anything to elucidate or defend the doctrine of mediate imputation. These New England theologians did reject immediate imputation. In that respect they were at one with the exponents of mediate imputation. It may be that their rejection of immediate imputation logically involved the rejection also of mediate imputation and they were consistent in bringing to a logical issue what is implicit in the denial of the doctrine of immediate imputation. In that event the New England development of thought brought to its logical result what was inherent in the classic doctrine of mediate imputation as propounded by Placaeus. But our concern is not with the logical consequences which proceed from the doctrine of mediate imputation but with this doctrine itself as it was understood and propounded by its representative proponents. Mediate imputation does maintain that the sin of Adam was imputed to posterity, that posterity was involved in Adam's sin, and that the sin of the one man Adam was the sin of all. And the question is whether this involvement is *directly* based upon the relation which Adam sustained to posterity or whether it is mediated through the inheritance from Adam of a corrupt nature. It is with that restricted question in view that we turn to the exegetical data.

2. Immediate Imputation

It is assumed on the basis of earlier study in this series that the only feasible interpretation of Romans 5:12-19 is to the effect that the one trespass of Adam is the sin of all, that when Paul says "one sinned" and "all sinned" he refers to the same sin viewed in its twofold aspect as the sin of Adam, the one man, and the sin of all his posterity. Our question now is simply whether there are any considerations in this passage, or others, which bear on the mode of imputation. Is it mediate or immediate? It is well to have the question sharply focused: does the evidence indicate that the sin of Adam is reckoned as the sin of all through the medium of inherited depravity? Or does the evidence point to the immediacy of conjunction which the doctrine of immediate imputation has maintained? The following propositions, it will surely be granted, are germane to the question at issue, and, if they are shown to be well grounded, they determine the question.

(i) *The immediate conjunction of the sin of Adam and the death of all.* Romans 5:12, 15, 17, furnish the basis for this inference.

In verse 12 the particular point of significance for our present interest is the force of καὶ οὕτως in the middle of the verse. It is, as shown earlier, coordinative and continuative. But in οὕτως there is the note of comparison, though not the kind of comparison that would supply the apodosis to ὥσπερ at the beginning of the verse. What then is this comparison? In the first two clauses reference is made to the sin of Adam and to the death which was its consequence. Summarily the thought is: Adam sinned and he died. In the case of the individual, Adam, we may not interject any medium between his sin and the death inflicted upon him. No other sin than that which the apostle refers to repeatedly as the one sin of the one man Adam needs to be intruded to explain or validate the death of Adam. Furthermore, it would be alien to the sustained thought of the whole passage to intrude any other aspect of Adam's sinfulness as the ground of his death. Far less would it be consonant with the passage to think of Adam's subsequent depravity as the medium through which death came to lay its hold upon him. This is just saying that here there is an immediate juxtaposition of Adam's sin and the death that followed. Now the force of καὶ οὕτως, introducing the next two clauses, is to institute a parallelism. Just as sin and death entered with Adam, so sin and death became the lot of all men. Adam sinned and he died – there is immediate conjunction. All sinned (in Adam, as argued already) and they died – there is the same immediate conjunction. It would be just as arbitrary and indefensible to interject the thought of mediating depravity in the latter case as it would be in the case of Adam himself. To suppose that any other factor is interposed between the involvement of all in the sin of Adam and the death of all that results would interfere with the analogy expressed in οὕτως. And the conclusion to which we are driven is that when Paul says "death penetrated to all men" it is quite contrary to the terms of verse 12, as well as of the entire passage, to think of inherited depravity as the medium through which the death contemplated is conceived of as penetrating to all. But if mediate imputation is correct this is what must be done. For if inherited depravity mediates the imputation of Adam's sin it must also mediate the death which is its consequence. In verse 12 it is impossible to interject any other consideration as the reason for the death of all than the one sin of Adam in which all are regarded by the apostle as involved.

In verse 15 – "by the trespass of the one the many died" – the death of all is brought into immediate conjunction with the one sin of Adam. This scarcely needs argument. The supposition that inherited depravity intervenes as the medium through which the trespass of the one man takes its effect would contradict Paul's emphasis. For, in that event, we should have to suppose that posterity is reckoned as sinful and therefore as inflicted with death before the sin of Adam is imputed and takes its effect. But what Paul is saying is that it is by the trespass of the one that the many died, and if this does not have the priority, if the trespass of the one and the death of the many do not stand in such close relationship that they are self-explanatory, then the patent purpose and emphasis of the apostle break down.

In verse 17 – "by the trespass of the one death reigned through the one" – we are again confronted with the one sin of Adam as the explanation of the universal reign of death. And even more pointedly, perhaps, than in verse 15 do we detect how alien to the conjunction which the apostle is so intent upon asserting is the intrusion of hereditary depravity between "the trespass of the one" and the reign of death through the one. The conjunction is of the kind that comports only with the doctrine of immediate imputation.

(ii) *The immediate conjunction of the sin of Adam and the condemnation of all.* This appears from verses 16 and 18.

When the apostle says in verse 16 that "the judgment was *from one* unto condemnation" it is not immediately apparent whether he means the one man Adam or the one sin of Adam. In the preceding clause δι' ἑνὸς ἁμαρτήσαντος refers to Adam as having sinned and it could be that the ἐξ ἑνὸς of the next clause has in view the one man Adam rather than the one trespass of Adam. But the contrast drawn in the second and third clauses would distinctly favour the view that ἐξ ἑνὸς refers to the one trespass. For ἐξ ἑνὸς is contrasted with ἐκ πολλῶν παραπτωμάτων – "from many trespasses" – and one trespass can more suitably be contrasted with many trespasses than can one man. But even if we allow doubt to remain as to the reference of ἐξ ἑνὸς in verse 16 there can be no doubt as to the import of verse 18. There it is explicitly stated that "through one trespass" δι' ἑνὸς παραπτώματος – judgment came "upon all men unto condemnation". This is an unambiguous assertion to the effect that the ground, or, if we will, the medium, of the condemnation of all is the one trespass of Adam. To intrude the medium of inherited depravity would introduce another factor, namely, another sin or aspect of sinfulness, which would plainly violate the emphasis that it was from the *one trespass* that the judgment of condemnation came upon all. In other words, the interjection of inherited depravity, which, on the premises of mediate imputation, is the crucial and explanatory consideration, posits an addition which is palpably inconsistent with the apostle's emphasis upon the singularity of the trespass from which universal condemnation proceeded. This is just saying that no other sin or aspect of sinfulness can be allowed to interfere with the conjunction of the one trespass of Adam and the condemnation of all. And this means immediate conjunction. If we may return to verse 16, it is therefore Paul's doctrine that the judgment was from one trespass unto condemnation whether this is what he expressly says in verse 16 or not. And even if we suppose that the ἐξ ἑνὸς of verse 16 refers to Adam (as is not probable for the reason mentioned above) rather than to the one trespass, we must remember that it is Adam *as sinning* who is in view, namely, the δι' ἑνός ⸀ἁμαρτήσαντος of the preceding clause, and the *sinning* contemplated can be none other than the one trespass of verses 15 and 18. Hence the express or clearly implied thought of verse 16 is that the condemnation of all proceeded from the one trespass of Adam and the same kind of conjunction appears in verse 16 as is unmistakable in verse 18. It is immediate imputation, therefore, that verses 16 and 18 establish in respect of the *modus operandi* of universal condemnation.

Since then we have found that both death and condemnation are immediately grounded upon the one trespass of Adam, we would have to infer that the sin of Adam would in like manner be brought into immediate conjunction with the sin of all. But the apostle does not leave this climactic feature of his doctrine to good and necessary inference. He deals with it expressly.

(iii) *The immediate conjunction of the sin of Adam and the sin of all.* This is apparent from verses 12 and 19.

In verse 12 Paul says, "all sinned". We found already that this is but another aspect from which the one sin of the one man Adam may be viewed. The one explanation of this twofold aspect from which the sin of Adam may be viewed is the solidarity existing between Adam and his posterity. Pertinent to our present question, the intrusion of hereditary depravity as a mediating instrument is entirely unnecessary once we recognize the fact of solidarity. And, besides, hereditary depravity as an explanation is not only unnecessary; it would also be extraneous and disturbing. Hereditary depravity emanates from the solidarity; it is a process subsequent to the solidarity. It is therefore the solidarity itself and not a process emanating from it that adequately and suitably explains the "all sinned" of verse 12. Verse 19, however, puts the thesis in clearer focus. "Through the disobedience of the one man the many were constituted sinners." When the apostle says, "constituted sinners" he has surely in mind that which is logically first in our becoming or being reckoned sinners. And when we ask how were men thus constituted? The answer is at hand; it was "through the disobedience of the one man". In terms of the context it is the one trespass of the one man Adam. Mediate imputation asserts that what is basically and logically first in constituting men sinners is hereditary depravity and not the disobedience of the one man. The same kind of incompatibility appears at this point as we noted already in connection with death and condemnation. Paul brings the sin of all into direct relation to the sin of Adam; mediate imputation denies this conjunction and the contradiction is overt. In Paul's thought not only is death inflicted upon all by the *one trespass* of Adam, not only is condemnation pronounced upon all by this *one trespass*, but by that same trespass, in verse 19 called disobedience, all are constituted sinners. As we contemplate the sin, condemnation, and death of all, in other words the universal reign of sin, condemnation, and death, we have nothing in this passage to provide the explanation but the one sin of Adam. These two facts are brought into direct relation to each other. And the only consideration left for inference on our part is that they stand in this relationship to each other because there is the solidarity of the race in the sin of Adam. Paul leaves no room for any other factor or constitution.

These conclusions may be correlated with what is implicit in 1 Corinthians 15:22: "In Adam all die". That death is the wages of sin (Rom. 6:23) and that death cannot be conceived of as existing or as exercising its sway apart from sin is the Pauline principle. When he says that "in Adam all die" it is impossible, on Pauline premises, to exclude the antecedence of sin and the only way in which the antecedence in this case could obtain is that all are conceived of as having sinned in Adam. Otherwise the statement "in Adam all die" would be without the foundation which Paul's principles demand. As we correlate this premise of 1 Corinthians 15:22, namely, that "in Adam all sinned", with the teaching of Romans 5:12-19 there is only one conclusion: all sinned in Adam in his one trespass. And the immediacy of conjunction established by so many distinct lines of argument from Romans 5:12-19 is the same kind of conjunction which suits the proposition presupposed in 1 Corinthians 15:22 and, in reality, is the kind of conjunction which the proposition would naturally be understood to imply.

(iv) *The analogy supports immediate imputation.* The parallel instituted in Romans 5:12-19 as a whole is that between the way in which condemnation passes upon men through the sin of Adam and the way justification comes to men through the righteousness of Christ. In the case of the righteousness of Christ (designated δικαίωμα in verse 18 and ὑπακοή in verse 19) this righteousness comes to the justified through no other medium than that of union with Christ; it is not mediated through the righteousness inwrought in the believer in regeneration and sanctification. To use the language of imputation, it is not by mediate imputation that believers come into the possession of the righteousness of Christ in justification. It would be contradictory of Paul's doctrine of justification to suppose that the righteousness and obedience of Christ become ours unto justification *because* holiness is conveyed to us from Christ or that the righteousness of Christ is mediated to us through the holiness generated in us by regeneration. The one ground upon which the imputation of the righteousness of Christ becomes ours is the union with Christ. In other words, the justified person is constituted righteous by the obedience of

Christ because of the solidarity established between Christ and the justified person. The solidarity constitutes the bond by which the righteousness of Christ becomes that of the believer. Once the solidarity is posited there is no other mediating factor that could be conceived of as necessary to the conjunction of the righteousness of Christ and the righteousness of the believer. This is to say that the conjunction is immediate. If the case is thus on that side of the analogy which pertains to justification, we should expect the *modus operandi* to be the same in connection with condemnation. To put the argument in the order underlying the parallelism, immediate imputation in the case of Adam's sin provides the parallel by which to illustrate the doctrine of justification and is thus eminently germane to the governing thesis of the apostle in this part of the epistle.

Chapter Four

IN these studies we have been concerned with the subject of the relation which Adam as the first man sustained to the members of the human race and, more particularly, with the relation which the members of the race sustain to the first sin of Adam. The various aspects of the subject already discussed lead up to the concluding question: what is the character of the involvement on the part of posterity in Adam's trespass? In terms of *sin* what was entailed for posterity? If all sinned in Adam, how are we to define this sin of all in the sin of Adam?

V. THE SIN IMPUTED

When we speak of the sin of Adam as imputed to posterity, it is admitted that nowhere in Scripture is our relation to the trespass of Adam expressly defined in terms of imputation. And since this is the case the biblical teaching respecting the involvement of the race in the first sin of Adam must not be prejudiced or distorted by the use of the term "imputation" if it does not adequately or accurately convey the biblical meaning. The word has been widely used, however, in this connection and there is no good reason for abandoning its use. The Scripture does employ the notion of imputation with reference to the judgment which God entertains and registers in the case of the person who has sinned or is a sinner. This is true in both Testaments (*cf.* Lev. 17:4; Ps. 32:2; Rom. 4:8; 2 Cor. 5:19). The negative expressions to the effect that God does not impute sin to those whose sins are forgiven imply that God does impute sin and that the blessedness of forgiveness consists in the reversal of this imputation. We may not forget, furthermore, that even in the passage with which we are particularly concerned the idea of imputation is clearly enunciated. "Sin is not imputed when there is no law" (Rom. 5:13), implying, of course, that sin is imputed wherever the transgression of law obtains. Hence the judgment of God with reference to sin can be scripturally stated by saying that God imputes sin, and this means that he reckons the sinner to be guilty of the sin which belongs to him or is committed by him. If we say that the trespass of Adam is imputed to posterity, all we can strictly and properly be regarded as meaning is that the sin of Adam is reckoned by God as the sin also of posterity. The same sin is laid to their account; it is reckoned as theirs. We may not allow any arbitrary associations which may be attached to the word "imputation" to perplex or obscure this simple meaning of the term "impute". If it is applied in its scriptural import to the relation we sustain to Adam's sin, it means simply that this sin is reckoned by God as our sin. We have already found that the teaching of Paul is to the effect that the trespass of the one was the sin of all, that when Adam sinned all sinned. If all sinned in Adam, it is esteemed by God to be so; it is judged by God for what it is. Nothing less or more is meant by the imputation of Adam's sin to posterity. And if we restrict ourselves to the biblical notion of imputation, the use of the term throws no more light upon the questions that arise and which we proceed to discuss than do these other synonymous expressions. In other words, we may not think that the term "imputation" itself possesses some differentiating notion that supplies the solution to the question of the precise character of our involvement in the sin of Adam. So our question now is: what was reckoned in the divine judgment as having occurred in the case of posterity when Adam fell? God's judgment is always according to truth, and what he reckoned as having occurred did actually occur. The question is then: what did happen? And this is to say, what was imputed to posterity?

Perhaps we can discover the *status quaestionis* if we consider, first of all, the rather emphatic position taken by Charles Hodge. In the nineteenth century no one entered the lists in defence of the doctrine of immediate imputation more vigorously than Dr. Hodge. In dealing with the question of that which was imputed to posterity he says: "As he (Adam) fell from the estate in which he was created, they (posterity) fell with him in his first transgression, so that the penalty of that sin came upon them as well as upon him.

Men therefore stood their probation in Adam. As he sinned, his posterity came into the world in a state of sin and condemnation."[1] This would rather clearly amount to the assertion that posterity sinned and fell in Adam. In his commentary on the epistle to the Romans there is repeated use of such formulae as these: that "all sinned when Adam sinned", that they "were regarded and treated as sinners on account of his sin",[2] that by the sin of Adam all "were set down in the rank or category of sinners".[3] Thus there can be no question but Dr. Hodge would affirm that all sinned in Adam and fell with him in his first transgression. However, when Hodge explicates this statement he is also insistent that this sin of posterity or, in other words, the sin of Adam imputed to posterity consists simply in *the obligation to satisfy justice.* "To impute", he says, "is to reckon to, or to lay to one's account.... To impute sin, in Scriptural and theological language, is to impute the guilt of sin. And by guilt is not meant criminality or moral ill-desert, or demerit, much less moral pollution, but the judicial obligation to satisfy justice."[4] Since Dr. Hodge elsewhere elaborates on this question in the most polemic fashion,[5] we are not left in any doubt

---

[1]*Systematic Theology*, vol. II, p. 196.

[2]*Commentary on the Epistle to the Romans* (Edinburgh, 1864), p. 151.

[3]*Ibid.*, p. 173; *cf.* also *Essays and Reviews* (New York, 1857), pp. 49 ff., in which we find repeatedly such formulae as the following: "all men are regarded and treated as sinners, on account of Adam's sin" (p. 60); "we are treated as sinners on his account, or, in other words, have his sin put to our account" (p. 82; *cf.* pp. 61, 63, 79, 81).

[4]*Systematic Theology*, II, p. 194. William Cunningham might be quoted to a similar effect. "The peculiarity of the doctrine of imputation, as generally held by Calvinistic divines, is, that it brings in *another* species of oneness or identity as subsisting between Adam and his posterity ... so that, while there was no *actual* participation by them in the moral culpability or blameworthiness of his sin, they became, in consequence of his failure to fulfil the covenant engagement, *rei*, or incurred *reatus*, or guilt in the sense of legal answerableness, to this effect, that God, on the ground of the covenant, regarded and treated them as if they had themselves been guilty of the sin whereby the covenant was broken; and that in this way they became involved in all the natural and penal consequences which Adam brought *upon himself* by his first sin" (*Historical Theology*, Edinburgh, 1870, vol. I, p. 515). *Cf.*, also, Thomas Ridgeley: *A Body of Divinity* (New York, 1855), vol. I, p. 406.

[5]*Cf. Theological Essays: Reprinted from the Princeton Review* (New York and London, 1846), pp. 128-217. "And if there is anything in which Calvinists are agreed, it is in saying that when they affirm 'that the guilt of Adam's sin has come upon us,' they

– he conceived of the imputation of Adam's sin to posterity as consisting in the obligation to satisfy justice. The involvement of the race in the sin of Adam is, therefore, to be interpreted in these restricted terms and the imputation to posterity is to be equated with the obligation to satisfy justice. To use the Latin terms, the imputation was not the *culpa* of Adam's sin, nor the *demeritum*, but simply the *reatus*, specifically the *reatus poenae*.

Dr. Hodge in his polemic for this interpretation of the import of imputation could enlist and appeal to the statements of others in the reformed tradition. He quotes, for example, from John Owen who does say quite plainly that "nothing is intended by the imputation of sin unto any, but the rendering of them justly obnoxious unto the punishment due unto that sin".[6] There are, however, questions that arise in connection with this equation. The first is one of exegesis. Are we justified in interpreting the pivotal expressions "all sinned" and "the many were constituted sinners" (Rom. 5:12, 19) in this restricted sense, namely, "were placed under the obligation to satisfy justice"?

There is, of course, no question but the imputation of sin carries with it the *reatus*, the obligation to satisfy justice. But we may not overlook the fact that Paul in Romans 5:12-19 uses not only expressions which imply the penal consequence of sin but also the expressions which imply involvement in sin itself. As has been observed repeatedly in other connections in the course of this study, Paul not only takes account of *death* as penetrating to all and as reigning over all by means of the one trespass (vv. 12, 14, 15, 17) and not only of *condemnation* as coming upon all through the one trespass, but also of the fact that all were constituted *sinners*. That is to say, not only does the wages of sin come upon all, not only does the judgment of condemnation pass upon all, but all are indicted with the sin which is the basis of condemnatory judgment and of which death is the wages. If the imputation referred to in verse 13 meant merely the obligation to satisfy justice, the *reatus poenae*, then it would have sufficed for Paul to speak of death and condemnation. In reality he is not content with the thought of

---

mean, exposure to punishment on account of that sin" (p. 140; *cf. passim* where this thesis is presented and argued *in extenso*).

[6]John Owen: *The Doctrine of Justification by Faith, Works*, ed. Goold (Edinburgh, 1862). vol. V, p. 324; ed. Russell (London, 1826), vol. XI, p. 400.

penal consequence; he lays the foundation for all predication in terms of consequence in the propositions, "all sinned", "the many were constituted sinners" (vv. 12, 19), and, by implication, "sin was imputed to all" (v. 13). It is this distinct progression of thought that prevents us from taking for granted that propositions to the effect that "all sinned" or were "constituted sinners" may be interpreted to mean simply, "were placed under the sentence of condemnation" or "were made judicially liable to the sanctions of justice".

It is true that there are expressions in the Old Testament in which the term for sin is used in the sense of being counted as a sinner. To these Dr. Hodge appeals (Gen. 43:9; 44:32; I Kings 1:21) and concludes, "To sin, therefore, or to be a sinner may, in Scriptural language, mean to be counted an offender, that is, to be regarded and treated as such".[7] But it is not apparent that these texts mean simply to be liable to the punishment which the respective situations contemplated, and we may not assume that to be counted a sinner, in the usage of Scripture or theology, may be reduced to the notion of obligation to satisfy justice. Furthermore, though it were conceded that "visiting the iniquity of the fathers upon the children" (Exod. 20:5; 34:7; Num. 14:18; *cf.* Jer. 32:18; Lam. 5:7) refers to no more than bearing the penalty of the sins of the fathers, we may not conclude that no more is implied in the Pauline expressions of Romans 5:12, 13, 19 than that posterity is subject to the punishment of Adam's sin."[8] To say the least, therefore, we are placed under the necessity of exercising caution and hesitation before we grant that the terms "sinned" and "were constituted sinners" (Rom. 5:12, 19) are to be construed as merely denoting *the obligation to satisfy justice.*

There is another consideration derived from the parallel which the apostle institutes in this passage which should arouse suspicion as to the adequacy of the formula which Hodge employs. The parallel to the imputation of Adam's sin is the imputation of Christ's righteousness. Or, to use Paul's own terms, being "constituted sinners" through the disobedience of Adam is parallel to being "constituted righteous" through the obedience of Christ. In justification, according to reformed theology and Dr. Hodge's own

[7] *Commentary* as cited, p. 152.

[8] *Cf.* Hodge's discussion in *Theological Essays*, pp. 153 f.

position, it is not merely the *judicial benefit* of Christ's righteousness or obedience that is imputed to believers but the righteousness itself. It would be to evacuate Paul's doctrine of justification of its most precious and central significance to reduce the imputation to the judicial consequence. The judicial consequence flows from the imputation of the righteousness itself, and the two may not be equated. We should expect this same distinction and sequence to obtain on the other side of the parallel, namely, the imputation of Adam's sin. And it is the same kind of distinction that the Pauline expressions bear out.

It is beside the point at the present stage of our discussion to appeal to the fact that we are not made subjectively and morally righteous by the imputation of the obedience of Christ. For the question now is whether our being constituted righteous through the obedience of Christ involves more than the judicial consequence of that constituting act and whether the latter is but the result of an antecedent fact which must, in the nature of the case, be distinguished from the judicial consequence. The only observation necessary at this stage is that there is surely room for a concept of being "constituted righteous" other than that of being made subjectively and morally righteous, a concept which falls into the category of forensic relationship and one that is not to be explicated in terms merely of the corresponding award or consequence. And, in like manner, we must leave room for a concept of being "constituted sinners" that is antecedent to our obligation to satisfy justice and may not be reduced, in its definition, to this resulting obligation.

It can readily be understood why Dr. Hodge in his vigorous defence of the doctrine of immediate imputation should have defined imputation as consisting in the obligation to satisfy justice. He was confronted with the objection that immediate imputation involved the notion that thereby we are represented as *personally* and *voluntarily* participating in the first sin of Adam. And to such a supposition there is the obvious objection that when Adam sinned we, his posterity, did not exist as personal voluntary agents and could not be conceived of as acting thus personally and voluntarily. Furthermore, he was required to deal with the objection that immediate imputation supposed the transfer of moral character from Adam to posterity. He was emphatic in his denial of any such implication on the ground, with which his opponents agreed, that the moral quality of an action cannot be transferred from the perpetrator to another who is not the actual perpetrator. Denying, therefore, both of these allegations with respect to the import of immediate imputation he was under the necessity of defining the imputation in terms which would patently steer clear of both of these notions. The concept which appeared to him to define this differentiation and at the same time conform to biblical teaching was that of *reatus*, the obligation to satisfy justice.

There was also another reason why Dr. Hodge was so jealous for this defining concept. It is the analogy between the imputation of Adam's sin to posterity and the imputation of our sins to Christ in his vicarious sin-bearing. This argument appears again and again in his polemics. One quotation will suffice. "When it is said that our sins were imputed to Christ, or that He bore our sins, it is not meant that he actually committed our sins, or that He was morally criminal on account of them, or that the demerit of them rested upon Him .... And when it is said that the sin of Adam is imputed to his posterity, it is not meant that they committed his sin, or were the agents of his act, nor is it meant that they are morally criminal for his transgression ... but simply that ... his sin is the judicial ground of the condemnation of his race."[9]

The question remains, however, whether Dr. Hodge, in guarding against misunderstanding and misrepresentation of the doctrine of immediate imputation, has done justice to the biblical data and in his zeal for sharp differentiation between imputation, on the one hand, and personal participation or transfer of moral character, on the other, has not oversimplified the problem and left out of account a certain implicate of our relation to Adam's sin, enunciated, for example, in Paul's expression "constituted sinners" (Rom. 5:19). And there is also the question whether the analogy of the vicarious sin-bearing of Christ provides a basis for the precise inference which Dr. Hodge elicits from it. After all, there is a uniqueness to Christ's sin-bearing, and while there is undoubtedly analogy it may well be that we shall have to discover discrimination at the point where Dr. Hodge insists upon identity.

[9]*Systematic Theology*, II, pp. 194 f.

In connection with Hodge's insistence that the obligation to satisfy justice defines for us what is involved in the imputation to posterity of Adam's sin, there is not only the question of exegesis; there is also the question as to whether Hodge's position adequately represents the thought of reformed theologians and, more particularly, the thought of those who have been the exponents of immediate imputation. It must be admitted that this is not a simple question. There is particularly the difficulty connected with the precise import of the word "guilt" as used in this connection. And of considerable importance is the definition of the Latin term *reatus* and its relations to *culpa*, on the one hand, and *poena*, on the other.

If we examine the teaching of John Owen to whom, for example, Hodge made appeal, we shall find that certain positions taken by Owen in his exposition of imputation would appear, at least, to be considerably different from those of Dr. Hodge. The quotation already given from Owen accords with the insistence of Hodge that the guilt imputed to posterity is the obligation to satisfy justice. More might be quoted from Owen along this line. However, in the context of that same quotation Owen also says: "But that men should be liable unto death, which is nothing but the punishment of sin, when they have not sinned, is an open contradiction. For although God, by his sovereign power, might inflict death on an innocent creature, yet that an innocent creature should be guilty of death is impossible: for to be guilty of death, is to have sinned. Wherefore this expression, 'Inasmuch as all have sinned,' expressing the desert and guilt of death then when sin and death first entered into the world, no sin can be intended in it but the sin of Adam, and our interest therein: 'Eramus enim omnes ille unus homo;' and this can be no otherwise but by the imputation of the guilt of that sin unto us."[10] The thought to be noted here is the insistence that there can be no obligation to the penalty of sin without the sin which is the proper ground of that obligation. This means that the obligation to penalty cannot obtain unless there is antecedent sin. And surely this implies that the imputation of Adam's sin to us cannot be defined in terms of the obligation to penalty; the latter is the effect of the

[10]*Works*, ed. Goold, V, p. 325; ed. Russell, XI, p. 401.

imputation. Again, in reference to the distinction between *culpa* and *poena*, Owen says: "Much less is there any thing of weight in the distinction of 'reatus culpae' and 'reatus poenae;' for this 'reatus culpae' is nothing but 'dignitas poenae propter culpam' .... So, therefore, there can be no punishment, nor 'reatus poenae,' the guilt of it, but where there is 'reatus culpae,' or sin considered with its guilt..."[11] This latter quotation conveniently introduces us to what may well be considered as the consensus of reformed theologians of the sixteenth and seventeenth centuries.

Owen's rejection of the distinction between *reatus culpae* and *reatus poenae* reflects a widespread antipathy to this distinction among Protestant theologians. This antipathy sprang from recoil against the Romish abuse of the distinction by which a foundation was laid for the doctrine of penitential and purgatorial satisfaction – in the pardon of sin the *culpa* is remitted but for the temporal *poena* of post-baptismal sins satisfaction must be made either in this life or in purgatory."[12] But of more importance for the subject in hand is the way in which reformed theologians conceived of the relations of *culpa*, *reatus*, and *poena* and, most particularly, their insistence that there can be no *poena* or, for that matter, no *reatus poenae* apart from *culpa*.

On the relations of these three elements, the definition of Van Mastricht is representative and, in any event, most succinct: "*Reatus* is therefore the *medium quid* between *culpa* and *poena*, for it arises from *culpa* and leads to *poena*, so that it is at the same time the *reatus* of *culpa* and of *poena* and, as a medium, intervenes between these two termini and takes its name from both equally".[13] *Reatus* is

---

[11]*Ibid.*, V, p. 199; XI, p. 247.

[12]*Cf.* Francis Turretine: Institutio Theologiae Elencticae, Loc. IX, Quaest. 111, §VI; M. Leidecker: *Medulla Theologica*, Cap. IX, §XV (Utrecht, 1683, pp. 150 f.). James Henley Thornwell, though rejecting the Romish doctrine, defends the propriety of the distinction and maintains that it is really the distinction, which Protestant theologians made, between *reatus potentialis* and *reatus actualis*, the former being the intrinsic demerit and the latter that arising from the ordination of God; *cf. Collected Writings*, vol. I, p. 423.

[13]*Theoretico-Practica Theologia*, Lib. IV, Cap. II, VII (Amsterdam, 1724, Tom. I, p. 444). To the same effect is the formulation of the *Synopsis Purioris Theologiae*, known as the Leyden Synopsis, which reads: "Primum est *Reatus*, quo nomine intelligitur obligatio ad poenam, sive vinculum illud inter peccatum et poenam, quasi medium interjectum, quo peccator ad subeundam poenam, et quamdiu

therefore the liability in punishment arising from the *culpa* which sin entails. While it is not improper to speak of the *reatus culpae*, yet this may not be thought of as a *reatus* distinct from *reatus poenae* for, in reality, the *reatus culpae* is simply the *reatus poenae*. In our terms, the liability entailed in blameworthiness is nothing other than the obligation to penalty, the obligation to satisfy justice. We should expect from this definition of the relations of *culpa*, *reatus*, and *poena* that *reatus poenae* could not be conceived of apart from *culpa*. But the reformed theologians have been very jealous to insist upon this principle and it is not superfluous to cite some of the copious evidence which the reformed theology furnishes in support of this principle.

The principle in question is clearly enunciated in Calvin. In the first few chapters of the second book of the *Institutes* he is dealing specifically with the subject of original sin and hereditary depravity, and it is in this connection that he gives expression to the axiom concerned. Yet it is stated as a principle that holds true in general. Of the original sin with which infants are afflicted he says: "Whence it follows that it is properly accounted sin in the sight of God because there is no *reatus* without *culpa*".[14] This is to say that there is no liability to penalty without blameworthiness. From this, as a general principle, he argues for the sinfulness of the depravity with which infants are born.

Jerome Zanchius, in dealing with the imputation to us of the disobedience of Adam, is explicit. His words are: "We therefore say that this disobedience, although it could not pass to us as act, nevertheless did pass to us as *culpa* and *reatus* through imputation, inasmuch as that sin of Adam as our head God imputes to us, and that most justly, as the members".[15] Again, "the disobedience of Adam comes upon us as *culpa* and *reatus*".[16]

The Leyden Synopsis is equally explicit when it says: "The form of original sin consists in that transgression and disobedience by which all who were in Adam ... sinned with him; the disobedience

---

durat reatus, ad poenae quam subit, durationem, arctissime obligatur" (Disp. XV, XXXVII).

[14]"Unde sequitur, proprie coram Deo censeri peccatum quia non esset reatus absque culpa" (*Inst.*, II, i, 8).

[15]*Opera Theologica*, 1613, Tom. IV, col. 36.

[16]*Ibid.*, col. 38; *cf.*also coll. 39, 41.

and *culpa* with its resulting *reatus* were justly imputed by God as judge to all the sons of Adam, inasmuch as they all were and are one with him".[17]

Although Amesius does not make use of the term *culpa* in this connection, yet it is of interest to note the terms in which he speaks of imputation and how he distinguishes between imputation and the communication that takes place through natural generation. "This propagation of sin consists of two parts, namely, imputation and real communication.

"By imputation the same singular act of disobedience, which was Adam's, becomes also ours.

"By real communication the same singular sin is not derived to us, but the same in kind or of like reason and nature."[18]

Turretine, also, affirms the same principle in at least two different connections. In reflecting on the falsity of the Romish distinction between *reatus culpae* and *reatus poenae* he says that "the vanity of the distinction is apparent from the nature of both; for since *culpa* and *poena* are related and *reatus* is nothing else than obligation to *poena*, which springs from *culpa*, they both stand or fall together, so that if *culpa* is removed and with it its *reatus* the *poena* itself ought necessarily to be removed, for *poena* can never be inflicted except on account of *culpa*...."[19] Perhaps of greater relevance is a later comment in connection with 1 Corinthians 15:22 – "in Adam all die" – where we read: "Therefore in him (Adam) they also sinned and are held with him in a common *culpa*. For no one can merit the penalty of death in another unless with that other person and in him he has sin, which is the cause of death, in common with him. Nor is it sufficient to say that all die in Adam *efficienter* because we derive from Adam original sin, which is the cause of death. Because for the same reason we could be said to die in our parents ... from whom we directly derive sin, and this the Scripture never says, but only from Adam. This is so because we were in Adam in a peculiar manner, not only as our seminal root but also as our representative head. So we are said to have sinned in him not only by reason of *efficiency*, as the cause by which

[17]Disp. XV, XXIV.

[18]*Medulla Theologica*, Cap. §§XVII, 2-4.

[19]*Op. cit.*, *Loc.* IX, Q. III, §VI.

sin is propagated to us, but also by reason of *demerit*, because his (Adam's) *culpa* has brought *reatus* upon us."[20]

There can be little doubt, therefore, that the most representative of reformed theologians were jealous to maintain that *reatus* and *poena* and, if we will, *reatus poenae*, always presuppose *culpa* and that, therefore, our involvement in the *reatus*, the obligation to penalty, of Adam's sin means that we were also involved in the *culpa* of his sin. To use Turretine's formula, "poena ... nonnisi propter culpam potest infligi". If we have the *reatus* in common with Adam we must likewise have his *culpa*.

---

[20]*Ibid., Loc.* IX, Q. IX, §XVIII. It is also to be noted how other representative reformed theologians declare in favour of this principle. David Pareur says: "Nos vero Adami culpam juste luimus. 1. Quia culpa sic est Adami, ut etiam sit nostra. Omnes enim in Adamo peccante peccauimus: Quia omnes in lumbis Adami fuimus. 2. Quia culpam Adami omnes natura trahimus, probamus, imitamur.... 3. Cum tota Adami natura sit rea, nos vero ex massa eius propagati simus, non possumus non etiam ipsi esse rei..." (*Corpus Doctrinae Christianae*, Para I, Quaest. VII, Hanover, 1634, p. 46). Again, in reference to Romans 5:12, he says: "Sic tria in eo concurrerunt: culpa actualis, reatus legalis, pravitas naturalis: seu transgressio mandati, poena mortis. et corruptio naturae, quae fuit amissio imaginis Dei .... An ullo horum posteritas mansit immunis, sed omnia simul ad posteros introierunt non una via, sed triplici: Participatione culpae, imputatione reatus, propagatione naturalis pravitatis. *Participatione culpae*, quia omnes posteri seminali ratione fuerunt in lumbis Adami. Ibi omnes in Adamo peccante peccaverunt .... *Imputatione reatus*, quia primus homo ita stabat in gratia, ut si peccaret, non ipse solus, sed tota posteritas ea excideret, reaque cum ipso fieret aeternae mortis .... Atque hoc est, quod primum Adae peccatum nobis imputari dicitur. *Naturali* denique *propagatione* seu generatione horribilis naturae deformitas cum tristi reatu in omnes posteros sese diffudit" (*In Divinam ad Romanos Epistolam Commentarius*, p. 119). Later on in this commentary, in referring to the first sin of Adam, Pareus says: "Non (inquit) ita fuit unius, quin et omnium fuit. In uno omnes illud admiserunt: alioqui mors in omnes transire non potuisset. Qui enim non peccant, hoc est, nulla culpa et reatu tenentur, ut Sancti Angeli: in eos mors nil iuris habet. Quia vero mors in omnes transiit omnes igitur peccaverunt, hoc est, culpa et reatu tenentur" (*ibid.*, p. 120). *Cf.*, also, B. de Moor: *Commentarius Perpetuus in Johannis Markii Compendium Theologiae Christianae*, (Leyden, 1765), Pars 111, pp. 254 f.; William Bucanus: *Institutions of Christian Religion* (E. T., London, 1606), pp. 158-161; Benedict Pictet: *Theologia Christiana* (London, 1820), p. 147. Robert W. Landis in *The Doctrine of Original Sin as Received and Taught by the Church of the Reformation Stated and Defended* (Richmond, 1884) deals at great length with this question and others related to it. This lengthy monograph is devoted to a large extent to criticism of Dr. Hodge's position, and particularly of what Landis calls the gratuitous imputation of Adam's sin to the race, a position which he considers to be that of Hodge.

It was not only the reformed theologians who maintained this correlativity of *culpa* and *poena*. The classic exponents of evangelical Lutheranism did likewise, and the similarity in mode of statement is apparent. David Hollaz can say: "The first sin of Adam, inasmuch as he is regarded as the common parent, head, root, and representative of the whole human race is truly and by the just judgment of God imputed to all his posterity for *culpa* and *poena*".'[21] And Quenstedt says to much the same effect: "For in the sin of the first man there concur: 1. actual *culpa*, 2. legal *reatus*, 3. natural pravity. All of these entered into the world at the same time, and into all Adam's posterity. For we are involved (1) in participation of the actual *culpa*, inasmuch as we all sinned in Adam, (2) in the imputation of the legal *reatus*, for the first man stood and fell as head ..., and (3) by propagation of natural pravity, because it spreads to all men through natural conception."[22]

We thus find that reformed and Lutheran theologians did not conceive of the *reatus* of Adam's sin as imputed to posterity apart from the *culpa* of the same sin. And this is simply to say that the relation of posterity to the sin of Adam could not be construed or defined merely in terms of the obligation to satisfy justice (*reatus poenae*) but must also include, as the antecedent and ground of that *reatus*, involvement in the *culpa* of Adam's transgression. Hence when Dr. Hodge says that the imputation of the guilt of Adam's sin to posterity does not mean the imputation of "criminality" or "demerit" but only of "the judicial obligation to satisfy justice", we discover what we are compelled to regard it as a divergence from the older reformed theologians in respect of a principle which they esteemed basic in the construction of the doctrine of our relation to the first sin of Adam. It is just precisely the involvement of posterity in the *culpa* of Adam's sin that Hodge is jealous to deny,

---

[21]*Examan Theologicum Acromaticum*, "Theologia". Pars II, Cap. III, Quaest. X (Leipzig, 1763, p. 513).

[22]*Theologia Didactico-Polemica* (Leipzig, 1715), Pars II, col. 914. The similarity of Quenstedt's terminology to that of Pareus, as quoted above, is quite apparent. *Cf.*, also, L. Hütterus: *Compendium Theologicum* as revised by G. Cundisius (Jena, 1652), p. 573; J. Gerhard: *Loci Theologici*, Loc. IX, Cap. III, §53 where the language is not the same as in the preceding but points in the same direction; Heinrich Schmid: *The Doctrinal Theology of the Evangelical Lutheran Church* (E. T., Philadelphia, 1889), pp. 247 ff.; Francis Pieper: *Christian Dogmatics* (St. Louis, 1950), vol. I, pp. 538 ff.

when these other theologians were insistent that *poena* and *culpa* are inseparable and that *reatus* arises from *culpa* and leads to *poena*. And it would appear that the difficulty which we found with Dr. Hodge's position from the standpoint of exegesis, specifically the exegesis of Romans 5:12, 19, lies close to this divergence on Hodge's part from the formulation of other reformed theologians. In other words, it may be that the shortcoming which adheres to Hodge's position in respect of exegesis is the shortcoming which the other reformed theologians sought to avoid by the very insistence which we have discussed. It can at least be said that if posterity are regarded as involved in the *culpa* of Adam's sin, then we have an additional factor in terms of which to interpret "all sinned" and were "constituted sinners".

To return to the question at issue, namely, the definition of that which is imputed to posterity or, in other words, the import of "all sinned" and "the many were constituted sinners" (Rom. 5:12, 19), it appears to the present writer illegitimate to restrict the imputation to "the judicial obligation to satisfy justice" or to what has often been called *reatus poenae*. The basic reason for this judgment has been indicated already. In the crucial passage (Rom. 5:12-19) Paul not only speaks of the wages of sin as penetrating to all, not only of the judicial condemnation as coming upon all, but also of all as implicated in the sin of Adam with the result that they became sinners. There is likewise the theological consideration to which the reformed theologians were sensitive that to impute penal liability without the imputation of that to which the penal liability is due is faced with a juridical objection. Although it is not ours to solve all mysteries and by no means ours to call in question the government of God in inflicting the whole race with the penal consequences of Adam's own sin, yet we have no need or right to complicate the mystery by making the kind of disjunction which the notion of the mere imputation of judicial liability entails. The Scripture does not make this disjunction and we may not lay upon our theological formulation a liability which the Scripture itself does not warrant and from which its express statements steer us away.

It is fully to be admitted that the doctrine of our involvement in the one trespass of Adam is one that has to be properly guarded against misconstruction and we may not lay it open to interpretations which conflict with other biblical principles. When we say that we are involved in the trespass of Adam and that it is reckoned to us as our sin, we must insist as jealously as did Hodge and other theologians that we, the members of posterity, did not personally and voluntarily as individuals eat of the forbidden fruit. And neither are we to posit any such notion as the *transfer* from Adam to us of the moral character involved in his trespass. At least we must not regard any such postulate as indispensable to the proposition that Adam's trespass is also ours in its character as sin. On the other hand, we must not so attenuate our involvement that what is conceived of as ours is merely the judicial liability or some other consequence of sin. Out of deference to the biblical teaching we shall have to recognize and make allowance for a real involvement on our part in Adam's sin that is not to be construed as actual, voluntary participation or the *transfer* of moral character, on the one hand, and yet is not to be reduced to the level of judicial liability, on the other. We must insist on the involvement of posterity in Adam's sin in a way that will place this involvement in the category of sin and yet maintain that it was Adam's trespass in a manner that is not ours. In the language of theology we must try to do justice to both considerations, that, in respect of posterity, Adam's trespass was both *peccatum alienum* and *peccatum proprium*.

In pursuing this inquiry it should be understood that we are doing so on the express assumption of the immediate imputation to posterity of Adam's sin, and the only question now is: what is entailed in that imputation so as to make it truly an imputation of *sin*?

The expression which Paul uses, "constituted sinners", is parallel and antithetical to the other expression in the apodosis of Romans 5:19, namely, "constituted righteous". The latter expression plainly refers to an action which falls within the ambit of justification. This is the theme with which Paul is dealing in this part of the epistle and to interpret "constituted righteous" in terms diverse from "the righteousness of God" (Rom. 1:17; 3:21, 22) brought to bear upon us unto justification, "the free gift from many trespasses unto justification" (Rom. 5:16), "the free gift of righteousness" (Rom. 5:17), "the one righteous act ... unto justification of life" (Rom. 5:18), and the grace that reigns "through righteousness unto eternal life" (Rom. 5:21) would be a travesty of exegesis. It is a legitimate question whether the constitutive act of Romans 5:19 is the logical antecedent of the justifying act or is embraced in the justifying act itself. But this question does not affect the fact that "constituted righteous" must derive its character from the nature of justification. Now, if anything is apparent from Scripture usage and from the teaching of Paul in particular, it is that justification is forensic – it has reference to a judicial sentence. It is no more subjectively operative in its import than is condemnation. Hence "constituted righteous" must have forensic import – it has reference to an act of God which contemplates forensic relationship, the relationship which a person is conceived of as sustaining to law and justice. Since it is obviously an act of God which is concerned with a radical change of relationship, it must mean that God constitutes a new judicial relation to himself in virtue of which the person may be declared to be righteous in his sight. And since it is by "the obedience of the one" that this relationship is constituted, there can be but one conclusion, that by an act of grace the obedience of Christ is brought to bear upon the person concerned in such a way that the judgment registered with respect to that person is the judgment which the obedience of Christ elicits and demands. To put it otherwise, the person is given property in the obedience of Christ with the result that his judicial status is that belonging to the obedience in which he has come to have property; this is the act of grace involved in being "constituted righteous".

The parallel antithesis, "constituted sinners", will have to be interpreted along similar lines. In relation to the precise inquiry being conducted it cannot be reduced to lower terms than those which we find, antithetically, in "constituted righteous". And perhaps the most relevant way of stating the case by way of parallel is that posterity came to have property in Adam's disobedience with the result that their judicial status is that belonging to the disobedience in which they have property. The disobedience of Adam is brought to bear upon posterity in such a way that the judgment registered upon them is the judgment which the disobedience of Adam elicits and demands. If we may speak in terms of imputation, there is as truly an imputation of the disobedience of Adam as there is of the obedience of Christ. As the latter imputation is not that of the benefit accruing but that the benefit accruing follows upon the imputation, so the former must not be conceived of as the liability entailed but the liability as flowing from the imputation. It is within the sphere of the forensic that the imputation takes place, but the imputation must not be defined in any other terms than those of disobedience and obedience. Viewed from the standpoint of personal, voluntary action the disobedience in the one case is that of Adam and the obedience is that of Christ. But the effect of the "constituting" act is that others, not personally and voluntarily engaged, come to have property, indeed propriety, in the personal, voluntary performance of another. It is both *alienum* and *proprium*, and neither aspect must be stressed to the exclusion of the other.

When we take account of what occurs in the realm of grace and appreciate the reality of the believer's property in the righteousness of Christ and the centrality of this truth in the gospel of grace, it is not only feasible but it is incumbent upon us to reckon with a parallel property in the sin of Adam. It is totally indefensible to exclude the possibility of a divine judgment and government by which the sin of Adam is reckoned to be as really and properly ours as is the righteousness of Christ in justification. And that this is actually the case is the witness of Scripture. It may be that this is the limit of revelation to us respecting the involvement of posterity in the one trespass of Adam. But even should this be the case it is sufficient to establish the reality of our property in nothing less than his sin, and, with the proper qualifications already stated, there does not appear to be any good reason why this property should not be called, as some of the older theologians stated, participation in the *culpa* of his transgression.

It may not be without warrant, however, to pursue the question still further. In any case theologians of the reformed family have done so and it may not be useless to conduct this pursuit.[23] The terms "constituted righteous" (Rom. 5:19) must be interpreted, as has been shown, within the ambit of justification and therefore forensically. We may not, however, overlook the fact that it is

---

[23]*Cf.* Thomas Goodwin: *Works* (Edinburgh, 1865), vol. X, pp. 47-55; Jonathan Edwards: *Works* (New York, 1855), vol. II, pp. 481-495.

in union with Christ that this constitutive action takes place. It is in virtue of union with Christ that believers come to have property in Christ's righteousness unto their justification. And though nothing must be pleaded to tone down the forensic nature of justification, yet with equal emphasis the virtue emanating from union with Christ must not be restricted to justification. All the grace bestowed upon believers finds it ground or basis in union with Christ in his death and resurrection. The subjective renewal which is concomitant with justification springs from this union, for it is in virtue of solidarity with Christ in his death and resurrection that the regenerative operations of the Holy Spirit take place in the believer, whether regeneration is logically prior to justification, as some maintain, or logically posterior, as others hold. In this way regeneration, though wrought by the agency of the Holy Spirit, stems from solidarity with Christ in his once-for-all accomplishment. If we follow this direction of thought and apply it to our union with Adam we may properly find that although "constituted sinners" (Rom. 5:19) cannot be made to express any more than the forensic relation to Adam's sin, yet solidarity with Adam implies more by way of involvement in sin than that expressed in forensic terms. We may not try to trace parallels in every detail; in the operations of redemptive grace there are factors which far transcend the operations of judgment in our relation to Adam's sin, as Paul observes in Romans 5:12-19. But a parallel to this extent is surely not without warrant, that as representative solidarity with Christ in his obedience unto death and in his resurrection secures and insures subjective renewal in regeneration, so representative solidarity with Adam in his sin involved for posterity their subjective depravity as well as the forensic judgment of their being "constituted sinners". In this way a basis may be laid for a better understanding of the relation which the infliction of posterity with depravity sustains to the one trespass of Adam. And depravity may not be conceived of so much as a penal infliction arising from the imputation of Adam's sin but as an implicate of solidarity with Adam in his sin. Pravity is thus itself a constituent element of identification with Adam in his trespass, and we can no more be exempted from the pravity which Adam's trespass involved than we can be relieved of the forensic judgment which passed upon it. It may contribute to elucidation and support of this position if we set forth the following theses.

(1) The members of posterity cannot be conceived of as existing when Adam trespassed. To posit any such supposition is to contradict the meaning of conception and generation as the divinely constituted means for the origin of all members of the race except the first pair. Yet all the members of the race were contemplated by God as destined to exist; they were foreordained to be and the certainty of their existence was thus guaranteed. It is important in this connection to bear in mind that as *thus contemplated* by God they were contemplated no otherwise than as members of the race in solidaric union with Adam and therefore as having sinned in him. In other words, they are not conceived of in the mind and purpose of God except as one with Adam; they are not contemplated as potentially but as actually one with Adam in his sin. And this proposition is basic to all further thought on the question.

(2) All the members of the race come to exist actually by the act or process of generation; this is the divinely constituted means whereby God's foreordained design comes to effect in the course of history. It is a capital mistake to interpose the question: when does each member of the race *become* actually sinful? For the truth is that each person never exists as other than sinful. He is eternally contemplated by God as sinful by reason of the solidarity with Adam, and, whenever the person comes to be *actually*, he comes to be as sinful. Sinfulness is correlative with his beginning to be as an individual in his mother's womb. If, for the moment, we speak of the soul as the seat of personality, it runs counter to all the implications of our solidarity with Adam to think of the soul as ever existing or as conceived by God to exist as a pure entity undefiled by sin. The soul or, to speak more properly, the person never exists apart from the sin of Adam's transgression.

(3) If we ask the question: when is the sin of Adam imputed? the answer is apparent. The imputation is correlative with the beginning to be. This is only another way of saying what was stated in the preceding paragraph. Sin is intertwined with our very existence in view of Adamic solidarity.

(4) When we attempt to define this involvement that is correlative with our origin as individuals, we cannot say less than

that we are reckoned as having sinned in Adam. It must be fully appreciated that theologians who define imputation in terms of the obligation to punishment are at the same time sustained and emphatic in the use of such formulae as "we sinned in Adam", "we are reckoned as having sinned in Adam", "the sin of Adam is imputed to us". And this is evidence that, although they are virtually deserting this ground when they define sin in terms merely of *reatus poenae*, they are yet unable to abandon the formulae which reflect the biblical teaching and which are demanded in their true and proper import if the implications of our solidarity with Adam are to be rightly assessed. It would appear that the reason why Dr. Hodge, for example, can temporarily waive the proper import of these formulae and adopt a definition that is on lower ground is that he had not been ready to entertain the implications which a valid use of these formulae involved.

(5) The sin of Adam was what all sin is, transgression of the law of God. As such it was pravity and perversity; it was *culpa* without mitigation. It is impossible to think of his trespass apart from these characterizations. When sin is predicated of him it would be an abstraction to posit such predication apart from these characterizing conditions. Likewise, when we think of the solidarity of the race with Adam in his sin, is it not an abstraction to think of posterity's involvement apart from these came characterizations? If we may not make this abstraction it means that the solidarity of the race with Adam's trespass requires us to infer that the pravity and perversity of sin are entailed for posterity in their identification with the original trespass. This is simply to say that when each member of the race comes to exist he exists, from the inception of his being, as depraved with that perversity which his solidaric identification with the sin of Adam involves.

If this analysis is correct, then the question of the relation of depravity to the imputation of the trespass of Adam is placed in a different perspective from that frequently supposed. The representation usually made by those maintaining immediate imputation is that the infliction of the race with depravity is the penal consequence of the imputation of Adam's sin. It is not so certain, however, that this is the most accurate analysis or that it rests upon a biblical basis. On the foregoing construction the case would be that the infliction with depravity is involved in the imputation of Adam's sin; our involvement in and identification with the sin of Adam carries with it as a necessary ingredient the pravity or perversity apart from which sin does not exist. In other words, the imputation of Adam's sin carries with it, not merely as consequence but as implicate, the depravity with which all the members of the race begin their existence as distinct individuals. The imputation is not thus conceived of as something causally antecedent to the depravity but as that which includes depravity as an element.

Furthermore, the relation of depravity to natural generation may also have to be formulated in a different fashion. It may not be strictly accurate to say that we become depraved by natural generation. It is true that *in* the act of generation we become depraved. This is true because it is by generation that we come to be as distinct persons. In this sense it would not be improper to say that we become depraved by natural generation. But natural generation is not the reason why we are conceived in sin. It is not an adequate explanation of our depravity to say that by the law of generation like begets like and since Adam became depraved it was inevitable that he should beget children in the same depraved condition. It is necessary, of course, to take account of this factor. But the *reason* why we are naturally generated in sin is that, whenever we begin to be, we begin to be as sinful because of our solidarity with Adam in his sin. Thus the relation of natural generation to depravity is that by the former we begin to be and having begun to be we are necessarily sinful by reason of our involvement in Adam's sin. Natural generation we may speak of, if we will, as the means of conveying depravity, but, strictly, natural generation is the means whereby we come to be and depravity is the correlate of our having come to be. We may not think that the most relevant biblical statements provide us with a different construction. "In sin did my mother conceive me" (Ps. 51:5), "that which is born of the flesh is flesh" (John 3:6), and "by nature children of wrath, even as others" (Eph. 2:3) point to the fact that we are conceived and born corrupt. But these texts do not go further than to establish the fact that we are depraved from our mother's womb and that natural generation inevitably produces corrupt human nature.

Objections to this construction of the relation of depravity to the imputation of Adam's sin are easily anticipated. Perhaps the most plausible is that the parallel between the imputation of Adam's sin to us and the imputation of our sins to Christ breaks down if this analysis is correct. For on no account may we give quarter to the suggestion or lend any support to it that in the imputation of our sins to Christ in his vicarious sin-bearing there was any such involvement as infliction with the pravity of sin. Our Lord was holy, harmless, undefiled, and separate from sinners; he was without spot and blameless and no pravity touched his soul. This is an axiom of Christian belief and to compromise here is to abandon Christianity. But to urge this as an objection to the formulation in question is quite invalid. There are several observations.

(1) The imputation of Adam's sin to posterity carries with it *in any event* the infliction of the race with depravity. Whether we conceive of this depravity as implicate of the imputation or as penal consequence, it is an inevitable result. There was no pravity resulting for our Lord from his vicarious sin-bearing. Since there is this radical and patent difference, the question at issue is not affected if we conceive of the depravity that comes upon posterity as something entailed in the imputation of Adam's sin. The implications of imputation in the respective cases are radically different in respect of the pravity in connection with which the objection is raised. Hence the objection has no validity.

(2) The vicarious sin-bearing of Christ and the imputation which it presupposes are in a unique category. We must not allow this uniqueness to be prejudiced by drawing the parallel to the imputation of Adam's sin in such close terms that we virtually obliterate the differences. These differences are so basic that to discover a radical differentiation in this matter of pravity would exemplify the unparalleled features of Christ's vicarious sin-bearing.

(3) In interpreting the sin-bearing of Christ we have too limited a conception of its involvements for him if we view it in terms merely of *penal* satisfaction. Christ indeed bore the penalty of the sins of his people. But the tendency to restrict his sin-bearing to the bare notion of penalty impoverishes our appreciation of what his vicarious sacrifice demanded and entailed. Suffice it to

be reminded that the Scriptures do not describe his undertaking as consisting only in the endurance of our penalty; "he bore our *sins*". "The Lord hath laid upon him the iniquity of us all." He stood in the closest relation to our *sins* that it was possible for him to sustain without becoming himself defiled thereby, and this is the mystery of humiliation, of grace, and of love that eternity will not exhaust. This perspective with respect to Christ's vicarious sin-bearing is parallel in this locus of doctrine to the other contention in connection with the imputation of Adam's sin, namely, that the latter is not to be construed as consisting simply in *reatus poenae*. A deeper appreciation of the meaning of Christ's sin-bearing and of the imputation it involved points to a more inclusive concept of what is entailed in the imputation of Adam's sin.

(4) On the point of the objection it must not be overlooked that the precise expressions used in Scripture with reference to the solidarity of the race in Adam's sin are not paralleled in connection with Christ's sin-bearing. With reference to posterity we read that "all sinned" and "the many were constituted sinners". But, though Christ is said to have been "made sin for us" (2 Cor. 5:21), to have been "made a curse" (Gal. 3:13), to have borne our sins (1 Pet. 2:24) to have been sent "in the likeness of sinful flesh and for sin" (Rom. 8:3), yet we do not read that he sinned or was constituted a sinner. There is in this discrimination an index to the difference that must be posited between imputation as it applies to Adam's sin and as it applies to Christ's sin-bearing. To find differentiation, as it pertains to pravity, in the precise manner formulated above is not only consonant with the difference but exemplifies the same in a way that is most appropriate.

It may be that thought on this question of our relation to the sin of Adam has been given too restricted a direction by excessive concentration on the notion of imputation. If we keep in view what lies at the basis of imputation, namely, union or solidarity with Adam and therefore solidarity with Adam in his trespass, we are given a concept that provides for and points in the direction of a more inclusive definition of what is involved for posterity in the imputation of Adam's sin.

If the involvement of posterity in the first sin of Adam is recognized to carry with it as implicate or ingredient the pravity which Adam's trespass implied, this construction performs a threefold service. First, it provides us with a line of thought which imparts to the idea of the sin of all in the sin of Adam an import that measures up to the definition of sin. The sin of posterity is not that of mere *reatus* abstracted from the only proper basis of *reatus*, namely, sin itself. Secondly, it brings the doctrine of the immediate imputation of Adam's sin to its logical rights because this construction finds in the depravity with which posterity is inflicted the direct implicate of solidarity with Adam's sin – pravity is itself an ingredient of the solidaric sin. And, thirdly, it vindicates the analysis which was characteristic of both reformed and Lutheran theologians that *reatus poenae* presupposes *culpa*. On the foregoing analysis *culpa* is clearly exhibited in solidaric pravity.

List of Contributors

Sinclair B. Ferguson is Distinguished Visiting Professor of Systematic Theology at Westminster Theological Seminary, Pennsylvania. He has degrees from the University of Aberdeen and in addition to his work at the seminary he has a pastoral ministry at the First Presbyterian Church, Columbia, South Carolina. He has authored many books including *Taking the Christian Life Seriously; Discovering God's Will; Children of the Living God; John Owen on the Christian Life; Daniel (Communicator's Commentary); Healthy Christian Growth; Deserted By God?; The Holy Spirit; The Big Book of Questions and Answers; Let's Study Philippians; Let's Study Mark; The Big Book of Questions and Answers About Jesus* and has co-authored *If I Should Die Before I Wake.*

Richard B. Gaffin, Jr., is Professor of Biblical and Systematic Theology at Westminster Theological Seminary, Pennsylvania. He holds degrees from Calvin College and Westminster Theology College; and has completed graduate studies at Georg-August Universität, Göttingen. He has authored *The Centrality of the Resurrection (= Resurrection and Redemption)*, *Perspectives on Pentecost*; and *Calvin and the Sabbath.*

Lane G. Tipton is Associate Professor of Systematic Theology at Westminster Theological Seminary, Pennsylvania. He holds degrees from Southwestern Oklahoma State University, Westminster Seminary, California and Westminster Theological Seminary, Philadelphia.

Peter A. Lillback is Professor of Historical Theology and President of the Seminary at Westminster Theological Seminary, Pennsylvania. He has degrees from Cedarville College, Dallas Theological Seminary and Westminster Theological Seminary, and has authored *The Binding of God: Calvin's Role in the Development of Covenant Theology* and edited *The Practical Calvinist: An Introduction to the Presbyterian and Reformed Heritage.*

Carl R. Trueman is Professor of Historical Theology and Church History at Westminster Theological Seminary, Pennsylvania. He holds degrees from St Catharine's College, Cambridge and the University of Aberdeen, and in addition to his work at the seminary he is editor of *Themelios* and council member of Alliance of Confessing Evangelicals. He has authored *Luther's Legacy: Salvation and English Reformers, 1525-1556*; *The Claims of Truth: John Owen's Trinitarian Theology*; *Reformation: Yesterday, Today, Tomorrow*; *The Wages of Spin: Critical Writings on Historic and Contemporary Evangelicalism.* He has also co-edited *Protestant Scholasticism: Essays in Reassessment, Solid Ground: Twenty-five Years of Evangelical Scholarship*; and *The Trustworthiness of God.*

Jeffrey K. Jue is Associate Professor of Church History at Westminster Theological Seminary, Pennsylvania. He holds degrees from the University of California at Irvine, Westminster Theological Seminary in California, and University of Aberdeen, and has completed graduate studies at the University of Geneva. He has authored *Heaven upon Earth: The Millenarian Legacy of Joseph Mede (1586-1638)*.

William Edgar is Professor of Apologetics at Westminster Theological Seminary, Pennsylvania. He has degrees from Harvard University, Westminster Theological Seminary, and Université de Genève, and has authored *In Spirit and in Truth: Ten Bible Studies on Worship*; *Taking Note of Music*; *Reasons of the Heart: Recovering Christian Persuasion*; *If You Seek Me*; *The Face of Truth*; *Truth in All Its Glory: Commending the Reformed Faith.*

K. Scott Oliphint is Professor of Apologetics and Systematic Theology at Westminster Theological Seminary, Pennsylvania. He has degrees from West Texas State University and Westminster Theological Seminary. He has authored *The Battle Belongs to the Lord: The Power of Scripture for Defending Our Faith* and co-authored *If I Should Die Before I Wake.*

John Stafford Carson has been minister of First Presbyterian Church, Portadown, County Armagh, Northern Ireland since June 2005. He is a graduate of the University of Ulster, Queen's University, Belfast, and Westminster Theological Seminary, Pennsylvania. Mr Carson served as minister of Kells and Eskylane Presbyterian Churches, Carnmoney Presbyterian Church, and from 2000 to 2005 was Executive Vice President of Westminster Theological Seminary in Philadelphia.

Alexander Finlayson is Professor of Theological Bibliography and Director of Library Services at Westminster Theological Seminary, Pennsylvania. He has degrees from the University of Toronto and Tyndale Seminary.

John Murray (1898-1975) earned his M.A. from Glasgow University in 1923, his Th.B. and Th.M. from Princeton Theological Seminary in 1927. While studying theology at New College, Edinburgh, Murray was invited by Caspar Wistar Hodge to join him as an assistant in systematic theology at Princeton Seminary in 1929. Serving one year at Princeton, Murray was invited by Machen to teach systematic theology at the one-year-old Westminster Theological Seminary. He taught systematic theology at Westminster Theological Seminary from 1930 until his retirement on January 1, 1967. Upon retirement, Murray returned to Scotland where he married, fathered two children, and carried on preaching and pastoral ministries until his death.

Scripture Index

Subject Index

mentor
DCD
THE PRACTICAL CALVINIST
An introduction to the Presbyterian and Reformed Heritage
In Honor of
D. Clair Davis'
Thirty Years at Westminster Theological Seminary
Contributors include:
• Sinclair B Ferguson • Robert Godfrey •
Edmund Clowney • Richard Gaffin
• William Barker •

The Practical Calvinist:

An introduction to the Presbyterian and Reformed Heritage

For thirty years D. Clair Davis taught church history at Westminster Theological Seminary in Philadelphia. His influence will not be fully known until the next life, but as a measure of the esteem that he is held in this remarkable volume has been prepared.

Section 1 consists of five articles written by D. Clair Davis himself looking anew at the five points of Calvinism.

Section 2 looks at the Reformed heritage through church history.

Section 3 is a revealing, charming and often amusing collection of anecdotes by colleagues, students and friends of Dr. Davis.

Section 4 is a bibliography of Dr. Davis' wide and varied writings. A useful reference source in itself.

"*...a feast, both appetising and satisfying, of contemporary reflection on the Presbyterian and Reformed heritage. Articles from a galaxy of scholars lead us into matters historical, theological, homiletical and pastoral.*"

Edward Donnelly, Professor of New Testament,
Reformed Theological College, Belfast

"*Festschrifts usually suffer from lack of cohesion and variable quality. This work doesn't, and in fact provides an excellent introduction to the Reformed Heritage especially for readers who are not part of that tradition.* "

James Grier, Academic Dean,
Grand Rapids Baptist Seminary, Grand Rapids, Michigan

"*Anyone concerned to understand and to maintain the heritage of conservative reformed Christianity will find many engaging essays that fit their interests.*"

George M. Marsden, Francis A McAnaney Professor of History,
University of Notre Dame, Indiana

"*A marvellous collection of superb essays by some of the leading scholars of the reformed tradition. Here is scholarship and pastoral theology at its best – both done in the service of the church.*"

Timothy George, Dean,
Beeson Divinity School, Samford University,
Birmingham, Alabama

ISBN (10) 1-85792-814-8/ISBN (13) 978-1-85792-814-3

Christian Focus Publications

publishes books for all ages

Our mission statement –

STAYING FAITHFUL
In dependence upon God we seek to help make His infallible Word, the Bible, relevant. Our aim is to ensure that the Lord Jesus Christ is presented as the only hope to obtain forgiveness of sin, live a useful life and look forward to heaven with Him.

REACHING OUT
Christ's last command requires us to reach out to our world with His gospel. We seek to help fulfil that by publishing books that point people towards Jesus and help them develop a Christ-like maturity. We aim to equip all levels of readers for life, work, ministry and mission.

Books in our adult range are published in three imprints.

Christian Focus contains popular works including biographies, commentaries, basic doctrine and Christian living. Our children's books are also published in this imprint.

Mentor focuses on books written at a level suitable for Bible College and seminary students, pastors, and other serious readers. The imprint includes commentaries, doctrinal studies, examination of current issues and church history.

Christian Heritage contains classic writings from the past.

Christian Focus Publications Ltd,
Geanies House, Fearn, Ross-shire,
IV20 1TW, Scotland, United Kingdom
info@christianfocus.com
www.christianfocus.com